The Bible:
A History

The Bible:

A History

THE MAKING AND IMPACT OF THE BIBLE

Stephen M. Miller & Robert V. Huber

A LION BOOK

The Bible in a Rapidly Growing Church

The Book of the Reformation

The Bible in the Modern World

Introduction

On the brink of execution, the apostle Paul wrote what many believe is his last surviving letter. He addressed it to his close friend Timothy, leader of a church in what is now Turkey. 'All scripture is inspired by God,' Paul wrote, 'and is useful for teaching, for reproof, for correction, and for training in righteousness' (2 Timothy 3:16).

The jailed apostle was talking about Jewish scripture, which Christians today call the Old Testament. Little did he know that one day Christians would consider his private letter part of sacred scripture. Paul was probably no exception in this regard. As far as scholars can tell, none of the biblical writers knew their words would become part of the Holy Bible.

Yet in time, people of faith came to recognize the word of God in these laws, history, poetry, wise sayings, prophecy, Gospels and letters. How people came to this awareness remains a mystery. We do know that not all Jews agreed on which writings belonged in their Bible, and that Christians debated what to include in the New Testament. It was not until the late AD 300s that the majority of church leaders ruled in favour of the collection of writings that make up the Bible today. Yet even now there is disagreement. Roman Catholics have an enlarged Old Testament, which includes several books and parts of books found in the Septuagint, the ancient Greek translation of Hebrew scripture. Eastern Orthodox churches add a few more.

No matter which collection of scriptures is studied, there is astonishing consistency in these books that were written by countless authors over a stretch of more than 1,000 years. The unifying element is God – his character and his continuing plan of salvation, a strategy for reaching out to people and saving them from sin and the harm it causes. Even the Old Testament and New Testament – writings compiled by the different theological camps of Jews and Christians – unite in the seamless story of who God is and what he is doing to help humanity.

Why is the Bible so consistent when it comes to talking about God? And how has the Bible managed to survive for so many centuries? People of faith say that the answer lies with God himself. This is his story. It rests patiently on leather scrolls hidden in caves for 2,000 years. It outlasts flames kindled to silence it, and fuels the passion of believers who make more copies. It survives critical study by sceptical scholars. And it drives missionaries to take it to the ends of the earth, and translators to turn spoken languages into written languages, for the sole purpose of letting others read God's story for themselves.

The Bible: A History is not the story in the Bible. You can read that in scripture itself. This is the story of the Bible – of how it came to be, how it survived, and how it changed the world throughout the centuries. It is a remarkable story.

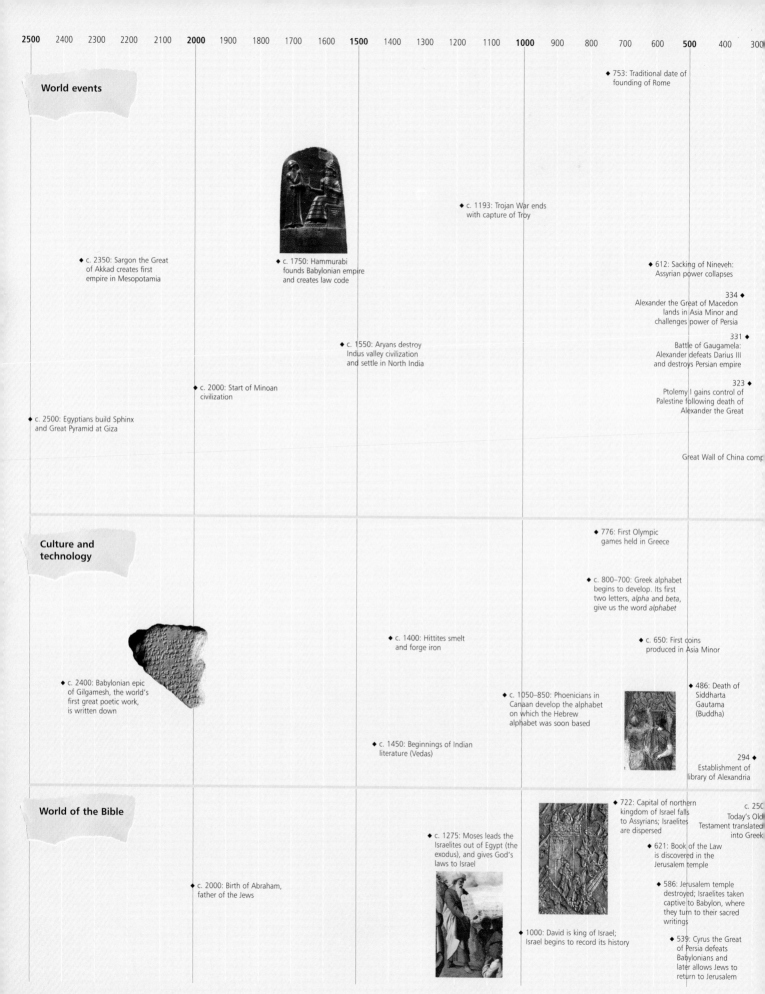

| 2500 | 2400 | 2300 | 2200 | 2100 | **2000** | 1900 | 1800 | 1700 | 1600 | **1500** | 1400 | 1300 | 1200 | 1100 | **1000** | 900 | 800 | 700 | 600 | **500** | 400 | 300 |

World events

◆ 753: Traditional date of founding of Rome

◆ c. 1193: Trojan War ends with capture of Troy

◆ c. 2350: Sargon the Great of Akkad creates first empire in Mesopotamia

◆ c. 1750: Hammurabi founds Babylonian empire and creates law code

◆ 612: Sacking of Nineveh: Assyrian power collapses

334 ◆
Alexander the Great of Macedon lands in Asia Minor and challenges power of Persia

331 ◆
Battle of Gaugamela: Alexander defeats Darius III and destroys Persian empire

◆ c. 1550: Aryans destroy Indus valley civilization and settle in North India

323 ◆
Ptolemy I gains control of Palestine following death of Alexander the Great

◆ c. 2000: Start of Minoan civilization

◆ c. 2500: Egyptians build Sphinx and Great Pyramid at Giza

Great Wall of China comp

Culture and technology

◆ 776: First Olympic games held in Greece

◆ c. 800–700: Greek alphabet begins to develop. Its first two letters, *alpha* and *beta*, give us the word *alphabet*

◆ c. 1400: Hittites smelt and forge iron

◆ 650: First coins produced in Asia Minor

◆ c. 2400: Babylonian epic of Gilgamesh, the world's first great poetic work, is written down

◆ c. 1050–850: Phoenicians in Canaan develop the alphabet on which the Hebrew alphabet was soon based

◆ 486: Death of Siddharta Gautama (Buddha)

◆ c. 1450: Beginnings of Indian literature (Vedas)

294 ◆
Establishment of library of Alexandria

World of the Bible

◆ 722: Capital of northern kingdom of Israel falls to Assyrians; Israelites are dispersed

c. 250
Today's Old Testament translated into Greek

◆ c. 1275: Moses leads the Israelites out of Egypt (the exodus), and gives God's laws to Israel

◆ 621: Book of the Law is discovered in the Jerusalem temple

◆ c. 2000: Birth of Abraham, father of the Jews

◆ 586: Jerusalem temple destroyed; Israelites taken captive to Babylon, where they turn to their sacred writings

◆ 1000: David is king of Israel; Israel begins to record its history

◆ 539: Cyrus the Great of Persia defeats Babylonians and later allows Jews to return to Jerusalem

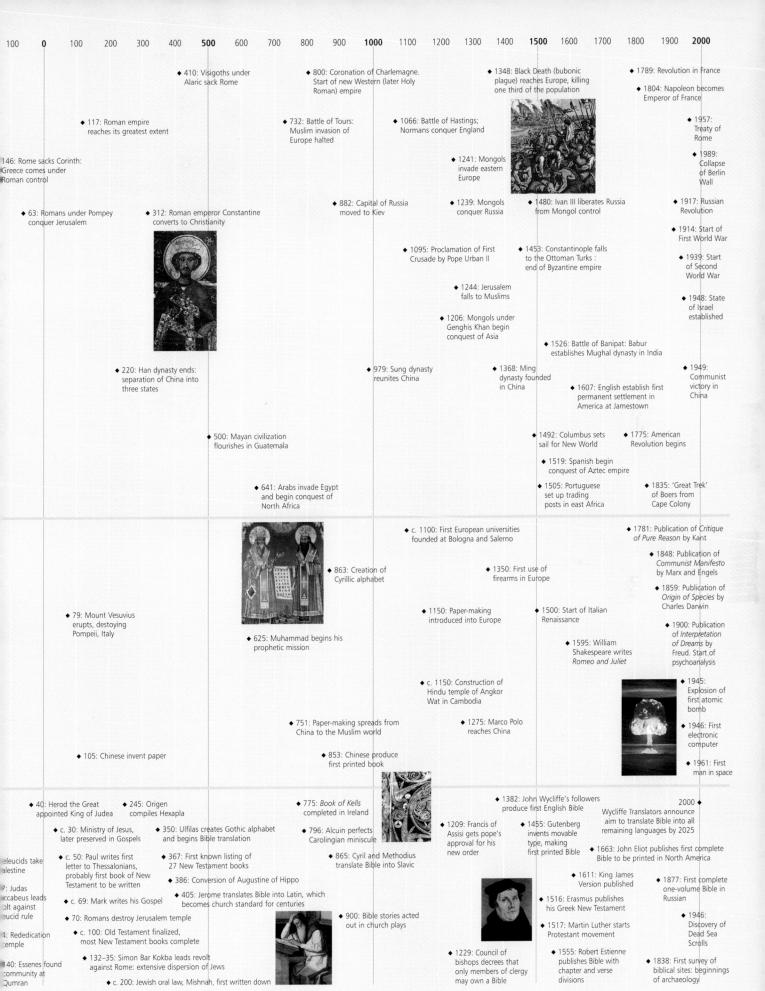

100   0   100   200   300   400   **500**   600   700   800   900   **1000**   1100   1200   1300   1400   **1500**   1600   1700   1800   1900   **2000**

◆ 410: Visigoths under Alaric sack Rome

◆ 800: Coronation of Charlemagne. Start of new Western (later Holy Roman) empire

◆ 1348: Black Death (bubonic plague) reaches Europe, killing one third of the population

◆ 1789: Revolution in France

◆ 1804: Napoleon becomes Emperor of France

◆ 117: Roman empire reaches its greatest extent

◆ 732: Battle of Tours: Muslim invasion of Europe halted

◆ 1066: Battle of Hastings; Normans conquer England

◆ 1957: Treaty of Rome

◆ 1989: Collapse of Berlin Wall

◆ 1241: Mongols invade eastern Europe

146: Rome sacks Corinth: Greece comes under Roman control

◆ 882: Capital of Russia moved to Kiev

◆ 1239: Mongols conquer Russia

◆ 1480: Ivan III liberates Russia from Mongol control

◆ 1917: Russian Revolution

◆ 63: Romans under Pompey conquer Jerusalem

◆ 312: Roman emperor Constantine converts to Christianity

◆ 1914: Start of First World War

◆ 1095: Proclamation of First Crusade by Pope Urban II

◆ 1453: Constantinople falls to the Ottoman Turks : end of Byzantine empire

◆ 1939: Start of Second World War

◆ 1244: Jerusalem falls to Muslims

◆ 1948: State of Israel established

◆ 1206: Mongols under Genghis Khan begin conquest of Asia

◆ 1526: Battle of Banipat: Babur establishes Mughal dynasty in India

◆ 220: Han dynasty ends: separation of China into three states

◆ 979: Sung dynasty reunites China

◆ 1368: Ming dynasty founded in China

◆ 1949: Communist victory in China

◆ 1607: English establish first permanent settlement in America at Jamestown

◆ 500: Mayan civilization flourishes in Guatemala

◆ 1492: Columbus sets sail for New World

◆ 1775: American Revolution begins

◆ 1519: Spanish begin conquest of Aztec empire

◆ 641: Arabs invade Egypt and begin conquest of North Africa

◆ 1505: Portuguese set up trading posts in east Africa

◆ 1835: 'Great Trek' of Boers from Cape Colony

◆ c. 1100: First European universities founded at Bologna and Salerno

◆ 1781: Publication of *Critique of Pure Reason* by Kant

◆ 1848: Publication of *Communist Manifesto* by Marx and Engels

◆ 863: Creation of Cyrillic alphabet

◆ 1350: First use of firearms in Europe

◆ 1859: Publication of *Origin of Species* by Charles Darwin

◆ 79: Mount Vesuvius erupts, destoying Pompeii, Italy

◆ 1150: Paper-making introduced into Europe

◆ 1500: Start of Italian Renaissance

◆ 1900: Publication of *Interpretation of Dreams* by Freud. Start of psychoanalysis

◆ 1595: William Shakespeare writes *Romeo and Juliet*

◆ 625: Muhammad begins his prophetic mission

◆ c. 1150: Construction of Hindu temple of Angkor Wat in Cambodia

◆ 1945: Explosion of first atomic bomb

◆ 751: Paper-making spreads from China to the Muslim world

◆ 1275: Marco Polo reaches China

◆ 1946: First electronic computer

◆ 105: Chinese invent paper

◆ 853: Chinese produce first printed book

◆ 1961: First man in space

◆ 40: Herod the Great appointed King of Judea

◆ 245: Origen compiles Hexapla

◆ 775: *Book of Kells* completed in Ireland

◆ 1382: John Wycliffe's followers produce first English Bible

2000 ◆ Wycliffe Translators announce aim to translate Bible into all remaining languages by 2025

◆ c. 30: Ministry of Jesus, later preserved in Gospels

◆ 350: Ulfilas creates Gothic alphabet and begins Bible translation

◆ 796: Alcuin perfects Carolingian miniscule

◆ 1209: Francis of Assisi gets pope's approval for his new order

◆ 1455: Gutenberg invents movable type, making first printed Bible

◆ c. 50: Paul writes first letter to Thessalonians, probably first book of New Testament to be written

◆ 367: First known listing of 27 New Testament books

◆ 865: Cyril and Methodius translate Bible into Slavic

◆ 1663: John Eliot publishes first complete Bible to be printed in North America

eleucids take alestine

◆ 386: Conversion of Augustine of Hippo

◆ 1611: King James Version published

◆ 1877: First complete one-volume Bible in Russian

7: Judas ccabeus leads olt against eucid rule

◆ c. 69: Mark writes his Gospel

◆ 405: Jerome translates Bible into Latin, which becomes church standard for centuries

◆ 1516: Erasmus publishes his Greek New Testament

◆ 70: Romans destroy Jerusalem temple

◆ 1517: Martin Luther starts Protestant movement

◆ 1946: Discovery of Dead Sea Scrolls

4: Rededication emple

◆ c. 100: Old Testament finalized, most New Testament books complete

◆ 900: Bible stories acted out in church plays

◆ 1555: Robert Estienne publishes Bible with chapter and verse divisions

40: Essenes found community at Qumran

◆ 132–35: Simon Bar Kokba leads revolt against Rome: extensive dispersion of Jews

◆ 1229: Council of bishops decrees that only members of clergy may own a Bible

◆ 1838: First survey of biblical sites: beginnings of archaeology

◆ c. 200: Jewish oral law, Mishnah, first written down

1

THE
OLD TESTAMENT
TAKES SHAPE

The Old Testament took shape slowly, over a period of more than 1,000 years, and many inspired writers, editors, scribes and others were involved in its making. First, stories of the creation and of the early days of Judaism were passed on by word of mouth. Later, after the Hebrew alphabet had been developed, these stories began to be set down in writing and other stories, laws, prophecies and poetry were added to them. Over the centuries, these writings, which describe God's involvement in human history, were revised and combined and slowly took on the form they have today.

Moses Receiving the Tablets of the Law by Lorenzo Ghiberti, 15th century.

By Word of Mouth

'We have heard with our ears, O God, our ancestors have told us, what deeds you performed in their days, in the days of old.'

PSALM 44:1

Before men and women could read or write, they passed along stories about their people's past by word of mouth. Travelling shepherds tell such stories in their camp, in a painting entitled *The Arab Tale-Teller*, by Emile Jean Horace Vernet (1789–1863).

In the beginning there was no written word. There was only the spoken word, and – as it was later to be recorded in the book of Genesis – God created the universe by speaking words into the void. God's earliest worshippers could not write down their thoughts about God or their experiences of God, but they could speak them, and speak them they did. Long before they invented their own writing system, and even long afterwards, Hebrews told and retold stories, many of which were later to appear in the Bible.

CLINGING TO BELIEFS

At first, fathers and mothers probably told their children stories about their own parents and grandparents. Abraham himself must have engaged in such storytelling. When he was called by the Lord to leave Ur and move to Canaan, Abraham must have wanted to preserve memories of his old life and to convince his family and new neighbours that the Lord was the one true God and that the many gods being worshipped by the people around them were lifeless idols. Abraham probably repeated stories of how the Lord created the universe and saved Noah and his family from the flood. He must have told of his own calling, repeating God's promise to make him the father of a great nation. Later, his son and grandson, Isaac and Jacob, would have continued the tradition, adding their own stories. When their descendants were forced by famine to move to Egypt, where they later became slaves, they would have had even more reason to preserve their heritage, clinging to their beliefs in order to endure.

The Hebrews were not the only people to pass along stories orally. A number of ancient

Babylonian narratives parallel those in the Bible. One such tale, later set down as a poem, the 'Enuma Elish', tells of the creation of heaven and earth, but it also tells of a multitude of battling gods who are eventually subdued and ruled by Marduk, the principal god of Babylon. On the other hand, the creation account of the Hebrews affirms that the one true God created everything and holds all creation in his grasp. This vision of God makes the Hebrews unique in the ancient world.

Storytelling, then, was not merely for entertainment. Rather, it was a way of preserving the culture of the people, of letting them know who they were, how they differed from their neighbours. The stories reminded the Hebrews of what made them special. As time went on, storytelling moved out from the family to larger

Adding to the story

In order to make a point, storytellers sometimes supplemented their narratives with unrelated stories from other traditions. Some of these stories have survived independently of the Bible. One of them may be the ancient Egyptian 'Tale of Two Brothers'. In this tale a woman tries to seduce her brother-in-law. When he rejects her advances, the woman is afraid of what will happen if her husband finds out what she has done. And so, as soon as her husband comes home, she accuses his brother of rape, and the brother is forced to flee for his life. Some scholars say that a Hebrew storyteller may have borrowed this story and adapted it for use in the saga of Joseph, who, having been sold into slavery by his brothers, is accused of rape and imprisoned after he refuses the sexual advances of the wife of his master, Potiphar. If a Hebrew storyteller did deliberately incorporate the Egyptian tale into the Joseph narrative, he was not trying to falsify history, as we understand it. He was probably only attempting to illustrate that Joseph was an upright and moral man and that God would take care of him no matter how cruelly he was treated by the outside world. For Genesis goes on to tell how Joseph ultimately rises to power and is able to help his own people in time of famine.

groups, and professional storytellers became common. Often these storytellers recited their texts at community gatherings or to celebrate special feasts. As they told their stories, they may have embellished them to stimulate the interest of their audiences, but they dared not wander far from the point or alter any essential truths. If they tried, listeners would have objected, as they had heard these recitations often enough to be familiar with their contents, and would not tolerate significant deviations – for it was their faith and culture that was being passed on in these stories.

THROUGH THE CENTURIES

The oral tradition, as this ancient type of storytelling is now called, continued after the Hebrews were delivered from slavery in Egypt and eventually moved into the land that God had promised them. Stories of Moses and the exodus, the conquest of Canaan and heroic feats in the days of the judges were added to the repertoire. Even though writing was becoming widespread, only bits and pieces of the biblical texts were being written down. In fact, scholars say that none of the books of the Bible were written down in their final form until at least the time of King David. But even later, centuries after the last of the books of the Bible had been written, people continued using word of mouth to pass on stories, laws, principles and teachings of all kinds.

More than stories
Stories were not the only type of material passed on by storytellers. There were also proverbs, prayers, lyric poems, songs, laws and even riddles (such as Samson's riddle in Judges 14:14) and etiologies – stories that explain how some person or place was named, or how so many languages came into the world.

First Writings

Cuneiform

The word cuneiform comes from the Latin *cuneus*, which means 'wedge', referring to the shapes of the signs used in cuneiform.

While the Hebrews were passing on their culture by word of mouth, the world's first writing systems were being put to use. In Mesopotamia (now Iraq), where Abraham received the Lord's call, a type of writing called cuneiform was being used. In Egypt, where the descendants of Jacob were laboring as slaves, hieroglyphs were in use.

WRITING IN CUNEIFORM

The first of these writing systems was probably an early form of cuneiform, which appeared in Mesopotamia about 3200 BC. Cuneiform is a system of writing in which symbols known as signs are cut into wet clay tablets, which are then left to dry or are baked in a kiln. Signs were pushed into the clay using a reed stylus with a wedge-shaped tip. The earliest signs were rough pictograms, vaguely resembling the objects they represented, but as time went on the signs became more and more stylized. By the eighth century BC they were made up of varied configurations of wedges and lines. The tablets themselves varied in shape and thickness and ranged in length and width from

Fragment of the Babylonian epic of Gilgamesh, dating from the 15th century BC, which was found at Megiddo.

The formation and evolution of cuneiform signs.

two centimetres (three-quarters of an inch) to 30 centimetres (one foot). Sometimes cuneiform was also scribed onto wax-covered tablets or chiselled into stone monuments.

Because of the enormous number of signs involved, cuneiform was difficult to master and was generally reserved for professional scribes in palaces and temples. Early cuneiform employed some 800 signs but later cuneiform used thousands. The earliest signs represented persons, animals or objects. Actions were sometimes represented by grouping symbols for objects. For example, the verb 'to eat' was represented by combining the symbol for 'mouth' with the one for 'food'. Two shortened signs for 'reed' were shown with their ends against a tablet-like rectangle to represent the verb 'to write'. As time went on, some signs came to represent the sounds of monosyllabic words, rather than their meanings, so that words of more than one syllable could be represented by combining these signs.

The earliest surviving cuneiform writings do not preserve history or literature. They are administrative records that discuss animal husbandry, grain distribution, land management and the processing of fruits and grains. A few other texts appear to be manuals for teaching the writing craft. As time went on, however, cuneiform writing was inscribed on monuments and used to preserve history and poetry.

Archaeologists have recovered several large libraries of ancient cuneiform writings, helping us understand the way of life in biblical times. The most important of these libraries, found in the ruins of the ancient Assyrian capital of Nineveh, contains more than 1,500 texts, including some of the most ancient surviving cuneiform writings. They were collected by King Ashurbanipal, who ruled from 668 to 627 BC. The most famous work from the library is the epic poem 'Gilgamesh', which is preserved on 12 tablets. This first great poetic work of all time, though written about 2000 BC, brings together tales that are far older. They tell of a tree of life and an evil serpent, and recount many adventures, including one about how a man survives a great flood by building a boat and bringing animals aboard – like Noah, this man also sends out birds to see if the flood waters are receding. Perhaps the Hebrew account of Noah and the flood is an adaptation of the Gilgamesh

		Archaic Uruk c. 3000	Presargonic Lagash c. 2400	Neo-Assyrian c. 700
KA	'mouth'			
GU	'to eat'			
GI	'reed, to render'			
SAR	'plant, to write'			

It is due largely to the heroic efforts of a young English army officer, Sir Henry Rawlinson, that cuneiform can be read today. While stationed in Persia during the 1830s and 1840s, Rawlinson became fascinated by a huge monument cut into the stone face of a peak in the Zagros Mountains. There, scenes of heroic life from the time of Darius I of Persia (about 500 BC) were accompanied by cuneiform inscriptions in three languages – Old Persian, Elamite and Akkadian. In order to copy the text, Rawlinson had to stand at the top of a ladder that was precariously perched on a narrow ledge high above the valley floor. At times he had to steady himself with his left arm, while holding his notebook in his left hand and writing with his right hand. Rawlinson then spent decades deciphering the work he had copied, opening the way to the study of cuneiform and the languages it preserves.

consonants. About 700 different hieroglyphs were used in Egypt during much of the Old Testament period. Hieroglyphic writing was usually done with a pen and ink on papyrus, but hieroglyphs were also used on the walls of palaces, tombs and monuments.

The Hebrews must have seen both cuneiform and hieroglyphic writing, as they were displayed in public places. However, it is likely that very few Hebrews were able to read or write. Their time of literacy was to come with the invention of the alphabet.

tale, with the Hebrew concept of the divine added to it, or perhaps it is an independent account of the flood that archaeologists believe inundated the area around Ur in about 3400 BC.

HIEROGLYPHIC WRITING

Shortly after the time the Mesopotamians were developing cuneiform (or perhaps even a little earlier), the Egyptians were developing their own writing system. Although it is possible that the Egyptians got the idea of writing from Mesopotamia, their system, which consists of pictographs called hieroglyphs, is entirely unrelated to cuneiform. Some hieroglyphs convey meaning. For example, a circle with a second, small, circle at its centre was the sign for 'sun', but it could also be used to mean 'day'. The sign of a man with his hand to his mouth might mean either 'eat' or 'be silent'. Other signs represented sounds. For example, the words for 'man' and 'be bright' contain the same consonant sound, hg, and were represented by the same hieroglyph. There were also signs that stood for certain combinations of

Hieroglyphic writing is combined with a depiction of a married couple in this Egyptian funerary stele.

Writing Hebrew

Because of the huge number of symbols used in early writing, scribes were generally the only people who could read and write before the invention of the alphabet in the late Bronze Age (1525–1200 BC). Of the early alphabets, the most significant were developed in Canaan.

THE HEBREW ALPHABET

Although the earliest surviving alphabet was created before the Phoenicians arrived in Canaan (about 1200 BC), the Phoenicians produced the most extensive body of surviving texts using an alphabet. These texts date from about 1050 to about 850 BC. Consequently, the writing system developed in ancient Canaan is generally referred to as the Phoenician alphabet. The Hebrew alphabet is its direct descendant. As the Hebrews settled in their new land, after 40 years in the wilderness, they developed their own method of writing by adapting the Phoenician alphabet to their own language. This was probably not difficult, as Hebrew, like Phoenician (and Ugaritic), is a Canaanite

Illuminated page from Exodus from a 13th-century Hebrew Bible.

The Hebrew alphabet

Hebrew letter	name	Transliteration
א	'aleph	(none)
ב	beth	b, bh
ג	gimel	g, gh
ד	daleth	d, dh
ה	he	h (or none)
ו	waw	w (or none)
ז	zayin	z
ח	heth	ḥ
ט	teth	ṭ
י	yodh	y (or none)
כ	kaph	k, kh
ל	lamedh	l
מ	mem	m
נ	nun	n
ס	samekh	s
ע	'ayin	ʿ
פ	pe	p, ph
צ	ṣadhe	ṣ
ק	qoph	q
ר	resh	r
שׂ שׁ	śin, shin	ś, sh
ת	taw	t, th

Note: some letters take on a different form when positioned at the end of a word.

The oldest words in the Bible

Although the biblical books we have today were probably written relatively late in Israel's history, earlier bits of writing were incorporated into the final text. Among the oldest of these, scholars believe, was the Song of Miriam. After the Israelites had passed through the miraculously parted waters of the Red Sea, Miriam, Aaron's sister, picked up a tambourine and danced: 'Sing to the Lord,' she sang, 'for he has triumphed gloriously; horse and rider he has thrown into the sea' (Exodus 15:21). Another ancient piece of writing found in the Bible is the Song of Deborah (Judges 5), a magnificent piece of poetry that offers a slightly different version of the battle described in Judges 4, which immediately precedes the song.

language that, along with Aramaic, makes up the language group known as West Semitic.

The Hebrew alphabet consists of 22 letters. All of them are consonants, for only consonants are written in Hebrew. Most words in ancient Hebrew have roots that contain three consonants. Readers had to supply the vowel sounds to make up the intended word, which was suggested by the context. For example, if English were to be written in this fashion, without vowels, a word written as 'vctn' could be read as either 'vocation' or 'vacation'. However, the context would usually alert the reader to the correct choice. A person would go on a vacation but follow a vocation. In addition, Hebrew is written from right to left. And so, the English words 'vocation' and 'vacation' would be written backwards in Hebrew, as 'ntcv'.

KEEPING THE LANGUAGE CONSTANT

All the books of the Old Testament are written in Hebrew, except for a few scattered chapters and verses. But even though these books were written over a period of nearly 1,000 years – and incorporated even older, oral traditions – there is strikingly little difference between the oldest texts and the newest. This is astounding, as most languages change constantly. For example, English literature of 1,000 years ago is totally unreadable today by someone with no special training. To the untrained eye, the text of the Old English poem 'Beowulf' looks more like obsolete German with a sprinkling of strange symbols added. Not so the Old Testament. The reason for the consistency of Hebrew writing

may be that the texts of scripture were so revered that they had a profound effect on the language itself, keeping it constant.

There may also be other reasons for this consistency, however. Some of the earlier biblical passages may have been somewhat updated as writers or editors of the tenth to sixth centuries BC shaped the official version of stories that had long been transmitted by word of mouth. For example, we know that some ancient place names, which would have been unknown to most readers at the time the text was being written down, were replaced by more current names. In Genesis 14:14 we read that Abram went as far as Dan, but Dan did not exist in Abram's day; the territory in question would be named Dan, after one of Abram's great grandsons, only centuries later. The author or editor of this passage from Genesis must have quietly substituted 'Dan' for the region's older name 'Leshem', which would have been known to Abram but totally unknown to most later readers. In other passages, both old and newer names are used together. For example, 'And Sarah died at Kiriath-arba (that is, Hebron) in the land of Canaan' (Genesis 23:2).

Another possible reason for the unparalleled consistency in the Hebrew language is that after a time it ceased to be a living language in the strict sense. From the fifth century BC on, the Israelites began to speak Aramaic, the language of their Persian conquerors, and as time went by Hebrew was used solely for worship and holy scripture. As a result, the language was less subject to change than the language used for everyday business and conversation.

Even after Hebrew stopped being used in daily life, however, it continued to be highly revered as the language of sacred texts, and the scriptures continued to be preserved in the older language. Although many nonbiblical texts were written in Hebrew in ancient times, none of these writings survive today. Aside from some inscriptions on monuments and walls and writing on ancient coins, the only ancient Hebrew writing that survives is found in the Old Testament.

First alphabet

The earliest writings using what appears to be an alphabet were actually left by a group of northwest-Asian prisoners of war who were working in turquoise mines in the Sinai Peninsula about 1600 BC. The writings have not been clearly deciphered, but they seem to be religious in content. So far, however, no connections have been made between this earliest alphabetic writing and later systems.

Unlocking language mysteries

Although almost no ancient Hebrew writing survives outside the Bible, archeologists have uncovered a large trove of writings on clay tablets at Ugarit on the Syrian coast. Although these writings use a cuneiform-style alphabet instead of an alphabet made up of lines, the Ugaritic language is so close to Hebrew that scholars are able to use these texts to help solve problems in deciphering unclear Hebrew words of the Old Testament.

Not quite an alphabet

Technically, the collection of symbols, or letters, used in writing Hebrew is not an alphabet, but an *abjad*. An *abjad* is the equivalent of an alphabet that has no symbols to represent vowel sounds.

Moses Gives the Law

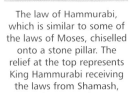

The law of Hammurabi, which is similar to some of the laws of Moses, chiselled onto a stone pillar. The relief at the top represents King Hammurabi receiving the laws from Shamash, the sun god.

Moses gave his people hundreds of laws preserved in the first five books of the Bible. He said these laws came directly from God – and the Israelites had good reason to believe it.

Before Moses presented his people with the first and most famous of these laws – the ten commandments engraved in stone – God personally delivered those same laws in a spectacular speech before the entire nation. It was dawn, and as instructed by Moses, the people assembled at the base of Mount Sinai to meet God. Thunder and lightning filled the sky as a dense cloud lowered itself on the mountain. God appeared as a fire, cloaked in billowing smoke. The long blast of a ram's horn announced his arrival, and the mountain shook with a violent earthquake. The people trembled in terror.

Then God spoke. With a voice that filled the plain, he delivered the ten commandments for all to hear. The experience was so frightening that the people pleaded with Moses to serve as intermediary between them and God. 'You speak to us, and we will listen; but do not let God speak to us, or we will die' (Exodus 20:19). Moses agreed and delivered the remaining laws on God's behalf.

LAWS THAT DEFINE A NATION

Those ten laws that Moses later carried down the mountain on stone tablets became the fundamental laws of Judaism, on which all other Jewish laws are based. Many of the more than 600 subsequent laws probably came to Moses during the months the Israelites camped at Mount Sinai. Some of these laws are distinctive enough that they actually define the nation. People could tell a person was an Israelite by the way the Israelite looked and behaved. As the law required, Israelite males were circumcised. Israelites did not eat certain common foods, such as pork and rabbit. Israelites did not work from sundown on Friday until sundown on Saturday.

Other law codes in the ancient Middle East covered only secular matters, such as penalties for stealing and procedures for getting a divorce. But Jewish law covered both secular and religious matters, showing that God ruled both domains. Other law codes also operated on the basis of class

distinction, with the upper classes drawing milder penalties than commoners. Under Jewish law, aristocrats and commoners were treated alike. Even slaves had some rights. Jewish law was also unique in ordering people to protect the helpless, especially widows and orphans.

There are two types of Jewish law. The first and most common are laws that apply to specific cases. 'When someone steals an ox... the thief shall pay five oxen' (Exodus 22:1). The second are broad principles designed to help people live in harmony with one another and remain faithful to God. These laws are not related to any specific cases and they do not have any stated punishment. The best-known examples are the ten commandments, which serve as the core of moral teaching for both Jews and Christians, and are today reflected in the laws of many nations.

Behind the Jewish law was the people's conviction that they served a holy God who lived among them, first in the tabernacle (a tent worship centre), and later in the temple. 'Sanctify yourselves therefore,' God said, 'and be holy, for I am holy' (Leviticus 11:44). By carefully observing God's rules and rituals, the Israelites maintained their holiness, and found forgiveness when they failed. The high standards and unique laws of Moses set Israel apart as 'a priestly kingdom and a holy nation' (Exodus 19:6). Like priests, their purpose was to serve God. In return, God promised to bless them.

ORAL LAW

Jewish tradition says that many of the laws and explanations that God gave Moses were not written, but were passed along by word of mouth. The oral law, as it became known, included supplemental laws and guidance that reinforced the written law. For instance, the written law said to honour the sabbath by not working. The oral law defined what was and was not work. As times changed, religious leaders adapted and expanded these oral laws. For instance, when Rome destroyed the temple in AD 70, Jews could no longer obey laws about offering sacrifices at the temple. So the oral law was expanded, teaching the people they could offer sacrifices of prayer – in keeping with a prophet's direction, 'we will offer the fruit of our lips' (Hosea 14:2).

Moses Presents the Ten Commandments to the Israelites by Raphael (1483–1520).

By about AD 200, the collection of oral laws had grown so large that Jewish scholars realized they needed to write it down. The result was the Mishnah, the first authoritative collection of Jewish legal traditions, and the most revered Jewish document after the Bible.

TEN COMMANDMENTS WRITTEN IN STONE

The book of Exodus says little about what the ten commandments looked like, except that they were two stone tablets written on both sides (Exodus 32:15). They probably were not as large as those shown in paintings and movies, otherwise Moses would have had a hard time carrying them down Mount Sinai.

Some Bible scholars suggest the tablets may have been slabs of limestone, a relatively light rock common in the region. Somewhat like shale, limestone can be broken into thin, flat slabs. People throughout the ancient Middle East often used small pieces of limestone as we use paper, recording words or pictures with ink or inscriptions.

The stone tablets containing Israel's most basic laws were to be kept in a gold-plated box called the ark of the covenant. This chest, which became Israel's most sacred relic, measured about one and a third metres (four feet) long and two-thirds of a metre (two feet) wide and high.

The ark, with the ten commandments inside, was put in the Holy of Holies – the most sacred room in the tabernacle tent, and later in the temple. Babylonian invaders apparently stole the ark when they captured Jerusalem in 586 BC. But a Jewish book, written perhaps in the first century BC, said the prophet Jeremiah hid the ark in a cave on the mountain where Moses died, in what is now Jordan (2 Maccabees 2:4–8).

'What other great nation has statutes and ordinances as just as this entire law that I am setting before you today?'

MOSES IN DEUTERONOMY 4:8

Papyrus: Paper from the Nile

In Bible times, tall, slender papyrus reeds grew in dense clusters along the River Nile. You will not find them growing wild along the Nile today because civilization destroyed their natural habitat. Ironic, since papyrus nourished human civilization by providing a great way for people to communicate and preserve their history.

Papyrus was the world's first lightweight, inexpensive and durable writing material. That assured it a major role in the story of the Bible. In fact, many of the oldest copies of Bible books, including some of the Dead Sea Scrolls that are more than 2,000 years old, survive on paper made from papyrus reeds.

By about 3000 BC, Egyptians discovered they could make paper from the columns of soft, mushy pith inside papyrus reed stems. These reeds grew throughout the Mediterranean, but

> *'Civilization – or at the very least human history – depends on the use of papyrus.'*
> ROMAN HISTORIAN PLINY THE ELDER, FIRST CENTURY AD

Source of 'paper'

Our word 'paper' comes from the word 'papyrus'.

Papyrus by the water.

the papyrus reeds in Egypt were best suited to making paper for two reasons. First, the supply seemed endless – especially in the Nile Delta. Second, stems of the Egyptian plants were biggest: five metres (10 to 15 feet) high and up to five centimetres (two inches) thick. This meant Egypt had pretty much a monopoly on the industry.

HOW TO MAKE PAPYRUS PAPER

As ancient Egyptian wall paintings show, men harvested papyrus reeds by pulling them from the river bottom and hauling them in bunches on their back. Craftsmen then cut the stems into short sections of about a third of a metre (one foot) long, or a little longer. Next they cut away the outside layer of the stem, exposing the soft cylinder of white pith inside.

The pith, still moist, was then sliced lengthwise into thin strips, normally about one to three centimetres (a quarter of an inch to one and a quarter inches) wide. These strips could be dried and stored for use later, or they could be immediately worked into papyrus sheets.

To make a sheet, strips were laid side by side on a hard surface, such as a board. The parallel strips were just touching or slightly overlapping. Then a second row was laid on top, with its strips running crossways to the first layer. Craftsmen then hammered and pressed the moistened strips until the pith fibres intertwined, binding the two layers. Afterwards, the sheets were dried in the sun, forming a strong, flexible, creamy white writing surface.

Scribes could write on individual papyrus sheets. But the sheets were often glued end to end with flour paste to form a scroll, or roll, generally about 20 sheets long. Scribes preferred to use the side with the horizontal strips, so they could move their pens with the grain. But many ancient papyrus scrolls have writing on both sides.

LONG-LASTING INK

Ink was made of natural minerals that did not fade easily. The clearly legible writing on the Dead Sea Scrolls written centuries before the time of Jesus is a tribute to the quality of the ink.

Black ink came from carbon deposits,

An Egyptian scribe's palette, containing reed pens and holes for red and black ink.

such as soot scraped off lamp tops or pot bottoms. Carbon also came from charcoal or burnt bones ground into a fine powder. Whatever the carbon source, it was mixed with a binding agent such as gum arabic, a water-soluble sap from acacia trees. This mixture was dried into small cakes. When a scribe was ready to write, he rubbed a moistened pen or brush over the ink cake.

Scribes commonly used red ink as well. It was made from iron oxide, red ochre or other minerals found in the soil.

When scribes made a writing mistake, they could erase the fresh ink by wiping it with water. If the ink had already dried, they could scrape it away with a rock. These methods of erasing worked because dried papyrus plant juices form a protective barrier on the surface of the sheet, keeping the ink from sinking deep into the fibres.

A PEN TO CHEW ON

Pens first used for writing on papyrus paper were more like small paintbrushes. They were cut from rushes, tiny plants that grew in the marsh. The pens were cut to different lengths, often anywhere from about 15 to 40 centimetres (6 to 15 inches). Scribes would chew on the pen tip to loosen the tiny fibres and form them into a delicate brush.

When the scribes wrote, they looked more like artists at work because they did not generally rest their hands on the sheet, but held the pen like a brush against a canvas. By New Testament times, writers used reeds sharpened to a point and split like a quill pen. Pens and dried cakes of ink were often kept together in long, narrow pen boxes made of wood. Ink cakes were also kept in small stone inkwells.

Two figures and hieroglyphs decorate a sheet of papyrus. Holding the sheet up to the light reveals that it is constructed by laying strips of papyrus stems at right angles to each other.

The Bible's name

The Bible owes its name to papyrus. Greeks called papyrus rolls *biblia*, after Phoenicia's seaport of Byblos – a major exporter of papyrus. In time, the word came to mean 'book' and eventually 'the Book', the Bible.

David and His Royal Writers

'... the account of the Annals of King David.'

1 CHRONICLES 27:24

King David commissioned a written history of the Israelites. This act was possibly even more significant than his defeat of the Philistine giant Goliath, which is depicted here.

David's most important contribution to the Bible may not have been the psalms attributed to him, or even his starring role in dramatic stories, such as his mortal combat with the giant Goliath. His biggest contribution may be that he started the almost millennium-long process of writing the Bible, by commissioning a history of the emerging nation he led.

No one is sure when the first Israelite put pen to papyrus and started writing down the stories, songs and other genres of Israelite tradition that became the Bible. Moses is the first person the Bible identifies as a writer. After the Israelites repelled an attack, God told Moses, 'Write this as a reminder in a book and recite it in the hearing of Joshua' (Exodus 17:14). Joshua may have needed to hear the words because, like most Israelites of the time, he probably could not read or write.

Moses – educated in the Egyptian palace – may also have written many other stories about Israel's great exodus, though the Bible does not say so. Yet any writing that was done probably was not preserved in a national archive. Instead, the stories and traditions were kept vividly alive in the minds of the Israelites through storytelling. This honoured God's request: 'Keep these words that I am commanding you today in your heart. Recite them to your children and talk about them' (Deuteronomy 6:6–7).

WRITERS IN DAVID'S CABINET

By about 1000 BC, King David secured Israel's borders. That done, he probably set out to preserve the nation's place in history. He must have anticipated a long future for Israel since God had said of David, 'I will establish the throne of his kingdom forever' (2 Samuel 7:13). Among the royal cabinet members David appointed were two writers: 'Jehoshaphat son of Ahilud was the recorder; Sheva was secretary' (2 Samuel 20:24–25).

The Bible does not describe the jobs of these two men, but scholars suggest the officials directed two departments of scribes. The recorder was probably responsible for writing down and circulating the king's decrees – acting as a royal spokesman who communicated the king's wishes to the people. The secretary may have been in charge of David's correspondence with individual Israelites and with rulers of other nations.

David, and later the son who succeeded him, Solomon, also probably assembled a group of scribes to write down and preserve the nation's well-known stories and laws. Possibly, the scribes who worked with the royal recorder and secretary were part of this scholarly team. The Bible never actually says David and Solomon created such a team of history-preserving scribes. But the Bible hints at it, as indicated below.

CLUES OF DAVID'S INFLUENCE

The book of Judges seems tailored to reveal more than Israel's chaotic history during the early days in Canaan, before the people had a king. The history was turbulent, with one crisis after another – each resulting in the people repenting of their sins and God sending a heroic leader, such as Gideon and Samson. But the final words of the book speak of anarchy and seem to hint that what the nation really needed, for long-term stability, was a king. 'In those days there was no king in Israel; all the people did what was right in their own eyes' (Judges 21:25).

In the two books of Samuel and the two books of Kings, writers carefully preserved stories about Israel's earliest kings, clearly showing that God chose David to rule the nation. Because it was customary for the king's oldest surviving son to inherit his father's throne, many people probably thought the throne of Israel should have passed from Saul, the nation's first king, to a son of Saul. But events reported in Israel's early history show that the prophet Samuel told Saul, 'Because you have rejected the word of the Lord, he has also rejected you from being king' (1 Samuel 15:23).

In dramatic stories, which possibly drew from first-person accounts by Samuel and David, the

writers tell of Samuel going secretly to young David's home town in Bethlehem and anointing him as Israel's next king – an anointing that took place at God's command. During this anointing, 'the spirit of the Lord came mightily upon David from that day forward' (1 Samuel 16:13).

The stories that follow offer compelling evidence that David was, indeed, blessed of God, since he rose to power and greatly expanded the nation's boundaries. This carefully preserved record is among the most intriguing and finely crafted writing in the Bible, packed with action, drama and riveting conversation.

Although the stories certainly helped deflect opposition to David's rule, later stories continue the saga and include some staggering failures of David, most notably his adultery with Bathsheba, followed by the murder of her husband.

This ancient history, initially preserved by word of mouth, eventually prompted Israel to create its own national literature. And later, when the scrolls began to crumble and fade with time and repeated use, scribes made exact copies on new scrolls, so their nation's history – and the lessons learned from it – would never be lost.

Early Aramaic inscription found in Dan, dating from the ninth century BC. The emphasized line reads 'Beit David', meaning, 'The House of David'.

David was no myth

Some Bible scholars once speculated that David was a mythical hero, much like Hercules, since there was no evidence he ever lived. But in 1993, a stone fragment that mentions the 'House of David' was found in northern Israel. The stone appears to commemorate a victory of the Arameans (in what is now Syria) over the Israelites. Dated about 200 years after the time of David, this inscribed stone became the first evidence outside the Bible that Israel had a king named David.

Since then, other references to David have been discovered – including an Egyptian wall inscription from about 50 years after David's death. The hieroglyphic inscription identifies a place that, according to some Egyptologists, says 'the Heights of David'. Jerusalem, David's capital city, is located in the hills of Judea.

The acts of Rehoboam, and all that he did, are they not written in the Book of the Annals of the Kings of Judah?'

1 KINGS 14:29

Psalms: Israel's Hymn Book

'It was the custom in Scotland for boys to wear the kilt to church on Sunday... I can recall singing the words of Psalm 147:10... "neither delighteth he in any man's legs".'

PETER C. CRAIGIE,
UNIVERSITY OF CALGARY

Psalms is not a book designed for people to read, like other Bible books. It is a book to sing. Psalms is a collection of 150 worship songs – masterfully crafted poetry set to music. These are songs the ancient Hebrews sang on a variety of occasions.

There are songs for walking to Jerusalem to attend religious festivals. Ancient superscriptions (words above the verses) refer to these road songs as 'songs of ascent', since no matter what direction people approached the hilltop city of Jerusalem from, they had to climb. There are also songs for the king's coronation, for weddings and for temple rituals.

SONGS FOR ALL OCCASIONS

Many songs are praises to God, thanking him for creation, protection and healing. Probably for this reason, the ancient Hebrew name of the book is Tehillim, which means 'praises'. Surprisingly, when you break the songs into categories, you have to file the thickest stack of songs under 'complaint'. These laments are poignant expressions of sorrow or fear over the treachery of friends, the threats of enemies, sickness, loneliness and the sense of being forsaken by God.

Because the book covers so many topics, it later became known as Psalms, from the Greek word *psalmos*, meaning 'song' or the 'twanging of

A psalm to Ishtar

A hundred years ago, some Bible scholars doubted that David had anything to do with the Psalms. The scholars argued that the songs could not be that old, and were probably written 400 years or more after David. Recent archaeological discoveries suggest otherwise.

There are striking similarities between some of the Hebrew psalms and songs found among the literary works of other ancient cultures: Egyptians, Canaanites, Babylonians and Assyrians. The parallels are sometimes so obvious that scholars suspect people in ancient times occasionally borrowed songs from other cultures and adapted them to fit their beliefs.

Here are excerpts from Psalm 13, quoted from the King James Version, and compared with excerpts from the Prayer of Lamentation to Ishtar. Goddess of war, Ishtar was worshipped by the Babylonians. The prayer to Ishtar is on a scroll from several hundred years after David. But a note on the scroll said it belonged to a Babylonian temple and was copied from an older version. Scholars say the prayer dates back hundreds of years, perhaps to the time of David or beyond. The Babylonian civilization started about 700 years before David.

Psalm 13
How long wilt thou forget me, O Lord? for ever?
how long wilt thou hide thy face from me?...
how long shall mine enemy be exalted over me?

Prayer of Lamentation to Ishtar
How long, O my Lady, wilt thou be angered
*   so that thy face is turned away?*
* How long, O my Lady, shall my adversaries*
*   be looking upon me?*
In truth and untruth shall they plan evil against me.
* Shall my pursuers and those who exult over me*
*   rage against me?*

Singers' guilds
Some psalms are attributed to singers' guilds, either the Sons of Korah or the Sons of Asaph. Occasionally, a psalm is attributed to an individual member of one of these guilds. Psalm 88, for example, is attributed to Heman of the Sons of Korah. As the names suggest, each guild was made up of members of a family, whose job was to sing at worship services.

It is not clear whether the guild members composed psalms or merely preserved and performed them. It seems likely, however, they composed some psalms, preserved a few classics, and revised others to fit new circumstances. The argument for revision is bolstered by the fact that some psalms are repeated with only minor changes: Psalm 40:13–17 repeats Psalm 70, following a section of 12 other verses.

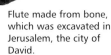

Flute made from bone, which was excavated in Jerusalem, the city of David.

strings'. In fact, the book includes brief instructions to musicians, occasionally instructing that stringed instruments or flutes should accompany a particular song.

DAVID, THE SINGING KING

Almost half the psalms are attributed to King David, a celebrated musician who, as a youngster, was often invited to King Saul's palace to play the lyre – a soothing, harp-like instrument that calmed Saul's bouts with depression. 2 Samuel preserves two of David's songs: a tribute to Saul and Jonathan killed in battle (1:17–27) and a song of thanks to God (22:1–51). 1 Chronicles says David later organized the temple music ministry, and selected the musicians.

David, however, may not have written many of the 73 psalms attributed to him. The Hebrew designation that bears his name is 'leDavid'. 'Le' is a preposition that can mean 'by', 'for' or 'about'. Yet if David did not write these psalms, at least his life inspired them. Many scholars say these superscript references to David were probably added by editors long after the psalms were composed.

A THOUSAND YEARS OF MUSIC

No one knows when the songs were written, but they seem to span nearly a millennium, from the exodus through the exile, when the Jews were defeated and banished to Babylon in 586 BC. Psalm 90 is the only song attributed to Moses, and may have been written by him, though it could well have been written later as a prayer in the spirit of Moses. Another psalm, speaks of the exile in Babylon as in the past: 'By the rivers of Babylon – there we sat down and there we wept when we remembered Zion' (137:1). This psalm was certainly written after the exile.

The individual songs of this book were probably used in public and private worship long before they were collected into a single volume. How and when the songs were compiled remains a mystery and may have taken place over several centuries – with new songs being added after they gradually became an established part of Jewish worship tradition. The final compilation took place sometime after the exile in Babylon. Among the famous Dead Sea Scrolls is one of Psalms, which was copied sometime between AD 30–50, about the time of Jesus. This version of Psalms includes three previously unknown songs. Other songs are not in the same order as they are in today's Bible, and there are some minor differences in the wording.

For more than 2,000 years, the psalms have been copied, carefully preserved and treasured by Jews and Christians alike. In this way, songs of ancient poets become the songs of today, as people continue using them to express their deepest feelings to God.

This seventh-century BC relief is from the palace of Ashurbanipal in Nineveh, and it shows Assyrian musicians with their instruments.

This Egyptian wall painting from the tomb of Rekhmere (a court official) shows female musicians with harp and stringed instruments.

Bible Poems

'Poetry provides imagery and tone for inspired writers to drum God's word home to his people.'

DONALD K. BERRY, PROFESSOR OF RELIGION, UNIVERSITY OF MOBILE, MOBILE, ALABAMA

'Poetry' was not in the ancient Hebrew vocabulary – there is no word for it. But poetry fills Hebrew literature. More than a third of the Old Testament is made up of poems, written to be sung or recited with expressive emotion.

Even before writing became common in Israel, the people crafted magnificent poetry that they memorized and passed along from generation to generation. Scholars say the oldest words in the Bible are poems:

❧ Miriam's song of praise after God parted the Red Sea (Exodus 15:21).

❧ Deborah's song after defeating an invasion force (Judges 5:1–31).

❧ David's funeral song for King Saul and Jonathan (2 Samuel 1:19–27).

These songs – all believed to be more than 3,000 years old – bear strong similarities to other Middle Eastern poetry of that era.

From Genesis to Malachi, almost every book of the Old Testament has at least some poetry. Several books have nothing but poetry: Psalms, Proverbs, Song of Solomon and Lamentations. Job is almost all poetry; and Ecclesiastes is about half poetry. In the Prophets, most messages from God are poems.

REPEATED THOUGHTS, NOT SOUNDS

Poetry written today often rhymes and has rhythm. We can hear the convergence of sounds, and feel the beat of each line. Hebrew poetry is not like that. It does not generally repeat sounds or march to the cadence of an easily recognizable beat. (Scholars are unsure how the words were pronounced, and where the accents fell. So it is unclear what kind of beat may have existed. But in the English translations, there is often no beat at all.)

What Hebrew poetry usually does, however, is repeat or balance ideas. With figurative language, the poet makes a statement in the first line and then says it again – another way – in the second line, and perhaps in later lines as well.

Bible scholars call this unique feature 'parallelism'. Hebrew writers used the technique in several ways.

Identical thoughts

The most obvious kind of poetic repetition is one that Bible scholars call 'synonymous parallelism', in which the second line means the same thing as the first line.

One well-known example comes from a prophet's plea for the corruption-plagued nation of Israel to do the right thing:

Let justice roll down like waters,
*   and righteousness like an ever-flowing stream.*
Amos 5:24

Knowing about this poetic technique can help readers interpret confusing statements in Bible poetry. But readers who are not aware of it can get confused. For instance, the prophet Zechariah predicted Jesus would ride into Jerusalem on what could sound like two animals at once. Zechariah said the king comes:

humble and riding on a donkey,
*   on a colt, the foal of a donkey.*
Zechariah 9:9

The seasons of life

One of the most famous examples of Hebrew poetry comes from a wise man searching for the meaning to life.

The words do not rhyme, in English or Hebrew. And there is no consistent beat. But in these words, it is easy to see the most prominent feature of Hebrew poetry: repetition of thought. The idea in the first line of each stanza is repeated in the second line:

For everything there is a season,
and a time for every matter under heaven:
a time to be born, and a time to die;
a time to plant, and a time to pluck up what is planted;
a time to kill, and a time to heal;
a time to break down, and a time to build up;
a time to weep, and a time to laugh;
a time to mourn, and a time to dance;
a time to throw away stones, and a time to gather stones together;
a time to embrace, and a time to refrain from embracing;
a time to seek, and a time to lose;
a time to keep, and a time to throw away;
a time to tear, and a time to sew;
a time to keep silence, and a time to speak;
a time to love, and a time to hate;
a time for war, and a time for peace.

ECCLESIASTES 3:1–8

Miriam's song of praise after the parting of the Red Sea, which is preserved in Exodus 15, is considered among the oldest poems in the Bible. *The Story of Moses (The Dance of Miriam)* by Lorenzo Costa (c. 1459/60–1535)

Suffering from A to Z

One kind of Hebrew poetry is an acrostic. The first verse starts with the first letter of the Hebrew alphabet, the second verse starts with the next letter, and so on – through the 22-letter alphabet. Psalm 25 is an acrostic-style plea for help, suggesting the writer knows suffering from A to Z.

Contrasting thoughts

A second common technique is one that scholars have named 'antithetical parallelism'. Here, the poet strengthens his first line by contrasting it with the exact opposite in a second line.

The Lord watches over the way of the righteous,
but the way of the wicked will perish.
Psalm 1:6

A build-up of thought

Perhaps the hardest kind of parallelism to identify is one called 'constructive' or 'synthetic' parallelism. Usually, there's no repetition at all. Instead, each line builds on the one before it.

Like a gold ring in a pig's snout
is a beautiful woman without good sense.
Proverbs 11:22

In another passage, a poet uses the same technique to describe people who obey God's law:

They are like trees
planted by streams of water,
which yield their fruit in its season,
and their leaves do not wither.
In all that they do, they prosper.
Psalm 1:3

Not all Hebrew poetry has parallel ideas. Instead, the words simply feel like poetry – dancing with power and grace. Since the Hebrew language itself is almost poetic by nature, and rich with imagery, alliterations and other literary devices, it is sometimes hard to tell the difference between poetry and prose.

New Testament poems

The New Testament, written in Greek instead of Hebrew, has very few poems. Two of the most beautiful are the Beatitudes and the Lord's Prayer.

Sources of the Pentateuch

Although much was written down during the time of King David and his son, Solomon, accounts of the origins of the Israelites and their beliefs were probably still being circulated by word of mouth during the heyday of the kingdom of Israel. These accounts would eventually be preserved in written form in the first five books of the Bible, known as the Pentateuch (from the Greek for 'five-book work'). For many centuries it was believed that Moses had written the Pentateuch, and it was often referred to as the Five Books of

That's another story

Refutation of Moses' authorship of the Pentateuch came as early as the first century AD. In chapter 14 of 2 Esdras, one of the books of the Apocrypha (books that did not quite make it into the Old Testament), God speaks to Ezra from a bush, telling him to assemble five scribes and to dictate to them what God will inspire him to say. Ezra dictates for 40 days, and his scribes copy down the 24 books of the Old Testament plus 70 other sacred books. Early Christian writers – the Fathers of the Church – interpreted this passage as showing that Ezra, not Moses, had written the Pentateuch, and that he had done so under direct inspiration from God. However, 2 Esdras was written hundreds of years after the time of Ezra, and the Fathers are known for not paying much attention to historical and scientific details. Today the passage from Esdras is generally regarded as a myth.

Moses. Today scholars believe the Pentateuch was not written down until well after the time of Moses and that it was the work of numerous authors. But this idea is not entirely new. From early times it was suspected that, even though Moses is certainly the spirit behind the texts, he did not personally write the books credited to him.

QUESTIONING MOSES' AUTHORSHIP

Problems with Moses' authorship started early. Although the New Testament speaks of the law of Moses it does not specifically say that Moses wrote the five books of the Pentateuch. Soon, however, this idea seemed to catch hold, even though it seemed that parts of the text had been written later than the time of Moses. In about AD 400 Jerome, whose Latin translation of the Bible, the Vulgate, was to remain in use for 1,500 years, held that Moses was the original author of the Pentateuch but that the books had not been given their final shape until about 400 BC, the time of Ezra, the priest who instituted religious

Then and now

Aside from the doublets in the Pentateuch, there are other indications that these books were not written by Moses. One such sign is the frequent use of the phrase 'to this day' in referring to the continued use of place names or customs. As used in the text, 'this day' obviously refers to a time far later than that of Moses.

reform among the Jews who were returning to Jerusalem after exile in Babylon.

By the seventh century more serious doubts arose about Moses' authorship. One early objection was that the book of Deuteronomy contains an account of Moses' death, and Moses could not have written such an account himself. Later commentators, including the 17th-century philosopher Thomas Hobbes, suggested that the first five books of the Bible had indeed been written by Moses but that later scribes had added material to the text, including the description of Moses' death. Hobbes's contemporary, Baruch Spinoza, held that the Pentateuch had been compiled by Ezra, using older materials, some of which might have been written by Moses.

In his studies of the Pentateuch, Spinoza noticed doublets (the presence of two versions of a single story). Some of the most obvious are found in Genesis. There are two accounts of the creation, for example. In Genesis 1:11–27, God creates plants, then animals, and then he creates man and woman together. In Genesis 2:7–22, God creates man, then plants, then animals, and then he creates a woman out of the man's rib. The story of the flood offers another clear example. In Genesis 7:2–3, Noah takes aboard the ark seven pairs of each kind of clean animal and bird but only one pair of each kind of unclean animal. In Genesis 6:19–20 and 7:8–9, he takes aboard only one pair of each kind of animal and bird, whether clean or unclean.

These doublets and other elements – such as minor contradictions in dates, place names and other details – suggested that the Pentateuch was not written by a single author, whether Moses or someone else. Over the next two centuries, scholars examined the biblical texts, paying close attention to the doublets, and came up with numerous theories about the origin of the ancient texts.

FOUR SOURCES

As scholars separated the strands of narrative indicated by the doublets, they began to realize that some accounts used the name Yahweh for God while others used the word Elohim. This led them to believe that at least two traditions were interwoven in the Pentateuch. Other scholars found more. In 1878 the German scholar Julius Wellhausen studied all the viable theories and proposed a schema called the Documentary Hypothesis, which is still widely used today.

Wellhausen saw four basic sources, which he named J, E, P and D. The letter J stands for Jahveh, the German spelling of Yahweh, the name generally used for God in this source. E stands for Elohim, the Hebrew word meaning 'god'. P stands for priestly, because these writings focus on priests and worship. Finally, D denotes the book of Deuteronomy, which makes up the fourth source.

The J, E, P and D sources had been written as separate accounts at different times, in different places, and by different people, as will be discussed on the following page. They themselves incorporated even earlier sources, both written and oral. Some of these primary sources probably go back to Moses, while others are even older. J, E, P and D were not to be combined to make up the books we have today until at least the time of the Babylonian captivity in the sixth century BC.

According to Genesis, Noah either took aboard the ark seven pairs of each kind of clean animal and bird, along with one pair of each kind of unclean animal, or he took one pair of each kind of animal and bird, whether clean or unclean. Catalan illustration of Noah's ark (illuminated c. 970/75).

Shaping the Pentateuch

The Pentateuch, the first five books of the Bible, was not written, as long supposed, by Moses or any other individual. Rather it probably interweaves four sources, identified by the letters J, E, P and D, as explained on the preceding pages. The time and place in which these sources were written is uncertain, but there is a general agreement on some points.

HOW THE SOURCES DIFFER

J, the oldest source, probably dates back to the ninth century BC, after Israel had split into the southern kingdom of Judah, which continued to be ruled by the descendants of David, and the northern kingdom of Israel, which had its own, non-Davidic kings. J stresses the monarchy by focusing on God's promise to bring the Israelite tribes together under one king, thus implying criticism of the secession of the north. Theologically, J is the simplest source, viewing God as a compassionate being who communicates face to face. Its literary style is lively and colourful. J stresses stories and traditions of the southern tribes, including those of Abraham, who lived in the southern city of Hebron.

E, which probably dates to the eighth century, focuses on the leadership of Moses and the prophets rather than kings. Its style is more sophisticated than J's and God is less personal, communicating through angels or in dreams. E stresses traditions and characters from the northern kingdom. Sometime after the northern kingdom fell to the Assyrian conquerors, copies of E may have been taken south to Jerusalem. E was combined with J sometime in the mid-seventh century.

D, or at least a large part of it, probably made up the book of law that was found in the temple in 621 BC, and read to King Josiah (2 Kings 22:8). The remainder of D may have been written later. D emphasizes the need for central worship, as advocated by Josiah, and several references seem to be to the reign of Josiah. Scholars say that

Joseph is sold into slavery by his brothers to either Ishmaelite or Midianite traders. The event is depicted in this woodcut by Julius Schnorr von Carolsfield (1794–1874), from *Die Bibel in Bildern*.

North against south

There are many reasons for believing that the J source of the Pentateuch was written in the south after Israel had been split into northern and southern kingdoms. However, the story of how the Israelites acquired the city of Shechem, which was later to become the capital of the northern kingdom, makes it dramatically clear. According to J, the land was acquired through treachery. This account (now Genesis 34) tells how Shechem, the prince for whom the city was named, raped Dinah, the daughter of Jacob, but then repented and offered to marry her and make peace. Dinah's outraged brothers slyly pretended to agree to this plan, but only if Shechem and all his men would be circumcised. But while the men were still sore from their circumcisions, Jacob's sons killed them and plundered their city. According to the northern E source, however, Jacob simply bought land at Shechem, which was to become the northern capital (Genesis 33:18–19), and omits the ugly story told in J.

D was added to the combined J and E in the mid-sixth century.

P may have been added to the earlier sources during the Babylonian exile, in the sixth century, by priests who were attempting to demonstrate and preserve the origins of temple rituals. In the P texts the priest is the ultimate authority; prophets play no part. According to P, only Aaron's descendants are priests, while in the other sources all Levites, whether descended from Aaron or not, are priests. In addition to a lot of material on the role of priests, there are more than 200 references to the tabernacle (a tent worship centre, and the forerunner of the temple in Jerusalem), while the tabernacle is mentioned only three times in E and never in J and D. P is more rigid in tone than J or E. There are no angels, talking animals or dreams in P, and no references to God mixing with humans – or wrestling with them. Instead, there is an interest in ages, dates and measurements not found in the other sources.

Some scholars believe that P was not added to the other sources until the Israelites returned to Jerusalem from Babylon. At that time it might have been composed by a priest who was attempting to re-establish rituals and customs while the temple was being rebuilt. That priest may even have been Ezra, offering some modest basis for the fanciful story, told in 2 Esdras, of his dictating the entire Old Testament to scribes.

CLOSELY KNIT TEXTS

The editors of the Pentateuch, whoever they were, did a masterful job of pulling the texts together. In some cases, stories from the various sources are simply placed one after the other, as in the two versions of the creation in Genesis 1 and 2. In other places, however, sources are so closely knit together it is hard to separate them.

For example, in the story of Joseph, E and J versions are entwined. Genesis 37:21–24 reports that Reuben keeps his brothers from murdering their younger brother Joseph by convincing them to throw him into a pit, planning to rescue him later. Reuben's plans will be thwarted when the other brothers sell Joseph into slavery to a group of Midianites. But Genesis 37:25–27 says that it is Judah who saves Joseph's life, suggesting that he be sold to a band of Ishmaelites. Then these two traditions come together in a verse that seems to name both the Midianites and the Ishmaelites as the traders who bought Joseph: 'When some Midianite traders passed by, they drew Joseph up, lifting him out of the pit, and sold him to the Ishmaelites for 20 pieces of silver' (Genesis 37:28). This passage also demonstrates the northern and southern biases of J and E. For in the E version Reuben, whose descendants settled in the north, saves Joseph, while in the J version Judah, whose descendants settled in the south, does so.

In places, the editors of the Pentateuch pieced together strains of the various sources by simply linking them with phrases or even single words – such as adding 'again' to justify repetitions. In other places they repeated a sentence from one source after inserting something from a different source, thus bringing the reader back to the earlier point. In other cases, they separated accounts by adding genealogies or other supplemental material. In all they did, however, the editors took care never to significantly change or delete material from their sources. In fact, the editors held their material in such high regard that they incorporated seeming contradictions and awkwardnesses into the text rather than change essential materials for a smoother read.

And then she wrote...

Harold Bloom, a prominent literary scholar, speculates that the author of the J source of the Pentateuch may have been a woman. To be sure, J seems to be more sympathetic towards women than E, P and D, but most biblical scholars discount Bloom's view, and hold that J was written by a male scribe.

Prophets and Scribes

Then Jeremiah called Baruch son of Neriah, and Baruch wrote on a scroll at Jeremiah's dictation all the words of the Lord that he had spoken to him.'

JEREMIAH 36:4

Right: Scribes generally closed their scrolls with tiny chunks of clay, called *bullae*, into which they impressed their seals. The *bulla* shown here is believed to contain an impression of Baruch's seal, as it identifies Baruch by his name, his occupation and his father's name.

In the early days of their history, the Israelites had no king. Or rather, the Lord God was their king, and he kept in touch with his people through prophets – men and women who spoke for him. There were probably thousands of Israelite prophets, but only a small number of them are known today.

In the 200 years or so after the Israelites settled in the Promised Land, prophets advised the judges who ruled the land – or even, like Deborah, ruled as judges themselves. The last judge-prophet was Samuel, who under God's guidance, chose and anointed Israel's first two kings, Saul and David. But even in the days of the kings, prophets wielded power, advising the people and their leaders and, at times, even boldly confronting kings who disregarded God's will. Stories of these prophets are found in the books of Samuel and Kings, where bits and pieces of their prophecies are recorded. The words of later prophets, the so-called writing prophets, are recorded in biblical books that bear their names.

THE WRITING PROPHETS

The earliest writing prophets were Hosea and Amos, who called for religious and social reforms in the northern kingdom of Israel. (The land of the Israelites had split into two kingdoms after the death of Solomon, Israel's third king.) Hosea and Amos assured the people that the Lord would protect them if they turned back to him, stopped worshipping idols, and started to care for the needy. In addition, the prophets Micah and Isaiah condemned the injustices and idolatry they found in both Israel and the southern kingdom of Judah. The great prophet Isaiah also warned that God would send the Assyrians to invade Israel as punishment for the sins of the people. All these prophets went unheeded and, as Isaiah had foreseen, the Assyrians obliterated the northern kingdom of Israel. After 721 BC it no longer existed.

Later prophets turned their attention to the surviving kingdom of Judah, generally begging the people to remember the Lord and follow his

Baruch the scribe

Baruch was born in Jerusalem to a prominent family of scribes. And even though his brother, Seraiah, who was a minister in the king's court, could have secured him an important position, Baruch gave up court life and dedicated himself to the thankless and often painful job of following the unpopular prophet Jeremiah. Throughout the turbulent final years of the fiery Jeremiah's career, Baruch faithfully acted as the prophet's secretary, refusing to desert him while he was in prison, helping him escape the murderous plots of rival court prophets, and even defying the king by reading Jeremiah's unwelcome prophecies in public. After the fall of Jerusalem in 586 BC, Baruch went with Jeremiah a few miles north to the small town of Mizpah. When trouble erupted there, Jeremiah's supporters urged the prophet to flee with them to Egypt. When Jeremiah refused, the people accused Baruch of inciting the prophet against them in an attempt to get them all exiled to Babylon, and they forced both Jeremiah and Baruch to go with them to Egypt. While in Egypt, Baruch probably shaped much of the biblical book of Jeremiah.

word. They included Zephaniah, Nahum, Habakkuk and the unstoppable Jeremiah, who advised Judah's last five kings.

In 597 BC, after the first of two invasions of Jerusalem, the Babylonians brought home 8,000 captives, including Ezekiel. From exile Ezekiel prophesied the destruction of Jerusalem's temple, but his people ignored him until the temple did fall during the second Babylonian invasion of Jerusalem in 586 BC. From then until his death, Ezekiel preached hope, reassuring his people that God would resurrect Israel, like a pile of dry bones coming back to life. In 539, Babylonia was conquered by Cryus the Great of Persia, who allowed the Israelites to return to Jerusalem to rebuild it.

SETTING IT DOWN

Generally, prophets delivered their prophecies spontaneously, perhaps accompanied by music and dancing. But their words were later written down in highly structured poetic form, and no one knows by whom. The prophets themselves may have later written down and polished their own pronouncements, but in many cases, it is believed, disciples of the prophets wrote down their teachers' words for later study and teaching. Often these disciples edited the texts to fit new circumstances and, in certain cases, probably even added to the prophecies. The book of Isaiah suggests this process, as its writings cover a period of some 200 years. Not only is this far too long a period for one man to have prophesied, but there are obvious differences in writing style that strongly suggest the work of two or even three writers. Only the prophecies in chapters 1 to 39 of the biblical book of Isaiah are believed to have been made by the historical Isaiah.

Prophetic works were also preserved by scribes. This method of preservation is vividly described in chapter 36 of the book of Jeremiah. We read there that when King Jehoiakim of Judah forbade Jeremiah to enter the temple to proclaim his prophecies, God told the prophet to write down all his words and have them read to the king. Jeremiah then dictated all his past prophecies to his scribe, Baruch, who copied them down in a scroll. Baruch then went to the temple, where he publicly read Jeremiah's words. When officials of the king heard about this, they sent for Baruch, had him read the prophecies to them, then took the scroll from Baruch and told him to go into hiding along with Jeremiah. The officials then went to the royal palace and fearfully read the prophecies to the angry king, who promptly burned the scroll. But the prophecies were not lost, for God ordered Jeremiah to have the scroll rewritten, and Baruch again took down his master's words. The new scroll probably formed the basis for the first 25 chapters of the book of Jeremiah.

In 582 BC Jeremiah and Baruch were forced to take refuge in Egypt. There, Baruch continued as Jeremiah's secretary-scribe, writing down the prophet's pleas that the Israelites be faithful to the Lord. While in exile Baruch probably wrote most of chapters 26 to 45 of the book of Jeremiah. According to a later tradition, Baruch also wrote the book of Baruch, a work found in the Apocrypha. However, scholars now believe that the book of Baruch was written centuries after the scribe's death.

The North Rose window of Chartres Cathedral illustrates Old Testament prophets (in circles) and kings (in squares).

Unflattering History

'[David] saw from the roof a woman bathing [Bathsheba]; the woman was very beautiful... So David sent messengers to get her, and she came to him, and he lay with her.'

2 SAMUEL 11:2–4

King David watches Bathsheba bathe, an act that led to adultery and murder. Israel recorded its history, good and bad, with the hope that future generations would learn from the mistakes of their ancestors. Fifteenth-century illumination from a Book of Hours.

Hired priests

Israel moved so far from God during the time of the Judges that priests were for sale. One man actually hired a Bethlehem priest to take charge of his personal shrine, complete with an idol (Judges 17).

Israel disappeared from the world map about 1,500 years after God told Abraham, in Canaan, 'All the land that you see I will give to you and to your offspring forever' (Genesis 13:15). But in 586 BC, the Babylonian army invaded and wiped out the last vestiges of a Jewish nation. Soldiers levelled the cities – including Jerusalem and the temple – and dragged survivors off to exile in Babylon.

More than 1,000 kilometres (600 miles) from home, the Jews lost their identity as a nation. They had no king to rule them, no city to call their own, and no temple in which to offer their sacrifices of repentance. They were just another race of conquered people stirred into the racially diverse soup of the Babylonian empire.

In exile, after the destruction of nearly everything that set the Jews apart as a unique nation chosen by God, they began to re-evaluate their faith. They wanted to know how this tragedy could have happened, and if it was permanent. So they studied their traditions, laws, and history – searching for answers.

They were apparently treated well and could do as they pleased in the communities where they settled. Scholars speculate that the Jews started synagogues during this time, as a substitute for the temple. Though Jewish law permitted sacrifices only at the temple altar in Jerusalem, the people could gather at the synagogues – often in people's homes – for fellowship, study, and worship.

POLISHING OLD TESTAMENT TEXTS

It was during this time of exile that the Jews compiled and edited much of the Old Testament stories and teachings into the written text we have today. Among the books polished into final form were those of earlier prophets who had warned that the nation was headed for destruction if the people did not abandon their idols and evil behaviour, and return to God. Also finalized during these years were the books of Israel's history, from Joshua to 2 Kings. Even the five books of Moses, from Genesis to Deuteronomy, were probably moulded into their final form during and shortly after the exile. Collections of psalms were probably put together during this time, and formed the basis of what was to become the book of Psalms. Lamentations was written at this time, giving a heartbreaking description of the fall of Jerusalem and the temple.

Understanding the likely setting behind these books helps explain why the Jews preserved so much of their unflattering history. For in these stories and teachings they found the answers they sought about their disastrous exile. So they made a point of preserving what was so relevant to their situation.

THE REASON BEHIND THE HORROR

Exiled Jews wanted to know what they had done to deserve such a horrifying fate. The stories they studied clearly showed that they broke their covenant with God – they were in breach of contract. During the exodus, the Israelites agreed to set themselves apart from other nations as a people devoted to God and his laws. In return, God promised to bless them with national prominence, prosperous harvests, large families and victory over enemies. Disobedience, however, would produce the exact opposite. Listed among the many sad consequences was this: 'You shall be plucked off the land... The Lord will scatter you among all peoples, from one end of the earth to the other' (Deuteronomy 28:63–64).

This is exactly what happened to them. After centuries of disobedience – idolatry, injustice, immorality – the Jewish people got the punishment they had been warned about. The stories of their history show God's patience with them, expressed by his many attempts to turn them away from sin by sending corrective punishment. This is especially clear in Judges, a book featuring repeated cycles of sin, followed by oppression at the hands of enemies, followed by the Israelites calling on God for help, followed by deliverance. This cycle repeated itself over and over.

Even the stories of David's adultery and of Solomon's idolatry late in life are preserved, to show that God punishes sin even among revered heroes. David's son born from the adulterous affair died. And Solomon's kingdom was later split in two: Israel in the north and Judah in the south.

As later kings and their people continued ignoring their covenant – especially by worshipping idols – God sent prophets to warn them about what would happen. In 722 BC, Assyrian invaders decimated the northern nation of Israel and scattered the people abroad. Jews watching in Judah failed to see the connection between sin and judgment there, and in 586 BC suffered the same fate at the hands of Babylonians.

WERE THE JEWS STILL CHOSEN?

Stories compiled during the exile clearly showed that the Jews lost their nation because of their long history of sin. The follow-up question was whether or not they were still God's chosen people. Would God take them back after what they had done?

The implication in their tradition was that whether or not the Jews were devoted to God, he was devoted to them. He would punish sin, but he would forgive and restore:

When all these things have happened to you, the blessings and the curses that I have set before you, if you call them to mind among all the nations where the Lord your God has driven you, and return to the Lord your God, and you and your children obey him with all your heart and with all your soul… then the Lord your God will restore your fortunes and have compassion on you, gathering you again from all the peoples.
Deuteronomy 30:1–2

This was exactly what the Jews in exile needed to hear. So they became determined to preserve these teachings and stories – along with some embarrassing history – as a source of hope for themselves and a sacred warning for the generations to come. These writings helped the Jews preserve their faith, re-establish their commitment to following God's laws, and restore their national identity.

'By the rivers of Babylon – there we sat down and there we wept when we remembered Zion.'

PSALM 137:1

The Assyrian attack on the Judean city of Lachish in 701 BC is shown in this stone relief from King Sennacherib's palace in Nineveh: 'In the 14th year of King Hezekiah, King Sennacherib of Assyria came up against all the fortified cities of Judah and captured them' (2 Kings 18:13). The Bible says God punished the Israelites' sin by sending such invaders.

History with a Viewpoint

The biblical books of Joshua, Judges, 1 and 2 Samuel, and 1 and 2 Kings relate the history of the Israelites from the time they entered and conquered Canaan, the land that God had promised them, until they lost the land and were carried off to exile in Babylon. For about 2,000 years students of the Bible assumed that these books were written by different authors at different times. Then, in 1943, all of that changed. A German biblical scholar, Martin Noth, showed that these books had a uniform style and outlook, and concluded that they constitute a single ancient history. Furthermore, Noth claimed that Deuteronomy, which shares the same style and outlook, had been written as an introduction to the history, connecting it to the Pentateuch; it had not been written as part of the Pentateuch, as formerly believed. Today many scholars agree, though most believe that the history, now known as the Deuteronomistic History, evolved gradually.

A SINGLE, LONG HISTORY

The Deuteronomistic History as it appears in the Bible today was probably shaped during the Babylonian exile, when the Israelites were struggling to understand why God had seemingly abandoned them, his chosen people. The first edition may have been started centuries earlier. Soon after Israel was divided into two kingdoms, Jeroboam, the first king of the northern kingdom of Israel, built shrines containing images of calves, scandalizing orthodox believers who considered it against the law of Moses to do so. To make matters even worse, Jeroboam also appointed priests from among the people instead of using priests from the tribe of Levi as required. According to a recent theory, the Levitic priests who were replaced by these new appointees joined together to preserve their revered traditions. Their descendants, who continued this work, eventually moved to Jerusalem sometime before the northern kingdom completely fell to the Assyrians in 721 BC. These so-called Deuteronomists may have started to write their history soon after the fall of the northern kingdom, to explain why the northern kingdom had fallen.

In writing their history, the Deuteronomists made use of various ancient sources, including chronicles and court histories, military records, territorial lists, cycles of stories about the prophets Elijah and Elisha, and ancient songs (including the Song of Deborah). The first version of the history was probably completed during the reign of King Josiah of Judah, and it presented Josiah as a model king whom God would use to restore his relationship with the Israelites. This early version stressed the need to keep the law of Moses and to rid worship of all pagan influences. The texts did not represent themselves as actual histories, but merely as theological commentaries on history. Each king was judged only on his relationship with God. His strictly political accomplishments, the Deuteronomists said, could be read in other books – books that are now lost. For the Deuteronomists, if a king allowed pagan worship, he was evil. If he supported God's law and worshipped only him, he was good. Most of the kings of Israel were bad, and so Israel fell. Under Josiah, however, the kingdom of Judah would prosper with God offering full support.

Sculpture of the prophet Jeremiah on the central pillar of a doorway in Moissac Abbey Church in France.

HOPES DEFLATED

The optimism of the Deuteronomists was suddenly dashed when Josiah was killed in battle. The next four kings were not good ones, and finally Jerusalem fell to the Babylonians and by 586 BC most of the Israelites had been carried off into exile. In order to make the history understandable in the face of these tragic circumstances, the Deuteronomists' texts needed revision. The early version of the history had blamed bad kings for the troubles of the people, but there were no more kings. Consequently, an editor or group of editors reworked the history and brought it up to date. The changes show that it was not merely the kings who had done wrong, but the people as a whole. The role of the people is greatly expanded in the revised texts, and it is made clear that God had established his covenant with the people themselves and not merely with their rulers. God remained faithful to his covenant even though the people continuously broke it by refusing to listen to God's word and by disobeying his laws. But

---

Jeroboam did not turn from his evil way, but made priests... from among all the people; any who wanted to be priests he consecrated... This matter became sin to the house of Jeroboam, so as to cut it off and to destroy it from the face of the earth.'

1 KINGS 13:33–34

Jeroboam's Idolatry by Jean-Honoré Fragonard (1732–1806).

Josiah, an ideal king

When his father, Amon, was assassinated in 640 BC, the eight-year-old Josiah became king of Judah in his place. In time Josiah came to revere God, though his father had not. He undertook a restoration of the temple, financing it with money collected from the people. In 622 BC, as the work proceeded, a book of the law, probably an early version of the book of Deuteronomy, was found, and Josiah was so inspired by it that he instituted far-reaching religious reforms – with the backing of the prophet Jeremiah. Because the law required all sacrifices to be offered in Jerusalem, Josiah destroyed all altars outside the temple, including the one Jeroboam had erected at Bethel. In 609 BC Josiah went to war with Egypt and was killed in battle. The Bible concludes: 'Before him there was no king like him, who turned to the Lord with all his heart, with all his soul, and with all his might, according to all the law of Moses; nor did any like him arise after him' (2 Kings 23:25).

when trouble came and the people repented, God always forgave them. The history seems to end on a note of hope that if the people turn back to God during this time of exile, he will again forgive them and again restore them to his favour.

No one really knows who wrote the Deuteronomistic History or who edited it during the exile. Some scholars believe that the prophet Jeremiah might have done the revisions from his exile in Egypt. They point out that the books are careful to say nothing about their author and that Jeremiah does not enter into the history even though he was a major figure who advised the last four kings of Judah. This omission may have been deliberate because Jeremiah did not want to bring himself into the history that he was writing. Jeremiah's own work is covered in the separate book that bears his name.

After the exile ended the revised text was probably returned to Jerusalem, where it was joined to the Pentateuch, with more changes and additions being made to smooth out the fusion. The final text, which we have today, shows a loving God who continues to care for his people, even though they constantly move away from him. God is always seen as loving and faithful in the Deuteronomistic History.

Later Prophecies and History

'Ezra had set his heart to study the law of the Lord, and to do it, and to teach the statutes and ordinances in Israel.'

EZRA 7:10

First the northern kingdom of Israel and then the southern kingdom of Judah had been conquered, and the Israelites were being held captive by the Babylonians, far from their homeland. But conquerors can be conquered too. In 539 BC Cyrus the Great of Persia defeated the Babylonians, and much of the Near East came under Persian rule. Soon after this conquest, Cyrus allowed some of the Israelites to return to Jerusalem, and rebuild their city and temple.

LAST PROPHETIC WRITINGS

The book of Isaiah contains predictions of Cyrus's saving action. These predictions and the rest of chapters 40 to 55 of Isaiah were probably written by an anonymous prophet, using the name of the earlier prophet Isaiah, shortly before Cyrus's victory. Later, from Jerusalem, either the same prophet – sometimes referred to as Deutero (Second) Isaiah – or an entirely different prophet wrote the passages contained in chapters 56 to 66 of the book of Isaiah. This 'Third Isaiah' encouraged the Israelites to rebuild Jerusalem, telling them that God's salvation would come not only to them but to all the world.

In addition, five other prophets made their

Ezra, the second lawgiver

A direct descendant of Moses' brother Aaron, Ezra was given a commission by King Artaxerxes of Persia to return to Jerusalem and teach the people the law of Moses. He travelled to Jerusalem with a large group of other Israelite exiles, and when he arrived he immediately began his work of re-establishing the Jewish religion there. When he discovered that many of the Israelites had taken pagan wives, he was horrified and convinced most of them to divorce these idol worshippers. Then he read from the book of Moses (the Pentateuch) in Hebrew, while an interpreter translated into Akkadian, the language the exiles had begun speaking in Babylon. The people of Jerusalem had never heard, or had forgotten, much of what they heard in these readings, but quickly adopted it. From that time to this the law of Moses has been the focal point of Jewish worship. Moses had been the Jewish people's first lawgiver. Ezra, by restoring the Mosaic law to them, is considered their second lawgiver.

Ezra the Scribe, illustration from a seventh to eighth-century illuminated manuscript from Italy.

The Cylinder of Cyrus, dating from 536 BC, which tells of the decree recorded in the book of Ezra permitting the Jews who were transferred to Babylon to return to Judah and rebuild the temple.

voices heard during the period following the return from exile. Obadiah condemned the Edomites, a neighbouring people, for not having helped the Israelites when the Babylonians had invaded and taken them into exile. Haggai and Zechariah urged the returning Israelites to rebuild the temple. A little later, Joel described a plague of locusts as a punishment from God and urged repentance, and Malachi told the people that God loved them and pointed to the coming of the Messiah. The prophecies of each of these men are preserved in individual books of the Bible.

REWRITING HISTORY AND EXTENDING IT

Not all of the exiled Israelites returned home during Cyrus's rule. Some never returned. Daniel, the prophet, and Esther, who married a later king of Persia, were among those who stayed. And the many who did return did so slowly, over a period of about a century. Among the most important of the later returnees were Ezra, a priest and scribe, and Nehemiah, who served as governor of Judah. Nehemiah saw to the rebuilding of Jerusalem's walls, which had been destroyed by the Babylonians in 586. Ezra instituted religious reforms and promoted the book of the law, which many scholars believe to have been the Pentateuch in its present form. Accounts of Ezra and Nehemiah are found in the biblical books that bear their names – a single volume called Ezra-Nehemiah in the Hebrew Bible.

During the time of Ezra and Nehemiah, a new history of the Jewish people appeared, known in the Bible as Chronicles. In the Hebrew Bible this is a single book, but in Christian Bibles it is divided into two parts. 1 Chronicles traces the history of the Israelites from the creation of the world to the death of King David. Most of this history is given briefly in the form of genealogies and lists of priests, military leaders and officials. The reign of David, however, is given in more detail, but David's blemishes are

ignored. For example, even though vast portions of the books of Samuel and Kings are repeated in Chronicles, often verbatim, the story found in 2 Samuel 11–12, of David's adulterous affair with Bathsheba and its consequences, is missing from 1 Chronicles. In fact, David is not presented realistically at all but merely as a model against which all future kings can be measured.

2 Chronicles begins with an idealized history of Solomon's reign. The account of the divided kingdom that follows pays scant attention to the northern kingdom of Israel, which is seen as totally false to God. The kings of the southern kingdom of Judah, on the other hand, are judged by whether or not they follow God's law. Judah finally falls to the Babylonians because so many of its kings fail in their duty. The book ends with an account of the destruction of Jerusalem and the exile of the people, but it offers some hope. Prompted by God, Cyrus decrees that the Jews may return to Jerusalem and rebuild their temple.

Many scholars believe that the books of Chronicles, Ezra and Nehemiah were created as a single work by a single author, who is generally refered to as the Chronicler. Certainly, the texts of Ezra-Nehemiah complete Chronicles by adding the history of Judah after the return from exile, and Ezra begins where 2 Chronicles ends – with Cyrus's decree. No one knows who the Chronicler was, but many believe it was Ezra himself. If not, it was probably some other temple official writing around 400 BC.

Evidence Supporting the Bible

Most archaeologists who dig through the ruins of ancient biblical cities in the Middle East are not on a mission to prove the Bible. In fact, they argue that historical records cannot prove the most important teachings of the Bible – such as the existence of God. What archaeologists are looking for are clues about what life was like in biblical times. But in their quest for insight, they sometimes stumble across evidence that supports Old Testament history as the Bible reports it.

Here are a few of the most famous discoveries, listed in the order they appear in biblical history.

ISRAEL'S FIRST MENTION OUTSIDE THE BIBLE

How odd that history's first-known reference to Israel is an Egyptian king's exaggerated boast that he wiped out the nation: 'Israel is laid waste'.

The bragging pharaoh is Merneptah. The quotation – chiselled into a black granite slab more than two metres (seven feet) high – was commissioned by the king to commemorate his alleged victory over several enemies in Canaan, the Israelites included. The monument, now on display in the Cairo Museum, was erected in Thebes, Egypt in about 1210 BC. That is after the exodus, when the Israelites arrived in Canaan – perhaps in the time of the Judges.

This evidence lends support to the biblical story of the exodus, which says the Israelites fled Egypt and settled the region that today includes Israel and parts of neighbouring Arab nations.

ANOTHER KING BRAGS OF DEFEATING ISRAEL

In 1868, nomadic herders in Jordan found a stone monument that looks a bit like a tombstone more than a metre (three feet) high. Chiselled into the black stone monument, now famous as the Moabite Stone, are the exploits of King Mesha who claims to have 'utterly destroyed forever' the descendants of 'Omri, king of Israel'. Omri was King Ahab's father, and the first of a three-generation dynasty of Israelite rulers.

The Bible confirms that Mesha led his people, the Moabites (in what is now Jordan), in a rebellion against Jehoram, Omri's grandson and the last ruler of Omri's dynasty. Jehoram invaded Moab to quell the rebellion in this neighbouring nation that paid taxes to them. But the Israelite army was driven back (2 Kings 3:27). Contrary to Mesha's boast, Jehoram was not killed in the fighting. Jehoram died later in a coup.

The Moabite Stone, dating from the 800s BC, confirms the Bible's report of Omri's dynasty and of Mesha's victory over Israelite forces led by a descendant of Omri.

AN ISRAELITE KING BOWING

Found in the ruins of Assyria's capital city of Nimrud (in northern Iraq) is yet another monument to a king's domination of Israel. The stone monument has a picture of an Israelite king, Jehu, bowing to an Assyrian king, Shalmaneser III. The picture, accompanied by a caption, is engraved onto a four-sided, black marble pillar that stands about one and a half metres (five feet) tall and is on display in the British Museum.

The caption below the picture describes the gifts that the Israelite king brought: 'The tribute of Jehu son of Omri: silver,

gold, a golden bowl, a golden beaker, golden goblets, golden pitchers, tin, staves for the king's hand, javelins.'

Jehu was not actually a descendant of King Omri, but was the king who succeeded Omri's grandson, Jehoram. Shalmaneser's Obelisk, as the monument is called, confirms the existence of two Israelite kings that the Bible says lived during the 800s BC, when Assyria dominated the Middle East.

HEZEKIAH CAGED

The Bible says that the Assyrian king, Sennacherib invaded the Israelite kingdom of Judah, overran all the fortified cities, and then surrounded Jerusalem – the capital, where King Hezekiah lived. The Bible adds that the Assyrian army suddenly fled one night after the angel of the Lord came to the Assyrian camp and killed thousands of their soldiers (2 Kings 19).

Sennacherib's own version of this invasion is recorded in one of the best-preserved records of the ancient Middle East: a six-sided clay cylinder covered in cuneiform writing. Sennacherib's prism tells about eight of his military campaigns, including the one in which he besieged Jerusalem. Here are excerpts from his Judean campaign in 701 BC:

As for Hezekiah the Judahite, who did not submit to my yoke: 46 of his strong, walled cities, as well as the small towns in their area, which were without number, by levelling with battering-rams and by bringing up siege engines, and by attacking and storming on foot... I besieged and took them... [Hezekiah] himself, like a caged bird I shut up in Jerusalem, his royal city.

Sennacherib confirmed the Bible's account that he took Judah's fortified cities and surrounded Jerusalem. But he stopped short of claiming he captured Jerusalem.

CYRUS FREES POLITICAL PRISONERS

When the Persian conqueror Cyrus overpowered Babylon in 539 BC and started the Persian empire, he issued a decree that freed all prisoners of the Babylonian empire. 2 Chronicles and Ezra say that among these prisoners were the Jews who survived the annihilation of their country when in 586 Babylon levelled the Judean cities – including Jerusalem – and took the survivors back to Babylon as spoils of war.

A clay cylinder inscribed with cuneiform writing and dating from Cyrus's reign confirms that he conquered Babylon and that he released all Babylonian prisoners so they could go back to their homelands, rebuild their temples, and worship their gods:

I returned to these sanctuaries on the other side of the Tigris [River] – the sanctuaries which had been ruins for a long time – the images which used to live therein and established for them permanent sanctuaries. I also gathered all their former inhabitants and returned them to their homes.

Furthermore, Cyrus asked these people and their gods to pray for him: 'May all the gods whom I have resettled in their sacred cities ask daily [my gods] Bel and Nabu for a long life for me!'

In response to Cyrus's policy, many Jews returned to their homeland and began rebuilding Jerusalem and its temple, as the Bible said.

'He is dirtier than vines or pigs from treading under his mud... He is simply wretched through and through.'

DESCRIPTION OF A SLAVE BRICK-MAKER (POSSIBLY A HEBREW) FROM A WALL PAINTING IN AN EGYPTIAN TOMB

Sennacherib's clay prism, which confirms that the Assyrians attacked Jerusalem during Hezekiah's reign, as the Bible reports.

Lost Books of the Bible

'In one sense these books were never truly lost... the stories have survived in Jewish tradition from ancient times to the present as "the legends of the Jews".'

DUANE L. CHRISTENSEN, PROFESSOR OF BIBLICAL STUDIES AND NEAR-EASTERN HISTORY, WILLIAM CAREY INTERNATIONAL UNIVERSITY, PASADENA, CALIFORNIA

There are 39 books in the Old Testament. As many as 23 others – all of which are named in the Old Testament – are missing. We can read excerpts of a couple of these books, because the Bible briefly quotes them. But we cannot read the books themselves because they have not survived.

All the missing books are believed to cover some chapter in ancient Israel's sacred history: wars, the reigns of certain kings and the stories of individual prophets. Also, the missing books were quite old – obviously written before the books that mentioned them. That means they pre-date some of the earliest stories in Israel's history, including one of Joshua's first battles for the Promised Land – in which Joshua apparently quoted a war cry from a lost book.

Bible scholars speculate that there are not really 23 missing books, but only about half a dozen, because some books were probably known by

Joshua's prayer during the Battle of Gibeon – for the sun to stand still so that Israel would have time to defeat the enemy – may have been written in the lost Book of Jashar before the book of Joshua was ever written. *The Battle of Gibeon*, from the Spanish Bible, c. 1400–25.

ancient, and are exquisitely crafted poems. If these excerpts are a true sampling of the Book of Jashar, the world lost a masterpiece.

In the Bible's first reference to this book, Joshua, Israel's commander, apparently quoted a prayer from the book, asking God to prolong the daylight or darkness to give the Israelites time to defeat their enemy. Or it may be that Joshua's prayer was recorded in the Book of Jashar before it was written in the book of Joshua:

'Sun, stand still at Gibeon,
and Moon, in the valley of Aijalon.'
And the sun stood still, and the moon stopped,
until the nations took vengeance on their enemies.
Is this not written in the Book of Jashar?
Joshua 10:12–13

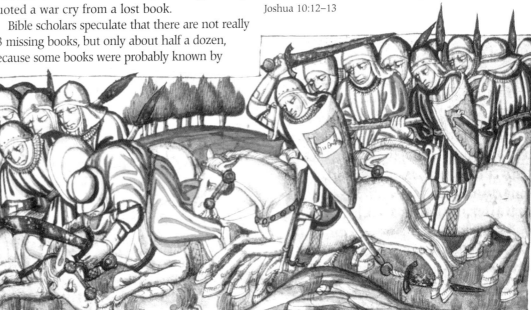

several names. Many of the titles were not actually book titles, the scholars explain, but probably descriptions of the contents. If so, the 18 different lost books mentioned in 1 and 2 Chronicles – such as the book of the Kings of Israel, and the record of the prophet Nathan – might actually correspond to different sections in a single book spanning centuries of Israel's history. Most of these book descriptions or titles refer to national leaders: kings, prophets and royal advisors. So the writers compiling the book or series of books may have drawn heavily from palace records.

BOOK OF JASHAR

There are two, possibly three, Bible quotations from the Book of Jashar. All are considered very

This prayer sounds much like one in Homer's *Iliad*, a war story set in about the time the Israelites invaded and settled Canaan. In the *Iliad*, King Agamemnon, commander of the Greek forces in the Trojan War prayed, 'Grant that the sun may not go down, nor the night fall, till the palace of Priam is laid low.'

A second poem quoted from the Book of Jashar is David's poignant funeral song for King Saul and Jonathan (2 Samuel 1:17). A third poem, also possibly from Jashar, is part of King Solomon's dedication of the temple (1 Kings 8:12–13). An early Greek translation of the Bible says this poem is from the book of song – a title scholars say might be an accident. The Hebrew letters for 'song' are 'syr' and for 'Jashar' are 'ysr'. So the first two letters may have been switched. Whether the title of the lost work was the Book of Jashar or the Book of Song, it is possible that nothing was actually written down, but that the stories were preserved in memorized lyrics and passed from generation to generation by ballad singers and storytellers.

Based on these three excerpts of the lost book, scholars suggest the book contained the epic literature of ancient Israel, celebrating the nation's heroes, history and God.

BOOK OF THE WARS OF THE LORD

Before anyone wrote Numbers – a book tracing the Israelite exodus towards Canaan – there was the Book of the Wars of the Lord. The description of this lost book, as well as the single quotation from it in Numbers, suggests it was a collection of poems about Israel's early wars of conquest – as the migrating nation marched towards Canaan, and then later invaded. Some scholars suggest this book is the same as the Book of Jashar.

The poem quoted in Numbers is so old that it is almost impossible to translate the words in a way that makes much sense. But it seems to be identifying the terrain in Moab (now Jordan), which the Israelites passed through (Numbers 21:14–15). Some scholars say the two poems that follow were probably also in this lost book: the Song of the Well (21:17–18) and the Song of Heshbon (21:27–30).

Though it is no longer possible to read these lost books in the flowing lyrics that once existed – if only in songs never written down – it is likely that at least some of the stories were preserved in the Old Testament books of Israel's history.

23 Lost Books

Here are the names of the lost books, and where they are referred to in the Bible:

1. *Book of the Wars of the Lord* – Numbers 21:14.

2. *Book of Jashar* – Joshua 10:13; 2 Samuel 1:18.

3. *Book of the Acts of Solomon* – 1 Kings 11:41.

4. *Book of the Annals of the Kings of Israel* – 1 Kings 14:19 (and 14 other references).

5. *Book of the Annals of the Kings of Judah* – 1 Kings 14:29 (and 17 other references).

6. *Book of the Kings of Israel* – 1 Chronicles 9:1; 2 Chronicles 20:34.

7. *Records of the Seer Samuel* – 1 Chronicles 29:29.

8. *Records of the Prophet Nathan* – 1 Chronicles 29:29.

9. *Records of the Seer Gad* – 1 Chronicles 29:29.

10. *History of the Prophet Nathan* – 2 Chronicles 9:29.

11. *Prophecy of Ahijah the Shilonite* – 2 Chronicles 9:29.

12. *Visions of the Seer Iddo* – 2 Chronicles 9:29.

13. *Records of the Prophet Shemaiah and of the Seer Iddo* – 2 Chronicles 12:15.

14. *Story of the Prophet Iddo* – 2 Chronicles 13:22.

15. *Book of the Kings of Judah and Israel* – 2 Chronicles 16:11.

16. *Annals of Jehu son of Hanani* ('which are recorded in the Book of the Kings of Israel') – 2 Chronicles 20:34.

17. *Commentary on the Book of the Kings* – 2 Chronicles 24:27.

18. *Acts of Uzziah* (written by 'the prophet Isaiah') – 2 Chronicles 26:22.

19. *Book of the Kings of Israel and Judah* – 2 Chronicles 27:7.

20. *Vision of the Prophet Isaiah* (written 'in the book of the Kings of Judah and Israel') – 2 Chronicles 32:32.

21. *Annals of the Kings of Israel* – 2 Chronicles 33:18.

22. *Records of the Seers* – 2 Chronicles 33:19.

23. *Book of the Annals* – Nehemiah 12:23.

'Now the rest of the acts of Ahab, and all that he did, and the ivory house that he built, and all the cities that he built, are they not written in the Book of the Annals of the Kings of Israel?'

1 KINGS 22:39

Writings: Last But Not Least

The 'Esther scroll' and noisemakers used in the Feast of Purim. During this joyous festival, the story of Esther is read to celebrate deliverance from a Persian holocaust.

The Jewish Bible – which Christians call the Old Testament – is divided into three parts: Law, Prophets and Writings. No one knows when or how these divisions emerged, but Bible scholars speculate that they reflect the order in which the Jewish people accepted the books as divinely inspired and sacred.

First came the laws of Moses, the first five books of the Bible. Then came the writings of prophets, who pleaded with the people – usually in vain – to obey those laws. And finally came the collection of miscellaneous books known as the Writings – teachings and stories devoted to helping people live good and righteous lives, which became recognized as inspired.

ELEVEN SACRED BOOKS

Eleven books make up the Writings. Early Jewish rabbis often divided these into three categories, which determine the order of the books in the Jewish Bible:

❧ Three 'big writings' – Psalms, Proverbs and Job.

❧ Holiday books, arranged in the order of the religious holidays at which they were read in the synagogue – Song of Solomon, Ruth, Lamentations, Ecclesiastes and Esther.

❧ History books – Daniel, Ezra and Nehemiah (combined into one book), and 1 and 2 Chronicles (one book).

EARLY WORKS AND LATECOMERS

Although these 11 books were probably the last to be accepted as sacred enough for inclusion in the Jewish Bible, not all of them were the last to be written. Parts of two 'big writings' – Psalms and Proverbs – are at least as old as some books of the prophets, and perhaps nearly as old as the law.

For instance, the old age of the 30 sayings of the wise men (Proverbs 22:17 – 24:22) is reflected in their similarity to 30 sections of an Egyptian work called 'The Wisdom of Amenemope', a sage who lived sometime between 1200 and 1000 BC.

Here is the first proverb from the wise men:

Do not rob the poor because they are poor,
or crush the afflicted at the gate.
Proverbs 22:22

Tales of men like Job

Job's story of lost health, family and possessions may be one of the oldest in the Bible. This is evidenced by the fact that there are similar stories of suffering that reach far back into the antiquity of Egypt and the Persian Gulf region of Mesopotamia. One such story dates from before 2000 BC. It is called 'A Man and His God', but is more commonly known as the Sumerian Job. (Sumer was a Persian Gulf kingdom in what is now southeast Iraq.)

Like Job, the unidentified man in this short story said he had done nothing wrong, but he was suffering terribly. In agony, he prayed: 'Tears, lament, anguish and despair are lodged within me. Suffering overwhelms me like a weeping child. In the hands of the fate demon my appearance has been altered.'

As Job had cursed the day of his birth (Job 3:1), the Sumerian Job expressed a similar depth of misery: 'Let my mother who bore me not cease lamenting for me before you. Let my sister, truly a sweet-voiced ballad singer, narrate tearfully to you the deeds by which I was overpowered. Let my wife voice my suffering to you. Let the singer expert in chanting unravel my bitter fate to you like a thread.'

In the end, like Job, the man is delivered and praises his god: 'I have set my sights on you as on the rising sun,' the man prays. 'You looked on me from a distance with your good life-giving eyes.'

In this coloured woodcut from the 16th century, Job is in pain, and his wife urges him to curse God so he can die and end his suffering.

Here is a similar proverb from the beginning of the Egyptian book:

*Do not steal from the poor
nor cheat the cripple.*

Although some sections of the Writings may well come from Israel's earliest history, most books are thought to have been written a century or more after Babylon destroyed Jerusalem in 586 BC and exiled the survivors to Babylon. Several of the books are clearly set in those times.

Esther is a queen of Persia, the empire that defeated the Babylonians. Her heroic story of saving the Persian Jews from a holocaust launched the springtime festival of Purim, the most fun-filled Jewish festival of all. Jews read the book aloud in synagogues and happily celebrate their deliverance with noisemakers, costume parties and gifts.

Ezra and Nehemiah, which scholars say the priest Ezra may have written, is set 150 to 200 years after Babylon's 586 defeat of the Jewish nation. These books tell of Jews returning to their homeland to rebuild Jerusalem's temple and, later, the city walls.

Stories of the religious persecution of Daniel and his Jewish friends also took place at the end of Babylonian times and the beginning of the Persian empire. But it is unlikely the stories were compiled until a later time of persecution for the Jews: the Maccabean revolt in 167 BC, when a Seleucid (Syrian) king tried to wipe out the Jewish religion and replace it with worship of Greek gods such as Zeus.

The tender story of Ruth – King David's great grandmother, who was a non-Jew from what is now Jordan – may have been written in David's time, to provide some family history about the king. But many scholars say the story was more likely recorded centuries later, in the time of Ezra. If so, Ruth's story would have provided a compelling argument against Ezra's command for Jewish men in the re-emerging nation of Israel to divorce their non-Jewish wives. For it is incredibly clear that God blessed Ruth and selected this non-Jew to found the royal line of Israel's most revered king.

'If God has something against me, let him speak up or put it in writing!'
JOB 31:35, CONTEMPORARY
ENGLISH VERSION

Jewish Worship and the Bible

When the Israelites started worshipping their God, as an emerging nation on their exodus to the Promised Land, there was no written Bible they could use. In fact, there was not even a place for this nation-on-the-road to worship.

Jewish tradition, preserved in scripture, says God changed this. He had the people build a tent worship centre, called the tabernacle. And he began giving them laws. The ten commandments – the building blocks on which all other Jewish laws were constructed – were stored in a sacred chest in the worship centre's holiest room. Hundreds of other laws and teachings followed, which God delivered through Moses.

Bible music in worship

'Make a joyful noise to the Lord, all the earth,' proclaims Psalm 100. 'Worship the Lord with gladness; come into his presence with singing.' And the people did.

King David, to whom many psalms are attributed, organized religious choirs and appointed a professional musician to direct them. These full-time priestly musicians were to inspire Jewish worshippers with song, accompanied by harps, lyres, trumpets and cymbals.

Music echoed from the Jerusalem hilltop, as priests offered the morning and evening sacrifices and as private worshippers brought their offerings. Some arrived singing what became known as Songs of Ascents (Psalms 120–134) – songs for the road that Jews sang on their pilgrimage to Jerusalem. The songs were called 'ascents' because no matter what direction people approached Jerusalem, they had to climb.

'I will lift up my eyes to the hills,' says Psalm 121, 'from where will my help come? My help comes from the Lord.'

No musical notation survived with the lyrics, but the wide range of poetry – from despair to elation – suggests the music was rich and deeply moving.

These laws guided Jewish worship, telling them when and how to offer sacrifices – the principal method of worship at the time.

WORSHIP AT THE TEMPLE

After the Jews built a permanent worship centre in Jerusalem – the temple – the Bible began to take on a bigger role in worship. One reason for this change is that the Jewish laws and many sacred stories, songs and poetry were already preserved in writing on scrolls kept in the temple, so worship leaders had ready access to them.

The Jews used scripture in a variety of ways. Sometimes they recited it. God had told them to do so. When worshippers brought to the temple their offerings from the early harvest, they were to quote from Deuteronomy 26:3–11. Presenting the offering to the priest, the worshipper recited God's acts that had brought the Jews into the Promised Land, and then declared, 'So now I bring the first of the fruit of the ground that you, O Lord, have given me.' A similar ritual, which worshippers were to recite when they brought their tithe to the temple, is preserved in Deuteronomy 26:13–15.

Psalms was Israel's hymnbook, a source of music for the temple choirs that sang to worshippers every day. The worshippers who came to bring their offerings and pray probably sang along, and sometimes sang personal solos of praise or lament in the sprawling courtyard:

Create in me a clean heart, O God,
  and put a new and right spirit within me.
Psalm 51:10

Teachers of the Jewish law and tradition lingered in the courtyard, giving lectures and answering questions about their sacred scriptures – as they did when 12-year-old Jesus impressed them with his knowledge (Luke 2:46). It was near the temple, in the city square, that the scholar Ezra stood on a wooden platform during a New Year's worship service and read the Jewish law aloud for all those who had returned from exile in Babylon. As he unrolled the scroll, the crowd stood in honour of the scripture (Nehemiah 8:5). They wept when he read, perhaps in gratitude or repentance.

WORSHIP AT THE SYNAGOGUE

During exile in Babylon, the Jews had no place to worship. The Jerusalem temple was in ruins,

---

'The heads of ancestral houses of all the people, with the priests and the Levites, came together to the scribe Ezra in order to study the words of the law.'

NEHEMIAH 8:13

A tithe prayer

I have removed the sacred portion from the house, and I have given it to the Levites, the resident aliens [needy foreigners in Israel], the orphans, and the widows, in accordance with your entire commandment (Deuteronomy 26:13).

and hundreds of miles away. Bible scholars suspect that it was during this exile, in what is now the Persian Gulf region, that synagogues emerged as a substitute for the temple.

The word 'synagogue' comes from the Greek for 'assembly'. Unlike the temple, synagogues were not run by priests, nor could people offer sacrifices there – Jewish law permitted sacrifices only at the temple. But the synagogue is where Jews stayed in touch with their sacred teachings and traditions.

Typically, a synagogue service included readings from the law of Moses (the first five books of the Bible), followed by readings from other books of the Hebrew Bible (which Christians call the Old Testament). There were also usually prayers and a sermon. Visitors were often invited to read from the sacred scrolls and address the worshippers. It was after reading an excerpt from Isaiah, which predicted the coming era of the Messiah, that Jesus declared the prophecy fulfilled (Luke 4:21). The apostle Paul later took advantage of the visitor-friendly custom by telling the assembled Jews about Jesus – a practice that seemed to generate few converts, but a great deal of opposition towards Paul.

After the Jewish temple was destroyed by the Romans in AD 70, it was never rebuilt, and Jews could no longer sacrifice animals or make crop offerings. Instead, when they meet in their synagogues they do as the prophet predicted: 'We will offer the fruit of our lips' (Hosea 14:2). That fruit is prayer, read from the Hebrew Bible and reinforced in sermons by rabbis.

Jewish men meet in the synagogue to study scripture and ancient commentaries by revered Jewish teachers. Reading the Bible is a key part of Jewish worship.

The First Bible Translation

The Jews lived under Persian rule for about 200 years – from the time that Cyrus overthrew the Babylonians until Alexander the Great conquered the Persian empire in 332 BC. Beginning in 323, when Alexander died, Palestine and Egypt came under the control of Alexander's former general Ptolemy I, who was succeeded by his son, Ptolemy II in 285. Ptolemy II was a great ruler who fostered learning. His capital at Alexandria, Egypt, became the chief centre of learning in the Mediterranean world, noted for its extensive library.

By Ptolemy's time, large numbers of Jews had left their home to work and study in foreign lands, including Egypt, and they spoke the Greek language, received a Greek education, and adopted many Greek customs. In time, these dispersed Jews, known as the Jews of the Diaspora (Greek for 'dispersion'), found themselves unable to read their own scriptures, which were written in Hebrew. A translation into Greek was sorely needed, and one was produced in the third century BC. It was the first translation of the Bible ever made.

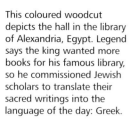

This coloured woodcut depicts the hall in the library of Alexandria, Egypt. Legend says the king wanted more books for his famous library, so he commissioned Jewish scholars to translate their sacred writings into the language of the day: Greek.

A LETTER TELLS A TALE

According to an ancient account, the Hebrew scriptures were translated into Greek at the request of King Ptolemy II. This account is the subject of an ancient document, known as the *Letter of Aristeas*. The author, Aristeas, claims to be writing from Alexandria to a brother he calls Philocrates. Aristeas tells his brother that King Ptolemy had wanted his librarian Demetrius to acquire a copy of every book in the world for his famous library in Alexandria. After collecting 200,000 volumes, Demetrius appraised the king of his progress, adding that he hoped to increase the number of books in the library to 500,000. Among the books still missing, Demetrius said, were the lawbooks of the Jews, which were worthy of translation and inclusion in the royal library.

Anxious to possess a translation of the Jewish books, Ptolemy ordered that a letter be written to Eleazar, the Jewish high priest in Jerusalem, asking him to send 72 of his best scholars to

The Septuagint may have been commissioned by Ptolomy II, shown above with his sister (and later wife), Arsinoe II, in an Indian sardonyx cameo from 287 BC.

Alexandria to make an accurate translation of the Jewish law (the five books of Moses) into Greek. When the 72 scholars arrived in Alexandria (there were six scriptural scholars from each of the 12 tribes of Israel), they were served sumptuous feasts and treated almost as royalty. They were then given a quiet place to work on a small island a mile out into the Mediterranean Sea. The scholars divided the work among themselves, consulting one another as they progressed. They completed their translation in 72 days. When the translation was read to an assembly of local Jews it was lavishly praised. In fact, it was declared to be so accurate that a curse was placed on anyone who dared change anything about it. King Ptolemy, too, was pleased with the translation, marvelling at the genius of the lawgiver. He sent the scholars back home weighed down with rich gifts.

Whether the *Letter of Aristeas* is authentic or not is debatable. Some scholars consider the letter to be fictitious and believe that it was actually written after the time of Ptolemy, possibly in the second or first century BC. To add to the confusion, later, far more fanciful versions of the story also exist. In some early Christian versions of the tale the translation is made by only 70 scholars – paralleling the 70 elders who were with Moses at Mount Sinai (Exodus 24:1–14) and the 70 disciples Jesus sent out (Luke 10:1–20). It may be from these Christian versions of the tale that the translation receives its name, the Septuagint (Greek for 'seventy').

However it was done, the translation known as the Septuagint was definitely made, and it soon became the standard Greek translation of the Jewish scriptures. But the translation referred to in the *Letter of Aristeas* was only of the Pentateuch, or law (the first five books of the Bible). Over the next 200 years or so, the remaining books of the Hebrew Bible were also translated into Greek, and are generally considered part of the Septuagint.

INFLUENCE OF THE GREEK SCRIPTURES

The early Christians used the Septuagint when referring to the Hebrew Bible. In the New Testament, which is written in Greek, nearly all quotations from the older scriptures are taken from the Septuagint. As a result, Christians gained great respect for this translation and it was soon regarded as a Christian version. For this reason some Jews of the early Christian era

Philo's variation on the tale

In the first century BC, the Jewish philosopher Philo elaborated on the tale told in the *Letter of Aristeas*. According to Philo, the translators were housed on the secluded island of Pharos, where there were no distractions besides nature itself to interrupt their work. (It was on that same island of Pharos that King Ptolemy II also built the lighthouse of Alexandria, one of the seven wonders of the ancient world). Unlike the scholars in the story told by Aristeas, Philo contends that all 72 of the scholars translated every word of the text. Despite the probability that each scholar would have used different words in translating a particular passage, every one of the 72 scholars used exactly the same Greek words to translate the entire Hebrew text. Miraculously, their translations were exactly the same even though they had not consulted one another, as Aristeas holds they had. This proved that the Septuagint was inspired by God. Philo ends by stating there is an annual festival on Pharos, when Jews and Gentiles come from afar to thank God for the translation made by the 72 scholars.

'As the books were read, the priests stood up... and said, "Since this version has been made rightly and reverently, and in every respect accurately, it is good that this should remain exactly so, and there should be no revision."'

LETTER OF ARISTEAS, DEFENDING THE NEW TRANSLATION

Books in the Septuagint

The Books of the Septuagint are shown below. Those preceded by an asterisk (*) were not included in the later canon of the Hebrew scriptures, but today most of them are included in Roman Catholic, Greek Orthodox and Slavonic Bibles, and are printed in a separate section of many Protestant Bibles called 'the Apocrypha'. The only books not in the Catholic, Greek and Slavonic Bibles (nor in the Apocrypha) are: 1 Esdras, the Prayer of Manasseh, 3 and 4 Maccabees, Odes and the Psalms of Solomon. However, Greek Orthodox and Slavonic Bibles include 1 Esdras, the Prayer of Manasseh and 3 Maccabees. In addition, the Greek Bible also includes 4 Maccabees in an appendix.

LAW AND HISTORY

Genesis

Exodus

Leviticus

Numbers

Deuteronomy

Joshua

Judges

Ruth

1–4 Kingdoms (the books of Samuel and Kings)

1–2 Paralipomena (Chronicles)

*1 Esdras

2 Esdras (Ezra-Nehemiah)

Esther

*Judith

*Tobit

*1–4 Maccabees

POETIC AND PROPHETIC BOOKS

Psalms

*Odes

*Prayer of Manasseh (included in Odes)

Proverbs

Ecclesiastes

Song of Solomon

Job

*Wisdom of Solomon

*Ecclesiasticus (or Sirach)

*Psalms of Solomon

Hosea

Amos

Micah

Joel

Obadiah

Jonah

Nahum

Habakkuk

Zephaniah

Haggai

Zechariah

Malachi

Isaiah

Jeremiah

*Baruch

*Letter of Jeremiah (included in Baruch)

Lamentations

Ezekiel

Daniel

*Prayer of Azariah (included in Daniel)

*Song of the Three Jews (included in Daniel)

*Susanna (included in Daniel)

*Bel and the Dragon (included in Daniel)

Authorized version?

Some biblical scholars believe that the *Letter of Aristeas* was written (long after the events it describes) to defend the authority of the Greek translation of the Hebrew Bible. It may have been used to fight against proposals to make a new translation or to radically revise the original one. This is suggested by the fact that a great deal of space is spent on showing the importance of the translators and their work and on praising the quality of the translation. On the other hand, very little space is devoted to describing the translation process itself.

✤

began to grow dissatisfied with the Septuagint, and in the second century three important new Greek translations of the Hebrew Bible appeared. They are attributed to the Jewish scholars Aquila, Symmachus and Theodotion. Aquila's translation was slavishly faithful to the Hebrew original, retaining a sense of the original Hebrew language, but the Greek was awkward and not easy for most people to read. Theodotion also tried to stay close to the Hebrew text. Instead of finding Greek words for difficult Hebrew terms, he simply transliterated the words into Greek, using Greek letters to capture the sound of the original Hebrew words. Symmachus, whose translation survives only in fragments, was less concerned with giving a literal translation of the Greek than with making his version readable. As a result, his translation was the most elegant and graceful of the three second-century Greek translations of the Hebrew Bible.

VARIATIONS OF TWO KINDS

The official Jewish version of the Hebrew Bible was established sometime after the completion of the Septuagint. As a result, there are differences. Most importantly, the Septuagint contains books that are not found in the standard Hebrew Bible (which has remained the same since the second century AD). These include books found in some Christian Bibles (see 'Books in the Septuagint' on page 50) plus the Psalms of Solomon – a collection of psalms from the first century BC, which sing of a messiah who will conquer Israel's enemies – and odes – a collection of 15 songs or prayers found elsewhere in the Bible, except for the Prayer of Manasseh (a plea for forgiveness by the sinful King Manasseh) and one other.

There are also major variations in the contents of the books. For example, while the book of Job is shorter in the Septuagint than in the standard Jewish text, the books of Esther and Daniel are longer in the Septuagint, and even include entirely new stories, such as the tale of Susannah and the Elders, and a number of prayers. The book of Jeremiah is even arranged differently in its two versions, and the Septuagint version has material that is missing from the standard version. In fact, the standard version is 20 per cent longer than the Septuagint translation. It follows, some scholars argue, that the book of Jeremiah went through two or more versions and that the translation found in the Septuagint is from an earlier version. A later, expanded version was to find its way into the official Hebrew Bible. These major differences in the two versions of Jeremiah dramatically show that the Bible was not written once and for all and never revised. Before being established as a definitive text, a biblical book sometimes went through two or more versions.

Scholars who have made close studies of biblical texts believe that at least parts of the Septuagint translation were made from earlier versions of the Hebrew books than those of the standard texts. In some cases, the earlier versions are felt to be more accurate, and they help textual scholars to understand better passages that are unclear in the traditional texts. And so the texts of the Septuagint remain important today in helping us fully understand the word of God. In addition, to translate any text into a different language a person must interpret it to some degree to make it understandable in the second language. And so the translators who produced the Septuagint had to interpret the biblical books they worked on, thus showing us how they understood the Hebrew texts. As such, their translations represent the earliest surviving commentary on the Bible.

Fragment of the Septuagint from the second century BC.

Philo of Alexandria

P hilo of Alexandria, also known as Philo Judaeus (Philo the Jew), was probably the greatest Jewish writer of the first century. A philosopher steeped in Greek learning, the majority of his works (all written in Greek) are interpretations of the Hebrew scriptures. Philo was highly respected in his time, and his writings had a strong influence on a number of early Christian writers.

A PHILOSOPHER'S LIFE

Little is known of Philo's life. He was born about 20 BC into a rich and prominent Jewish family in Alexandria, Egypt, which was then home to the largest Jewish community outside Palestine (as many as a million Jews may have been living there). Philo received a thorough Greek education in Alexandria, and lived in that city all his life. He probably visited Jerusalem only once, to worship at the temple.

In AD 40, after Flaccus, the Roman viceroy of Alexandria, instigated incidents of anti-Jewish violence, Philo headed a delegation that went to Rome to protest the injustice to Emperor Gaius Caligula. Philo later wrote detailed accounts of this mission, which ended in the bloody death of the offending viceroy, in *Flaccus* and *On the Embassy to Gaius*.

Right: The port of Alexandria, Egypt, as it appears today.

'Behold, therefore, I venture not only to study the sacred commands of Moses, but also with an ardent love of knowledge to investigate each separate one of them, and to endeavour to reveal and to explain to those who wish to understand them, things concerning them which are not known to the multitude.'

PHILO, ON THE SPECIAL LAWS III, 6

Engraving of Philo of Alexandria by Thevet, 1584.

Philo did not succeed in politics, though some of his relatives did. Instead, he devoted himself to study and writing, and was eager to show that Jewish thought was in no way inferior to the prevailing Greek philosophy of the day. Although he was a contemporary of Jesus and Paul, Philo gave no sign in his writings of ever hearing of them. He died about AD 50, perhaps at the time that Paul was writing his first letter to the Thessalonians, the first written book of the New Testament.

PHILO'S COMMENTARIES

Although Philo sometimes wrote on non-biblical topics, including the treatise 'On the Contemplative Life', he mainly devoted himself to writing about the Pentateuch, or the law of Moses, or basing his work on the (Greek) Septuagint translation. Philo's main concern in life was to reveal to his readers what was not generally known about the law of Moses. Many of his writings paraphrase biblical passages, expanding the texts and adding his own views on various matters.

Philo's biblical commentaries can be organized into three groups. The first group offers allegorical, or symbolic, interpretations of the first 17 chapters of Genesis, interpreting the stories of the creation, Cain and Abel, the flood and Abraham in terms of morality and the quest of the soul for God. These allegorical interpretations are strongly influenced by the philosophy of Plato and his concept of the ideal.

The second group of Philo's biblical commentaries includes explanations of the Jewish laws. Although he interprets the laws symbolically, Philo also insists on their literal observance. For example, he admits that the sabbath is a symbol of the power of God the creator and is meant to show that we created beings are entitled to rest, but he insists that we must still follow the laws governing observance of the sabbath. He concedes that circumcision is a symbol of abandoning things of the flesh, but says that its symbolic nature is not an excuse for annulling the law of circumcision.

The third group of commentaries consists of questions and answers about passages from Genesis and Exodus. Philo generally answers these questions by first giving a literal explanation, and then a symbolic one.

In addition to preserving some examples of how the Bible was being interpreted in Jesus' time, Philo's writings tell us a lot about the way Jews of the first century thought. As such, Philo's works are invaluable aids in studying both Old and New Testaments.

Emergence of biblical commentaries

Although Jews probably discussed the meaning of their scriptures since the first scroll was copied, their views were passed down only by word of mouth – from teacher to student – and not written down.

Some biblical texts may be seen as the earliest written commentaries. For example, when the author of Chronicles rewrote much of Samuel and Kings, he cleaned up the images of David and Solomon, showing that he believed they should be seen only as model monarchs. In doing so he was subtly commenting on the earlier books, which show those kings warts and all.

In a similar way, the Greek translation of the Hebrew Bible (the Septuagint) was a kind of commentary, as it used words of a different language to interpret for Greek readers the (to them) unreadable Hebrew texts.

In the first centuries BC and AD the Essenes, a community of Hebrew men who lived ascetic lives in the desert, may have written the first true biblical commentaries, called *pesharim* in Hebrew (one such commentary is a *pesher*). In these scrolls the Essenes typically quoted a biblical passage and then wrote an interpretation, often relating it to their own community, the coming of a liberating messiah, and the end of time. The *pesharim* were not known outside the Essene community of Qumran until they were discovered about half a century ago hidden with many other ancient scrolls in caves near the Dead Sea.

The first widely known commentator on the Bible was Philo, who wrote in the first half of the first century AD. Then, about the time of Philo's death, Christians began to write accounts of Jesus' life and teachings, seeing them as fulfilment of the Hebrew scriptures. The four Gospels are filled with references to the Hebrew scriptures, which are interpreted as prophecies of Jesus' coming and of his mission. The letters included in the New Testament also rely heavily on the Hebrew Bible. The letter to the Hebrews, in particular, carefully cites biblical passages and then comments on them in the light of Jesus. Some say its style was influenced by Philo.

Settling the Jewish Bible

Jews carrying a Torah scroll to be read at a Bar Mitzvah ceremony at the Western Wall, or Wailing Wall, in Jerusalem. The Torah, a collection of the first five books of the Bible, is considered especially important because it contains God's laws. These books were probably the first that the Jews declared as inspired by God and revered as scripture.

No one knows how the books of the Old Testament were chosen, or when. The Bible does not say, nor do the ancient writings of the rabbis. There are, however, clues from history that allow Bible scholars to speculate about the process.

'Canon' is a Greek word scholars use to identify the list of accepted books. It means 'measuring rod', and refers to those sacred books that 'measure up' to a standard of excellence that shows the writers were directed by God.

There are 24 books in the Jewish canon. These books are divided into three sections: Law (Torah), Prophets and Writings. Hints from history suggest that it took the Jewish people several centuries to settle on which 24 books to include in their Bible – from about 600 BC to the first century AD.

The books seem to have been approved one section at a time, in the order described by Jesus: 'the law of Moses, the prophets and the psalms', with psalms referring to the Writings, of which Psalms is the first and largest book (Luke 24:44).

A three-part approval process would help explain why some Bible books seem out of place in their assigned sections. Daniel, for example, is a book of prophecy. But in the Jewish Bible it is in the Writings section instead of Prophets. The reason, scholars say, is because Daniel probably was not finished until the second century BC, long after the Prophets section had been established. So it was added to the last canonized section of the Jewish Bible. The same is likely true for Chronicles, listed among the Writings though it is very much like Kings, which is listed among the Prophets.

ACCEPTING THE LAW

It is impossible to know when the first five books of the Bible were assembled into a collection that the Jews said contained the laws and teachings of God. Many scholars say it probably took a national crisis – like the Babylonian exile in 586 BC – to make this happen. With Jerusalem and its temple destroyed by the Babylonian army, Jewish survivors were taken from their homeland to Babylon.

In exile, or perhaps a few decades later when many returned to Israel to re-establish their nation, the Jews felt they needed to discover which of God's laws and Jewish traditions were essential. The reason this is likely is because before the exile the prophets had predicted the catastrophe, warning that God promised what would happen if the Jews did not honour the covenant that their ancestors made with God. 'You shall be plucked off the land,' God had said through Moses. 'The Lord will scatter you among all peoples, from one end of the earth to the other' (Deuteronomy 28:63–64). Centuries later, on the brink of the Babylonian invasion, the prophet Jeremiah complained that he had been preaching God's message to the people for 23 years, but they did not listen. So now God was going to carry out his ancient threat by sending the Babylonians to conquer the Jewish homeland and enslave the survivors for 70 years (Jeremiah 25:3–11).

After returning to their decimated homeland, the Jews did not want to repeat their mistake. So to celebrate the Jewish New Year, they asked the priest Ezra to read aloud 'the book of the law of Moses' (Nehemiah 8:1).

ACCEPTING THE PROPHETS

Israel certainly had more prophets than those whose ministry is detailed in Bible books. There were associations or schools of prophets called the 'company of prophets' (1 Kings 20:35). And the Bible mentions some prophets by name, such as David's seer, Gad and the prophet who opposed Jeremiah, Hananiah.

For guidance in deciding which prophetic books carried God's stamp of approval, the Jews may have turned to a passage in the law that tells the people how to recognize a true prophet: 'If a prophet speaks in the name of the Lord but the thing does not take place or prove true, it is a word that the Lord has not spoken' (Deuteronomy 18:22).

Scholars say the long process of recognizing and accepting the authority of books in this section of the Jewish Bible probably began after the exile, perhaps by the fifth century BC. This was about the time the last book in this section was written – Malachi. The canon on this section was probably closed before Daniel is thought to have been finished, in the 100s BC. Another clue that the canon on the prophets was closed by then is found in the introduction (prologue) of Ecclesiasticus (also known as Sirach), a Jewish book written in about 130 BC and included in the Apocrypha. It says, 'Many great teachings have been given to us through the Law and the Prophets and the others that followed them.'

In the Jewish Bible, the prophetic books are divided into two categories: Former Prophets and Latter Prophets. The Former Prophets may have been accepted first, since they are books about early Jewish history. The Latter Prophets were books from later times, and deal more with the lives and ministry of individual prophets.

ACCEPTING THE WRITINGS

This section of the Jewish Bible may have been the last to be canonized. But that does not mean these books were the last written. Some of the Psalms and Proverbs may have been written early in Israel's history. And Job resembles Egyptian and Persian Gulf region stories written

Organizing the Old Testament

The Jewish Bible and the Protestant Old Testament are the same, although they are arranged in a different order. In the Roman Catholic and Eastern Orthodox Churches, the Old Testament also includes several other ancient Jewish works. These additional books, known as the Apocrypha, appeared in an early Greek translation of sacred Jewish writings, but the Jews later decided against keeping them in their Bible. So Protestants later followed suit, dropping them from their Bible.

The Hebrew scriptures (24 books)

THE LAW

Genesis

Exodus

Leviticus

Numbers

Deuteronomy

THE PROPHETS

Former prophets

Joshua

Judges

Samuel

Kings

Latter prophets

Isaiah

Jeremiah

Ezekiel

The Twelve (the collection of Hosea, Joel, Amos, Obadiah, Jonah, Micah, Nahum, Habakkuk, Zephaniah, Haggai, Zechariah and Malachi).

THE WRITINGS

Psalms

Job

Proverbs

Ruth

Song of Solomon

Ecclesiastes

Lamentations

Esther

Daniel

Ezra-Nehemiah

Chronicles

Protestant Old Testament (39 Books)

HISTORY

Genesis

Exodus

Leviticus

Numbers

Deuteronomy

Joshua

Judges

Ruth

1, 2 Samuel

1, 2 Kings

1, 2 Chronicles

Ezra

Nehemiah

Esther

POETRY

Job

Psalms

Proverbs

Ecclesiastes

Song of Solomon

PROPHECY

Isaiah

Jeremiah

Lamentations

Ezekiel

Daniel

Hosea

Joel

Amos

Obadiah

Jonah

Micah

Nahum

Habakkuk

Zephaniah

Haggai

Zechariah

Malachi

'Make public the 24 books that you wrote first, and let the worthy and the unworthy read them.'

2 ESDRAS 14:45

Passover pilgrimage: a procession of Samaritans on Mount Gerizim. Samaritans consider only the first five books of the Bible to be sacred.

centuries before the Israelites came to the Promised Land.

The earliest mention of a Jewish Bible containing 24 books appears in 2 Esdras, a Jewish work written in the first century AD and included in the Apocrypha. A Jewish historian who lived at that time, Josephus, says there were 22 books, but scholars say he was probably combining Ruth and Judges (whose stories take place in the same time) and Jeremiah and Lamentations (both said to have been written by Jeremiah).

Other Jewish writings appeared on the scene too late to be included in the Writings. They were, however, included in the Septuagint – the Greek translation of revered Jewish writings that began in the third century BC with the translation of the Law and that continued into the first century AD with other books. The Jews, however, decided these late-arriving books did not carry the same authority as the earlier ones. The late books are included in Roman Catholic and Eastern Orthodox Bibles. In Protestant Bibles, these books are generally left out or are grouped together as the Apocrypha, the Greek word for 'hidden'.

Some scholars say the canon of the Jewish Bible was closed late in the first century AD by Jewish leaders convened at the Council of Jamnia (Jabneh). Other scholars insist no such council meeting ever took place. Jamnia, they argue, was a Jewish academic centre where rabbis studied and debated many topics, including the reliability of theologically troubling books, such as Ezekiel, Proverbs, Ecclesiastes, Esther and the Song of Solomon.

The order of books in the Jewish Bible does not match the order of Old Testament books in most Christian Bibles today. In Christian Bibles, for example, Daniel is among the prophets and Chronicles comes after Kings as a history book. This follows the pattern set by the Septuagint, the Greek Bible translation popular among early Christians.

The Abisha scroll, the most sacred relic among Samaritans. This scroll of the Samaritan Bible is signed by Abisha, who claims to be the great-grandson of Aaron, the brother of Moses. But scholars date the lettering style to about 2,500 years after Aaron.

Samaritan Bible

Jews in late Bible times considered the Samaritans to be a pagan people of mixed race and distorted faith. Samaritans, the Jews said, were a product of Assyrian invaders who took over northern Israel in the 700s BC and married the surviving Jews. But the Samaritans argued they were the only faithful remnant of Israel, and guardians of the true scripture.

Like the Jewish Sadducees, Samaritans considered only the first five books of the Bible sacred. But their version of those five books has some important differences from the traditional Hebrew version. The most important is that it identifies Mount Gerizim – not Jerusalem – as the proper place to worship God. It is even written into their ten commandments.

To support their religious claims they turn to their most sacred object: an ancient scroll signed by a scribe named Abisha. He said he was the great grandson of Aaron, who was Moses' brother and Israel's first high priest. Abisha claimed he wrote the scroll in the door of the tent worship centre at Mount Gerizim 13 years after Israel arrived in Canaan. Many scholars question this claim because the lettering style of the signature dates from the AD 1100s. Some of the few scholars allowed to examine the scroll say it is a patchwork of fragments and restorations written over many centuries by different people.

The Samaritan Bible is based on some of the oldest known Hebrew writings. But many scholars say the Samaritan version was revised to defend Samaritan traditions. The Samaritans, however, say the Jewish Bible is the one that has been revised.

Several hundred Samaritans still live in Israel, and each year conduct Passover sacrifices on Mount Gerizim, which overlooks the city of Nablus (ancient Shechem).

Who wrote Daniel?

Some scholars say Daniel did not write the book named after him. They say references to a Syrian ruler in the 100s BC show the book was written long after the time of Daniel (500s BC) by someone using his name, so the book would become an instant ancient classic. Other books written about the same time did not make it into the Jewish Bible because they were considered too new. Some scholars, however, argue that Daniel was able to predict several centuries into the future and wrote the book himself.

Books That Did Not Make It

'And then they brought me to the place of darkness, and to a mountain whose peak reached heaven. And I saw the places where light is stored, the treasuries of the stars and thunder. In the deepest part of the place there was a bow of fire and arrows in their quiver, a sword of fire, and every type of lightning.'

1 ENOCH 18:2–3

Naming the extra books

In the early fifth century, when preparing his great Latin translation of the Bible (the Vulgate), Jerome included books from the Septuagint that were not in the Hebrew canon. But, in separate prefaces, he indicated that these books were non-canonical – he was the first to call them 'Apocrypha'. Jerome's prefaces were later dropped, and the apocryphal works were gradually incorporated into the Catholic canon. Catholics now refer to these works as deuterocanonical, meaning 'later added to the canon'.

'And then the two men lifted me up to the seventh heaven. There I saw a great light and fiery troops of great archangels, bodiless forces, dominions, orders, governments, cherubim and seraphim, thrones and multi-eyed beings, nine regiments of them... and the Lord at a distance, sitting on his high throne.'

2 ENOCH 20:1–2

The books included in the official canon of the Hebrew Bible were not the only ancient Jewish texts that were widely read by Jews – and later by Christians. Dozens of highly respected works never made it into the Bible. The most important of these are generally divided into two groups. The first group contains the works that were included in the first, Greek, translation of the Bible (the Septuagint), but were not accepted in the later canon; most of these writings are included in the Old Testament by Catholics, but are not considered canonical by Protestants, who call them the Apocrypha (from the Greek for 'hidden'). The second group consists of more than 50 other works of diverse nature.

THE APOCRYPHA

The books of the Apocrypha were written at various times between 300 BC and AD 70. They include romantic stories, histories and books of wisdom.

The romantic stories are found in the books of Tobit and Judith. Tobit is a delightful adventure story with a moral. The book of Judith tells of a Jewish heroine who helped her people defeat the Assyrians by single-handedly beheading their leader, Holofernes.

The first and second books of the Maccabees relates the history of the heroic Hasmonean family who overthrew the Seleucid dynasty (the Syrians) in the second century BC, and ruled the Jews independently until the Romans came in 63 BC. They were called the Maccabees, from the Greek word for 'hammer', because their most ferocious fighter, Judas, struck his enemies like a hammer.

The book of Sirach, modelled on the wisdom literature of the Old Testament, presents the teaching of Jesus Ben Sira, a Jewish scholar living in Egypt, who wrote in Hebrew in about 180 BC. This work strongly resembles the book of Proverbs, but Ben Sira also incorporates much other Old Testament teaching into his writing, and includes long poems to Wisdom, which he equates with love of God and fulfilment of his law. The Wisdom of Solomon, which was written in the first century BC (some nine centuries after the time of Solomon), personifies Wisdom as the saviour of Israel's ancestors and emphasizes God's power and mercy. It also speaks of God's gift of immortality

The book of Tobit

Some of the books that did not make it into the Bible are good reading. One of these, the book of Tobit, is a folkloric adventure story with a moral. It tells of an old man of Nineveh who loses his wealth because he defied the orders of the Assyrian king and buried an executed fellow Jew. Tobit also loses his sight when bird droppings fall into his eyes as he sleeps in the open. After he prays for help, his son, Tobias, accompanied by the angel Raphael in disguise, travels to Media, where he succeeds in collecting money owed to Tobit. During the voyage Tobias meets Sarah, who has married seven times only to have her husbands murdered by an evil demon on their wedding night. With the angel's help, Tobias kills the demon, marries Sarah, and returns home. He then restores his father's eyesight using the gall of a man-eating fish, and everyone lives happily ever after. Tobit, who risked everything to give a neighbour a decent burial, is seen in this tale as a model of a charitable man. The story clearly demonstrates that goodness is rewarded and evil is punished.

to the righteous, a concept that was rare in Jewish thought but was to be at the centre of Christian beliefs.

The book of Baruch may originally have been three separate works by different authors. The first part tells the story of how the prophet Jeremiah's scribe Baruch wrote a prayer of confession to be read at the temple in Jerusalem. The second part is a poem that reproaches Israel for having forsaken God's law, thereby earning exile. The concluding part is a poem encouraging the exiled Israelites in Babylon. A letter purportedly written by Jeremiah to the exiled Israelites in Babylon is sometimes included in the book of Baruch, but sometimes presented separately.

The Apocrypha also includes additions to the books of Esther and Daniel. The Daniel material includes the story of Susannah and the Elders, which tells how Daniel wisely discerned the falsity of a slanderous accusation against an innocent young woman; and tales of how Daniel slew a 'dragon' (a large snake that was being worshipped) and uncovered a hoax by the priests of Bel (a pagan god). The added material in Esther includes many plot developments plus a dream and its interpretation and prayers. Interestingly, the official Hebrew text never mentions God, but in the additions, the words 'Lord' or God' appear more than 50 times.

'PSEUDO' WRITINGS

The other books that did not make it into the Hebrew Bible are often grouped under the name pseudepigrapha – that is, 'pseudo' writings. Dating roughly to between 200 BC and AD 200, most were written under an authoritative pseudonym (pen name) – such as Moses, Solomon or Isaiah – or were written in imitation of earlier biblical books.

About 20 of these works belong to the type of visionary literature known as the apocalypse (from the Greek *apocalypsis*, meaning 'revelation'). The most notable of these are the three books of Enoch, which tell the story of the fallen angels briefly alluded to in Genesis 6:1–4 and speak of eternal life for the righteous. Typically, an apocalypse is set in a past period of turmoil, such as the years of captivity in Babylon, and is narrated by a prominent biblical figure, such as Adam, Abraham or Elijah. It generally demonstrates, through visions, that God is always in charge, guiding events according to his own plan. Generally, apocalypses were written during times of persecution, applying examples from the past to show that God would guide his people through their current problems and that good would triumph in the end.

The pseudepigrapha also include extensions of Old Testament stories and associated legends, including Jannes and Jambres, the story of the Egyptian magicians who opposed Moses and Aaron in the pharaoh's court, and 'The Martyrdom and Ascension of Isaiah'. There are also various testaments of Old Testament figures, such as 'The Testament of the Twelve Patriarchs', in which each of Jacob's sons gives moral advice as he nears death. Finally, there are books of wisdom, prayers and hymns and various fragments.

Although Jewish in origin, some of the pseudepigrapha were later expanded or revised by Christians. In fact, all the pseudepigrapha,

and the Apocrypha as well, are important to Christians today, as they demonstrate the attitudes and beliefs of Jews at the time of Jesus and contain ideas that found their way into the New Testament.

Susanna and the Two Elders by Lorenzo Lotto (c. 1480–1556). In the story of Susanna, two Jewish elders try to pressure Susanna into sex. When she refuses, they retaliate by publicly accusing her of sleeping with a young man. Daniel defends her and exposes the lie. The elders suffer the fate Susanna was saved from: execution.

Josephus, Jewish Historian

Volumes of history produced by this first-century Jew – history that fills in the gaps between the Old and New Testaments – would likely have been lost had it not been for passing references to Jesus, John the Baptist and James the brother of Jesus. Secular writers in the early centuries after Josephus rarely quoted him. And Jews ignored his work, probably because they considered him a traitor. But Christian writers preserved his work because they saw in it evidence supporting the New Testament.

THE RELUCTANT SOLDIER

Joseph ben Mattathias, better known by his Roman name of Flavius Josephus, was born into the well-to-do family of a Jerusalem priest in AD 37, about seven years after the crucifixion of Jesus. He had an excellent education, and studied the teachings of several Jewish groups before joining the Pharisees.

At the age of 27 he was sent to Rome to negotiate the release of Jewish priests who were imprisoned there. He accomplished this by getting help from a Jewish sympathizer who was Emperor Nero's mistress.

When he returned home, Jewish resentment against the Roman occupation erupted into a revolt. Although Josephus had seen Rome's power and argued against the war, he was put in charge of Jewish forces in Galilee – the first place Syrian-based Roman forces would attack. Josephus's militia were overrun, and he was captured. But he predicted that the Roman commander, General Vespasian – whom he knew was the empire's most respected Roman soldier – would become the next emperor. When that happened, during this very war, Josephus was freed. Josephus then

Panel from the Arch of Titus in Rome, depicting Roman soldiers in triumphant procession, carrying the golden menorah and other artefacts looted from the Jerusalem temple before its destruction. Josephus witnessed and recorded the fall of Jerusalem in AD 70.

Josephus on John the Baptist

Josephus confirms the Bible's claim that Herod Agrippa executed John the Baptist. The historian adds that some Jews said the defeat of Herod's army, which came later in a battle against Arabians, was 'as a punishment for what he did against John, that was called the Baptist: for Herod slew him, who was a good man, and commanded the Jews to exercise virtue, both as to righteousness towards one another, and piety towards God, and so to come to baptism'.

joined the military entourage of Vespasian's son, General Titus, as a valuable aide who helped Rome crush the rebellion in AD 70. Tragically, the magnificent Jewish temple was destroyed (and has never been rebuilt).

THE PAMPERED HISTORIAN

In recognition for his service to Rome, Josephus was granted Roman citizenship, an apartment in Vespasian's palace and a lifetime pension. He spent the rest of his life, nearly 30 years, writing history. His surviving works are:

- *The Jewish War*, seven books about the doomed Jewish revolt.

- *The Antiquities of the Jews*, 20 books about Jewish history, from creation to the first century AD.

- *Life*, a short postscript to *The Jewish War*, focusing on his role in the war.

- *Against Apion*, two books refuting slanders against the Jews led by a speaker named Apion.

In his writings, Josephus tried to bridge the gap between Romans and Jews. He especially tried to help Romans understand and appreciate the Jews. For example, he attributed the Jewish war to a group of fanatics reacting to corrupt Roman officials the emperor had condemned. There were, however, many other important factors he did not mention, such as a passionate desire for an independent Israel that would be led by a Jewish king like David.

Despite Josephus's attempts to convince Romans to respect Jewish traditions, the Jews considered him a despicable traitor, and he never saw his homeland again.

Josephus on Jesus

There are at least two versions of what Josephus wrote about Jesus. The most widely circulated is one that many scholars claim was later edited by Christians to reinforce their views about Jesus. The excerpt has Josephus implying Jesus was more than a human, and declaring he was the Messiah who rose from the dead after three days. A similar version, written in Arabic during the 10th century, appears to have escaped the light editing. It reads:

At this time there was a wise man who was called Jesus, and his conduct was good, and he was known to be virtuous. And many people from among the Jews and the other nations became his disciples. Pilate condemned him to be crucified and to die. And those who had become his disciples did not abandon their loyalty to him. They reported that he had appeared to them three days after his crucifixion, and that he was alive. Accordingly they believed that he was the Messiah, concerning whom the Prophets have recounted wonders.

Josephus, depicted in a copper engraving from 1737.

Bust of Vespasian from the first century AD. Vespasian became a lifelong patron of Josephus after the latter correctly predicted that this top Roman general would become the next emperor.

Scripture in Jesus' Language

'All the people gathered together into the square before the Water Gate. They told the scribe Ezra to bring the book of the law of Moses, which the Lord had given to Israel. Accordingly, the priest Ezra brought the law before the assembly... The scribe Ezra stood on a wooden platform that had been made for the purpose... And Ezra opened the book in the sight of all the people, for he was standing above all the people; and when he opened it, all the people stood up... So they read from the book, from the law of God, with interpretation. They gave the sense, so that the people understood the reading.'

NEHEMIAH 8:1–2, 4–5, 8

By the time the Israelites had returned from exile in Babylon to rebuild the temple and the city of Jerusalem, they had lost touch with much of their heritage – including their ancestral language. Instead of Hebrew, most of the Israelites could speak only Aramaic, the language of the Persian empire, and many Jews would continue to do so through the time of Jesus. When the scribe Ezra called the people together to read the book of the law, he realized that most of them would not understand the Hebrew text. Consequently, he first read the text in Hebrew and then had someone repeat what he had just read in Aramaic. The entire scene is vividly described in chapter 8 of the book of Nehemiah.

SCRIPTURE FOR THE PEOPLE

Because the language problem continued, especially among the Jews who remained in Babylon after the exile, the practice of translating scripture into Aramaic became customary. At some point, Aramaic translations were prepared for use during synagogue services, in which one man read from scripture and another gave a translation or interpretation of the reading. These Aramaic versions came to be called Targums, from the Hebrew word meaning 'translation' or 'interpretation'. By the early Christian era, there were Targums for the entire Hebrew Bible except for the books of Ezra, Nehemiah and Daniel.

In the beginning the Targums may have been preserved by word of mouth. Later they were written down and frequently revised. The chief purpose of all the Targums was to communicate the message of the biblical text to the people. Some were straightforward translations of the biblical texts, while others incorporated additional stories or current Jewish teachings into the text. For example, one verse from the Pentateuch reads simply: 'Give ear, O heavens, and I will speak; let the earth hear the words of my mouth' (Deuteronomy 32:1). One Targum translates this verse simply and literally, but another greatly expands it, explaining at length why Moses is speaking and adding detailed references to the much later prophet Isaiah. The earliest surviving Targums, found among the Dead Sea Scrolls, include one covering parts of the book of Job, which differs significantly from the standard text. Not all Jews of ancient times accepted the validity of all the Targums. Rabbinic literature tells the story of how the great rabbi Gamaliel the Elder (Paul's teacher), examined a Targum of Job, and then promptly ordered a mason to hide it among the stones in the temple.

WHAT DID JESUS READ?

The Gospel of Luke 4:16–20 colourfully describes Jesus' participation at a synagogue

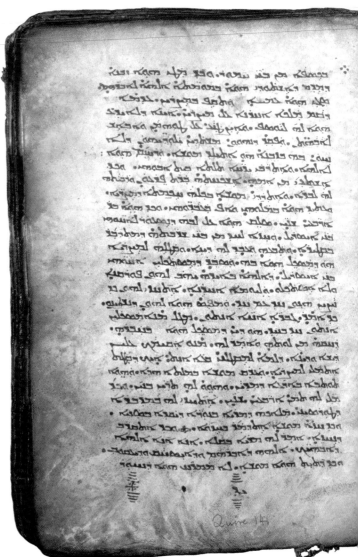

service in Nazareth. According to Luke, when Jesus went to the synagogue, an official asked him to read from the book of Isaiah, handing him the appropriate scroll. Jesus not only read from the scroll, he also preached on it. If it was the custom to read a Targum at this point in a service, Jesus, whose native language was Aramaic, may have done so. Luke makes no mention of a Targum, but he also fails to mention a reading from the Pentateuch, which would have been part of the service. It may be that Luke also skipped over the detail of the Targum to sharpen his main point – Jesus' comments about Isaiah.

But whether Jesus used the Targums or not, they are written in the language he usually spoke and their study is important to us. To begin with, the Targums give us an idea of the early Jewish interpretations of the texts, and the Targums that stay close to the biblical texts help us ascertain the correct word intended in Old Testament passages that are unreadable because the ancient Hebrew texts are marred by tears or inkblots.

There are also hints that New Testament writers made use of the Targums. For example, the images of God the creator as the Word and as Light are found in both the prologue to John's Gospel and in one of the Targums. In addition, careful consideration of the Targums helps us

A professional scribe copies scripture onto a parchment scroll by hand.

bridge the chasm between the Old and New Testaments, as they offer insights into how Jewish interpreters from Jesus' time understood the Hebrew scriptures.

The Peshitta: the Bible in a new tongue

In the years just before the birth of Jesus, Syriac, a new language closely related to Aramaic, developed in and around Edessa (modern Urfa in south-eastern Turkey). In the first and second centuries, the Hebrew Bible was translated into Syriac and later called *peshitta* ('simple' or 'pure') to distinguish it from later Syriac translations made from the Greek Septuagint. The books of the Peshitta were created by different writers in different places, but all were probably completed by the end of the first century or shortly after. Some of the books of the Peshitta, especially those of the Pentateuch, reveal the influence of the Aramaic Targums. In the case of the book of Proverbs, the Peshitta, and not the Hebrew text, seems to be the source for the Targum translation. The various ancient copies of the Peshitta remained consistent, making the text important in helping to establish correct texts for obscure Hebrew readings. New Testament translations were added to the Peshitta in the second century. Today, the Peshitta remains the official Bible of the Syrian Orthodox and Maronite Churches, and of the Church of the East.

Manuscript pages from the Peshitta version of the Acts of the Apostles. This particular manuscript dates to about 1216.

2

The New Testament Takes Shape

Jesus of Nazareth was born about 6 BC. Some 30 years later he engaged in a ministry of teaching and healing, then was arrested and put to death as a criminal. But three days later Jesus rose from the dead, and his disciples realized that he was the Messiah promised by the prophets. At first, no one wrote anything down about Jesus, but later, as a new church began to emerge, Jesus' followers began to write letters and accounts of Jesus' ministry. Some of these writings were read along with the Hebrew scriptures during Christian liturgies. In the centuries that followed a certain number of these works came to be grouped together and regarded as the New Testament – a fulfilment of the Hebrew scriptures, which were from that time on regarded by Christians as the Old Testament.

Jesus with New Testament writers Luke and Paul and the apostles Peter and Andrew in a Byzantine mosaic from the apse of the church of San Paolo Fuori le Mura, Rome, by Venetian artists, c. 1220.

Spreading the Good News

When Jesus was crucified, his disciples despaired. The Gospel according to Luke describes how two of them left Jerusalem on the Sunday after the crucifixion, walking to the nearby village of Emmaus 'and talking with each other about all that had happened' (Luke 24:14). On the road they met the risen Jesus, whom they did not recognize.

St Peter Preaching by Masolino da Panicale (1383–1447).

When Jesus asked what they were discussing, one of the disciples, Cleopas, sadly told the story of how Jesus had been condemned and crucified, dashing their hopes that he was the Messiah who would liberate Israel. Cleopas added that some women had found Jesus' tomb empty that morning and were told by angels that Jesus had risen from the dead, but there was no reason to believe this was true. Jesus admonished the disciples for not believing. When they recognized him, their doubts vanished and they rushed back to Jerusalem to tell their story to the other disciples.

This incident illustrates how stories about Jesus must have been passed along in the early years of Christianity. Men and women who had known Jesus – but who, unlike Cleopas, already believed and rejoiced in the risen Christ – would describe or even proclaim what they had witnessed to others wherever they went. In this way they spread the good news of Jesus by word of mouth.

A CHRISTIAN ORAL TRADITION

The first proclamations about Jesus were probably simple and to the point. Jesus had died and was raised from the dead. More elaborate proclamations, such as Peter's first sermon (Acts 2:14–36), probably identified Jesus as Lord and Messiah and demonstrated how the Messiah's (Jesus') death and resurrection were foretold by the prophets. Later proclamations also pointed out that Jesus had died for the forgiveness of our sins and that he would come again in glory to judge the living and the dead. The basic proclamations were eventually formed into short creeds, or recitals of essential beliefs about Jesus. These creeds were included in sermons, used to teach new converts, and probably recited at baptisms. They may also have been used in worship.

After hearing the basics included in the proclamations and creeds, people must have wanted details about who Jesus was and what he did and said. Perhaps groups gathered around Jesus' disciples here and there, as they repeated personal recollections of Jesus. In such gatherings the first Christians would have resembled the Hebrews in the days of the patriarchs, who gathered around storytellers to hear about the creation and the flood. In a short time, to satisfy new Christians, fuller accounts of

Jesus' resurrection and of his trial and death probably surfaced. To these were added memories of his miraculous healings, which would have attracted people who had hopes of being healed themselves. And, of course, the sayings of Jesus were repeated.

No need to write

Nothing about Jesus was written down in the first two decades after his time on earth, and there were probably several reasons for this. First of all, Jesus left no writings and he never instructed any of his followers to write about him. Then, too, the early followers of Jesus did not consider themselves to be part of a new religion that needed its own scriptures. They were mostly good Jews who accepted the Hebrew scriptures and believed that Jesus was a fulfilment of those scriptures – the Messiah promised by the prophets. When Gentiles (non-Jews) were drawn to follow Jesus, they adopted Judaism as their religion.

The major reason for not writing, however, may have been a practical one. The early Christians believed that Jesus would come again in the immediate future, and so they saw no reason to write down anything. They could keep the traditions about Jesus alive by word of

Fitting the format

As stories about Jesus were told and retold, they were often restructured to make them fit specific patterns. For example, stories involving miraculous healings followed a set format used in the Old Testament: first, the ailment is described; secondly, the afflicted person meets the miracle worker and asks for a cure; thirdly, the healing is accomplished by means of words or touch; fourthly, proof of the healing is supplied; and fifthly, the spectators are amazed. The healing of the leper as recounted in Mark 1:40–45 clearly shows this structure.

Often the incidents from Jesus' life were made to fit these formulas even if the facts had to be carefully chosen, rearranged, or even elaborated to make them fit the mould. This was not a distortion of the truth, for the storyteller's intention was not to give a detailed description of Jesus' actions, but rather to point out the power Jesus had over life and death, health and disease. By fitting a story about Jesus into a recognizable form the central message of the story was made clear to those who heard the good news.

mouth during the brief time before he returned again in glory to judge the living and the dead and bring his kingdom to completion.

Grouping the Jesus traditions

In the earliest years of Christianity, accounts of Jesus may have been related only by the men and women who had known him personally, and they would have reported on Jesus' life from their own points of view. As belief in Jesus spread, however, others must have been needed to carry the accounts of Jesus to distant places.

In order to organize the traditions about Jesus, this second generation of Christian teachers often grouped them together. For example, they kept Jesus' sayings separate from accounts of his miracles, and even the sayings were grouped together by type. Sayings about the law were grouped separately from prophetic sayings, and parables were often told in groups of three, sometimes sharing a theme or image, such as sowing seed. Stories relating to Jesus' actions were similarly grouped. There were stories about his baptism or his passion and death and stories about his miracles, which were broken down into nature miracles (such as calming the storm) and healings.

In about AD 50, some 20 years after Jesus' resurrection, Paul of Tarsus, who had been travelling extensively to spread the good news throughout Asia Minor and Greece, began to write letters to churches he had earlier helped to establish. These letters – later to be included in the New Testament – were probably the first Christian writings. However, it is possible that some early collections of stories about Jesus or collections of Jesus' sayings had been written down by this time. Although none of these collections survive, some of them may have been used later by the authors of the Gospels.

'Philip went down to the city of Samaria and proclaimed the Messiah to them.'

ACTS 8:5

The apostle Philip spread the good news throughout Samaria, and even converted an Ethiopian eunuch, whom he is seen baptizing in this illustration by Claude Lorrain (1600–82), *St Philip Baptizing the Eunuch.*

Paul's Letters to the Gentiles

Paul Preaching in Athens, fresco by Adolph Spangenberg von Gustav (1828–91). Paul usually stayed just a few days or weeks in a city – long enough to teach the basics of Christianity. He gave further teaching through his letters.

'He [Paul] is an instrument whom I have chosen to bring my name before Gentiles.'

ACTS 9:15

Right: Paul wrote letters to Gentile churches in the cities shown on this map, as well as to churches scattered throughout the territory of Galatia, in what is now Turkey.

God's plan for Gentiles

Isaiah delivered this message from God to the Jews: 'I will give you as a light to the nations, that my salvation may reach to the end of the earth' (Isaiah 49:6).

Whenn Paul was about 30 years old, hot-headed, and a Pharisee – one of the most intolerant branches of ancient Jewish religion – he probably would not have given Gentiles much more than the wake of his sudden exit.

Many strict Jews, as Paul and other Pharisees were, avoided all contact with these non-Jews. Some taught that even touching a Gentile would render a Jew unfit to worship God until cleansing rituals were performed. The rift between Jew and Gentile was so obvious that Tacitus, a Roman historian from Paul's century, said Jews 'regard the rest of mankind with all the hatred of enemies'.

Paul learned to love those enemies. His turning point came in a vision while he was on his way to Damascus to arrest Jews who had joined the Christian movement, which he believed was dangerously heretical. Suddenly, at about noon, a light brighter than the sun struck him and a voice rang out, 'I am Jesus, whom you are persecuting.' Jesus then appointed Paul to preach to the Gentiles, 'to open their eyes... so that they may receive forgiveness of sins and a place among those who are sanctified by faith in me' (Acts 26:15–18).

FROM SERMONS TO LETTERS

At first, Paul's ministry was limited to public speaking. He probably told the story of his vision, what he had learned about Jesus from the apostles, and how Jesus fulfilled Old Testament prophecies about the Messiah that God promised to send. Paul shared pastoral duties with Barnabas, ministering to a mixed congregation of Jews and Gentiles in Antioch, Syria. This church apparently had been started by travelling Christians who brought news about Jesus. In time, this church decided to spread the news to others. Directed by the Holy Spirit, the Antioch congregation commissioned Paul and Barnabas as missionaries. This launched the first of Paul's three known missionary journeys, during which he covered some 10,000 miles throughout the Middle East and southern Europe.

On his second journey, Paul recognized he had a serious problem. Generally, he had been staying in towns just a few days or weeks. That was long enough to teach the basics of the Christian religion. But it was not long enough to produce mature believers. After Paul left town, disagreements sometimes erupted, or travelling preachers arrived and offered a different slant on the gospel message, confusing and dividing churches. Sometimes the churches sent messengers with questions for Paul.

Rather than rushing back to the church – which was sometimes several hundred miles away – Paul took pen in hand and wrote letters. About half the books of the New Testament are letters from Paul. Because they survive, we have a vivid portrayal of his developing faith and of the emerging Gentile church.

Paul's letters are probably the oldest books in the New Testament, written before the stories of Jesus were ever penned. Many scholars say that 1 Thessalonians is Paul's oldest letter. After Paul

Tychicus, Paul's courier

When Paul or any other person outside the Roman government wanted to send a letter, they needed to find their own courier. The Roman empire's postal service was for official business only. Paul often used associates who worked alongside him. Tychicus was one such man.

A citizen of Ephesus, Tychicus travelled and worked with Paul during the third missionary journey. He delivered at least two of Paul's letters: Ephesians and Colossians.

In writing to Colossian believers, Paul explained why he chose Tychicus as the messenger: 'Tychicus will tell you all the news about me; he is a beloved brother, a faithful minister, and a fellow servant in the Lord. I have sent him to you for this very purpose, so that you may know how we are and that he may encourage your hearts' (Colossians 4:7–8). Paul's letter to the Ephesians has a similar note (Ephesians 6:21–22).

left Thessalonica, during his second missionary journey in about AD 50, the believers apparently sent him a message. They were confused about Jesus' second coming. And they were worried about what would happen to believers who died before Jesus came back. Would the dead be saved or lost? Paul assured the believers that when Jesus returns, 'the dead in Christ will rise first' (1 Thessalonians 4:16).

WHICH LETTERS DID PAUL WRITE?
Thirteen letters claim Paul as their writer. And a 14th – Hebrews – has sometimes been attributed to him, although he is not identified as the writer and some of the earliest Christian scholars doubted Paul's authorship. In the AD 200s, a theologian named Tertullian quoted Hebrews and said it was written by Barnabas.

Exactly which letters Paul wrote is a matter of continuing debate. Although Paul's name is on 13, it was common in ancient times for students to write in the name and spirit of their mentor, as a means of honouring that person and applying their teachings to newly developing situations. That is what many modern scholars say happened with books such as 2 Timothy and Titus, which are different from Paul's other letters in several ways – including the writing style.

By about a century after Paul's death, his letters were being collected and bound into individual books, and then circulated throughout the Church. The earliest known copies usually included 10 or 11 letters, sometimes including Hebrews and sometimes excluding 1 and 2 Timothy along with Titus. Paul's letters were generally arranged in order of length, from longest to shortest: Romans, Hebrews, 1 and 2 Corinthians, Ephesians, Galatians, Philippians, Colossians, 1 and 2 Thessalonians and Philemon.

In time, the order of Galatians and Ephesians was switched, the letters to Timothy and Titus were added and put in front of the shorter letter to Philemon, and Hebrews was moved to the end because it did not identify the writer.

Gentiles and barbarians

The word 'Gentiles' means 'nations'. Jews used it to identify non-Jews, just as Greeks used *barboroi* (barbarians) to identify non-Greeks.

Why Paul stopped preaching to Jews

When the Jews in one city rejected Paul's message he replied, 'It was necessary that the word of God should be spoken first to you. Since you reject it and judge yourselves to be unworthy of eternal life, we are now turning to the Gentiles' (Acts 13:46).

First-Century Letter Writing

If we eliminated letters from the Old Testament, we would not remove very much. No Old Testament books are letters, although there are references to some letters, such as dispatches sent by kings (Esther 1:22). But if we eliminated letters from the New Testament, we would lose 21 of the 27 books – everything except Matthew, Mark, Luke, John, Acts and Revelation.

In Paul's day, philosophers, religious leaders and other thinkers used letters as a tool for spreading their teachings to a wider audience. These instructional letters came to be known as epistles, from a common Greek word for 'letters'.

Ancient Roman fresco portrait of a young woman with a stylus and a book. There was no postal system except for official Roman documents. Roman citizens wanting to send letters to friends and relatives had to rely on caravans and other travellers to deliver the letters.

Paul, who wrote most of the New Testament letters, depended heavily on such letters to supplement his ministry. Since he travelled so much, starting churches throughout the Roman empire, letters allowed him to minister in more than one place at a time. While preaching in one city, he wrote to distant congregations and pastors, usually intending his letters to be read aloud during worship services, and occasionally to be circulated among other churches. He told the church at Colossae to pass his letter on to the Laodiceans (Colossians 4:16).

Greek words in the Bible

As in English, Greek has capital letters (called majuscules) and lower case letters (minuscules). Early Bible manuscripts used mainly capital letters, like those below:

Greek word	Pronunciation (transliteration)	English translation
ΘΕΟΣ	theos	God
ΊΗΣΟΥΣ	Iesous	Jesus
ΧΡΙΣΤΟΣ	christos	Christ, or Messiah
ΑΓΑΠΗ	agape	love

Paul generally dictated his letters to a scribe, sometimes adding a sentence or two at the end in his own handwriting. Although the Romans had a postal system, it was for official use. Citizens had to rely on caravans, other travellers, and – in Paul's case – associates, who often delivered the letter and stayed a while to help the congregation put Paul's advice into practice.

HOW TO WRITE A LETTER

When we write letters today, we usually follow a pattern, which includes the date along with a common style of greeting and closing. Writers in Paul's day did much the same, although they had a different pattern. It is a pattern Paul generally followed, although he felt free to adapt it.

Opening

Most letters written in the Greek style started by identifying the writer and the recipient, followed by the word 'Greetings'. James used this style (James 1:1). But Paul added a twist. Instead of 'Greetings', he opened with a blessing: 'Grace to you and peace from God our Father and the Lord Jesus Christ' (Romans 1:7).

Introduction

In the more personal Greek letters, writers often began by offering thanks, especially to the gods. Paul, on the other hand, often began by giving thanks to God and by praising the recipients. 'I give thanks to my God always for you'

Languages of Paul's day

Four languages were used in New Testament times – Hebrew, Aramaic, Latin and Greek.

In Paul's day, most Jews did not speak much Hebrew any more. That is because the language was rarely used during their generation-long exile in Babylon in the 500s BC. Jewish scholars, however, still preferred Hebrew. So did some of the priests and rabbis, who regularly led worship services in Hebrew, and read scripture in the traditional Jewish language (especially in Jerusalem, the centre of Jewish traditionalism).

Jews picked up Aramaic during their exile in the Persian Gulf area. Most Jews in Palestine spoke it as their everyday language. It was probably the language Jesus used.

Romans spoke Latin in their homeland and among themselves. They also used it in formal proclamations and on inscriptions. But abroad, they used the prevailing language of Greek.

Nearly everyone in the Roman empire knew Greek – the language in which the New Testament was written. Greek emerged as the dominant language after Alexander the Great and his armies swept through most of the Mediterranean world in the 300s BC.

The widespread popularity of Greek is one reason the New Testament writers chose that language – it promised the widest possible readership. Another reason is that by the time Christians got around to writing the New Testament, the Old Testament version they had grown to love was the Septuagint, a Greek translation of the Hebrew scriptures. When New Testament writers quoted the Old Testament, they quoted it from the Septuagint.

Although New Testament writers used Greek almost exclusively, there are plenty of indications that all four languages were still in use. They appear in words, phrases and other references. The most famous is the sign Pilate had posted on the cross of Jesus. It read: 'Jesus of Nazareth, the King of the Jews' and was written 'in Hebrew, in Latin and in Greek' (John 19:19–20).

(1 Corinthians 1:4). He also tended to add short prayers for the recipients: 'I pray that the God of our Lord Jesus Christ, the Father of glory, may give you a spirit of wisdom and revelation as you come to know him' (Ephesians 1:17).

Body

The main message of Greek letters often began with a concise statement about the letter's purpose. Paul followed this pattern in his letter to the Corinthians, when he appealed for them to stop arguing with each other (1 Corinthians 1:10).

Paul intended his written message to carry as much authority as he would have commanded in person. In fact, some critics charged that he was even more domineering in his letters than he was when he had to look the people in the eye – a charge Paul denied, vowing to prove it when he arrived (2 Corinthians 10:10–11).

Closing

It was common for Greek letters to close with a wish of good health for the recipient and a 'Farewell'. Paul, instead, closed his letters with a benediction – a short prayer of blessing and hope like those offered by many modern ministers at the end of a worship service: 'The grace of the Lord Jesus Christ, the love of God, and the communion of the Holy Spirit be with all of you' (2 Corinthians 13:13).

An angry letter
Paul's stern letter to the Galatians skipped the customary, polite introduction. Instead, Paul jumped directly to the problem, declaring he was shocked that the people had already rejected the true gospel he had taught them.

Writing Down the Good News

'Mark became Peter's interpreter and wrote accurately all that he remembered of the things said and done by the Lord, but not in order, for he had not heard the Lord.'

PAPIAS IN EUSEBIUS'S
HISTORY OF THE CHURCH

In his letters, Paul touched on events in Jesus' life and the words and deeds of Jesus may have been copied down into a few collections by the early AD 60s, but no full-scale work had yet been written about Jesus. Most of the traditions about Jesus were were still being passed on by word of mouth. By the mid-60s, however, many of the most famous of the men and women who had known Jesus or witnessed to the risen Jesus had died – including Peter and Paul and James, the brother of Jesus. Those who remained to pass on what they knew about Jesus had weaker bonds with the historical figure of Jesus. At the same time, it was becoming obvious that Jesus' second coming was not imminent, and it must have seemed a good idea to write a structured account of Jesus' words and deeds. So, sometime between AD 68 and 73, the first surviving 'Gospel' was written.

MARK MAKES HIS MARK

Although the Gospel according to Matthew appears first in the New Testament, as it has come down to us, the Gospel according to Mark was probably written first, as it seems to have served as a major source for the Gospels of Matthew and Luke. No one knows for sure who wrote this early Gospel. Although the name

Mark is found with the title of the Gospel in the earliest surviving manuscripts, there is nothing to indicate which Mark was meant, and Mark was a popular name in the first century. According to an early tradition, the author was John Mark, who helped Paul and Barnabas for a time, and then became associated with the apostle Peter, who called him 'my son Mark' (1 Peter 5:13) – meaning son in a spiritual sense. According to Papias, a second-century bishop (who is quoted in Eusebius's fourth-century *History of the Church*), Mark wrote his Gospel based on what Peter taught him. While this may be an exaggeration, Mark probably did use some of what he learned from Peter in writing his Gospel.

INVENTING A FORM

Writing the first Gospel was a huge and innovative task, as it involved inventing a new literary form. Biographies existed at the time, notably the Greek collection *Parallel Lives* (relating the achievements of famous Romans and Greeks), which was being written by the Greek Plutarch at about that time. But the Gospels that appear in the New Testament are not biographies or even histories in the strict sense. Not enough was known about Jesus to construct a day-by-day account of what he did and said. His life and ministry was preserved in disconnected memories, tales and quotes, plus a few lengthier narratives. The task of the first Gospel writer, and those who followed, was to tie the available materials about Jesus together to form a cohesive whole and to introduce a point of view.

Mark's point of view was almost surely influenced by the situation of the Christians for whom he was writing – a pattern that was to hold true for the later Gospels. No one can be sure of when and where Mark wrote his Gospel or for whom, but it is possible that Mark was with Peter just before his death in Rome in AD 64, and that he remained in Rome and wrote his Gospel there a few years later. Scholars have pointed out that Mark's Jesus predicts that his followers will face persecution, leading some to fall from faith (Mark 4:16–17 and 13:9–13). This was indeed the case in Rome at the time Peter and Paul were martyred. So Mark may have written his account of Jesus' ministry and death for Christians living in Rome, to prepare them

What does 'gospel' mean?

The word 'gospel' is an Old English (Anglo-Saxon) translation of the Greek word *evangelion*, which means 'good news'. The Greek word was used in ancient times to refer to the birth of an emperor-god. In the Old Testament the equivalent Hebrew term was used to tell of naming a king (1 Kings 1:24), the birth of a son (Jeremiah 20:15), and victory in battle (1 Samuel 31:8–10). Isaiah's Servant Songs predict that the servant would proclaim the good news of deliverance and a new age (Isaiah 40:1–5; 52:7–10). In the New Testament, after John's arrest, Jesus came 'proclaiming the good news of God, and saying, "the time is fulfilled, and the kingdom of God has come near; repent and believe in the good news"' (Mark 1:14–15). Here good news (gospel) means the announcement of the inbreaking of the new age of God's rule. In the early Church the gospel focused on the proclamation of Jesus' death and resurrection. Belief in it brought everlasting life. 'Gospel' is so used some 60 times in Paul's writings. Then Mark used the term in the opening verse of his work: 'The beginning of the gospel of Jesus Christ, the Son of God.' In later times the gospel, or good news, was taken to be Mark's entire account of Jesus' mission, death and resurrection, and other such accounts as well.

for facing persecution and even death, emphasizing the need to take up one's cross. The cross, in fact, is at the centre of Mark's Gospel.

Unable to construct a chronological narrative, Mark structured his work by grouping events as happenings: first, in Galilee, secondly, on the way to Jerusalem, and thirdly, in Jerusalem. Often he grouped similar events or sayings together, as is seen in the three parables about seeds related in chapter 4. Some scholars believe that Mark made use of a passion narrative (account of Jesus' trial and crucifixion) that already existed. A large part of Mark's Gospel is taken up by the account of Jesus' passion and death, and the Gospel ends abruptly in early manuscripts, with the women at Jesus' empty tomb saying nothing of what they witnessed, 'for they were afraid' (Mark 16:8).

This ending bothered Christians from the beginning because of its seeming negativity – why did the women not rejoice over the resurrection? In response, someone in the second century added the verses that are found in most Bibles today (Mark 16:9–20), drawing the material from the other Gospels and the Acts of the Apostles. Ever since then scholars have speculated that the original ending of Mark's Gospel may have been lost or that Mark never

completed his Gospel. Today, however, some scholars believe it was the intended ending. Pointing out that Mark stressed the need for Christians to accept the cross of Jesus and the difficulty Jesus' followers had in believing in the need for the cross, they hold that Mark ended his Gospel on a like note. Perhaps, too, Mark wanted the Christian reader to react emotionally at this ending, calling out mentally to the women to believe that Christ had indeed risen.

Jesus' suffering is emphasized in Mark's Gospel, which includes the mocking of Christ, depicted in this illustration by Cristoforo de Predis from the *Predis Codex* of 1476.

Matthew and Luke Follow Mark

Mark's Gospel was highly appreciated, and copies were taken to Christian communities far from Mark's own. This must have spurred others to write works about Jesus, for the opening of Luke's Gospel tells us, 'many have undertaken to set down an orderly account of the events that have been fulfilled among us, just as they were handed on to us by those who from the beginning were eyewitnesses and servants of the word' (Luke 1:1–2). Luke certainly had in mind the Gospel of Mark and possibly that of Matthew (John had not yet written his Gospel), but the rest of the 'many' accounts he knew have been lost.

Chapter 25 of Matthew's Gospel describes the Last Judgment, shown here in a fresco by Giotto di Bondone (c. 1266–1337), from the Scrovegni Chapel, Padua.

MATTHEW FILLS OUT THE STORY

The Gospel according to Matthew was probably the first surviving Gospel to be written after Mark's. Matthew used Mark's Gospel as a starting point for his own. He incorporated most of Mark's text, sometimes rewriting it, but often repeating it word for word. What makes Matthew's Gospel significant are the additions to the Markan text. To begin, Matthew fills out the story of Jesus, adding sections about his birth and infancy and his appearances after the resurrection. The other major additions are in the form of five discourses, or sermons, given by Jesus, including the Sermon on the Mount, which features the Beatitudes and the Lord's Prayer, and a description of the Last Judgment in which Jesus separates the sheep from the goats (the saved from the damned) by judging whether or not individuals took care of those in need.

Because much of the material in the discourses appears in the Gospel of Luke, but not in Mark, scholars have speculated that Matthew drew this material from a lost source, a list of Jesus' sayings, which they have named Q, from the word Quelle (German for 'source'). In fact, scholars have gone so far as to try to reconstruct this hypothetical source and even speculate on a number of revisions. However, no one can be absolutely certain that such a single source existed – the material used by the Gospel writers may have come from several early sources, written and oral. Certainly both Matthew and Luke used material that is found in neither Mark nor in the supposed Q.

According to an early tradition Matthew, the tax collector whom Jesus called as an apostle, wrote this Gospel. However, the author does not seem to have been an eyewitness, as he relied on Mark and other outside sources for his material. The earliest to name Matthew as author was Papias, the second-century bishop who named John Mark as the author of the earlier Gospel. Papias claimed that Matthew compiled the 'sayings' (*logia*) of Jesus in the Hebrew language. However, the word 'sayings' does not suggest a Gospel like the one we have, but rather a list of sayings like Q. In addition, Matthew's Gospel is written in Greek, not in Hebrew, and it used Greek sources (certainly Mark).

Matthew's Gospel may have been written about AD 85, but earlier and later dates have been suggested. It seems likely that the Gospel was written in Antioch, the city where Jesus' followers were first called Christians (Acts 11:26). After the martyrdom of Stephen, large numbers of Jewish Christians relocated to Antioch, and Matthew's Gospel suggests that the community for which it was written was heavily Jewish. For example, the Gospel emphasizes respect for the Jewish law and fails to explain Jewish customs in places where Mark's Gospel does. Matthew also reflects some distancing between Jewish and Gentile Christians – speaking of the Jews and 'their' synagogues and depicting the Pharisees as hypocrites, for example – reflecting the later history of Antioch, where uneasiness broke out between Jews and Gentile Christians.

Matthew's Gospel emphasizes the Church. Rooted in the teaching of Jesus, the Church is built on rock and 'the gates of Hades will not prevail against it' (Matthew 16:18). Very quickly Matthew's Gospel became the primary teaching tool of the Church, which may account for it being positioned as the first book of the New Testament.

LUKE'S TWO-VOLUME GOSPEL

The third Gospel is actually in two volumes – the Gospel proper and the Acts of the Apostles, a volume that continues the story of the early Church after Jesus' ascension. The two books are written in a masterful Greek style that is carefully organized, drawing many parallels between the ministry of Jesus and that of Paul.

Like Matthew, Luke used much of Mark's Gospel, adding material of his own. Like Matthew, Luke adds an infancy narrative, but his departs from Matthew's in the stories it tells and in the perspective – while Matthew recounts his stories of the birth and infancy of Jesus from the viewpoint of Joseph, Jesus' foster father, Luke sees his early narrative through the eyes of Mary, the mother of Jesus. For this reason, some commentators have speculated that Luke knew Mary personally, and obtained much of his material from her. Luke also adds his own resurrection stories, ending with Jesus' ascension into heaven. The same scene is repeated at the beginning of Acts to connect the two volumes. Acts tells the story of the early Church from the ascension to Paul's arrival in Rome. Thus it moves from Jerusalem, the centre of the Jewish world to Rome, the centre of the Gentile world, underlining Luke's main theme, that Jesus came for all men and women, saints and sinners, Jews and Gentiles alike.

What is truth?

Sceptics have pointed out that there are inconsistencies in the Gospels that undermine their accuracy. But the Gospel writers were not trying to set down a chronology of Jesus' life. They were writing theological works that showed who Jesus was and what, and saw nothing wrong with changing a historical fact to make a theological point. For example, in the Gospels of Matthew, Mark and Luke Jesus' last supper with his disciples is a Passover meal, commemorating the last meal the Israelites ate before fleeing Egypt. In the Gospel of John this last supper is eaten the day before. Why the difference? The first three Gospels presented the last supper as a Passover meal in which the traditional bread and wine become the body and blood of Jesus. John, on the other hand, sees Jesus as the lamb that is to be eaten at the Passover feast, and so he has Jesus die at the time the paschal lamb would be slaughtered, thereby changing the day. What the evangelists were doing is giving symbolic meaning to the meal. They had little regard for the day the meal was eaten. Each Gospel showed aspects of Jesus and what he means to us. The truth of historical detail here is less important than the overall 'truth' the Gospels seek to teach.

In Luke's Gospel most of the remaining non-Markan material is found in two sections. The first describes Jesus' ministry in Galilee (Luke 6:17 – 8:3) and includes the Sermon on the Plain, a shorter version of Matthew's Sermon on the Mount. The second section (Luke 9:51 – 18:14) describes Jesus' journey from Galilee to Jerusalem to face death. It incorporates teachings from Q and material not otherwise known, including the parables of the Good Samaritan and the Prodigal Son.

The oldest surviving manuscripts of the third Gospel attribute it to Luke, who may be the companion that Paul refers to as 'the beloved physician' (Colossians 4:14). Luke was probably a Gentile convert from Antioch. He wrote his Gospel around AD 85, give or take five to ten years. While no one knows where Luke wrote his two-volume Gospel, it seems to have been a Greek congregation, perhaps one of the churches established by Paul while he worked with Luke. Certainly the church was made up of mainly Gentile Christians, as the text avoids Jewish expressions and customs that would be unfamiliar to non-Jews, and the thrust of Luke's text is to spread the good news to Gentiles as well as Jews, extending Jesus' message to all people far and wide.

Luke's predominance
Luke wrote more than any of the other New Testament writers. The Acts of the Apostles and the Gospel of Luke together make up more than one quarter of the New Testament.

'I too decided, after investigating everything carefully from the very first, to write an orderly account for you, most excellent Theophilus, so that you may know the truth concerning the things about which you have been instructed.'

LUKE 1:3–4

Gospel statistics
About 80 per cent of Mark's 661 verses are repeated in Matthew and 65 per cent of Mark's verses are also found in Luke.

The Fourth Gospel

Peter turned and saw the disciple whom Jesus loved following... This is the disciple who is testifying to these things and has written them, and we know that his testimony is true. But there are also many other things that Jesus did; if every one of them were written down, I suppose that the world itself could not contain the books that would be written.'

JOHN 21:20, 24–25

Matthew, Mark and Luke

Because the first three Gospels are so similar, they are called the Synoptic Gospels to distinguish them from the very different Gospel of John. The term 'synoptic', from the Greek for 'seen together', refers to the fact that scholars often examine these Gospels side by side to study the relationships of one to the other and to the hypothetical source Q. The questions arising from these relationships are referred to by scholars as the Synoptic Problem.

The fourth Gospel, which is attributed to John, is a more poetic and theological work than the other Gospels. It was the last of the Gospels to be written and it may have gone through at least two editions, as it contains material that was obviously added to the original Gospel at a later time. The added material may have been written by the same author as the original, or by a different writer.

AUTHORSHIP AND SOURCES

Once again, no one knows who wrote this Gospel. The Gospel itself tells us that the author was 'the disciple whom Jesus loved' (John 21:20), commonly referred to as the 'beloved disciple', and an eyewitness of the crucifixion (John 19:35). Although the beloved disciple is often mentioned in John's Gospel he is never named. In about AD 180, the Christian writer Irenaeus identified him as the apostle John, who lived in Ephesus until the time of Trajan (who became Roman emperor in AD 98). For many centuries, John was considered the author of the fourth Gospel. In the past century, however, many scholars felt that the apostle had not written the Gospel, although he may have been the founder of a church, or community of Christians who preserved his traditions. One of John's followers, they believe, wrote the Gospel, and later, one or more others wrote the additions.

Scholars have detected three major sources in John's Gospel. The first is a collection of miracles, which John calls 'signs' (because he believed that they point to Jesus' real identity as God). Most of these signs are different from the miracles found in the earlier three Gospels, and include the dramatic raising of Lazarus from the dead. (The only miracle found in all four Gospels is the multiplication of loaves and fishes.) The second supposed source for John is a collection of discourses, which are generally linked to a 'sign'. Typically, Jesus performs a miracle and this leads to some incident or a dialogue between Jesus and one or more individuals; in the end some aspect of Jesus as God is revealed. The final source is a passion story that differs in many places from the other Gospel accounts.

TIMES OF WRITING

Most scholars agree that the Gospel was written sometime in the 90s. Some believe that the added materials came later, in the first decade of the second century.

That there were two editions seems obvious from the texts we have. Often passages are repeated, sometimes with a different tone, leading scholars to believe that a later editor added them but so revered the original text that he dared not delete any of it, and so let the two texts stand side by side. Even more obvious is that chapter 21, which describes appearances of the risen Jesus in Galilee, was added, as chapter 20 ends with a very definite conclusion to the entire Gospel. Chapter 21, in turn, ends with a weaker conclusion to the Gospel. Why two endings from one author? Again, a later editor may have added chapter 21, which preserves a tradition about Jesus that was important to the members of his community at that time, placing it last so as not to disturb the original.

Is John's Gospel anti-Semitic?

Since John's Gospel so often speaks of 'the Jews' with such seeming animosity, many readers have regarded the Gospel as anti-Semitic. But this is not so. In fact, most of the Christians in the community that produced the Gospel were themselves Jews who had come to believe in Jesus. Because of their beliefs in the divinity of Jesus, however, they scandalized other Jews who saw the Christian views as violating the first commandment, which demands worship of only one God. In time, this disagreement caused dissension in the synagogues, where both groups prayed. Eventually the traditionalists expelled the Christians from their synagogues, leaving a bitter taste in the mouths of the Christians. Although they were still generally following Jewish law, including the first commandment, the Christians began to see the Jews who dismissed them and their views as the other side, and perhaps even the enemy. As a result, when they write harshly of 'the Jews', they are referring to the Jews who rejected them, transferring their resentment to the Gospel stories where the Jews who specifically rejected Jesus (not all Jews) are portrayed as villainous – certainly far more villainous than they actually were.

A final question relating to additions arises over the story of the woman taken in adultery (John 7: 53 – 8:11), which is missing from many early copies of John's Gospel – though the other additions are not. Some scholars believe that this is an ancient tradition that was left out of all four Gospels but that travelled with them. Perhaps, they speculate, some second-century editor, wishing to preserve the tradition, added it to John's Gospel, even though it does not properly belong to any of the four Gospels as originally written.

THE COMMUNITY THAT PRODUCED THE FOURTH GOSPEL

The community for whom the Gospel of John was written has been widely discussed, and Raymond E. Brown, the pre-eminent interpreter of John's Gospel and letters in the late 20th century, went so far as to put together a proposed history of the community. According to Father Brown, it went through four stages. A group of Jewish Christians gathered around the beloved disciple somewhere in Palestine, where they remained until sometime after the Roman invasion of Jerusalem in AD 70. While in Palestine, they attended the regular Jewish synagogues and stirred up controversy by declaring that Jesus was God. The traditional Jews in the synagogue saw this as a contradiction to the Jewish belief that there was only one God. Eventually animosity grew between the two groups and the traditionalists expelled the Christians from their synagogues. (This situation is reflected in the story of Jesus' healing of the man born blind in chapter 9 of John's Gospel.) A great deal of animosity arose between the two groups, and at some point at least some of the Christians from this community relocated, probably to the city of Ephesus in Asia Minor (now Turkey).

In their new home, members of the community absorbed some of the Greek culture that surrounded them, but took an ever more hard-nosed stand on the divinity of Jesus. It was at this time that the Gospel was first written – either by the beloved disciple himself or, more likely, another member of the community. The Gospel, of course, stresses the divinity of Jesus.

In the years that followed, some members of the community sought to stress the humanity of Jesus to temper the emphasis of his divinity found in the Gospel, and so give a rounder picture of Jesus. These ideas are found in the first two letters of John, which were written at this time. Finally, some members of the community revolted over the new emphasis on Jesus' humanity, and there was no authority in the community to draw strict lines. Consequently, in the fourth period of the community, some members emphasized the need for pastors, or leaders, suggesting that the Spirit was not the only spiritual guide. At this time John's third letter was written and someone made the additions to the original Gospel, including chapter 21. This final chapter focuses on Jesus' assigning Peter to feed his sheep. It was a tradition that needed to be added to the Gospel at this point to keep the community from falling apart rather than accepting a more structured kind of Church.

The Raising of Lazarus from the *Maestà* altarpiece by Duccio da Buoninsegna (c. 1255–c. 1318). Only John's Gospel mentions this miracle.

Letters Not Written by Paul

Paul wrote to individuals and specific congregations. But several other Christian leaders wrote what scholars call 'General Letters' intended for circulation among a general audience of Christians. These letters are James, 1 and 2 Peter, 1, 2 and 3 John, along with Jude.

Although these general letters and the letters by Paul were written by different people, at different times in early Christian history, and for different reasons, they all share a common purpose – to inspire and help fellow Christians.

JAMES

This book is considered to be the Proverbs of the New Testament because it is full of wise and practical advice about how to live a godly life. Exactly who is giving this advice remains unclear. The writer identified himself only as 'James, a servant of God and of the Lord Jesus Christ' (James 1:1). There are at least four men by this name in the New Testament, two of them apostles. But at least since the AD 300s, church leaders have attributed the book to the James identified in the Gospels as a brother of Jesus (Matthew 13:55; Mark 6:3), and in Acts and Paul's letters as leader of the Jerusalem church.

If this James was the writer, the letter was written before AD 62. Jewish historian Josephus reported it was in that year that Jewish leaders in Jerusalem stoned James to death.

Some scholars say the Jewish ideas running throughout James suggest the letter was written when most of the church was still made up of Jews. This means it could pre-date Paul's letters and be the oldest book in the New Testament. James addresses his letter to the 'twelve tribes in the Dispersion', which could mean Jews scattered around the empire. But it could also mean Jews and Gentiles alike as in the 'new Israel'.

1 AND 2 PETER

1 Peter was written to encourage Christians facing persecution, perhaps in the early 60s, when Christians became increasingly viewed as a radical cult instead of a legitimate branch of the Jewish religion. It could also have been written later, after Nero accused Christians of setting fire to Rome in AD 64.

The writer identified himself as the apostle Peter, whom church leaders said was executed during Nero's four-year persecution. Some scholars doubt Peter wrote the letter because the writing style is refined Greek, a surprising feat for a Galilean fisherman. Other scholars say Peter admitted he had help: 'Through Silvanus, whom I consider a faithful brother, I have written this short letter' (1 Peter 5:12). Silvanus is the Latin form of the Greek name Silas, a Christian who travelled with Paul throughout the Greek-speaking world (Acts 15:22). Scholars who doubt that Peter wrote this letter say the persecution could have been during the 90s, long after Peter's death.

The writings in about AD 95 of Clement, a church leader in Rome who was later known as Pope Clement I, referred to 1 Peter. Irenaeus, a church leader in the second century, did the same and added that Peter wrote it.

2 Peter, written to warn Christians about heretical teachers, has the feel of a last

testament from someone about to die. The writer, who identified himself as the apostle Peter, said he received word from heaven that he would die soon.

As early as the second century, church leaders began doubting Peter wrote the letter. The writing style is dramatically different from First Peter, with less refined Greek. There are striking similarities with Jude, both in content

---

'Peter... has left one acknowledged epistle, and, it may be, a second one, for it is doubted.'

ORIGEN, CHRISTIAN
THEOLOGIAN, AD 200s

Right: Tenth-century Byzantine illumination of the apostle Peter. Although he was the leader of the apostles, Peter's writings make up only a fraction of the New Testament: 1 Peter and perhaps 2 Peter.

and wording. And the writer implies that Paul's letters were already revered, because he associates them with 'other scriptures' (2 Peter 3:16). This leads some scholars to suggest 2 Peter was written in Peter's name by a follower, and was perhaps the last New Testament book written – possibly as late as AD 100 to 150. Writing in the name of a respected teacher was a common practice among Greeks and Jews. The opposite of plagiarism, it credits the teacher whose ideas are being applied to new situations.

1, 2 AND 3 JOHN

The three short letters of John seem to reflect a time when Jewish believers in Christ have been banned from worshipping with other Jews – an action taken by many synagogues late in the first century. The first two letters help Christians deal with attacks against Jesus' divine and human natures, and warn against false teachers. The third letter condemns a maverick church leader opposed to those who oversee the Christian movement.

The writer does not identify himself, but the writing style and wording – especially in 1 John – are similar to that of the Gospel of John, also an anonymous work but usually attributed to the apostle John. Church leaders in the second century quoted from the letters and said John wrote them late in life, while living in Ephesus.

JUDE

In this 25-verse letter, the writer identifies himself as 'Jude, a servant of Jesus Christ and brother of James' (Jude 1). Some scholars say Jude was a brother of Jesus. That would explain why he mentioned James, the well-known brother of Jesus who led the Jerusalem church. The Gospels say Jesus had four brothers, including James and Judas (Jude for short).

The letter attacks a heretical teaching that says it is all right for Christians to sin, perhaps referring to a movement that emerged later in the first century. For this reason, some scholars suggest another Jude, who was a respected church leader, wrote the letter.

Revelation

Revelation closes the book on the Bible, and human history. But it opens the door to a new age of peace in which God has defeated evil, and the faithful live for ever with him.

This final book of the Bible gets its name from the opening description: 'The revelation of Jesus Christ' (Revelation 1:1). In the original Greek, the word for revelation is *apocalypsis*, from which we get 'apocalypse'. This word used to mean 'an unveiling', but because of the earth-shattering events described in the book, it came to mean an extinction-level catastrophe.

The writer identifies himself as a Christian named John, exiled to the small and rocky island of Patmos (between Turkey and Greece) for preaching about Jesus. But which John? A Christian writer named Justin Martyr, who lived about AD 100–65, was the first-known person to go on record with an answer. He said the writer was the apostle John, one of Jesus' closest disciples and the presumed author of the Gospel of John and the three letters of John. Within about 100 years, other church leaders began to challenge this answer, arguing that the book was nothing like John's other works.

Whoever wrote it, Revelation was probably written in the final decade of the first century, when Emperor Domitian renewed the persecution of Christians, executing many and exiling others to penal colonies. The vexing symbolism in Revelation apparently allowed the writer to encourage the Christian churches without repercussions from Rome. The Christians understood the coded images, many of which were drawn from the Old Testament. But to Romans, it probably read like the fantasy of a lonely man with too much time on his hands.

This illustration from the 10th-century *Commentary on the Apocalypse of Beatus* shows the second trumpet announcing the fall of Babylon. Much of Revelation was written in what appears to be code words, to protect the writer from repercussions by political leaders. Babylon, for example, was a Jewish name for Rome. Both empires destroyed Jerusalem and levelled the Jewish temple.

The Apostolic Fathers

Who you know is not solely a modern concern. It has been important since ancient times. In fact, a whole group of ancient Christian writers are identified by who they knew. In the late second century, the Christian writer Irenaeus boasted of his boyhood memories of the aged Polycarp, the bishop of Smyrna who had been martyred in AD 155. In his own youth, Polycarp had known the apostle John and 'others who had seen the Lord'. Polycarp had told Irenaeus of his conversations with them, 'repeating their words from memory', and thus creating a direct link between Irenaeus and the apostles, from whom all knowledge of Jesus flowed.

St Polycarp, one of the Apostolic Fathers, and St Sebastian, an early martyr, destroy pagan idols in a Christian convert's home. *St Sebastian and St Polycarp Destroying the Idols* by Pedro Garcia de Benabarre.

SOMEONE WHO KNEW SOMEONE WHO KNEW JESUS

Since the 17th century, ancient writers who knew someone who knew Jesus have been called Apostolic Fathers. Irenaeus, though an important writer, is not one of the Apostolic Fathers. He did not personally know an apostle; he was only someone who knew someone (Polycarp) who knew someone (John) who knew Jesus. But even such a tenuous link to Jesus was worth boasting about, or so Irenaeus seems to have thought.

In addition to Polycarp, the Apostolic Fathers include Clement I (the bishop of Rome, who may have been appointed by Peter himself) and Ignatius, bishop of Antioch. These three men wrote important letters on Church policy, as did another author who was wrongly identified as Clement. This last author, who apparently lived in or near Alexandria, Egypt, in the middle of the second century, wrote the first full Christian sermon that has been preserved; it is generally referred to as *Clement's Second Letter*, or *2 Clement*.

Other prominent Apostolic Fathers are the authors of the *Letter to Diognetus* and the *Epistle of Barnabas* (probably not the apostle, as claimed), which discuss the relationship between Judaism and Christianity. Also in the group are the author of the *Didache*, or 'The Teaching of the Twelve Apostles', and Hermas, author of the *Shepherd of Hermas*. These last two works have a good deal to say about life in the second-century Church.

KNOWLEDGE OF NEW TESTAMENT BOOKS

By the time of the Apostolic Fathers (the late first and early second centuries), all the books of the New Testament had probably been written, but they were not yet considered scripture in the way the books of the Old Testament were. In fact, a New Testament canon would not be established for another two centuries. One of the criteria for deciding which books would be part of the New Testament, however, was to be that they were known and used by Christian churches. For the second century, we have only what the Apostolic Fathers wrote to tell us which books were generally read and used.

In his *Letter to the Philippians* (3:2), Polycarp openly refers to 'the blessed and glorious Paul', who had established the church at Philippi, urging the Philippian Christians to carefully study the letters Paul had written to them (one of which is in the New Testament) in order

Ignatius is thrown to the lions

In about AD 69, before some of the New Testament books had been written, Ignatius was named bishop of Antioch (Syria). Although nothing is known of his life until his final year, Ignatius must have known and consulted with a number of the apostles and others who knew Jesus, qualifying him for the title of Apostolic Father. Then in about 107, during Emperor Trajan's persecution of Christians, Ignatius was arrested, condemned to death for being a Christian, and led by armed guard to Rome for execution – to be eaten by wild beasts. Along the way, he wrote seven letters, which show that Ignatius was ardently devoted to Christ and affirmed Christ's divinity and resurrection. Ignatius did not fear death, but looked forward to dying for his faith in Christ, and he begged those he wrote to not to interfere with his execution. In his letter to the Romans (4:2) he pleads:

I am voluntarily dying for God – if that is, you do not interfere. I plead with you, do not do me an unreasonable kindness. Let me be fodder for the wild beasts. That is how I can get to God. I am God's wheat and I am being ground by the teeth of wild beasts to make a pure loaf for Christ.

Ignatius, bishop of Antioch, was martyred for his Christian beliefs.

Ignatius was to get his wish. When he arrived in Rome he was thrown to the lions and quickly died. His letters remain as important witnesses of the early Church.

to 'grow in the faith delivered to you – "which is a mother to us all"' (the last seven words allude to Galatians 4:26). Generally, however, references to the New Testament books come as quotations from them or reflections of their ideas. Polycarp himself quotes from a wide variety of New Testament works, including Matthew, Luke and the letters of John and 1 Peter.

In his seven surviving letters, Ignatius is deeply influenced by Paul's letters, and freely quotes from them, but he infuses his Pauline thought with elements that are reminiscent of John. Barnabas's letter is similar in tone to Hebrews, and the *Didache*, a kind of church manual, seems almost to be an extension of concepts from Matthew's Gospel. The *Shepherd of Hermas* frequently reflects knowledge of Revelation, especially in its image of the Church as a woman and its foe as a beast, but it is less focused on the end times than on what is to be done as we await those times. The book also reflects familiarity with the Gospels of Matthew, Mark and John, and the letter to the Ephesians. Clement, in his letter to the Corinthians, alludes to Matthew, Mark, Luke, Acts, Romans, 1 Corinthians, Galatians, Philippians, 1 Timothy, Titus and 1 Peter.

Clement's Second Letter is important in that it cites two classes of writing in the Church – the Bible and the Apostles: 'The Bible, moreover, and

the Apostles say that the Church is not limited to the present, but existed from the beginning' (*2 Clement* 14:2). The letter is thus equating the Old Testament (here called the Bible) with the New (the Apostles). Similarly, the author introduces a citation that is found in Matthew's Gospel by saying 'And another scripture says, "I do not come to call the righteous, but sinners"' (*2 Clement* 14:2). This is the first clear instance we have of a New Testament passage being placed on a level with texts from the Old Testament. The author of *2 Clement* appears to be familiar with much of the New Testament as we know it, although some of the passages he cites are so short their sources cannot be pressed.

All in all then, many of our New Testament books were known to the Apostolic Fathers. However, one book, the Gospel according to Matthew, with its emphasis on the Church, seems to have been more popular. Perhaps this is why it was placed first among the books of the New Testament.

Candidates for scripture

In time, some of the writings of the Apostolic Fathers themselves came to be considered for inclusion in the New Testament, but in the end, although they are still considered important, they were dropped from the official canon.

Unwanted Gnostic Gospels

In 1945, two Egyptian brothers were digging in a cave near the Nile river town of Nag Hammadi. What they discovered was a literary treasure in a clay jar – a dozen leather-bound papyrus books from one of the first-known Christian heresies, Gnosticism. Gnostics got their name from the Greek word *gnosis*, meaning 'knowledge'. They earned the name because they believed people were saved through secret knowledge about spiritual matters, not through faith in Jesus.

Before this discovery, almost everything known about the Gnostics came from their opponents – early Christian leaders who wrote against the popular movement. But inside these dozen books are 52 ancient essays, most of which seem written by Gnostics themselves. The books were written in the AD 300s in Coptic, an Egyptian language, but were translated from Greek manuscripts probably written one or two centuries earlier.

What scholars discovered in studying these

The Gospel of Thomas

The most famous and controversial of the gnostic essays found at Nag Hammadi is the Gospel of Thomas. This 'Gospel' is not a neatly flowing story in the manner of the New Testament Gospels, but a list of sayings. It contains 114 sayings of Jesus, about half of which parallel sayings in the New Testament Gospels. Most of the other sayings point towards gnostic ideas.

In one saying, Jesus seems to deny that God's kingdom is located at a specific place and time:

If those who lead you say to you, 'Look, the kingdom is in the sky,' then the birds will get there first. If they say, 'It's in the ocean,' then the fish will get there first. But the kingdom of God is within you and outside of you. Once you come to know yourselves, you will become known. And you will know that it is you who are the children of the living father.

Saying number 70 seems to support the gnostic idea that humans are saved by awakening to the spiritual knowledge hidden within them: 'If you bring forth what is within you, what you bring forth will save you. If you do not bring forth what is within you, what you do not bring forth will destroy you.'

Scholars debate whether this collection of sayings is from first-century witnesses other than those of the New Testament Gospels, or if they grew out of those four Gospels and were written in the second or third centuries, during the peak of gnostic influence.

Fragment of the Gospel of Thomas from the *Nag Hammadi Codex II*, fourth century.

Heresies spur creeds

Heresies such as Gnosticism forced church leaders to define clearly what Christians believe. Basic tenets of the faith were drawn up in short statements, such as the Apostles' Creed, which required baptismal candidates to confirm their belief in the creator God, in Jesus and his resurrection, in the Holy Spirit, and in resurrection of the body for eternal life.

ancient documents is that Gnostics had been around almost from the beginning of Christianity, but were out of sync with traditional Christian teaching.

HOW DID GNOSTICISM BEGIN?

From the start, the Church fought distorted teachings that came from fellow members. Best known is the idea that Christians had to follow Jewish laws and traditions – a teaching the apostle Paul fought vigorously. Gnosticism appears to have developed a few years later, perhaps during the ministry of the first-century apostles. Paul seemed to warn Timothy about this pop theology: 'Avoid the profane chatter and contradictions of what is falsely called knowledge' (1 Timothy 6:20). Paul wrote similar warnings in letters to the Corinthians and Colossians.

Still, the movement attracted many Christians and became especially popular in the second century. By about AD 180 it was strong enough to provoke Irenaeus, a student of the apostle John and a bishop of Lyons (in what is now France), to write the first important essay on Christian theology, *Against the Heresies*.

WHAT DID GNOSTICS TEACH?

There were many gnostic groups, with a wide variety of teachings that drew from many religions: Christianity, Judaism, Greek mythology, as well as religions of Egypt and Persian Gulf lands. Gnostic groups did not always agree with each other. Yet there are several ideas that repeatedly show up in their writings, and that clash with traditional Christianity.

Creation is evil

Most Gnostics taught that the God of the Old Testament, who created the world, is not the Supreme Being. Instead, he is a lesser god; and everything he created – humans included – is evil. Physical bodies are described as burdens we have to endure until death frees us.

Because the world was portrayed as evil, many Gnostics became monk-like ascetics, depriving themselves of life's pleasures, such as food and sex. Other Gnostics did exactly the opposite. Arguing that the physical world did not matter and could not affect them spiritually, these Gnostics did whatever they wanted.

Jesus was not human

Many Gnostics believed Jesus was not the son of the 'inferior god' of creation. Instead, Jesus was a spirit being who only appeared human. He did not suffer pain. He did not die on the cross. And he did not rise from the dead.

We are saved by spiritual knowledge

To save humanity, Gnostics said, the ultimate God sent a redeemer from the ultimate kingdom to bring knowledge to the spirits trapped in human bodies. This entrapment is usually described as ignorance or sleep, not sin. And in order for humans to find salvation, they needed to be awakened from this ignorance – to recover the knowledge of their true identity as part of the ultimate God and his kingdom. Only then could they expect that after they died they would ascend to God's world of pure spirit.

Some Gnostics taught there were three kinds of people in the physical world. Some were born with this knowledge and could teach it to others. And some were capable of grasping the knowledge. But the vast majority of people were incapable of enlightenment.

Church leaders would have none of this. They would not discard the Old Testament God. Nor would they abandon the teaching that Jesus rose from the dead – a teaching Paul said was essential to the Christian religion (1 Corinthians 15:17). And church leaders refused to back away from the key Gospel teaching that opens the door of salvation to everyone, declaring that all who believe in Jesus will be saved (John 3:16).

GNOSTIC SAMPLER

Twenty-five of the 52 Nag Hammadi texts can be put into the category of apocalypses or revelations, which comes as no surprise given the gnostic emphasis on revealed knowledge. Among these essays are 'Apocalypses' said to be of Adam, Peter, James, John and Paul. Six essays are 'Gospels' about Jesus, including *The Gospel of Truth*, *The Gospel of Philip* and *The Gospel of the Egyptians*. Still other essays are wisdom writings, doctrinal teachings, prayers, hymns and reworked accounts of Old Testament stories.

Most writings clearly show a gnostic slant. *Testimony of Truth* portrays the creator as a villain. And *Apocalypse of Peter* attacks the Church. Other writings in the cache may not have been gnostic – *Discourse on the Eighth and Ninth*, for example, is about Egyptian legends. Who buried these writings and why remains a mystery.

'As children of the light of truth, flee from division and false teaching. Where the Shepherd is, there follow like sheep.'

IGNATIUS, BISHOP OF ANTIOCH

Gnostic amulet from the late Byzantine period depicting the sacrifice of Isaac. Such amulets were believed to have magical powers.

The Bible in Early Worship

The earliest Christians were also Jews and so they worshipped as the Jews did. After the destruction of the temple in AD 70, Jewish worship services were confined to the synagogues. The Gospel of Luke gives us a vivid description of part of a typical Jewish worship service at Nazareth. It was the custom to read from the Pentateuch, the first five books of the Hebrew Bible, and from the Prophets. Apparently, a synagogue official would choose someone from the congregation to do a reading and the reader would then give a talk, interpreting the passage he had just read. At the beginning of his ministry, Jesus was chosen to read from the prophets upon his return home. Luke's Gospel tells us:

When he came to Nazareth, where he had been brought up, he went to the synagogue on the sabbath day, as was his custom. He stood up to read, and the scroll of the prophet Isaiah was given to him. He unrolled the scroll and found the place where it was written: 'The Spirit of the Lord is upon me, because he has anointed me to bring good news to the poor. He has sent me to proclaim release to the captives and recovery of sight to the blind, to let the oppressed go free, to proclaim the year of the Lord's favour.' And he rolled up the scroll, gave it back to the attendant, and sat down. The eyes of all in the synagogue were fixed on him. Then he began to say to them, 'Today this scripture has been fulfilled in your hearing.' All spoke well of him and were amazed at the gracious words that came from his mouth.
Luke 4:16–22

Although Jesus' interpretation of the scripture he read was a bit disarming – he himself had come to fulfil Isaiah's prophecy – the scene beautifully evokes the typical synagogue service, as also observed by early Christians. Prayers, blessings and hymns, especially the psalms, would have been added to the service.

GATHERING TOGETHER ON THE LORD'S DAY

The earliest Christians attended synagogue but also gathered together – generally in each other's houses – to celebrate the eucharist, giving thanks for Jesus and remembering his breaking of bread at the last supper. As the Acts of the Apostles tells us of the early Christians: 'Day by day, as they spent much time together in the temple, they broke bread at home and ate their food with glad and generous hearts, praising God and having the goodwill of all the people' (Acts 2:46–47). At first, the breaking of bread was an entire meal and Paul was concerned that some Christians ate too much while others did not get enough food, and so he advised: 'So then, my brothers and sisters, when you come together to eat, wait for one another. If you are hungry, eat at home, so that when you come together, it will not be for your condemnation (1 Corinthians 11:33–34).

The *Didache*, a kind of church manual from the second century, instructs Christians to deal with their sins before coming to the eucharist. 'On every Lord's Day – his special day – come together and break bread and give thanks, first confessing your sins so that your sacrifice may be pure' (*Didache* 14:1). The order of the eucharist is more fully described by Justin Martyr, from Rome, in the mid-second century:

On the day called Sunday there is a meeting in one place of those who live in cities or the country,

The rite of baptism

Only baptized men and women were allowed to partake of the eucharist. From the early days, baptism incorporated the actions of John the Baptist and the words of Jesus, as he instructed his disciples to 'make disciples of all nations, baptizing them in the name of the Father and of the Son and of the Holy Spirit' (Matthew 28:19). The *Didache* gives definite instructions for baptisms, allowing variations to fit circumstances:

This is how to baptize: give public instruction on all these points and then 'baptize' in running water, 'in the name of the Father and of the Son and of the Holy Spirit'. If you do not have running water, baptize in some other. If you cannot in cold, then in warm. If you have neither, then pour water on the head three times 'in the name of the Father and of the Son and of the Holy Spirit'. Before the baptism, moreover, the one who baptizes and the one being baptized must fast, and any others who can. And you must tell the one being baptized to fast for one or two days beforehand.

Detail from *Baptism of Cornelius by the Apostle Peter*, a relief from the so-called sarcophagus of the 'miraculous source' from the late fourth century.

and the memoirs of the apostles or the writings of the prophets are read as long as time permits. When the reader has finished, the president in a discourse urges and invites [those in attendance] to the imitation of those noble things. Then we all stand up and offer prayers.

This part of the Christian service, then resembles the old synagogue services except that New Testament readings (the memoirs of the apostles) have been added to Old Testament readings (from the prophets), and the interpretation is given by the president, or head of the church, and not the reader. After the president's homily, Justin tells us, bread and wine and water are brought out, prayers are said by the president, and the bread and wine are distributed to those present and taken out to others by deacons. Justin explains that the service takes place on Sunday because it is the day on which God began the creation and the day on which Jesus rose from the dead. It seems likely that in the beginning, Jewish Christians had gone to the synagogue on Saturdays (the Jewish sabbath) and then gathered for the eucharist on Sundays, but by the mid-second century had combined the services into one on Sundays.

PRAYERS, HYMNS AND OTHER MATTERS
The prayers said at early Christian services were sometimes taken from the Gospels and Pauline letters. Paramount among them, of course, were the words Jesus spoke over the bread and the wine at the last supper, as reported in 1 Corinthians 11:24–25 and the Gospels of Matthew, Mark and Luke. Almost as important was the recitation of the Lord's Prayer, as found in Matthew 6:9–13. In addition, Philippians 2:6–11 preserves a prayer that may have been used in some early worship services. Scholars have pointed out a number of New Testament hymns that may have been used in these early worship services. They are found in Colossians 1:15–20, Ephesians 1:13–14 and 1 Timothy 3:16.

In the second century, worship services were long and included disconnected readings, but by the third century, the services had been shortened and, on feast days, the readings were chosen to fit the day being celebrated. For example, during the week before Easter, the readings came from Job because Job's suffering was seen in relation to Christ's, and on Easter, Jonah was read because Jonah's three days in the belly of the great fish were seen to predict Jesus' three days in a tomb. This was the beginning of the reform of Christian worship that was to stretch on through the centuries and continues today.

This early Christian wall painting from the catacomb of St Peter and Marcellinus shows a eucharistic love feast – a communal meal commemorating the last supper.

Giving thanks
The service of the Lord's Supper became known as the eucharist, from the Greek word meaning 'thanksgiving', in early times. Initially the word was used to describe only the prayers said at the service, but soon it became the name of the service itself.

From Scroll to Book

'When you come again, bring the cloak that I left with Carpus at Troas, also the books, and above all the parchments.'

2 TIMOTHY 4:13

Ink for parchment

Because the carbon-based inks generally used for writing on papyrus did not adhere well to parchment, inks made of iron sulphate and vegetable matter were used. Sometimes gum was added. These inks were applied with a reed pen, which sometimes did and sometimes did not have a metal tip.

Fourteenth-century Prussian manuscript illustration showing the Battle of Michael, the Battle against Gog and Magog, the Antichrist, the Last Judgment and the heavenly Jerusalem.

In Old Testament times the scriptures were written mostly on papyrus, but other materials were used for writing on. Laws and important pronouncements were carved into stone monuments or buildings. Sometimes important records were inscribed into stone that had been coated with plaster. Short sacred inscriptions were sometimes scratched in thin sheets of copper or even silver. Later wax-coated wood was used as a writing surface. Oddly enough people also wrote on pottery and on shards of broken pots, called ostraca, which were used the way we use scrap paper today.

Papyrus had remained the choice for scripture because its relatively large sheets could be joined together and rolled into convenient scrolls, each containing a full book. However, papyrus did not survive very long and it was largely imported from Egypt, with whom the Israelites were often at war, so new materials were sought to replace it. One material that was used in place of papyrus was leather. Tanned skins could be trimmed and stitched together to form a scroll with a smooth surface for writing, but leather was not an ideal replacement for papyrus, as it was thicker and harder to handle and its darker colour made it harder to read from.

Then, sometime before 500 BC, a new writing surface began to be developed in Perganum, a city off the western coast of Asia Minor (now Turkey). Called parchment, after the city in which it was developed, this product was also made from animal skins, but the process of preparing it was much more advanced.

MAKING PARCHMENT

Parchment was made in four major steps. First, the skin was taken from the animal and carefully washed. It was then soaked in clean water for a day or more. To complete the cleaning process, the skin was than transferred to a vat of water mixed with lime and left there for one to two weeks, or even more, to loosen the hair on the hide. During this period the solution was stirred several times a day with a pole or paddle.

Once the hair was sufficiently loosened, the second step began. The skins were removed from the vat and laid hair side up on a large log or beam that was tipped up at one end. The worker then stood behind the high end of the log and used a blunt two-handled curved knife

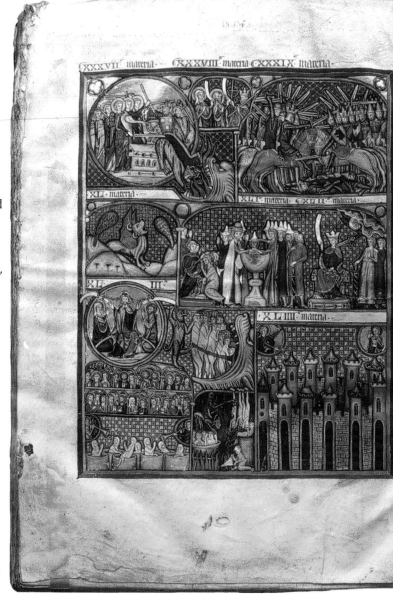

to scrape downward, pushing the hair off the skin. The skin was then turned over and the process repeated to get rid of any residue of flesh. The entire skin was again soaked in fresh water for a couple of days to remove the lime.

The third step involved stretching and refining. The skin was removed from the water and tied with short strings at various points to a wooden frame. The ends of the string on the frame were attached to adjustable pegs that could be turned to stretch the skin tighter across the frame. While the skin was on the frame, the worker used another special knife to scrape both sides of the skin once again, keeping it wet as he worked. Then he left the skin on the frame to dry in the sun, which stretched it further as a result of shrinkage.

The final step involved scraping the skin once again on both sides until it attained the desired thinness. The side that formerly had the hair tended to be shiny and required more scraping than the back surface. The skin was then removed from the frame and rolled up until needed. Just before it was to be used it was trimmed to size and buffed with pumice to whiten its surface.

As part of a living history programme in Wyoming, USA, a staff member, dressed in the clothing of the 1800s, demonstrates the making of parchment. Here, he stretches a hide over a fire to dry it.

The completed parchment was lighter in colour than papyrus and far more flexible. After use, it could also be scraped down and used again. Because it was less brittle, parchment was more easily folded. This made it ideal for use in a new form of manuscript, which was made up of smaller pages that were bound together – in place of single rolled scrolls. This new form was the codex, or the book as we know it.

DEVELOPMENT OF THE MODERN BOOK

By the time of Jesus, parchment had reached most parts of the Mediterranean world, and for Jews it was the preferred material for use in books read in public. When Jesus read from Isaiah in the Nazareth synagogue, he was probably reading from a parchment scroll. But at the same time, a new type of writing surface came into use – the book in the form that we know it today, with pages gathered together between covers.

This book form was developed from a much more primitive writing medium called the caudex (later codex) from the Latin word *caudeus*, meaning 'wooden'. The original codex, which was used by the Romans for record keeping and other forms of writing, consisted of several wooden boards that were hollowed out on one flat surface, filled with wax, and tied together to form a kind of crude notebook. The Romans wrote in the soft wax with the pointed end of a metal stylus and erased texts with the blunt end of the same stylus.

In time, papyrus and parchment sheets were used instead of the cumbersome waxed boards. At first, several sheets of papyrus or parchment were stacked and then folded in half to form simple notebooks. At about the time the books of the New Testament were being written, writers began to stitch together a number of these notebooks along their folds, thus creating a book with more pages, the codex. The first surviving reference to the codex is found in the *Epigrams* of the Roman poet Martial, which were completed in AD 98. Martial writes that bookshops sell 'Homer in parchment handybooks' and 'the *Iliad* and the tale of Ulysses... in many-folded skins'. He was surely referring to the works being in codex form.

CHRISTIANS AND THE CODEX

Judging from the number of codices surviving from the second century, Christians were quick to take up the new form of the book. Out of about 870 surviving codices from these times, all but 14 contain Christian writings. The earliest Christian codices were made from papyrus, but the superior durability and flexibility of parchment must have quickly made itself obvious, for most of the later codices were made with parchment and continued to be until the introduction of paper to the Christian world in the Middle Ages.

No one knows why the early Christians were so attracted to the codex. Some believe that they used the codex form to distinguish Christian writings from non-Christian works, or even from the Hebrew scriptures, which were written on scrolls. According to an ancient tradition, Mark first recorded his Gospel in a kind of codex, and other Christian writers followed suit.

As appealing as these theories may be, however, the real reasons for adoption of the codex were probably more practical. Scrolls were cumbersome. The reader had to hold onto one end of a scroll while unrolling the other end with his other hand. It was also difficult to mark

a place in a scroll for easy access to a particular passage. So when Jesus read from Isaiah at the synagogue in Nazareth, he would have had to have searched for the proper place and then held the scroll open as he read. If he had read from a codex, Jesus could have easily flipped through the pages and found the passage, perhaps aided by some sort of ribbon or other place marker. He would also have been able to leave the book open in front of him, rather than holding a scroll in place, freeing his hands for expressive gestures. This ease in keeping a codex open also made it easier for a reader to open two books side by side to compare readings.

Size might also have been a factor in preferring the codex to the scroll. The length of a scroll was limited, but a codex could be much longer. For example, the Gospel of Luke would take up more than 30 feet of scroll, about as much as a single scroll could accommodate. This means that the Gospels could not be collected in a single volume, nor could Luke and Acts, which are really two parts of a single work. On the other hand, scrolls had an advantage here for shorter works. If the work ended before the scroll was filled, the end of the parchment could be cut off and used for another work, while more parchment could be added if the scroll turned out to be too short for the work being copied. A codex was harder to add to or subtract from. To make a codex longer, an entire sheet of parchment had to be folded and added, often leaving the writer or copyist with more pages than he needed to complete the text he was copying. For this reason, bits of writing that are unrelated to the main text are often found at the ends of some ancient codices.

Whatever the reasons for their attraction to the codex, the Christians started a trend that was to endure. Although the Jews would continue to use scrolls in worship, and still do so now, the codex quickly became the form the book was to take throughout the Western world. It remains so today.

This side out

When a codex was put together the leaves of parchment were positioned so that the sides that formerly contained the hair were facing each other and the reverse sides were also together. This was done to make the facing pages of the manuscript uniform, because the two sides of the skins accepted ink differently.

❧

A Roman wax tablet from the fourth century.

Gospels and letters in book form

In the days just after the Gospels were written, they were mainly used by the communities in which they were written. But because of their great value for all Christians, they were soon circulated individually to other Christian communities. At some point they began to be bound together and circulated in the form of codices, or books. The same is true of Paul's letters. In the 1930s a group of long-lost codices of New Testament books were discovered and purchased by the scholar Chester Beatty. (The manuscripts are known as the Chester Beatty papyri after their founder and the material they are written on.) The most important of them, dating from the early third century, contains the Gospels. Interestingly, the order of the Gospels is Matthew, John, Luke, Mark and Acts, reflecting neither the order in which they appear in the New Testament, nor the order in which most scholars today think they were written. Another of these codices includes most of the letters attributed to Paul. The collection includes Hebrews (which later came to be contested as Paul's), but it is missing the epistles to Timothy and Titus. Perhaps the missing letters were unknown to the person who put the collection together, or perhaps he did not believe Paul wrote them.

ΚΑΤΑ

A page from *Codex Sinaiticus*, one of the oldest surviving Bibles.

Sheep to the slaughter

Scholars estimate that the *Codex Sinaiticus*, one of the earliest complete Bibles, contained at least 730 leaves and would have needed the skins of about 360 sheep and goats to provide enough parchment.

Our oldest Bibles

No one knows when the Old and New Testaments were first combined and copied into a single volume, but the two oldest surviving (almost) complete Bibles were created in the mid-fourth century. Known today as the *Codex Vaticanus* and the *Codex Sinaiticus*, they contain most of the text of the Septuagint (the first Greek translation of the Hebrew Bible), including the books later eliminated by the Jews and considered the Apocrypha by the Protestants, although the *Codex Vaticanus* is missing the books of the Maccabees. In addition, both codices contain all 27 books of the New Testament. The *Codex Sinaiticus* also includes the *Epistle of Barnabas* and the *Shepherd of Hermas*. The *Codex Vaticanus* was probably put together in Egypt around AD 350 and eventually ended up in the Vatican Library in Rome. The *Codex Sinaiticus* has a more exciting history. It was written in Egypt in the late fourth century and kept at St Catherine's Monastery at the foot of Jebel Musa (Mount of Moses), the peak believed to be Mount Sinai, where Moses received the ten commandments. It remained there unknown until 1844, when a visiting German scholar, Constantin von Tischendorf spotted it in a pile of trash that was waiting to be burned for fuel. When he realized what he had discovered, Von Tischendorf managed to salvage most of the manuscript. Because of their antiquity and near completeness, these two fourth-century codices are of invaluable help to biblical scholars today.

The monastery of St Catherine, Sinai, Egypt, built over the reputed location of the burning bush, has been a Christian religious site since the fourth century. It is an independent archbishopric within the Greek Orthodox Church.

The First Study Bible

Origen's study Bible usually had six versions of the Jewish scripture in parallel columns, allowing readers to compare one version against another, and earning it the name Hexapla. This early fragment of Psalm 22 preserves only four of the original six columns. (Cambridge University Library, T-S 12.182.)

Origen's hard lifestyle

Origen adopted a life of self-sacrifice, eating little, walking barefoot, and sleeping on the ground. He even went so far as to have himself castrated, according to Christian writer Eusebius – a report many modern scholars consider reliable. Eusebius said the reason for this drastic action was to 'prevent all suspicion of shameful slander on the part of unbelievers', since Origen taught women as well as men.

The first-known study Bible, completed in about AD 245, was not what most people would call reader-friendly. A mammoth project, it looked more like a set of encyclopaedias than a handy, single-volume study book. Its words filled an estimated 6,500 pages in perhaps 15 volumes. These numbers are estimated because – not surprisingly – no one ever made a complete copy of it. Some people did, however, copy parts of it. And a few fragments of those copies survive.

The project covered only the Old Testament, but it grew to massive proportions because it preserved six versions of the Jewish scriptures in side-by-side columns. This let readers compare one version of a Bible passage to another. The six-column format earned the work its name: Hexapla.

BRAINCHILD OF A SCHOLAR

The idea for this monumental endeavour came from the mind of a 45-year-old scholar – Origen,

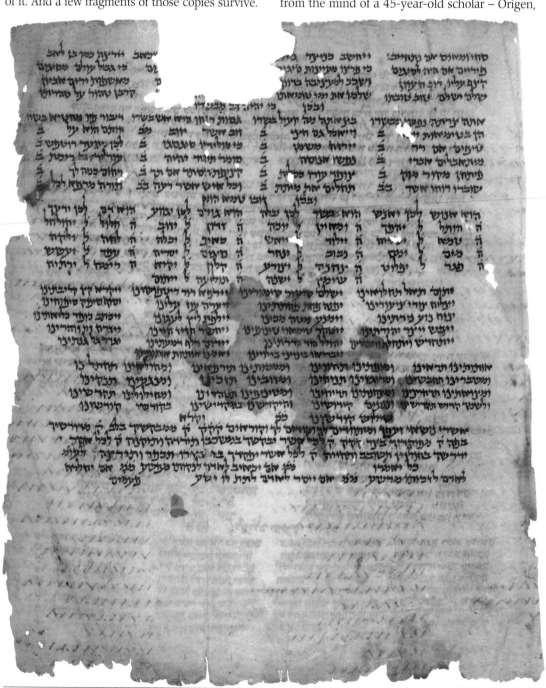

one of the greatest teachers and most prolific writers of the early Church.

Origen was born in about AD 185, the gifted child of well-to-do Christian parents in Alexandria, Egypt. Deeply loved by his parents and given an excellent education in Greek literature and Christian scriptures, Origen was 16 years old when his father was martyred and the family property confiscated. A wealthy Christian woman provided the money necessary for Origen to continue his studies and launch his life's work of teaching and writing about theology. At the age of 18, he was appointed head of a religion school in his home town.

Eventually, Origen settled in Caesarea, the Roman capital of Palestine on the coast of what is now Israel. This is where he spent the last 20 years of his life, lecturing and writing. It is also where he composed most of the Hexapla, working with a team of secretaries and copyists who worked in shifts to keep up with him.

The project began in about AD 230, and took some 15 years to complete. There were probably many reasons Origen embarked on such a consuming task. Primary was the fact that he was a life-long student of the Bible, and he wanted to understand the Old Testament. But there were many versions of it. There were various Hebrew versions, some containing passages that others did not have. And there were many Greek translations of the Hebrew scriptures, including several variations of the Septuagint, the first Greek translation. He decided to put the best of these in parallel columns for easier study. These are the versions he preserved, in six columns from left to right:

❧ The Hebrew text that Palestinian Jews considered the standard of their day, and that Origen believed was the text used to produce the Septuagint Greek translation.

❧ A transliteration of the Hebrew letters into Greek letters, to show how the Hebrew words were pronounced.

❧ A Greek translation by the scholar Aquila.

❧ A Greek translation by Symmachus.

❧ The Septuagint, as revised by Origen.

❧ A Greek translation by Theodotion.

In some sections of the Hexapla, Origen drew from three other Greek translations, sometimes producing seven or eight columns.

REVISING THE GREEK TRANSLATION

Origen spent most of his energy on the fifth column, revising the Septuagint. He explained his process: 'When I was uncertain of the Septuagint reading because the various copies did not tally, I settled the issue by consulting other versions and retaining what was in agreement.'

Some passages in the Septuagint did not appear in the Hebrew text; and other passages that appeared in the Hebrew text were missing from the Septuagint. Origen included everything in his revised version, with notes indicating which passages were missing from the Hebrew and which were added. Regarding these additions and notes, Origen wrote: 'Anyone who is offended by this procedure may accept or reject them as he chooses.'

Origen implied that one reason he undertook the project was to help him in his theological discussions with Jews. He did not read Hebrew – nor did most Jews of the time. But the Hexapla allowed Origen to know which passages from the Jewish Bible he could use to make a theological point to the Jews.

'I make it my endeavour,' Origen wrote in a letter while working on the Hexapla, 'not to be ignorant of their [the Septuagint's] various readings, lest in my controversies with the Jews I should quote to them what is not found in their copies, and that I may make some use of what is found there, even although it should not be in our own scriptures.'

Although Origen's massive work was never copied, the original lasted for several centuries before it disappeared in the early 600s, perhaps destroyed when Arabs invaded Palestine. However, copies were made and circulated of his revised Septuagint as well as sections of the Bible, such as the six-column version of Psalms.

All that is left today are fragments of his work. One such remnant is a reused parchment on which the ink of a 10th-century copy of the Hexapla Psalms is scratched off. In its place, a scribe from the 13th or 14th century wrote a different Greek text. But it is still possible to see the underlying words. The number of columns on the 10th-century manuscript varied from two to six, featuring about 150 verses on 35 pages. Because there were so many columns, each line could contain just a couple of words. A smaller fragment, of Psalm 22, contains all six columns.

Origen wrote many other works, including sermons and commentaries on books of the Old and New Testaments. He also wrote *On First Principles*, one of the first attempts to explain Christian teachings. His life's work ended when the Roman emperor Decius renewed the persecution of Christians in 251. Origen, then about 65 years old, was imprisoned and tortured. With his health broken, he died about two years later.

Origen, one of the best Bible scholars of his day, a prolific writer and creator of the first-known study Bible. He died of lingering health problems some two years after the Romans tortured him because of his faith. Engraving from 1584.

Quest for a Christian Bible

The creator of evils, lustful for war, inconstant in his attitude, and self-contradictory.'

MARCION, DESCRIBING THE
OLD TESTAMENT GOD

A piece of parchment found at Dura-Europas, Syria. This Greek text may be part of the *Diatessaron*, a Gospel that blends into one story the four Gospels of Matthew, Mark, Luke and John. The writer, some scholars say, was a second-century Syrian scholar named Tatian. His harmonized, composite Gospel became the preferred version for many Syrian churches.

Bad god, good God

There are two gods, Marcion taught – the wicked, lesser god of the Old Testament, and the loving, supreme God of the New Testament. To make his point, Marcion wrote a book, *Antitheses*, showing how Jesus and Paul clashed with the Old Testament: Jesus said, 'No good tree bears bad fruit' (Luke 6:43), and Isaiah declared the Lord said, 'I bring prosperity and create disaster' (Isaiah 45:7, NIV).

The reason Christians have 27 books in their New Testament, many scholars say, is because early church leaders did not like the 11 that a theologian named Marcion approved. Nor did they care for the claim of another theologian, Montanus, that God's revelation was continuing and there should be no end to scripture.

Opinions such as these, stretching from one extreme to the other, helped church leaders realize they had a problem. They needed to decide which Christian writings to accept as authoritative – as inspired by God and intended to guide Christians in their faith.

For the first 100 years after Jesus, there did not seem to be a problem. Christians were content with the eyewitness reports of Jesus' apostles, and the second-hand reports from followers of the apostles. This living memory, passed on from one person to another by word of mouth, had a powerful effect. In time, however, the memories grew fainter as the earliest generations of believers died. Christians started depending more on stories and teachings that had been written down, copied and distributed among the churches – collections of stories about Jesus (the Gospels), and letters written by Paul and other church leaders.

MARCION'S NEW TESTAMENT

The first-known list of 'acceptable' Christian writings was put together in about AD 140 by Marcion – four years before the Church excommunicated him as a heretic.

Marcion was a Gnostic. He taught there were two gods: the lesser and evil creator god of the Old Testament and the supreme and loving God revealed by Jesus and Paul. Marcion rejected the entire Old Testament, arguing that the spiritual

heroes and prophets in those books had been deceived by the creator god. He also argued that many of the Christian writings had been corrupted by false apostles who inserted their own bad ideas and deleted teachings they did not like. Careful work was needed to restore the Christian writings to their authentic state, Marcion said – work he undertook.

His finished product – the first New Testament – was a heavily edited Gospel of Luke along with 10 edited letters of Paul. Marcion's editing brought all these 11 writings in line with his increasingly popular gnostic teachings. Marcion, like other Gnostics, said Jesus was not really

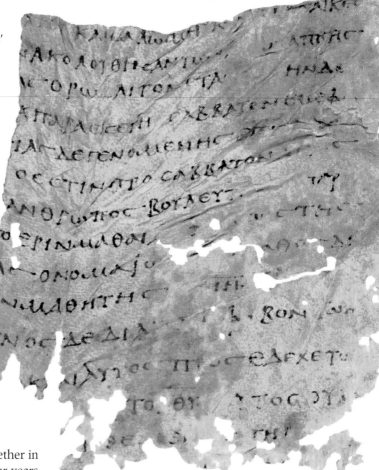

human, since everything physical was created by the evil god. Jesus was pure spirit, Marcion said, sent by the superior God. Jesus only appeared human. Marcion's Gospel of Luke, therefore, had no genealogy of Jesus, no story about his birth in Bethlehem or mention of his family, and no references to Old Testament prophecies Jesus fulfilled. Marcion also deleted from Paul's letters all references to Jesus taking human form and suffering for the sins of humanity.

As boldly heretical as Marcion may seem now, he was convincing in his day. Many scholars estimate that by the time he died in about AD 160 nearly half the Church believed much of what he taught.

TATIAN'S FOUR-IN-ONE GOSPEL

By the late 100s, the four Gospels about Jesus were circulating throughout the Church. Christian leader Justin Martyr, born in about AD 100, was one of the first to express knowledge and appreciation of these writings, though he did not seem aware of John's Gospel. In about 150 he referred to the Gospels as 'memoirs' of the apostles. Another Christian teacher from the same century, Basilides, pointed to passages in Matthew, Luke and John to support his arguments – showing the Gospels were becoming a source of authority.

Having four versions of the same story about Jesus was confusing. The flow of events did not always make sense, and details in one Gospel occasionally seemed to clash with details in another – as you might expect when comparing one witness's story with another's. Some early Christian scholars decided to resolve the confusion by blending the four Gospels into one harmonized story. The fact that they felt free to do this showed that as far as they were concerned the Gospels were not too sacred to refine.

One Syrian scholar who tried his hand at this was a gnostic Christian teacher named Tatian. In about 170 he finished his blended Gospel called *Diatessaron*, which means 'harmony of four'. Actually, it included more than four because Tatian added material from other sources that apparently had been passed along by word of mouth. His masterfully woven Gospel became the preferred version for many Syrian churches, and remained such until the early 400s, when a bishop in the region declared Tatian a heretic and ordered the churches to use other Gospel translations. Fragments of Tatian's work may survive today, although scholars debate this. Later copies and translations of the text, however, have also turned up.

MONTANUS'S NEVER-ENDING BIBLE

Near the end of the second century, Montanus, a priest from a pagan ecstasy cult in what is now Turkey, converted to Christianity. He brought with him his penchant for expressive zeal, starting a prophecy movement and claiming that he and his followers received messages directly

This Roman sandstone relief shows a priest making sacrificial offerings to the goddess Cybele. Before his conversion to Christianity, Montanus was a priest from such an ecstasy cult. He taught that God spoke directly to him and his followers, and he argued that the canon of scripture should remain open, to allow for new messages from God.

from God. These prophecies came to be written and compiled into books. Some of these messages went beyond anything previously found in Christian writings. Besides declaring that the end was near and Jesus would return soon, Montanus said the heavenly Jerusalem would descend to earth at his home region in Turkey.

Montanus gained a sizeable following. He convinced many that he and his followers were instruments of the outpouring of the Holy Spirit predicted by John: 'When the Spirit of truth comes, he will guide you into all the truth; for he will not speak on his own, but will speak whatever he hears, and he will declare to you the things that are to come' (John 16:13).

The Montanus movement, which continued for several centuries, taught that Christians should keep the canon of scripture open because God keeps the channel of revelation open through the continuing ministry of prophets. The Church eventually responded by arguing that all the revelations necessary for salvation are contained in the writings from the apostles.

'All scripture is inspired by God and is useful for teaching, for reproof, for correction, and for training in righteousness.'

PAUL, REFERRING TO THE OLD TESTAMENT IN 2 TIMOTHY 3:16

Settling the New Testament

There is no simple way to explain how Christians chose the 27 books that became the New Testament. It was not a knee-jerk response to heresies in the second century – although the scriptures that those heresies proposed certainly got people thinking about a New Testament. What followed were two centuries of debate among church leaders.

Yet, it was not the church leaders who decided this issue. In the end, they would only confirm the decision that the Church at large had reached gradually. When congregations gathered for worship, they read from the Jewish scriptures – especially prophecies that pointed to Jesus. They also started reading selected Christian writings – especially those stories and letters written by people closely associated with Jesus: apostles and followers of the apostles. The writings that were most respected, most in line with traditional Christian teaching, and most helpful for the local

The Acts of the Apostles, dating from the fifth century, and written in Sahidic Coptic, an ancient Egyptian language. As early as the third century, Acts – the story about the birth of the Christian church – was widely accepted as scripture.

churches were the ones read most often. These are the stories and letters that became dearest to believers in the first several centuries of the Church.

In the early 200s, the theologian Origen took a poll. It became a stepping-stone towards the New Testament canon. Origen wanted to know which Christian writings the churches were using. What he discovered led him to make a three-part list: accepted books, questionable books and unreliable books.

On his first list, of widely accepted Christian writings, were the four Gospels we now have,

the 13 letters of Paul we now have, and Acts, 1 Peter, 1 John and Revelation. On his second list, of questionable writings, were the six other books that complete our New Testament: Hebrews, James, 2 Peter, 2 and 3 John and Jude. His third list, of books widely considered unreliable, includes writings that never made it into the New Testament: Gospel of Thomas, Gospel of Egyptians and Gospel of Matthias.

EUSEBIUS AND THE EMPEROR

For almost 300 years, Christianity was an unwelcome religion in the Roman empire. Violent persecution came and went, depending on who was emperor. As Christian writings developed, the persecution branched out to include burning the revered Christian writings. Emperor Diocletian made this a standing order in the final years of his reign, from 303–306. But his successor – Constantine the Great – reversed Rome's attitude towards Christianity.

After Christ reportedly appeared to Constantine in a dream and assured him victory in the next day's battle, the emperor signed an edict of toleration in 313. From a banned religion, Christianity became the favoured religion. No more were Christian writings burned in bonfires. Instead, Constantine ordered extra copies: 50 Bibles for churches he planned to build in his capital city of Constantinople.

The emperor made his request to the renowned scholar Eusebius, bishop of Caesarea, the capital of Rome's province in Palestine. To fill this order, Eusebius had to decide which Christian writings to include in the Bible. As a young man, Eusebius had studied under Pamphilus, a student of Origen. So it comes as no surprise that Eusebius followed Origen's three-part division of Christian writings, and ended up with nearly the same list of approved books. In his first list were the books generally approved by the Church: the four Gospels, Acts, 14 letters of Paul (which included the anonymous book of Hebrews), 1 Peter, 1 John and Revelation 'if it seems desirable', which implies there was still considerable hesitation about this prophetic book. In his second list were disputed books, which included the rest of what is now in the

Books of the New Testament

GOSPELS

Matthew – Life and ministry of Jesus.

Mark – Probably the first story of Jesus.

Luke – Most complete story of Jesus.

John – Emphasizes the divinity of Jesus.

HISTORY

Acts – Beginning of the Church.

LETTERS OF PAUL

Romans – Summary of the Christian faith.

1 Corinthians – Instructions to a bickering church.

2 Corinthians – Paul defends his right to lead.

Galatians – Salvation is not earned by obeying laws.

Ephesians – The Church's job description.

Philippians – The joy of serving Christ.

Colossians – Faith in Christ saves.

1 Thessalonians – Teaching about the second coming.

2 Thessalonians – Second coming and holy living.

1 Timothy – How to be a pastor.

2 Timothy – Paul's last words.

Titus – How to pastor a difficult congregation.

Philemon – Forgive the runaway.

GENERAL LETTERS

Hebrews – Jesus brings grace to replace the law.

James – Show your faith by the way you act.

1 Peter – Endure suffering, as Christ did.

2 Peter – Watch out for false teachers.

1 John – Watch out for distortions about Jesus.

2 John – Do not support heretics.

3 John – Thanks for showing hospitality.

Jude – Watch out for false teachers.

PROPHECY

Revelation – God defeats evil once and for all.

New Testament: James, Jude, 2 Peter, along with 2 and 3 John. The third list was of rejected works that never made it into the New Testament.

Exactly which books Eusebius included in Constantine's 50 Bibles remains a mystery. None of the Bibles is known to have survived. Two exquisitely crafted Bibles from that era, however, have survived – the *Codex Sinaiticus* (found in the monastery at Mount Sinai) and the *Codex Vaticanus* (found in the Vatican, with part of the New Testament missing). But scholars say it is unlikely that these were among the 50 produced by Eusebius.

The Bible version he produced for Constantine may have drawn from Origen's six-column study Bible, the Hexapla, using the Greek translation of the Old Testament that appeared in the Septuagint column. For the New Testament, Eusebius may have included the approved writings from Origen's three-part list or those from his own list. It is possible he included the debated writings as well. The *Codex Sinaiticus* has all these Christian writings and several more.

Before the emperor Constantine came to power, Roman rulers ordered writings from the outlawed Christian church to be burned. But Constantine, in 313, ruled that Christianity was acceptable and ordered 50 copies of the Bible for churches he planned to build. Christianity soon became the empire's preferred religion. This 16th-century fresco from the Sucevita Monastery in Romania shows Constantine with his mother, Helena.

'Apply yourself totally to the text; apply the text totally to yourself.'

MOTTO IN 1734 EDITION OF A GREEK NEW TESTAMENT

Black Dwarf

'Black Dwarf' is what opponents of Athanasius called him. He was a short, dark-skinned Egyptian. Because of his fight against a popular heresy, he had plenty of opponents – enough to get him exiled five times by four Roman emperors, keeping him exiled 17 of the 45 years he served as bishop.

Wall painting of St Athanasius, an Egyptian bishop. His Easter letter of 367 is the first place in which all the books of the New Testament were listed together and identified as scripture.

Contenders for the New Testament

Early church scholars, councils and ancient editions of the Bible did not always agree on which books Christians should revere. Egyptian bishop Athanasius, in an Easter letter to his churches in AD 367, was the first person in history known to list the 27 books that Christians today call the New Testament. For most Christians, the issue was settled 30 years later at the Council of Carthage, although some disagreement lingered. The chart shows which books were included in various early lists.

▲ Marcion
c. 140

◆ Irenaeus
c. 180

✤ Origen
c. 250

✖ *Codex Sinaiticus*
(published Bible)
c. 325

● Athanasius
c. 367

■ Council of Carthage
c. 397

Matthew
- ◆ Irenaeus
- ✤ Origen
- ✖ Sinaiticus
- ● Athanasius
- ■ Carthage

Mark
- ◆ Irenaeus
- ✤ Origen
- ✖ Sinaiticus
- ● Athanasius
- ■ Carthage

Luke
- ▲ Marcion
- ◆ Irenaeus
- ✤ Origen
- ✖ Sinaiticus
- ● Athanasius
- ■ Carthage

John
- ◆ Irenaeus
- ✤ Origen
- ✖ Sinaiticus
- ● Athanasius
- ■ Carthage

Acts
- ◆ Irenaeus
- ✤ Origen
- ✖ Sinaiticus
- ● Athanasius
- ■ Carthage

Romans
- ▲ Marcion
- ◆ Irenaeus
- ✤ Origen
- ✖ Sinaiticus
- ● Athanasius
- ■ Carthage

1 & 2 Corinthians
- ▲ Marcion
- ◆ Irenaeus
- ✤ Origen
- ✖ Sinaiticus
- ● Athanasius
- ■ Carthage

Galatians
- ▲ Marcion
- ◆ Irenaeus
- ✤ Origen
- ✖ Sinaiticus
- ● Athanasius
- ■ Carthage

Ephesians
- ▲ Marcion
- ◆ Irenaeus
- ✤ Origen
- ✖ Sinaiticus
- ● Athanasius
- ■ Carthage

Philippians
- ▲ Marcion
- ◆ Irenaeus
- ✤ Origen
- ✖ Sinaiticus
- ● Athanasius
- ■ Carthage

Colossians
- ▲ Marcion
- ◆ Irenaeus
- ✤ Origen
- ✖ Sinaiticus
- ● Athanasius
- ■ Carthage

1 & 2 Thessalonians
- ▲ Marcion
- ◆ Irenaeus
- ✤ Origen
- ✖ Sinaiticus
- ● Athanasius
- ■ Carthage

1 & 2 Timothy
- ◆ Irenaeus
- ✤ Origen
- ✖ Sinaiticus
- ● Athanasius
- ■ Carthage

Titus
- ◆ Irenaeus
- ✤ Origen
- ✖ Sinaiticus
- ● Athanasius
- ■ Carthage

Philemon
- ▲ Marcion
- ✤ Origen
- ✖ Sinaiticus
- ● Athanasius
- ■ Carthage

Hebrews
- ✖ Sinaiticus
- ● Athanasius
- ■ Carthage

James
- ✖ Sinaiticus
- ● Athanasius
- ■ Carthage

1 Peter
- ◆ Irenaeus
- ✤ Origen
- ✖ Sinaiticus
- ● Athanasius
- ■ Carthage

2 Peter
- ✖ Sinaiticus
- ● Athanasius
- ■ Carthage

1 John
- ◆ Irenaeus
- ✤ Origen
- ✖ Sinaiticus
- ● Athanasius
- ■ Carthage

2 John
- ◆ Irenaeus
- ✖ Sinaiticus
- ● Athanasius
- ■ Carthage

3 John
- ✖ Sinaiticus
- ● Athanasius
- ■ Carthage

Jude
- ✖ Sinaiticus
- ● Athanasius
- ■ Carthage

Revelation
- ◆ Irenaeus
- ✤ Origen
- ✖ Sinaiticus
- ● Athanasius
- ■ Carthage

Shepherd of Hermas
- ◆ Irenaeus
- ✖ Sinaiticus

Epistle of Barnabas
- ◆ Irenaeus
- ✖ Sinaiticus

ATHANASIUS'S EASTER LETTER

The first time the exact 27 books of the New Testament were listed was in an Easter letter by an Egyptian bishop some 70 years old. In AD 367, Bishop Athanasius wrote the letter to churches in his jurisdiction, as he had done in Easters past to teach and encourage the believers.

In this memorable letter Athanasius wrote, 'As the heretics are quoting apocryphal writings, an evil that was widespread even as early as when St Luke wrote his gospel, therefore I have thought it good to clearly identify what books have been received by us through tradition as belonging to the canon, and which we believe to be divine.'

The bishop then listed the Old Testament books, followed by the New Testament books, from Matthew to Revelation. After listing the New Testament books, Athanasius wrote, 'These are the fountains of salvation, that they who thirst may be satisfied with the living words they contain. In these alone is proclaimed the doctrine of godliness. Let no one add to or take anything from them.'

Athanasius was not expressing just his personal opinion. He reported the prevailing attitude of the Church. This was confirmed when church leaders adopted his canon at several North African conferences: Hippo in 393, Carthage in 397, and at Carthage a second time in 419, in response to some leaders calling for the removal of Hebrews, James and Jude.

For most Christians, the question of the New Testament had been settled. The 27 books were almost universally accepted as the second part of the Bible. But lingering debate persisted. And there has never been complete agreement. Several decades later, the *Codex Alexandrinus* – a copy of the Bible from Alexandria, Egypt – included two letters Athanasius never mentioned: letters from Clement, a church leader from the late first century. Syrians continued using Tatian's second-century work *Diatessaron* – the four Gospels blended into one – well into the 400s (and beyond in many churches). Even today, some churches in eastern Syria exclude 2 Peter, 2 and 3 John, Jude and Revelation. The Ethiopian church, on the other hand, adds to the canon; it has 38 books instead of 27.

This page from *Codex Alexandrinus* shows the end of Luke 24. This fifth-century copy of the Bible from Alexandria, Egypt, was made several decades after the Egyptian bishop Athanasius named the 27 approved books of the New Testament. Even so, this version includes two more books. Both are letters attributed to a first-century church leader named Clement.

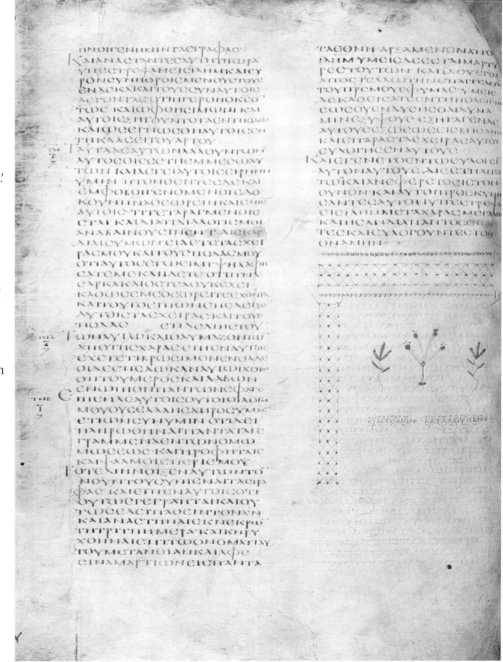

The 'Almost' Scriptures

Not all books that belong in the New Testament are there – at least not as far as some early church leaders were concerned.

Although many Christian writings did not make the final cut for the New Testament, some were serious contenders. And certain famous church leaders – such as Irenaeus, Tertullian and Origen – insisted that some of the missing books deserved as much respect and obedience as any other book in the Bible.

SHEPHERD OF HERMAS

Written in the mid-100s, this was a widely popular Christian book in the second and third centuries. Because it dealt with a wide range of moral issues that called believers to holy living and self-control, church leaders recommended it to new converts.

In this book, a celestial shepherd (presumably an angel) gives spiritual advice to a man named Hermas, a former slave turned businessman. Hermas was the brother of Pius, bishop of Rome in the mid-100s, according to a collection of Christian writings from about AD 200 (the Muratorian Canon).

There are three sections in this book: visions, sermons (called 'mandates') and parables (called 'similitudes'). Among the visions, which begin the book, is one apparently influenced by Revelation; it tells of an apocalyptic beast whose arrival foreshadows a terrible tribulation. The sermons and parables that follow cover religious topics such as sexual purity, repentance, patience and anger.

One notable question Hermes has for the shepherd is about sins committed after baptism. 'Some teachers say that there is no second chance beyond what was granted when we were blessed in the water of baptism and received remission for our previous sins,' Hermas said.

The shepherd replied, 'That is so; for he who has received remission for former sins ought never to sin again but live in purity.' The shepherd goes on to explain that there is a balance between God's justice and mercy, and that forgiveness after baptism is available – though only once and for a limited time.

Church leaders Irenaeus and Clement of Alexandria considered the book scripture, and so did Origen and Tertullian for a time. Even Bishop Athanasius, who later failed to include it in his

Good angel, bad angel

'Two angels accompany man,' said the celestial messenger in the *Shepherd of Hermas*:

The angel of righteousness is delicate, modest, meek and gentle. When he enters your heart, he speaks to you of purity, reverence, self-control and virtue. When these things come into your heart and good deeds flow from them, you know that the angel of righteousness is within you. Now observe the works of the angel of wickedness: he is ill-tempered, bitter and foolish.

Hermas replied to the heavenly messenger dressed in shepherd gear by saying he did not know how to tell when the bad angel was leading him. The shepherd answered:

When ill-temper and bitterness come over you, then you know that he is in you. When the lust for renown, feasting on heavy luxuries, a desire of women, covetousness, haughtiness and similar urges come into your heart, know that the angel of wickedness has slid into you. When you feel this, shake him out and cast him off.

In this 14th-century mural, *The Annunciation to the Shepherds*, angels announce the birth of Jesus. The *Shepherd of Hermas*, a book many early Christians considered to be scripture, was a collection of advice given to a shepherd by a celestial messenger, possibly an angel.

list of New Testament scriptures, continued to recommend it to new Christians. In the *Codex Sinaiticus*, a collection of the Old and New Testament books that was copied in the 300s, the *Shepherd of Hermas* was the last book of the Bible – after Revelation and the *Epistle of Barnabas*.

EPISTLE OF BARNABAS

The *Epistle of Barnabas* presents itself as a letter by an anonymous writer, but it reads more like an essay about how Christians fit into God's covenant with the Jews. The epistle's short answer is that the Jews forfeited their right to be God's people because they repeatedly rejected God in favour of idols, and they rejected the Messiah whom God sent. Christians, instead, became the rightful heirs of God's covenant, the writer claims. They are the new people of God who obey him and are blessed for doing so.

Proper Christian behaviour and the end times are also important themes in this essay. In addition, the writer reinterprets Old Testament passages to show the hidden (allegorical) meaning, which is presented as more reliable than the obvious, literal meaning. For example, the writer says that when Moses told the Hebrews not to eat pork, Moses meant that God's people should not become people 'who are like swine; that is, when they are in luxury they forget the Lord, but when they are in want they recognize the Lord, just as the swine when it eats does not know his lord, but when it is hungry it cries out, and when it has received food again it is silent'.

This essay was probably written sometime after the fall of Jerusalem in AD 70 but before Hadrian rebuilt it in 135. Who wrote it is unknown. Many early church leaders as well as some of the oldest known collections of Christian writings attributed the essay to Barnabas, one of Paul's associates. Among these were Clement of Alexandria, Origen, Jerome and the *Codex Sinaiticus*. Other scholars say it is unlikely that the Barnabas whom Paul described as observing Jewish traditions (Galatians 2:13) could write an essay like this that argues those traditions are obsolete.

DIDACHE

'Teaching' is what the Greek title of this early Christian writing means. And teaching is what it did. This was a slim handbook of instruction for new converts, training them in basic Christian beliefs, behaviour and worship rituals. Also known by its longer title, *Teaching of the Apostles*, this widely respected handbook was probably written in the closing decades of the first century or early

The Vision of the Trinity Appearing to Pope St Clement by Giovanni Battista Tiepolo (1696–1770). St Clement was the first-century writer of a letter many considered sacred.

in the second, when Christians and Jews were trying to distance themselves from one another.

Like the Jews, Christians were instructed to fast twice a week. 'Mondays and Thursdays are their days for fasting,' the handbook said of the Jews, 'so yours should be Wednesdays and Fridays.' Jews prayed three times a day, and the handbook said Christians should do the same. 'Your prayers', the handbook added, 'should be different from theirs.' Christians were to include the Lord's Prayer.

In 16 chapters, *Didache* also offers advice about appropriate Christian behaviour, baptism, Sunday worship, communion (eucharist) and the end times. In places, it quotes Jesus, calling for radical changes that seem nearly impossible – such as turning the other cheek when attacked. Elsewhere it offers what sounds like the gentle advice of an understanding pastor: 'If you can bear the Lord's full yoke, you will be perfect, but if you cannot, then do what you can.' Origen considered the *Didache* authoritative, but not canonical.

'Write down my commandments and my parables; and the other matters you will write down as I will show them to you.'

CELESTIAL MESSENGER,
SHEPHERD OF HERMAS

99

Popular Christian Writings

'A man of small stature, with a bald head and crooked legs, in a good state of body, with eyebrows meeting and a nose somewhat hooked, full of friendliness.'

ACTS OF PAUL AND THECLA – THE ONLY KNOWN DESCRIPTION OF PAUL

By the end of the first century, almost everyone who had ever seen Jesus was dead. Without the Jesus generation, there were no more eyewitnesses to his stories, teachings and miracles. So for spiritual guidance, Christians turned to the writings of the eyewitnesses and their close associates. By the early second century, Christians were familiar with nearly all of the 27 books in today's New Testament, as well as other early writings.

But the believers wanted more. They wanted details not covered in those earliest writings. They wanted to know about the life of Mary, the mother of Jesus. They wanted to know about Jesus' childhood. And they wanted to know more about the apostles themselves.

For the next two centuries or so, Christian writers obliged. Drawing from stories passed along by word of mouth and perhaps from well-intentioned imagination, they wrote scores of books: new Gospels about Jesus, new acts (histories) of the apostles, new letters from apostles, and new end-time prophecies.

Most of these books were never serious contenders for a slot in the New Testament. They did not meet the criteria of having been written by an apostle or a colleague of an apostle. Still, many of these books became immensely popular, were passed along, translated and sometimes read in church services.

INFANCY GOSPEL OF THOMAS

One popular Christian writing for inquiring minds was a short collection of miracles Jesus supposedly performed as a child between the ages of five and 12. The *Infancy Gospel of Thomas* claims to have been written by a Jew named Thomas. The miracles reported do not always portray Jesus as a saintly child. Instead, it shows his transformation from an immature and vindictive boy who used his supernatural powers for revenge to a compassionate adolescent who started using his powers to help others.

At the age of five, Jesus played in the mud, making little pools of water. Another boy came along and used a willow branch to drain the pools. 'What harm did the pools and the waters do to you?' Jesus asked. 'Behold, even now you will be dried up.' The boy withered and died.

Later, while Jesus was walking through the village, another boy bumped into him. Angry, Jesus said, 'You will not go back the way you came.' And the boy fell dead. The parents of the fallen boy went to Joseph and complained, 'Since you have such a child, it is impossible for you to live with us in the village; or else teach him to bless, and not to curse: for he is killing our children.' When Joseph urged Jesus to stop acting like this because it was making everyone hate them, Jesus struck his accusers blind. The people were afraid to speak out against him.

In time, Jesus learned to use his powers for good. When a playmate fell from a roof, Jesus raised him from the dead. When Joseph cut a beam too short for a couch he was making for a rich man, Jesus stretched the beam. And when a pitcher of water he was carrying home broke, he got more water and carried it in his cloak. Other miracles: healing his brother James who was dying of a snakebite, and raising more people from the dead, including a man who died of blood loss after accidentally cutting off part of his foot with an axe. Jesus healed the foot, too.

Paul's female disciple

Acts of Paul and Thecla is a story about an 18-year-old woman, Thecla, who broke off her engagement after hearing Paul preach about celibacy. Furious, her fiancé had Paul arrested, beaten and ordered out of town. No less furious was Thecla's mother, who cried out for her daughter to be burned alive. Tied to a pyre, Thecla escaped after a cloudburst washed out the fire. Thecla followed Paul on a missionary journey and miraculously survived many other attempts on her life, including an appearance in an arena. Later, she lived alone and became famous for healing the sick.

This engaging story was written by a church leader who was dismissed because of it, so said Tertullian, a theologian who lived in the early 200s. Tertullian did not explain why the man was removed from office, but scholars say it was probably because the story said Paul advocated celibacy over marriage – a teaching frowned on by most church leaders of the day.

St Thecla Delivering the City from Plague by Giovanni Battista Tiepolo (1696–1770). Thecla was the miracle-working heroine of the popular Christian story, *Acts of Paul and Thecla*.

It is unclear exactly when these stories were written. The earliest surviving manuscript is from the AD 400s. But in about 180, the church leader Irenaeus referred to a detail in one of the stories, saying only that his source was a writing other than 'the true scriptures'. He may have been referring to the widely distributed *Infancy Gospel of Thomas*, which was translated into at least 13 languages.

APOCALYPSE OF PETER

The *Apocalypse of Peter* is perhaps the most important example of Christian end-time literature outside the Bible, once rivalling Revelation in popularity. Part of the reason it was so well liked was because it provided incredible details about the afterlife.

The longest section of the work is a tour of hell, tracing 21 types of sinners and describing the punishment they received that was appropriate for their sin. People who spoke blasphemously against God's way of righteousness were hung 'by their tongues' over an 'unquenchable fire'.

And there were also others, women, hanged by their hair above that mire which boiled up; and these were they that adorned themselves for adultery...
And I saw the murderers and them that were consenting to them cast into a strait place full of evil, creeping things, and smitten by those beasts, and so turning themselves about in that torment. And upon them were set worms like clouds of darkness. And the souls of them that were murdered stood and looked upon the torment of those murderers and said: 'O God, righteous is your judgment.'

This visionary book claims to be a revelation that the resurrected Jesus gave to the apostle Peter. Most scholars say it was more likely written long after Peter's death. Clues in the text suggest it was probably written just after the self-proclaimed messiah, Simon Bar Kokhba, led the Jews in a doomed revolt against Rome (AD 132–35). The book was included in the Muratorian collection of scriptures (about AD 200), with the comment that 'some of us are not willing to have [it] read in church'. Other churches, however, continued reading it into the fifth century.

Hell from *The Garden of Earthly Delights* by Hieronymus Bosch (1450–1576). The longest section in the Apocalypse of Peter is a graphic tour of hell. Artists later transferred such word pictures to the canvas.

Debugged

Acts of John tells of the apostle John spending the night at an inn and ordering the bugs out of his room. 'O bugs,' John said, 'leave your abode for this night and remain quiet in one place.' The next morning John found a throng of bugs waiting outside his door. He told them that since they had behaved, they could go home. They skittered back into the mattress and disappeared.

Ways of Reading the Bible

The scriptures were composed by the spirit of God and... have not only a meaning that is manifest, but also another that is hidden as far as most people are concerned.'

ORIGEN, *DE PRINCIPIIS*

Criticizing the allegorists

In criticizing the allegorical approach to biblical interpretation, the Antiochene writer Theodore of Mopsuestia attacked the allegorists for their presumption. He notes that the allegorists claim that scripture points beyond the literal and historical to something spiritual that requires special understanding. They also claim that they can understand this spiritual meaning because they are spiritual. Where, Theodore asked, is the source of their understanding?

The early Christians writers all interpreted the Bible, both Old and New Testaments, but not all of these men used the same methods. The earliest Christian commentators continued to do what the New Testament texts themselves often do – find Jesus in the characters and events of the Old Testament.

Matthew's Gospel constantly refers to events in Jesus' ministry as in accordance with the prophets, and in the narrative of the holy innocents and the flight to Egypt, seems to parallel the infant Jesus with Moses. Paul sees the mothers of Abraham's two children as the mothers of the two covenants – Hagai repesents the Old Testament: slavery, Mount Sinai and earthly Jerusalem; while Sarah is the new Jerusalem, freedom and our mother. This type of reading is now called typology, as the Old Testament person or event is seen as a type of Christ or someone or thing associated with Christ (such as the new covenant). For example, because his father Abraham was willing to offer him up in sacrifice, Isaac is seen as the type of Jesus, whose heavenly Father offered him as a sacrifice on the cross. The passage through the Red Sea is a type of baptism.

Numerous writers of the second century pursued this same kind of typology, seeking more ties between Jesus and the Old Testament, often taking it to excess. For example, Justin Martyr, the respected writer who gave up his life for his faith in about AD 165, found types of Jesus' cross in almost every piece of wood mentioned in the Old Testament. Others seized on every mention of the word 'lamb' to apply it to Christ.

But finding types was not the only work for the early commentators. Often they wanted to explain obscure passages in the Bible or apply them to their own time. To do so, they needed other tools for interpretation.

ALLEGORICAL INTERPRETATIONS OF SCRIPTURE – FROM ALEXANDRIA

The tool some seized on was allegory, a kind of extended metaphor in which an event is given a meaning beyond the obvious. (Typology is a simple form of allegory, but much more limited.) Allegory was currently very popular in the Greek world, and the Jewish philosopher Philo of Alexandria had already used it in his own scriptural interpretations.

Not surprisingly, allegorical interpretations of scripture grew strongest in Alexandria, Philo's old home, where Greek culture was strong. Their most ardent adherent was Origen, the writer who had produced the Hexapla, or first parallel-text study Bible.

Figuring the transfiguration

The Gospels of Matthew, Mark and Luke all describe how Jesus took three of his disciples to a mountaintop, and was there transfigured before them, his face shining like the sun and his clothes becoming dazzlingly white, as white as snow. Writers of both the Alexandrian and Antiochene schools have written on this passage, showing how their methods of interpretation varied.

Origen, chief of the Alexandrian school, focuses on the fact that Jesus' garments were whiter than anyone could bleach them. He says that the workers who bleach material so inadequately may be the wise men of this world who cultivate the art of rhetoric (formal speech). They imagine their own poor thoughts to be bright and clean because their speech is adorned 'with verbal bleaching', but the One whose garments glisten is the Word, who exhibits in scripture the glistening of his thoughts. It is difficult for us today to relate wise men who use rhetoric to Jesus' transfiguration, but it was obviously clear to Origen.

John Chrystostom, of the School of Antioch, is more practical. In response to why Jesus' garments shone as white as snow, he says snow is the whitest thing we know. Similarly, Jesus' face shone like the sun because the sun is the brightest light we know. But then John takes this image one step further, albeit a more practical step than Origen would take. He asks, but did Jesus' face really shine like the sun does daily? No, he concludes, for the disciples were so dazzled that they fell on their faces. If Jesus' face had shone only as the sun normally shines, the disciples would not have fallen down, for they saw the sun shine every day without doing so. Consequently, Jesus' face shone brighter than the sun.

In his attempts to interpret scripture, Origen looked for three basic levels of meaning: the literal, or historical, meaning (the least important), the moral significance (what it means for us), and the symbolic meaning, which he arrived at through the use of allegory. Sometimes, however, Origen combined the last two meanings, referring only to the literal and spiritual meanings.

Origen could allegorize such simple things as a fishing boat. In one place he sees the boat carrying the apostles and Jesus as the Church. In another passage, where the progress of the apostles' boat is slowed by the wind, Origen sees the boat as 'the conflict into which anyone is constrained by the Word, and goes unwillingly'. He concludes that the 'Saviour wishes to train by exercise the disciples in this boat which is distressed by waves and the contrary wind.' These are simple transformations; others were more elaborate.

In the account of Jesus' feeding the 5,000, Jesus commands that the people 'sit down in groups on the green grass. So they sat down in groups of hundreds and of fifties' (Mark 6:39–40). Origen comments that the grass here represented the flesh and that the people sat on the grass in order to humble the flesh and prepare themselves to eat the loaves Jesus blessed. They are broken into groups because not everyone is equally nourished by the words they hear. Origen then tackles the numbers involved: 100 is a sacred number, he says, and is consecrated by God because of its completeness; 50, on the other hand, symbolizes the forgiveness of sins.

Origen believed in the need for allegorical interpretation because he was convinced that many biblical passages made no sense when taken at a strictly literal level. Most people, he held, were capable of reading the Bible only on the literal – and perhaps the moral level – but only special interpreters who were spiritually mature, could understand the texts on the spiritual level. Interpreting at this high level required allegory. Origen was followed in his approach by many other scholars, who are said to be of the School of Alexandria, the centre for this thinking.

A Byzantine depiction of John Chrysostom.

A MORE TEMPERED APPROACH – FROM ANTIOCH

The allegorical approach led to many excesses, and drew sharp criticism because it often wandered far from the written text or the intentions of the original writers. By the third century a number of Christian writers, centred in or trained at Antioch, Syria, began writing far more conservatively. Although they believed in multiple meanings in scripture, they insisted on keeping the text as written as the primary focus.

Perhaps the most important writer of the School of Antioch was the fourth-century scholar, Diodore of Tarsus, who had many brilliant students, including Theodore of Mopsuestia and the fiery preacher and charismatic bishop of Constantinople, John Chrysostom ('Golden Mouth'). Diodore took great pains to establish the historical circumstances in which the biblical books were written. (He even rearranged the psalms in an attempt to put them into historical order.) Only when he had established all he could of the circumstances under which a text was written did Diodore look for a higher meaning, which he (and his followers) called *theoria*. Diodore insisted that all *theoria* be rooted in the text and not be a figment of the interpreter's vivid imagination.

The influence of the School of Antioch was not long lived. It all but disappeared by the end of the fifth century, while the allegorists remained strong. However, the influence of the Antiochenes may be seen in the more tempered use of allegory by later writers, including Jerome and Augustine, the two greatest biblical scholars of ancient times.

Origen saw the storm that hit the apostles' boat as reminiscent of the daily conflicts we all face. Jesus allowed the storm to hit the boat to teach the apostles a lesson, but then he stilled the waters, as seen in this print by Gabriel Bodmeer.

'The cause of all evils is the failure to know the scriptures well.'
JOHN CHRYSOSTOM, *HOMILIES ON COLOSSIANS*

There are people who take great pains to twist the senses of the divine scriptures and... dream up some silly fables in their own heads and give their folly the name of allegory.'
THEODORE OF MOPSUESTIA, *COMMENTARY ON GALATIANS*

3

The Bible in a Rapidly Growing Church

Most of the Church, by AD 400, agreed on which books belonged in the Bible. The Christian Bible became a two-part book: the Old Testament, made up of the Jewish scriptures, and the New Testament, made up of 27 Christian works – stories, teachings, letters and prophecy.

That settled, the next 1,000 years were remarkable in the emerging story of the Bible. Christians began spreading their faith throughout the planet, and taking the Bible with them. Scholars standardized the text, since not all copies of individual books read in exactly the same way. Scribes made copies. Artists lavishly illustrated many of them. Linguists translated the text into other languages, sometimes inventing alphabets where no written language existed – just so people could have scripture in their own tongue. The Bible extended far beyond the Mediterranean, spreading throughout Europe. Wherever it went, people copied it over and over.

World map from the *Apocalypse of St Sever* (c. 1076), drawn by Stephanus Garcia.

Jerome the Fiery Scholar

'You urge me to revise the Old Latin version, and, as it were, to sit in judgment on the copies of the scriptures which are not scattered throughout the whole world; and, inasmuch as they differ from one another, you would have me decide which of them agree with the Greek original. The labour is one of love, but at the same time both perilous and presumptuous; for in judging others I must be content to be judged by all.'

JEROME, PREFACE TO THE FOUR GOSPELS, ADDRESSED TO POPE DAMASUS

Holy Land pilgrimage

When Jerome arrived in Bethlehem from Rome, he did not immediately settle down. First, he accompanied Paula and Eustochium, his friends from Rome, on a pilgrimage of all the biblical sites in the Holy Land. The three then travelled to Egypt to visit some early hermitages and monasteries before settling down and building their own monasteries.

'... tender and violent, gentle and rude, viciously proud and childishly humble, a man of deep hates and morbid passions whose brain was nevertheless permanently clear. He was a tissue of contradictions and he seems to have been aware of it himself.'

ROBERT PAYNE DESCRIBING JEROME IN *FATHERS OF THE WESTERN CHURCH* (1989)

In the fourth century lived two of the greatest biblical scholars of all time: Jerome and Augustine of Hippo. Jerome was a scholar of unapproachable genius, the finest of his age. As a man, however, he was a bundle of contradictions. He was self-centred and resentful, and often wrote vicious attacks against those who disagreed with him, yet he was also a loving friend and spiritual adviser to others. He could attack an opponent's physical defects in one breath, and gently advise a father on teaching his child the alphabet in another.

Jerome's full name was Sophronius Eusebius Hieronymus. He was born in about 347 in Dalmatia (now Slovenia), and at 12 he went to Rome to study the Greek and Roman classics. He was baptized in about 366, and soon he began to devote himself to lifelong study of scripture. In 377, after living as a desert monk for two years, Jerome was ordained a priest at Antioch. In 382, he returned to Rome as private secretary to Pope Damasus, who commissioned him to revise the current Latin translations of the Bible. While in

Rome, Jerome also preached against the Roman clergy and lax monks, and became the spiritual director of a group of wealthy Roman women. When Damasus died in 384, Jerome left Rome with two of his women friends, Paula and her daughter Eustochium, and took up residence in Bethlehem. There, Paula used her wealth to establish a monastery for women (under her own direction),

Monasticism emerges from the desert

Jerome was almost as dedicated to the ideals of monastic life as he was to the Bible, and he wrote an idealized biography of one of the first monks. *The Life of Paul* describes how the young Paul left his home in Thebes at the time of a persecution of Christians by the emperor Decius in 249–51. Paul fled to the desert, where he lived in a cave as a complete hermit for about 100 years, constantly praying and fasting. Another hermit, Antony of Egypt, came to him at the end and buried him. Because Paul is known only through Jerome's book, some people think he may be an idealized invention of Jerome, but Antony of Egypt was certainly real, and is generally regarded to be the father of monasticism, as he not only lived the life of a hermit, but gathered followers around him as well. Monasticism grew quickly. In the early fourth century, a native-born Egyptian named Pachomius established the first Christian community and wrote the first Rule (way of life) for monks, a Rule that Jerome later translated. Monasticism thrived and in time moved out of the deserts of Egypt and other barren places to the towns and countrysides of Europe. Monks became of vital importance in copying the Bible onto lavishly illuminated manuscripts.

and one for men, where Jerome spent the rest of his life. While in Bethlehem, Jerome completed his translation of the Bible. He died in 419 or 420.

BIBLICAL COMMENTARIES

In addition to his translation of the Bible, and a large number of letters and books on various topics, Jerome published a vast amount of biblical criticism – including substantial commentaries on each of the Prophets, Psalms, Ecclesiastes, Matthew, Galatians, Ephesians, Philemon and Titus. He also wrote a book on difficult passages in Genesis, handbooks of Hebrew names and places, and sermons on the Psalms and on Mark.

In his commentaries, Jerome followed Origen in freely using allegory. However, as he grew more familiar with the biblical texts through his translating work, he gained more and more respect for them, and always kept their literal meaning in mind. Although he continued to use allegory in interpreting scripture, he used it carefully, avoiding excesses. Typically, Jerome attacked those who did not follow him, complaining about heretics who used allegory to substantiate their own perverse teachings. The orthodox way of reading scripture, he said, is to tread a narrow path between the two extremes of over-literalism and over-allegorization.

'We are now busily occupied with our third book on Galatians, and... we are well aware of our weakness, and are conscious that our slender ability flows in but a small stream and makes little roar and rattle.'

JEROME, PREFACE TO
GALATIANS COMMENTARY

Jerome in art

Jerome is often depicted in the garb of a cardinal. This refers to his close association with Pope Damasus, who may or may not have named Jerome a cardinal. He is also sometimes shown beating his breast with a stone, in recognition of his devotion to a strict life of penance. Finally, Jerome is sometimes shown with a lion. This refers to a legend in which Jerome removed a thorn from the paw of a lion, who then followed him around like a pet.

The art of interpreting the scriptures is the only one of which all men everywhere claim to be masters. To quote Horace again, "the chatty old woman, the doting old man, and the wordy sophist, one and all take in hand the scriptures, rend them in pieces and teach them before they have learned them".'

JEROME, LETTER 53

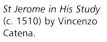

St Jerome in His Study (c. 1510) by Vincenzo Catena.

Jerome's Latin Bible

Jerome's messianic bent

In his Old Testament translations, Jerome emphasized the messianic content of some passages. Often the messianic references go beyond the original text, using terms that are not present in the Hebrew. Although such passages nourished Christian beliefs, they impeded the dialogue with Jewish scholars that Jerome hoped for.

🕊

Until Jerome's time, most Christians read the Bible in Greek, which was the language of educated men and women in Jesus' time. The New Testament had been written in Greek, of course, and the Old Testament was known almost exclusively through Greek translations, mainly in the original Septuagint translation known to the earliest Christians. By Jerome's time in the fourth century, however, Latin was being spoken throughout the vast Roman empire and a good Latin Bible was sorely needed. Although some Latin translations of the Bible had been made, they were poor ones, and it was left to the fiery Jerome to produce a good Latin Bible, known as the Vulgate because it was in the vulgar (common) language of the people. Jerome's translation proved to be so successful that it endured as the official Bible of the Catholic Church for more than 1,500 years.

TRANSLATING THE BIBLE

Jerome began his work on translating the Bible in Rome, after being commissioned to do so by Pope Damasus in 382 or 383. He quickly translated all four Gospels, using an Old Latin translation as the basis for his work and correcting it after studying the original Greek texts. His intention in making this translation, he said, was to 'correct the mistakes made by inaccurate translators and the blundering alterations of confident but ignorant critics, and further, all that has been inserted or changed by copyists more asleep than awake'. Judging from criticisms of the Old Latin translations made by Christians up to and including the pope, there were many such errors, alterations and accretions, and so Jerome had a hard job ahead of him. He was thoroughgoing in his work.

It is not certain that Jerome ever translated the rest of the New Testament, although some scholars believe that he did. The other New Testament books that came to appear as part of the Vulgate may have been translated by others. However, Jerome did translate the Old Testament in its entirety, and he turned his attention to this task soon after completing the Gospels. First, he made a quick translation of the Psalms. Again he used an Old Latin text, this time correcting it against the original Hebrew and an edition of the

Statue of St Jerome outside the Church of the Nativity, Bethlehem.

Greek Septuagint version, but this translation failed to satisfy him. At this point, he left Rome and settled in Bethlehem.

In Bethlehem, Jerome resumed his work by making a second translation of the Psalms. In working on this translation, he achieved greater accuracy by consulting Origen's Hexapla, the study Bible that gives various Hebrew and Greek versions of the Old Testament texts in six columns. Even though Jerome went on to make a third translation of the Psalms, it is this second version that was later used in the Vulgate. He then proceeded to translate Job, the three books attributed to Solomon and Chronicles, based on the Septuagint. Jerome then took a bold step and

Early reactions to the Vulgate

The public did not at first take to Jerome's translation of the Bible, preferring the versions they already knew from worship and study. Some deplored Jerome's abandoning of the Septuagint version for the Hebrew. Although Jerome had been careful to keep any terms from the Septuagint that had been the subject of theological discussion, critics were discontent because they considered the Greek text to be truer than the older Hebrew. In his Introduction to Proverbs, Ecclesiastes and the Song of Solomon (AD 393), Jerome responded to these critics:

If anyone is better pleased with the edition of the Seventy [the Septuagint], there it is, long since corrected by me. For it is not our aim in producing the new to destroy the old. And yet if our friend reads carefully, he will find that our version is the more intelligible, for it has not turned sour by being poured three times over into different vessels, but has been drawn straight from the press, and stored in a clean jar, and has thus preserved its own flavour.

In time, all objections to Jerome's work fell away and people began to realize how good his translation really was. For, far and away, it was the very best translation available at the time, and it soon became the standard Latin text of the Bible and a model for all future translators.

abandoned the Septuagint text, even though it had always been regarded by Christians as the definitive text of the Old Testament and was accorded an even higher place than the original Hebrew texts. From then on, it seems, instead of relying on the Greek of the Septuagint, Jerome translated directly from the Hebrew for the remainder of the Old Testament books.

After studying the books not accepted as part of the official Hebrew scriptures, yet found in the Septuagint, Jerome decided they were nonsensical. Even though he translated some of them, he rejected them as part of the Old Testament canon, and wrote introductions that labelled them Apocrypha. This was another bold step, as the books had long been accepted as scriptural by most Christians. Over the years, however, copies of Jerome's translation often dropped the introductions, and Christians continued to accept the Apocrypha as part of the Bible. It was not until the time of the Reformation that the canonicity of these books was seriously questioned again.

SAPIENTIAE

INCIPIT LIB SAPIENTIAE

EXPLICIUNT CAPITULA

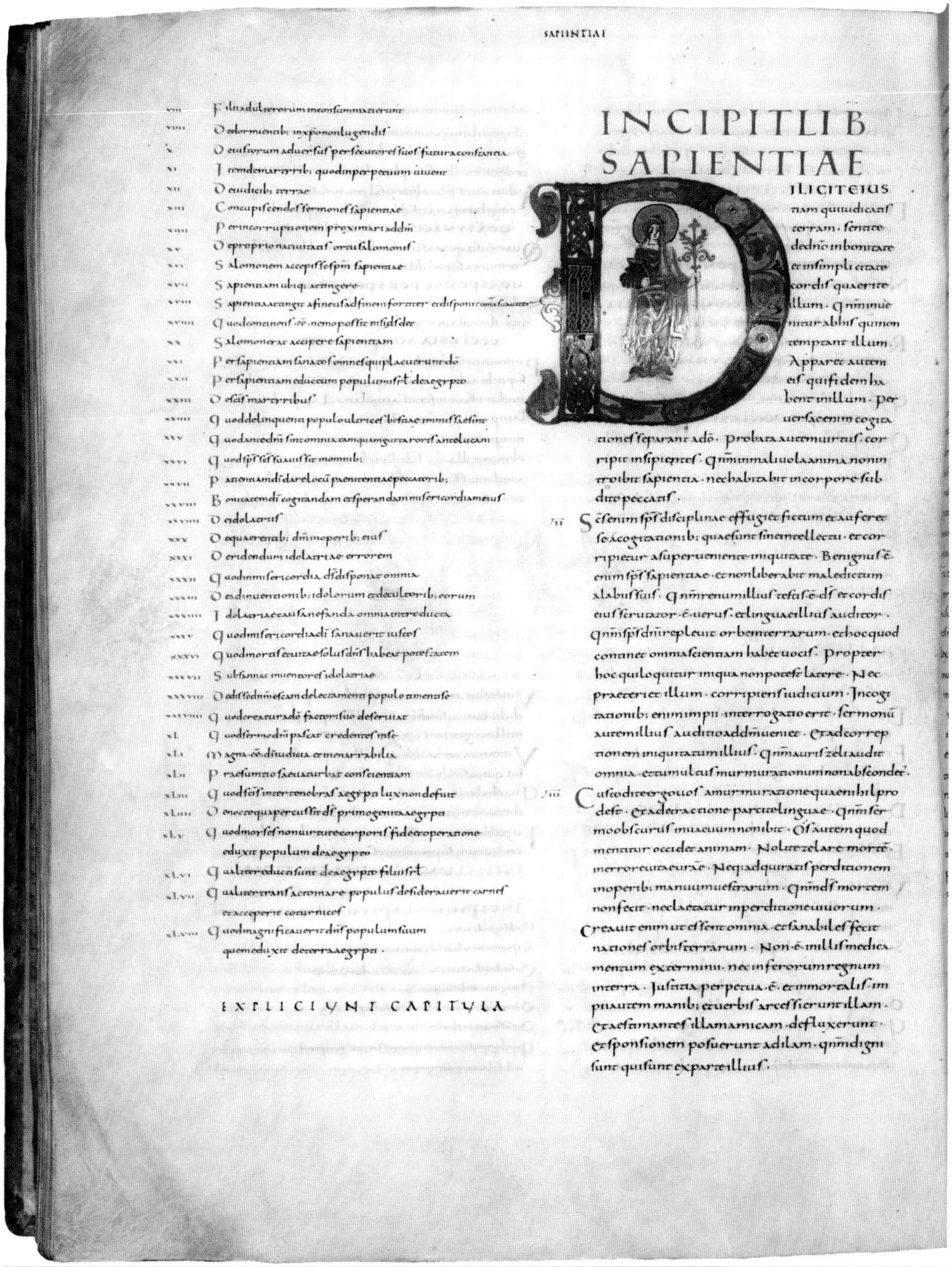

Page from a ninth-century edition of the Vulgate, Jerome's Latin Bible.

Augustine and the Bible

Augustine's mentor,
St Ambrose (339–97) by
Fiorenzo di Lorenzo
(c. 1490), from an altar in
Santa Maria Nuova in
Perugia, Italy.

'Let Thy scriptures be my chaste delights. Neither let me be deceived in them, nor deceive out of them.'

AUGUSTINE, CONFESSIONS

The Septuagint

Augustine gave his full support to the Septuagint, the ancient Greek translation of the Hebrew scriptures, believing that God inspired it, and that it was superior to the Hebrew. He therefore accepted the books Jerome labelled as Apocrypha, and he objected to Jerome's abandonment of the Septuagint and use of the Hebrew texts in translating the Bible into Latin.

❧

'The New Testament lies hidden in the Old; the Old Testament is enlightened through the New.'

AUGUSTINE, QUESTIONS ON THE HEPTATEUCH

Jerome's contemporary, the African bishop Augustine, started out as a sinful young man who disdained the Bible. He ended as a saint and the greatest theologian of the Western Church, who rooted his thoughts in scripture.

FROM SINNER TO SAINT

Augustine was born in the North African town of Thagaste (now Souk-Ahras, Algeria). His father, Patricius, was a pagan and his mother, Monica, a Christian. The local culture was Latin, and Augustine was educated in Latin literature. He also learned a bit of Greek, but he never knew more than a few words of Hebrew.

Although his mother Monica urged him to become a Christian and constantly prayed for her son's conversion, Augustine preferred to lead a life of pleasure. At the age of 17 he began a 15-year affair with a woman and fathered an illegitimate son. In 373, when he was 18, Augustine read *Hortensius*, a (now lost) work by the Roman orator Cicero, and felt spiritual stirrings. He then tried reading the Bible, but found the literary style distasteful. Of course, the version of the Bible he read would have been one of the notoriously poor Old Latin versions, which Jerome had not yet set about replacing with a standard text.

Instead of becoming a Christian, Augustine fell in with a group of Manichees, followers of the Persian heretic Mani, who disdained the Old Testament and believed in a cosmos made up of two battling kingdoms, one of darkness and the other of light. Augustine remained associated with this group for about 10 years, while he served in teaching posts at Carthage, Rome and Milan. In 385, his mother, Monica, arranged for Augustine to marry a 12-year-old heiress and convinced him to leave the woman he lived with. Augustine sent his mistress away, but while waiting for his fiancée to be old enough to marry, he took another mistress. In the end, he never married.

At about this time, Augustine became disillusioned with the Manichees and began to be swayed by sermons preached by the Christian bishop Ambrose, whose allegorical readings of

The Christian quarter of Hippo Regius, a Roman town in Algeria. On the hill in the distance is St Augustine's Cathedral.

scripture made Augustine realize that the Bible had merit after all. Slowly Augustine leaned ever closer towards Christianity. Then, one July day in 386, as he tells us, he was thinking things over in a garden in Milan when he heard a child's voice, coming from a nearby house, repeatedly chanting 'Take up and read, take up and read.' At first Augustine thought the child was playing some game, but could not imagine a game that used these words. He decided it was a message from heaven, and he picked up a copy of Paul's letters, opened it and read the first words that met his eyes: 'Let us live honourably as in the day, not in revelling and drunkenness, not in debauchery and licentiousness, not in quarrelling and jealousy. Instead, put on the Lord Jesus Christ, and make no provision for the flesh, to gratify its desires' (Romans 13:13–14). Augustine was instantly converted, 'by a light, as it were, of security infused into my heart – all the gloom of doubt vanished away'.

Augustine was baptized by Ambrose in 387. After his mother died later that year he returned to his home town, Thagaste, where he organized a group of laymen into a kind of monastic community. While visiting the nearby coastal town of Hippo Regius in 391, he was mobbed by the people, who admired him, and wanted him to be their bishop. He was ordained a priest more or less against his will. In 395, he was named bishop of Hippo. Augustine remained in Hippo, fulfilling all the duties of a bishop, writing, fighting heresies, and living in community with his clergy until his death in 430.

AUGUSTINE ON THE BIBLE

During his 35 years as bishop of Hippo, Augustine wrote a vast number of books, letters and sermons, many of them on biblical texts or rooted in the Bible. Chief among his works are his *Confessions*, an emotional personal account of his early years and conversion, which includes interpretations of the book of Genesis; and his monumental defence of Christianity against pagan critics, *The City of God*, which is grounded in scripture. In addition, Augustine wrote *A Harmony of the Evangelists*, which lays down principles for dealing with the differences among the Synoptic Gospels (those of Matthew, Mark and Luke); *On Christian Doctrine*, which gives guidelines for interpreting scripture, and various books of questions on scripture. He also wrote many biblical commentaries, including the very important *Tractates on John's Gospel* and *Homilies on the Psalms*.

Unlike Jerome, who focused on scripture chiefly as a scholar, most of Augustine's works of biblical interpretation were designed to awaken the understanding of the people of his diocese. Consequently, his style was less formal and more friendly. In his homilies, or sermons, on scripture, he used everyday language that was vivid in style and aglow with fervent love. As much as Augustine admired oratory or literary style, he preferred to sacrifice style in order to be sure the people understood him.

In his interpretations of scripture, Augustine followed Origen and others of the School of Alexandria in stressing the spiritual sense of scripture rather than the literal, but he generally used the term figuration in place of allegorization. On the other hand, he respected the literal meaning of scripture and was attentive to the text and the historical context in which it was written. For example, he pointed out that the order of the narratives found in the Gospels sometimes reflects general recollections rather than a strict chronological account. He also believed that the words of Jesus are often reported in a general way in the Gospels, reflecting the broad sense of what Jesus said rather than his exact words.

For Augustine the Bible speaks not only of promise and fulfilment in the person of Jesus, but contains answers – in literal or figurative ways – to all the basic questions of humanity. Augustine held that God gave us the scriptures to incite believers to a double love of God and neighbour, which is the goal of every soul's journey. On the other hand, Augustine realized that the complexities and ambiguities of human language make it difficult to interpret scripture, and he advised others to take particular care in doing so. His writings on scripture were widely circulated after his death, and they were carefully read and utilized throughout the Middle Ages.

St Augustine by Justus van Gent. From the Palazzo Ducale in Urbino.

A monk's habit

Although Augustine is usually portrayed in art wearing the full garments of a medieval bishop – including mitre, gloves, ring and staff – in real life he dressed in the grey habit of a monk, even when he celebrated the rites of the church.

'Wonderful is the depth of Thy oracles, whose surface is before us, inviting the little ones; and yet wonderful is the depth, O my God, wonderful is the depth. It is awe to look into it; and awe of honour, and a tremor of love.'

AUGUSTINE, *CONFESSIONS*

Rules for interpreting scripture

In *On Christian Doctrine*, Augustine laid down some basic rules for interpreting scripture that are still valid today. Among other things, he advises the interpreter to:

❧ apply Hebrew and Greek scholarship, for they are essential to interpreting the figurative language of scripture.

❧ become acquainted with the geography and natural history of the Holy Land, music, chronology, dialects and the science of numbers. Also become familiar with the writings of the ancient philosophers.

❧ remember that scripture is designed to have more than one interpretation.

❧ interpret obscure passages by the light of passages that are understood. This is preferable to interpreting by reason.

Finally, Augustine holds that the spirit and intent of the interpreter are more important than verbal accuracy and critical acumen. Mistaken interpretations are not necessarily bad: 'If a mistaken interpretation tends to build up love, which is the end of the commandment, the interpreter goes astray in much the same way as a man who, by mistake, quits the highroad, but yet reaches, through the fields, the same place to which the road leads.'

Pilgrimages to the Holy Land

Jerome the mapmaker

Jerome, who is known mainly for his Latin translation of the Bible (the Vulgate), was also a mapmaker who explored Palestine for 35 years. A 12th-century copy of one of his maps still survives. Made in AD 385, about the time the pilgrim Egeria travelled throughout the Bible lands, the map locates important sites mentioned in the Bible – including Jerusalem, the River Jordan, Nazareth and Bethlehem.

Facing page: One of the most famous early pilgrims to the Promised Land was Emperor Constantine's mother, Helena, who in 326 commissioned the building of several churches on holy sites. She is pictured here with Emperor Heraclius, who actually lived about 300 years later, and is said to have recaptured a piece of Christ's cross from the Persians and returned it to Jerusalem. *St Helena and the Emperor Heraclius at the Gate of Jerusalem*, 15th-century altarpiece of Santa Cruz de Bleza.

'Let me go rejoicing to the splendid sanctuary, the place where the noble Empress Helena found the divine Wood [of Christ's Cross]; and go up, my heart overcome with awe, and see the Upper Room.'

SOPHRONIUS, SYRIAN CHURCH LEADER, C. AD 600, EXPRESSING HIS DESIRE TO GO TO JERUSALEM

For many Christians, reading the stories about Jesus was not enough. They wanted to walk where he walked. They wanted to put themselves on the very stage where all the Bible scenes were played out. Doing so, they believed, would strengthen their faith by helping bring the stories to life.

Christians probably began taking trips to sacred sites as early as the first century. After crushing a Jewish revolt in AD 135, the Roman emperor Hadrian systematically began destroying all holy sites, Jewish and Christian. He replaced them with shrines to Roman gods. Over a cave stable in Bethlehem that was thought to be the birthplace of Jesus, he built a temple to Adonis – ironically, a god known for his death and resurrection. Each winter, according to Roman myth, Adonis went to the underworld. Each spring, he returned to earth.

The first pilgrimage on record took place a couple of decades later. Melito, the bishop of Sardis in what is now Turkey, wrote in a letter that he made a trip to Palestine to confirm names and places mentioned in the Bible.

THE EMPEROR'S MOTHER

Perhaps the most famous of the early pilgrimages was that of Emperor Constantine's mother, Helena, who came to Jerusalem in 326. Already in her seventies, she had become an ardent supporter of Christianity, the religion her son had legalized about a dozen years earlier. The Christian scholar Eusebius said she travelled around the region, identifying sacred sites and ordering the construction of churches and shrines to mark the locations.

Legend says she went to Jerusalem in search of the cross on which Jesus died, and that she found it buried on the hill of Golgotha. On this hilltop and over the nearby grave identified as the place Jesus was buried, Helena commissioned the building of the Church of the Holy Sepulchre. Among many other churches she apparently commissioned during this visit was the Church of the Ascension on the Mount of Olives, where Jesus ascended into heaven, and the Church of the Nativity in Bethlehem, over the cave stable where many believe Jesus was born.

PILGRIMAGES BECOME POPULAR

Some church leaders, such as Augustine, recommended against travelling to the Bible

Diary of a pilgrim

Few travellers to Bible lands have exhibited the same passion and energy for visiting religious sites as a mysterious woman named Egeria. She travelled for four years, from about 380 to 384. And she kept a journal describing the 63 Old Testament and 33 New Testament sites she visited in what are now Israel, Egypt, Syria and Turkey. Only part of her journal has survived, so scholars are left guessing where she came from. Some speculate that she was from France, because of the Latin dialect she used, and that she served as a nun, since she addressed her journal to 'reverend sisters'. Here are some excerpts from her diary:

These mountains are ascended with infinite toil, for you cannot go up gently by a spiral track, as we say snail-shell wise, but you climb straight up the whole way, as if up a wall, and you must come straight down each mountain until you reach the very foot of the middle one, which is specially called Sinai. By this way, then, at the bidding of Christ our God, and helped by the prayers of the holy men who accompanied us, we arrived at the fourth hour, at the summit of Sinai, the holy mountain of God, where the law was given.

EGERIA DESCRIBING MOUNT SINAI

We saw all the lands of the Sodomites and Zoar which is the only one of the five cities [which include Sodom and Gomorrah] that exists today. There is a memorial of it, but nothing appears of those other cities but a heap of ruins, just as they were turned into ashes. The place where was the inscription concerning Lot's wife was shown to us... the pillar [of salt] is said to have been covered by the Dead Sea.

EGERIA DESCRIBING SODOM AND GOMORRAH

You see there nothing but gold and gems and silk. For if you look at the veils, they are made wholly of silk striped with gold, and if you look at the curtains, they too are made wholly of silk striped with gold. The church vessels too, of every kind, gold and jewelled, are brought out.

EGERIA DESCRIBING JERUSALEM'S CHURCH OF THE HOLY SEPULCHRE, WHICH WAS BUILT ON THE SUPPOSED SITE OF CHRIST'S CRUCIFIXION AND BURIAL

lands, arguing that it undermined the teaching that God is everywhere. Others, like Jerome, insisted that it is natural to want to visit Jesus' homeland because it is 'part of the faith to adore where His feet have stood'.

Christians began coming from all over the Roman empire. They sought out key locations mentioned in the Bible, tombs of the prophets and monuments to saints and martyrs. One common pilgrimage was to go first to Mount Sinai and retrace the exodus to the Promised Land, and then visit the Bible sites in what is now Israel. But the most popular sites were in the Holy Land, the places Jesus walked.

Some pilgrims kept a diary of their travels. One of the first is by a man known only as the Bordeaux Pilgrim. He never identified himself, but scholars say he probably came from what is now Bordeaux, France, since his itinerary starts there. He travelled to Palestine in AD 333, and recorded brief notes about the 40 Old and New Testament sites he visited. His brief notes tell where he went, what he saw, the distance between locations, and places he rested or changed mounts. He did not seem especially interested in theological matters, and rarely commented on what he saw. He did, however, make notes about the newly constructed Church of the Holy Sepulchre:

On the left hand is the little hill of Golgotha where the Lord was crucified. About a stone's throw from thence is a vault wherein His body was laid, and rose again on the third day. There, at present, by the command of Emperor Constantine, has been built a basilica, that is to say, a church of wondrous beauty.

Church leaders and monks living in the Bible lands often served as guides, leading the pilgrims in prayer and reading to them relevant passages from the Bible. Monastic houses and churches served as rest stations and hotels. When the pilgrims returned home, they often took with them more than memories. They took cherished keepsakes to enhance those memories: water from the River Jordan, holy oil, sacred relics such as bone fragments, pieces of cloth and dust from the tombs of saints.

Writing Down the Spoken Law

Banned from Jerusalem

The Jerusalem Talmud was not collected and edited in Jerusalem. After the failed Jewish revolt of AD 135, the Romans banned Jews from the city and then repopulated most of what is now southern Israel with non-Jewish settlers. Most Jews moved north and the rabbis developed schools in several cities there, including Caesarea, Tiberias and Sepphoris. This is where the Jerusalem Talmud was born.

'Study of the Law is "life to you and length of days".'

RABBI AKIBA (C. AD 50–135)

A group of Jewish men meets at a synagogue in the Old City of Jerusalem to study their scriptures and the Talmud, which combines the Mishnah's collection of Jewish rules with a vast amount of other religious material, such as Bible commentary, history, teachings and rulings by ancient Jewish councils.

Not all religious laws that the Jews lived by were written in the Jewish Bible. Unwritten laws, passed on by word of mouth, carried the same authority as the Bible, and were believed to have come from God.

Rabbis taught their students that when God delivered the law to Moses – the rules preserved in the first five books of the Bible – God gave added instructions that Moses did not write down. For example, God told Moses that the people should not work on the sabbath. Moses put this in the written law. But the Jewish teachers said God also clarified for Moses what constituted work. On the sabbath, Jews were not to prepare food (they ate food prepared the previous day), draw drinking water, or carry anything to or from their home. There were dozens of such restrictions affecting just the sabbath.

Over time, this oral law expanded as new generations of Jewish religious leaders sought to interpret and apply the principles of God's laws to the ever-changing world.

SECOND TO THE BIBLE FOR JEWS

By the end of the AD 100s, the oral traditions had become so complex and impossible to memorize that many rabbis started making notes to help them remember the laws. Jewish custom said they should not, since Moses had not. But they realized if they did not start taking notes, some of the oral laws would be lost. In about AD 200, Rabbi Judah ha-Nasi decided to take the next logical step. He would undertake the enormous task of putting the oral law in writing. Assisted by teams of rabbis, Judah produced a document that Jews consider second only to the Bible in importance.

This document is the Mishnah, from an ancient Hebrew word that meant 'to recite', and later 'to teach'. A massive compilation, the Mishnah contained many centuries of interpretation, from the earliest oral laws to the laws and interpretations up to the time of Judah – although Judah preserved few of his own opinions.

The Mishnah is divided into six major sections, covering a wide range of Jewish life – from farming, to family, to faith. The six sections are:

❧ 'Seeds', which deals mainly with agriculture, covering laws about how to use the land.

❧ 'Appointed Seasons', which discusses the Jewish religious calendar, covering laws about observing the sabbath, religious festivals and fast days.

❧ 'Women', which talks mainly about laws affecting marriage, divorce and other aspects of family life.

🌢 'Damages', which covers civil and criminal laws, identifying when the law is broken and exactly what the punishment should be. There are also sections about idolatry and ethics.

🌢 'Holy Things', which covers worship rituals, especially sacrifices, offerings and temple services.

🌢 'Cleanliness', the final section, which focuses on laws of ritual purity and impurity, identifying what can make a person ceremonially contaminated and unfit for worship, as well as how to become ceremonially clean.

TALMUD LAW AND LORE

Detailed as the Mishnah was – with more than 500 chapters – it was only the beginning of putting the oral law into writing. Jewish scholars continued discussing the laws, often debating how the laws apply to life. These discussions and varied opinions were recorded, along with a variety of other subjects: Bible commentary, stories about rabbis, stories rabbis told about heroes of the Bible, teachings about demons, medical advice, science, history, legends and rulings handed down by the Jewish council about religious matters.

In time, these wide-ranging discussions were collected into a massive work known as the Gemara. This collection was combined with the Mishnah to form the Talmud. ('Talmud' and 'Gemara' are both from words that mean 'to study' or 'to learn'.)

There are two versions of the Talmud. That is

Rabbi Judah's sayings

Rabbi Judah ha-Nasi, a second-century Jewish leader, worked with other influential rabbis to put Jewish oral laws into a written collection called the Mishnah. Judah added some of his own sayings to this collection, as well as to other Jewish writings. These are some of his sayings:

What is the virtuous path that a man should follow? Whatever brings honour to his Maker and honour from his fellowman.

Contemplate three things and you will avoid sins: above you is an eye that sees, an ear that hears, and all your deeds are faithfully recorded.

Do not be deceived by the outward appearance of age or youth; a new pitcher might be full of good, old wine while an old one might be empty altogether.

A man should revere his father and mother as he reveres God, for all three are partners in him.

because there were two major centres of Jewish study. One was in what is now Israel. And the other was in the Persian Gulf region, where many Jews decided to stay after the Babylonians defeated the Jewish nation in 586 BC and took Jewish captives home with them. The Jerusalem Talmud, also called the Palestinian Talmud, is the shorter and less developed of the two. It was edited together in several rabbinic academies in various cities and was finished in about AD 450. The Babylonian Talmud – which is about three times longer and contains some two and a half million words – was finished about a century later, and became the more widely accepted version.

Throughout the 15 centuries since, this treasure trove of ancient Jewish thought has been a source of insight for Jews devoted to studying and applying God's law to their life. Even today, studying the Talmud remains a primary task in rabbinic schools throughout the world. Many Jews view the Talmud as a source of wisdom, although not on the same level as scripture. Most Orthodox Jews, on the other hand, consider the Talmud a vital and authoritative guide for living the Jewish life.

A well-preserved copy of the Mishnah from Palestine or Egypt, copied in the 12th or 13th century. The Mishnah is sacred to the Jews, and is second only to the scripture. It contains Jewish rules and traditions previously passed along only by word of mouth. But by AD 200 this oral law, as it was known, had grown so much that rabbis felt the need to preserve it in writing. (Cambridge University Library, T-S E2.67.)

Clarifying the Hebrew Bible

As late as Jesus' time, before the Romans invaded Jerusalem and destroyed the temple in AD 70, the texts of the Hebrew Bible were sometimes changed. Most of the changes were minor ones carried out by the scribes who copied the texts, but others were extensive. For example, the book of Jeremiah exists in two versions, one much longer than the other.

By the second century, everything changed and the texts started being copied with extraordinary accuracy, with no variations permitted. At that time the Jews were without a temple and dispersed around the Mediterranean. Consequently, they must have felt the need for a standardized text of their sacred books. Just as they began writing down their heritage during the days of captivity in Babylon, they must have worked to standardize the texts of their scriptures after they were again cut off from their land and had no temple.

Over the next few centuries, Jewish scholars worked hard to develop a correct text that could be copied with extreme accuracy. They were not allowed to change a single detail. One rabbi from this period warned his scribes that to eliminate or add a single letter to the sacred text would destroy the world.

PRESERVING GOD'S WORD

Between the years AD 500 and 1000 a special group of scribes developed and carefully preserved an official Hebrew text of the Old Testament that is still the standard today. Because they were considered to be the masters of the *masorah* ('what has been handed down'), they are called the Masoretes.

Like their predecessors, the Masoretes were careful not to change a single letter of the official texts. If they discovered an error, they copied it faithfully and added a note in the margin. A special symbol near the questioned word indicated a marginal note had been made. The note alerted readers to the possible problem or error, and they could decide for themselves whether or not to accept the established reading as correct.

The Masoretes also divided the texts into paragraphs, a division that probably extends back into antiquity. The divisions marked the passages to be used in readings from the Law and the Prophets in the synagogues. Two different cycles of readings were used at the time of the Masoretes. In Palestine, worshippers read through the Torah (the Pentateuch) once every three years, and so it was generally divided into 154 weekly sections. In Babylon, however, they read through the entire Pentateuch every year, and so the books were divided into 54 sections. In time, the one-year cycle became the standard.

VOWEL MARKINGS

The words the Masoretes worked so hard to preserve consisted only of consonants. In ancient Hebrew, the vowels were not written. Readers were expected to supply the correct vowels themselves in order to read the words correctly. As Hebrew was disappearing as a living language, and traditional pronunciations were being lost, there was a great need to develop a system of

A page from the *Aleppo Codex*. Dating from the 10th century, this manuscript is the earliest copy of the Hebrew Bible to use the Masoretic vowel markings.

indicating the vowel sounds so that readers would know how to vocalize the text properly. It was also important to indicate the vowel sounds because words using the same sequence of consonants may represent different words that are distinguished only by their vowel sounds. Traditionally, a reader identified the proper word by considering its context, but as fewer and fewer Jews were conversant in Hebrew, reading their ancient texts became ever more difficult.

Over the years three groups of Masoretes in three different locations developed systems of vocalization. The systems that prevailed came from Masoretes in the city of Tiberius, Palestine. They were developed in large part by members of two families, the ben Ashers and the ben Naphtalis. These systems of vowel markings use a number of symbols, generally various arrangements of dots that are placed above, below or between the consonants. These vowel markings are precise, indicating even subtle changes in pronunciation. In addition, accent marks are used to indicate pauses and stops and accented syllables. They were developed to help the reader fit the text to music during worship services. The system developed by the ben Naphtali family is found in some early manuscripts, but it eventually fell into disuse. The system used by the ben Ashers was widely used in the years to follow, and eventually became the standard.

Ezra reads the Law. Painting from one of the earliest-known synagogues, at Dura Europos, c. 245.

Five or six generations of the ben Asher family are known to have worked on this system. The last of these men, Moses ben Asher and his son, Aaron, did the final work in perfecting the system. In about 925, Aaron ben Asher himself used his system of notation in copying the manuscript known as the *Aleppo Codex* because it was kept for centuries by a Jewish congregation in Aleppo, Syria.

It is believed that the markings in the Aleppo Codex, the oldest surviving Masoretic text, preserve pronunciation and rhythms that go back to biblical times. In those days, Hebrew was a living language and such notations were unnecessary because fathers verbally passed on such knowledge to sons in an unbroken chain. The Masoretic vowel and accent marks help those who live in the wake of that oral tradition and who must struggle to learn Hebrew from books. But thanks to the Masoretes, today anyone with a good command of the Hebrew language can read the Old Testament as it was read in antiquity.

The battle over vowel markings

Today we know that Hebrew was written without vowels in biblical times, but about the time of the Reformation, many people believed that the vowel markings found in copies of the Hebrew Bible had always been used and no biblical text had ever been written without them. According to an ancient tradition, Moses received them by word of mouth from God and they were written down by Ezra, the priestly scribe who instituted religious reforms among the Jews returning to Jerusalem from Babylonian exile.

In the 16th century, when the Jewish scholar Elias Levita suggested that the vowels had been added to the biblical texts long after they had been written, he sparked a storm of protest that lasted two centuries. Although the Reformers welcomed Levita's findings, later Reformation scholars opposed them and accused the Catholics of using them to their own advantage. In 1678,

Switzerland passed a law forbidding anyone to preach who did not accept the integrity of the Hebrew text, including the divine origin of the vowel markings. It was only later, when scholars studied the matter dispassionately, that they found too much evidence on the subject to doubt Levita any longer. The main evidence centres on the fact that neither Jerome in the fourth century, nor any of a number of prominent Jewish scholars of the fifth century ever refer to the vowel markings even though they discuss vocalizations of the consonants at length. Today most scholars are convinced that the vowel markings were initiated by the Masoretes.

Scribal instructions

A book written in the eighth or ninth century, *The Tractate of the Scribes*, outlines rules and rituals a Masorete scribe must follow in copying scripture. They include ritual bathing and preparation of special parchment and writing tools. In addition, before writing the Hebrew word for God, he was required to say, 'I am writing the name of God for the holiness of his name.'

'So now, Israel, give heed to the statutes and ordinances that I am teaching you to observe, so that you may live to enter and occupy the land that the Lord, the God of your ancestors, is giving you. You must neither add anything to what I command you nor take away anything from it, but keep the commandments of the Lord your God with which I am charging you.'

MOSES IN DEUTERONOMY 4:1–2

In the middle of it all

Preserving an ancient tradition, a group of scribes called the Masoretes counted the number of words and letters in the Pentateuch (the first five books of the Bible that contain the Mosaic law). They faithfully indicated both the word (in Leviticus 13:33) and the letter (in Leviticus 11:42) at the exact centre of the Pentateuch.

A Bible for Warriors

Visigothic foot soldier with helmet, chain mail and spear. Illustration from the Monastery Santo Domingo de Silos in Spain – one of three countries where the converted warrior people settled.

Missionary translators

Ulfilas's creation of a Gothic alphabet – so he could translate the Bible into what was previously only a spoken language – opened the door to literature for Germanic people. Later missionaries did the same for other people, such as the Slavs. Today, this work continues around the world, especially in parts of Africa, Latin America and the Pacific Islands.

Page from a ninth-century Visigoth Bible, written in the Gothic alphabet invented by Ulfilas, the bishop to the Goths, in the fourth century.

In the first centuries after Jesus, when Christians were still debating which writings to include in the New Testament, a fierce, warfaring group of Germanic tribes along the Roman frontier could not have cared less. They were the Visigoths, meaning 'West Goths'. They knew little, if anything, about Christianity. And they did not even have a written language. Gothic existed only as spoken words. That would change – and the Goths would end up with a written language as well as a Gothic Bible – because of their raids into Roman territory.

The Goths migrated south from Sweden and settled in Dacia in what is now Romania, just north of the River Danube. With this region as their new homeland and base of operations in the AD 200s, they launched raids into Roman lands – and by 410 would sack Rome itself.

On one of their early raids, into what is now Turkey, they captured a Christian woman who

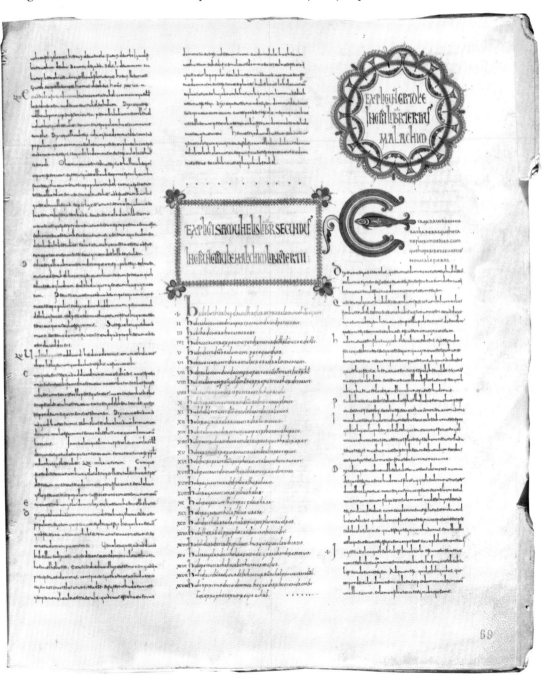

married a Goth. The son of this couple would bring the Goths Christianity as well as the Bible – written in their own language with an alphabet invented just for this purpose.

ULFILAS, THE LITTLE WOLF

Born in about AD 311, this child was given a warrior's name: Ulfilas (also translated as Wulfila), which means 'Little Wolf'. But instead of becoming a warrior, he became a minister.

For reasons unknown, when he was about 30 years old he went to the eastern capital of Rome: Constantinople, in what is now Istanbul, Turkey. Some speculate he went there as a hostage or perhaps as an ambassador on an assignment to meet the Roman emperor. Whatever the reason, he came home with a new title: bishop to the Goths. He was consecrated by Eusebius, the newly appointed Patriarch of Constantinople. Eusebius was an Arian, which was then a popular movement in Christianity that insisted Jesus was less than equal with God the Father – a movement later condemned as heresy. Whether or not Ulfilas was influenced by Eusebius, he proved himself a staunch Arian who made it his mission to take Arian Christianity back to his homeland.

Ulfilas ministered among the Goths for perhaps seven or eight years. But by 348, he and his followers were persecuted by unbelieving Goths. Ulfilas asked for and received the Roman emperor's permission to bring his congregation across the Danube River into Roman territory, where they settled in Moesia in what is now Bulgaria.

INVENTING AN ALPHABET

It was here that Ulfilas began the work for which he is most famous. For the last 30 years of his life, he translated the Bible into Gothic. But before he could start, he had to create a Gothic alphabet. He knew that neither of the two most common languages of the day would work: Greek and Latin (the language of Rome). So he mixed and matched. He chose from each of these alphabets the letters that corresponded to Gothic speech sounds. What he ended up with were 27 letters in the Gothic alphabet. Nineteen or twenty came from Greek. Five or six came from Latin. And two others were either invented or borrowed from runes, an ancient alphabet that some German peoples used.

Scholars do not agree about how much of the Bible Ulfilas translated. Philostorgius, a church historian from the 400s, said Ulfilas translated 'all the books of scripture with the exception of the Books of Kings [1, 2 Samuel and 1, 2 Kings], which he omitted because they are a

From Sweden to Spain

The Visigoths, who came from Sweden in the first centuries AD, gradually migrated south through Europe and then west. In the 400s, after defeating the Roman empire, they settled in what is now Spain, Portugal and southern France. With them they took the Christian faith they had been taught by the missionary, Ulfilas.

mere narrative of military exploits, and the Gothic tribes were especially fond of war, and were in more need of restraints to check their military passions than of spurs to urge them on to deeds of war.'

Yet there is no complete Gothic Bible to back up this claim. Ulfilas's original Bible was lost, perhaps burned in fires that the Church later ordered to destroy Arian writings. The oldest surviving Gothic Bibles are copies from the 400s and 500s, none of which is even nearly complete. Only a few chapters of the Old Testament remain, but there are larger portions of the Gospels and nearly all of Paul's letters. The most cherished copy is the *Codex Argenteus*, on display at the University of Uppsala in Sweden. It contains much of the Gospels, and was written in silver and gold letters on purple parchment.

These Bible fragments are the only known record of the Gothic language, which is now extinct. What the fragments reveal is that Ulfilas translated the Old Testament from the Septuagint Greek translation instead of the original Hebrew, and the New Testament from the original Greek.

When Ulfilas died aged about 70, in 382, most Goths were still unbelievers. But his followers continued the work, and Christianity spread throughout the Germanic tribes. By the time the Goths captured Rome, about 30 years later, even the Gothic king professed his faith in Christ.

'It was largely due to the work of Ulfilas that these plunderers [the Visigoths] became peacemakers.'

JAARS, A BIBLE TRANSLATION MINISTRY

Oldest Germanic writing

Copies of Ulfilas's Gothic Bible are the oldest surviving documents of any Germanic language. The Gothic alphabet was invented for the Bible, and the Bible was its first literature.

Capital showing Daniel in the lions' den, from San Pedro de la Nave, Campillo – one of the oldest Visigoth churches left in Spain, where many of the converted warrior people settled.

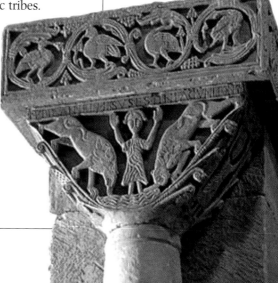

The Bible Goes East

❖ THE BIBLE IN A RAPIDLY GROWING CHURCH ❖

'O God, who has created heaven and earth, look down... on this your new people, and grant them, O Lord, to know you as true God, just as other Christian nations have come to know you.'

RUSSIAN PRINCE VLADIMIR
(AD 956–1015)

Brutal prince converts

Russian Prince Vladimir of Kiev, in what is now the Ukraine, was known for his brutality and is said to have taken part in human sacrifices. But in the late 900s he agreed to convert to Christianity for the privilege of marrying the sister of the Byzantine emperor. The prince became a changed man. He banned capital punishment, destroyed idols and built churches. Christianity became the state religion in a vast territory that stretched north to the Baltic Sea and east into Russia. Translations of the Bible and church rituals into the native Slavonic language helped the faith spread quickly.

Beyond the eastern border of the Roman empire was a tiny region that became the world's first Christian kingdom: Armenia. This tiny, landlocked nation lies just east of what is now Turkey, and north of Iran. At least a decade before the Roman emperor Constantine embraced Christianity and made it the empire's favoured religion in AD 313, the king of Armenia and members of his court became Christians – and the people of the nation began to follow suit.

One big problem for the Armenian believers, however, was the Bible. For a century, they did not have one in their native language. Some of the people spoke Greek and Syrian, especially in the villages, where travellers passed through. Greek and Syrian versions of the Bible were used in Armenian worship services – so much so that Greek and Syrian were starting to be considered 'Christian' languages.

This posed both a religious and a political problem. It was a religious problem because many people – especially those living outside villages – did not use those foreign languages, and could not understand the Christian writings when they were read. And it was a political problem because as the nation became increasingly Christian, the people gradually started moving away from their native Armenian language and towards the foreign, 'Christian' languages. That was a step away from national consciousness and towards assimilation into other cultures.

AN ARMENIAN BIBLE

There was a solution for both problems: create a Bible in the Armenian language. Unfortunately, as was the case in many eastern kingdoms outside the Roman empire, the Armenians had only a spoken language. In more ancient times, there apparently had been a written language, but it was lost.

In about 404, Mesrop, an Armenian monk who had studied the classical languages, decided to create an alphabet so he could translate the Bible into Armenian. With the blessing of the bishop of the Armenian church as well as the king, Mesrop began his work. Over the next year, he developed an alphabet of 36 letters, using as his model the 24-letter Greek alphabet. With his new alphabet, Mesrop could reproduce in writing the spoken sounds of Armenian.

Mesrop set out to translate the Old and New Testaments, a process that took about five years, with the help of a team of translators. Mesrop himself took responsibility for a large share of the work: the entire New Testament as well as

This mural depicting saints is in an 11th-century church in Georgia, on the tomb of Georgian King Marian. Seven hundred years earlier, a slave brought Christianity to this kingdom by converting King Mesrop, who then created an alphabet for translating the Bible into Georgian.

Proverbs. It is unclear what documents were used to make the translation. Some scholars today suggest they worked from Syrian copies of the Bible. Whichever language the translators used as a main source, Mesrop decided to refine the Armenian version they initially produced. He sent some of his colleagues on a search abroad for other copies of the Bible. They came back with Greek manuscripts, which Mesrop used to revise the initial work. What Mesrop produced has been called 'the queen of translations': a description that works on two levels. First, linguists consider it an excellent work; and secondly, historians say that by establishing a written language for the Armenians, Mesrop helped unite the nation – just as a queen could do.

In the years that followed, Mesrop started schools to teach people how to read and write Armenian. He also led the Church in developing books of liturgy, such as the rituals of baptism, communion, marriage, ordination and funerals.

TWO MORE ALPHABETS

Christianity followed a similar track in Armenia's neighbouring kingdoms to the north (Georgia) and east (Caucasian Albania, in what is now Azerbaijan). In Georgia, a captured slave in about AD 330 converted the king to Christianity – and the nation followed the king's example. Caucasian Albania was also practising Christianity at the time, as evidenced by surviving churches built during that era.

Surprisingly, it was Mesrop who created alphabets for both of these kingdoms. During missionary travels into Georgia, Mesrop created a 38-letter alphabet for translating the Bible and church rituals into Georgian. Though it is uncertain when the translation work started and who did the work, the Bible drew on Mesrop's alphabet. While in his sixties, Mesrop travelled to Caucasian Albania, where he created a third alphabet that was used to translate the Albanian Bible.

Mesrop died in 440, at about the age of 80. He left behind not only the three alphabets, the Armenian Bible and rituals, but also a collection of Bible commentaries, translations of the writings of the Church Fathers and hymns.

Today, citizens of Georgia still use the Bible in their native language, as do the Armenians. The Albanian Bible, however, did not survive. It disappeared – with the Albanian Church – during the Islamic invasions of the 600s. As Islam spread throughout the Middle East, Christianity moved north, taking the Bible with it to what is now central Europe and Russia.

Cyril and Methodius

'Many Christians have arrived in our midst… We pray you to send us someone capable of teaching us the whole truth.' This was the plea of the prince of Moravia (now Slovakia), in a letter he wrote in AD 862 to church leaders in Constantinople. German missionaries had been working in this Slavonic-speaking land, but with little success. They led the church rituals and Bible readings in Latin, a language most Slavs did not understand.

Cyril and Methodius, brothers and highly educated priests from Thessalonica, Greece, were sent on this goodwill mission. Cyril developed a Slavonic alphabet and began translating the Bible and some church rituals into the native tongue. The people loved worshipping in their own language. But the German missionaries opposed this practice. They held the traditional view, saying that since the sign on Jesus' cross was written in Hebrew, Greek and Latin, these should be the only languages used in church. The Germans appealed to the pope, who sided with the brothers. A second appeal to a later pope produced this papal response: 'We rightly praise the Slavonic letters invented by Cyril in which praises to God are set forth… for he who created the three principal languages, Hebrew, Greek and Latin, also made the others for his praise and glory.'

Cyril died of illness aged 42, but his brother completed the Slavonic Bible. After Methodius's death 15 years later, a new pope banned the use of the Slavonic language in church, forcing followers of the brothers to leave the country. They scattered throughout eastern Europe, taking their Slavonic language, Bible and liturgy into many neighbouring regions, including what is now Bulgaria, Yugoslavia, Romania and Russia. The two missionary brothers had laid the foundation for the Church in Slavonic Europe.

When the pope banned the use of the Slavonic language in Moravia during worship, many Slavonic-speaking Christians moved to neighbouring regions, taking their Slavonic Bibles with them.

A Bulgarian icon of St Cyril and St Methodius, Greek priests who produced a Slavonic Bible for people in what is now the Czech Republic, Slovakia, Bosnia-Herzegovina, Croatia, Yugoslavia, Bulgaria, Romania and Russia.

Mystics, Monks and the Bible

'Let us stand to sing the psalms in such a way that our minds are in harmony with our voices.'

THE RULE OF ST BENEDICT

Fifteenth-century illumination from the Psalter of Henry VII of England, showing monks in their stalls.

Early hermits – including those from the time of Jerome and Augustine – deliberately left society and went out into the desert or some other out-of-the-way place. There they led lives of prayer and fasting, seeking to devote themselves to God's word as revealed in the Bible. Few of these men and women owned Bibles and fewer still could read, but they regularly recited scripture passages from memory. Later, as these hermits began to group together into communities and move out of the desert into monasteries, their lives took on more structure and the written word became ever more important.

Rules devised for monks to live by were based on the Rule composed by the fourth-century Egyptian hermit Pachomius. The most influential Rule in the Western Church was written by Benedict of Nursia, abbot of the great Italian monastery of Monte Cassino, in about 575. Benedict's Rule, which stresses a life of work and prayer, is still followed today both in its original form and in dozens of variations, by monks and nuns.

LIFE OF A MONK

Under the Benedictine Rule – and its many variants – men lived together in community, pledging total obedience to the abbot, or head of the monastery, who was elected by the monks. The monks' waking hours were divided between work and prayer. Many monasteries supported themselves by farming, so most of the monks spent their working hours in the fields. Others were assigned to take care of the daily running of the monastery, working as cooks or porters or bell ringers. In some monasteries, the monks made wine. Whatever the monks did, they did for the glory of God, and they considered their work to be a form of prayer.

Formal prayer was of two types, private and community. Every day the monks put aside time for private prayer, which included prayerful reading. The form of private prayer and the texts for sacred reading were left up to the individual monk. Their community prayer centred on the so-called Divine Office, which Benedict called the *opus Dei* ('work of God'). It was also known as the Office of the Hours because its hymns, prayers and sacred writings were sung, chanted and read at specific hours of each day.

Each of the 'hours' consisted of prayers and readings from scripture, especially the Psalms. Generally the monks chanted all 150 psalms in the course of a week. There were also prayers for the Church and the community and for the needs of the surrounding neighbourhood. In fact, at some point the monks took onto themselves the obligations of prayer and penance neglected by more lax Christians.

A total of eight 'hours' were set aside for

Lectio divina – a way of reading scripture

Like everything else in their lives, reading was a form of prayer for the monks. In his Rule, Benedict put aside several hours a day for sacred reading, using a method known as *lectio divina* ('divine reading'). This is a form of contemplative prayer in which the monk would slowly and carefully read a passage from the Bible or some other Christian text and then concentrate on its meaning in his own life. It was not merely reading for information. While engaged in *lectio divina* the monk was expected to try to understand the why and how of Christian life in order to be able to respond to what God was asking of him. Since simple contemplation is difficult to sustain, the monk read to spur his spiritual thinking, as the text supplied specific ideas for consideration. Meditation engages thought, imagination, emotion and desire, and so involves the entire person, not just the mind. While meditating on the life of Jesus as revealed in the Gospels – a favourite topic – a monk could better understand the immensity of Christ's love for humankind, and begin to understand how he himself might become more Christlike.

the Divine Office. Long before dawn, the monks rose, went to the chapel, and chanted the prayers and listened to the readings assigned for the hour called matins (or Vigils). Then they slept again and returned shortly before dawn for lauds (from the Latin for 'praise'). After lauds, the monks spent time studying the psalms and readings used in the Divine Office. They then returned to the chapel to chant prime (considered the first hour of the day). The monks then had breakfast and began their daily work. They stopped work to pray the hour of tierce (mid-morning), and then devoted more time to reading. They then returned to the chapel for the hour of sext (noon) followed by a meal, after which they were allowed to rest or read quietly until it was time for the hour of none (mid-afternoon). Another period of work followed, ending with vespers (evening). Before retiring, the monks chanted the final hour, compline. After completing compline they were not allowed to speak at all, beginning the daily period known as the great silence. The great silence lasted until the chanting of lauds in the pre-dawn hours of the next day.

PRESERVING SCRIPTURE

Because they needed books for their private readings and for chanting the office, some monks were assigned to copying manuscripts for use in the monastery. While the other monks laboured in the fields or the kitchen, these scribes bent over sacred texts and painstakingly copied what they saw onto fresh parchment pages. They copied Psalters (the book of Psalms) for use in chanting the Divine Office, books of the Gospels and sometimes entire Bibles. In addition, they copied lives of holy men and women, sermons and biblical commentaries. Most of these manuscripts

were kept for use in the monastery, but the monks also copied manuscripts for wealthy patrons.

Because of the time and hard work needed to copy a manuscript, a monastery's books were considered its most treasured possessions. Some of the larger monasteries in later times boasted of separate libraries in which they kept these treasures – although these libraries generally contained no more than a few hundred volumes. Often these libraries were equipped with shelves that were built between arches, forming cubicles, or cells, in which the monks could sit and read. These cells were furnished with shelves (often two or three together) that could hold several books at a time.

Although lay men and women also copied manuscripts in the later medieval period, most of this work was done by monks. Like the Jewish scribes of their time, the monks pursued their work with the utmost seriousness. Because of their care the accuracy of holy scripture has been preserved through the centuries, and today we can feel confident that the word of God has come to us in its true form.

'We believe that the divine presence is everywhere and that in every place the eyes of the Lord are watching the good and the wicked (Proverbs 15:3). But beyond the least doubt we should believe this to be especially true when we celebrate the Divine Office.'

THE RULE OF ST BENEDICT

St Benedict Praying with His Monks by Sodoma (16th century).

A Bible-based Rule

The Benedictine Rule is filled with citations from the Bible. Rarely does Benedict make a point without backing it up with scripture.

Life as a Monastic Scribe

'If anyone take this book away, may he die the death, may he be fried in a pan, may the falling sickness and fever afflict him, may he be broken on the wheel and hanged.'

SCRIBAL NOTATION AT THE END OF A MANUSCRIPT

Bibles in parts

Before the 13th century, complete Bibles were rare. They were too time-consuming and too expensive to copy, and the resulting work was enormous, fit only to be read from a lectern. Instead, parts of the Bible were copied and bound together, such as the Pentateuch (the first five books of the Bible), the Psalms, the Prophets and – especially – the Gospels. In the 13th century, portable, compactly written Bibles appeared and quickly became popular.

The life of a monastic scribe was not easy. Between the times of required prayer and spiritual reading he spent long hours preparing parchment pages, making his own pens and ink, and laboriously copying texts. Working conditions were not good. The scribe spent hours on end in a cramped position and had to strain his eyes to see the manuscript he was copying. In the winter, he worked in the freezing cold. Fires for warmth and candles for better light were forbidden because the parchments they were working on were flammable and too valuable to be burned. The monk's comfort was secondary to the preservation of the manuscripts.

A scribe worked under the watchful eye of an overseer, who generally assigned the texts a monk would copy and kept a close eye on him as he worked, making sure he did not break any of the stringent rules imposed on scribes. A monk who produced a page of dirty parchment, wasted materials, or took another scribe's parchment was in trouble. His punishment for breaking the rules was meted out in deprivations or extra duties known as penances. The number of penances determined the type of punishment, including extra prayer or extra work. For severe lapses, such as neglecting his work, a scribe might be put on a bread-and-water diet.

GETTING READY

Once he was assigned a text to copy, a scribe began his work by preparing his parchment and writing tools. The parchment was made by the monks themselves, if their monastery raised animals, or acquired from a professional parchment maker. The scribe prepared the parchment by trimming it to size, smoothing its surface with pumice and rubbing it with chalk to remove any oil. This process would keep the ink from running. The scribe then added ruled lines to the page to guide his hand in copying. Horizontal lines helped the monk keep his writing straight, vertical lines marked the margins, and other lines cordoned off space for illustrations and decorations, which would be added later.

The monks had to make their own pens and ink. To make a pen the scribe selected a dried and hardened feather – preferably from a goose or swan. He then used a sharp knife to shape the tip of the feather, creating a sharp point and then flattening it slightly and cutting a slot in the centre. The end result resembled the nib of a modern fountain pen or the pens used for calligraphy. The pens did not hold their shape for long when in use and had to be sharpened

Charlemagne's scholar, Alcuin

The Anglo-Saxon monk Alcuin was a brilliant scholar and writer, and an innovator in the field of education at the time of Charlemagne. He was born in York in about 735 and died in Tours, France, in 804. In 767, he became head of the episcopal school at York, England, where he had received his own education. While on a journey to Rome in 780 he met Charlemagne, who persuaded him to join his court at Parma the following year. There Alcuin brought order to the educational system. He was a prolific writer, producing works on grammar, mathematics, philosophy and religion. He also wrote poetry and more than 300 letters, including many to Charlemagne. In addition, he revised the liturgy of the Frankish church, wrote biblical commentaries, and produced a revision of the Vulgate Bible.

In 796, Charlemagne appointed Alcuin abbot of the monastery of St Martin in Tours, France. There he supervised the scriptorium, making it the most productive in all of Europe. One of the reasons for increased productivity was the development of a new lettering style. Early manuscripts had been written in large capital letters, called majuscules. These letters were unconnected to the letters that preceded and followed, forcing the scribe to lift his pen after writing each letter. This slowed the writing down and took up a lot of space, resulting in bulky manuscripts requiring more parchment, which was costly. Earlier in the eighth century a new style of lettering called minuscule had come into use, and Alcuin is credited with perfecting it. In minuscule, the letters were connected and a scribe could write without stopping to lift his hand and begin again with each letter. Consequently, Carolingian minuscule, as Alcuin's version of the script is called, quickly became the standard script for European scribes.

constantly and replaced frequently. According to one report a scribe needed to prepare between 60 and 100 pens for a day's work.

There were a number of ways to make ink. The most common method of producing black ink – especially in the early centuries – was to mix charcoal or soot with plant gum or sap. Vermilion (red) ink was made from ground cinnabar, or mercury sulphide, which often occurs in volcanic veins in igneous rocks. This ink was used for chapter headings, titles, initials and any other writing that was not part of the actual text. Because they were written in this red colour, these extratextual materials were called rubrics (from the Latin for red). The inks were poured into pots or horns for use.

COPYING A MANUSCRIPT

When he was ready to start his actual copying, the scribe placed one of the prepared parchment pages on his work surface with the master text (the book he was to copy) alongside it. He also draped a weighted string across the master text to help keep his place as he copied it. A scribe generally sat at a slanted desk because the slanted surface helped him keep his pen perpendicular to the parchment page. He then crouched over his work and carefully copied the master text. He held the pen in one hand and a knife in the other, using the knife to sharpen the pen and scrape away any errors he made.

Copying was intense, exhausting work that was hard on the eyes and on the muscles of the neck and back. The scribe worked slowly, being sure his work was accurate, as any error he made might be picked up by future copyists. It was also an act of devotion for the monk, who accepted the biblical texts as the word of God, which should be rendered perfectly.

After the scribe had completed his work, he carefully proofread it and corrected any errors. A page with serious flaws was recopied. Repeated words, however, might be crossed out or under-lined with dots, or enclosed between the syllables of the Latin word *vacat* ('void'), which indicated that anything between 'va' and 'cat' should be ignored. Omitted words or phrases might be written in the margins or squeezed in above the place they belonged.

Corrections were not the only writings in the margins. Often the scribe added notes about the text and sometimes even personal notes, often complaints. In some cases, curses were penned, wishing harm to anyone who might damage, destroy or steal the manuscript he had worked so hard to copy. The completed manuscript, after all, represented a significant part of his life's work. It was also his personal prayer of praise to God. The high degree of accuracy in the old manuscripts shows how seriously the monastic scribes took their work. They had every right to be proud of it.

Part of a 13th-century French illustration showing an illuminator and a scribe.

Illuminating a Manuscript

'We, who are a light to faithful souls everywhere, fall prey to painters knowing naught of letters, and are entrusted to goldsmiths to become, as though we were not sacred vessels of wisdom, repositories of gold leaf.'

'COMPLAINT OF THE BOOKS' IN *PHILOBIBLION* BY RICHARD OF BURY, BISHOP OF DURHAM

The earliest Christian manuscripts contained only words and had no illustrations or decorations. Although these manuscripts were beautiful in their own way, they were somewhat off-putting to the reader who was not a dedicated scholar. To draw the reader into a text, scribes began to add visual elements. In time, these elements became more and more elaborate and even used thin sheets of gold and (more rarely) silver to brighten the page. The light reflected by the gold or silver lit up the page, or 'illuminated' it. For this reason, manuscripts with gold or silver came to be known as illuminated. At first only manuscripts with these precious metals were considered to be illuminated, but today any lavishly decorated manuscript is labelled as such.

DEVELOPMENT OF ILLUMINATION

The very earliest book illustrations were on Egyptian papyrus scrolls from the second millennium BC, or even earlier. The most famous of these works is the Book of the Dead with its illustrations of funerals and judgment scenes. No illustrated books survive after that time until the second century AD when Greek and Roman manuscripts included chronologically arranged scenes depicted in the text. The scenes were generally framed and often filled a page.

This illustrated Bible manuscript from the late 13th century shows the rules that were used for guidance when writing the text.

Christians started illuminating their manuscripts sometime in the fourth century. The early manuscripts reflected some of the elements found in Roman manuscripts. One of those elements – placing a portrait of the author at the beginning of each book – was carried over into books of the Gospels. The appropriate evangelist is depicted on the first page of each Gospel, a practice that continued throughout the history of illumination. As time went on the illuminations became ever more diverse and elaborate. They ranged from tiny decorative elements to full-page paintings. The margins were also sometimes filled with elaborate designs or scenes from the Bible.

Then, in the sixth and seventh centuries, the art of manuscript illumination declined as barbaric German tribes swooped down from the north and conquered much of Europe, decimating their culture. Unaffected by these invasions, however, Ireland and northern England continued to practise and develop the art of illumination.

In the late eighth century, book illumination again flourished in northern France and western Germany, as part of the cultural renaissance initiated by the emperor Charlemagne, who encouraged the increase of culture in his court, bringing in scholars from the British Isles and all over Europe. The renaissance continued in the ninth century under Charlemagne's successors. During this period a series of luxurious Gospel manuscripts were created featuring monumental evangelist portraits and large, elaborately decorated or illustrated initial letters (the first letter of a book or section).

In the centuries that followed, the Carolingian era (the time of Charlemagne and his successors), manuscript illumination continued to develop, taking on characteristics that reflected the cultures of the lands and times in which they were created. By the 13th century, illumination was mostly taken over by secular artists working for book dealers or individual patrons. After the invention of movable type in the 15th century, illuminated manuscripts gradually gave way to printed books with engraved illustrations.

TOOLS AND MATERIALS USED FOR ILLUMINATION

Illuminators who were working on elaborate designs sought out the finest parchment in order to display their work better. Because such parchment was expensive to make or buy, however, they sometimes created their illustrations on small patches of fine parchment and glued them into place on a manuscript copied on inferior parchment. Unfortunately, these patches often became detached and lost.

Later illuminators worked on entire pages, composed entirely of artwork, which they later inserted into the completed manuscript.

A collection of various handmade pens and brushes, together with the all-important knife, were the illuninator's chief tools. He also needed

Illuminated manuscript page showing Saul and the Battle of Mount Gilboa.

a sharp metal or bone stylus – or in later times, a kind of graphite pencil – for sketching out designs. In addition to black ink, he needed inks of various colours. Pigments for these colours came from a variety of sources, which the monk generally obtained from an apothecary, pounded into powder and mixed with egg or some other sticky substance. Red ink was made from cinnabar or sometimes from brazil wood or madder plants, and green came from verdigris – oxidized copper – or from malachite. Yellow ink was made from saffron, and white from white lead. Blue inks were often made from azurite or the seed of the crozaphora plant, but the very finest blue colour – an ultramarine – came from the semi-precious stone lapis lazuli, which is found naturally only in Afghanistan.

If the page was to include gold, the illuminator had to make his own gold leaf by pounding a gold coin into extremely thin sheets – as thin as the paint that was to be applied later. The sheets of gold leaf were so thin and lightweight that they could be blown away if someone breathed in their direction. More than 100 sheets measuring a few inches square could be made from a single gold coin. To hold the leaf in place on the page, a type of glue called glair was needed. Glair was made by whipping egg white until it was stiff, and then letting it revert to a sticky liquid. If a three-dimensional effect was desired, the artist needed a plaster-like substance known as gesso to build up the surface where the gold was to go. Finally, a tool made from a smooth rock or tooth was needed to burnish the gold until it shimmered.

ILLUMINATING A PAGE

Except for the very simplest illuminated manuscripts, the same person was rarely responsible for both the text and the art. Generally, a separate artist or group of artists

Jewish illumination

Jewish illumination had a late start. Because Mosaic law forbade the decoration of the Torah (the first five books of the Bible), Jews were reluctant to use illuminations in any of their writings. However, after a time, books (though not the Torah scrolls used in synagogues) began to utilize illuminations, and by the 13th century, illuminated Jewish manuscripts were plentiful, originating in far-flung places from Europe to North Africa and the Near East. Biblical books from outside the Torah, even in scroll form, were often highly decorated, especially scrolls of the book of Esther.

Styles of illumination varied with the locale, but most shared some common elements. The earliest illuminations focused on implements from the temple sanctuary, such as the menorah (seven-branched candelabra), the ark of the covenant or the entrance to the temple. Soon biblical commentaries in Europe began to illustrate legends involving biblical figures, as in the Esther scrolls. Nevertheless, Jews were reluctant to represent the human figure, believing that it was in violation of the first commandment. In some manuscripts, human figures are shown, but they have the heads of birds or other animals. God is represented symbolically with a ray of light or an outstretched hand. Also common were elaborate pages filled with intricate geometric designs. They were known as carpet pages because they resembled the designs found in oriental carpets. Because Hebrew has no capital letters, instead of illuminating initial letters in their manuscripts, Jewish artists decorated the entire opening word of a text.

This 13th or 14th-century illumination from a Haggadah (a book used during the Jewish Passover meal to recount the story of Israel's exodus from Egypt) depicts a celebration inside a synagogue.

created the illuminations. As manuscripts became more elaborate so did the division of labour. Usually, the monastery's best artist was assigned to paint the most elaborate and important illuminations, while an assistant created the other pieces. If the manuscript contained geometric margin designs, a specialist in this type of painting might create those designs, leaving space for another artist to add animal or human figures. And the work of applying gold leaf was often assigned to a separate artist. Sometimes one artist created the overall design of a page and left the application of colours to others.

The first step in creating illuminations was making a rough design. Staying within the areas blocked off by the scribe as he copied the text, an artist would block out the design using a sharp stylus, and then he would go over the outline with thin ink to 'crisp up' the design. Then he polished the areas inside the design to prepare them for decoration.

If the illumination was to include gold leaf, it was applied at this point, as burnishing the gold might damage the colours if they were done first. First, the artist brushed a thin layer of glair on the area to be covered with gold, in order to make it adhere to the page. Then he cut a piece of foil to the size needed, carefully picked it up with a flat brush, or the moistened handle of a brush, and positioned it on the page. Once the gold was all in position for a design, the artist burnished it with a special tool to bring out the lustre of the metal and seal it into place. Finally, the artist outlined the gold area with ink to smooth out any ragged edges and redefine the design.

The final major step in creating an illumination was adding the colour. If a number of artists were involved in the work, the chief artist or scribe sometimes indicated the colours desired for an area by adding a note or a daub of ink of the desired colour. The artist added the colours one at a time and layer by layer to create various tones and shadings. Sometimes, while waiting for one layer of ink to dry on one illumination the artist would move to another page, add a layer of colour to a different illumination, and then go back to the first. When all the colours had been added to an illumination, the artist highlighted the design with white ink.

When all the artists' work was done, the page that emerged was truly a work of art. Not only did the art work illuminate the page and draw the reader into the text; it illuminated the souls of whoever saw it. In a very beautiful way, it illuminated the word of God.

This initial letter 'A' incorporates an illustration of Belshazzar's feast, from the book of Daniel. From the English Winchester Bible, mid-12th century.

This initial letter 'B' begins a Psalter from the former monastery of Suben, Upper Austria.

Luxury Bible Covers

Bibles from medieval and Renaissance times did not usually come bound and covered. People paid extra for that. They picked up their Bible at the printer's shop and took it to a binder, sometimes in another town.

Some Bibles were not bound at all, but were merely wrapped in a protective covering, such as leather, and tied closed with a cord. Others were meticulously stitched together to form bound books covered with hardback masterpieces of intricate art – covers of fine leather with delicate artwork stamped or tooled into it, ivory sculptures, or thin gold plates etched in lacy patterns and studded with jewels. Artistry was limited only by the budget of the book owner and the skill of the artisan. For many of the wealthy, cost was no factor – they wanted nothing less than the best possible cover to encase the words of God.

The art and business of bookbinding developed in Egyptian monasteries in the second century AD. Monks took folded sheets of papyrus or parchment and attached them to other folded sheets by sewing them together. Then they put the stitched stack into protective leather-covered boards and tied them together, much as we might drop a stack of papers into a cardboard file folder and hold it all together with a rubber band.

In the Middle Ages, bookbinding rose to a high art that featured exquisite bindings – producing books that were the pride of their owners, just as they are now the pride of museums and book collectors. Monks, and later artisans, began the process of binding by stacking folded sheets of the Bible in order. Then they stitched these 'gatherings' with cord. Ends of the leftover cords were tied to what were often oak boards that provided the book's protective cover.

Surviving books show that the plain wood covers were decorated in a wide variety of ways. Some front covers became the showcase of a wood carving. Most were covered in fine leather, etched with intriguing patterns, floral motifs or some other artwork. Some covers were inset with ivory plaques carved with Bible scenes, such as the crucifixion. Others were carefully plated with thin layers of gold, silver or brass. Yet others were draped in embroidered cloth. Often, artisans combined several techniques, such as setting an ivory scene in a dazzling frame of precious metals and brilliant gemstones.

Royalty and other wealthy donors sometimes ordered luxury Bibles such as these and presented them as gifts to churches and monasteries. These treasures were often stored in the church treasury with other valuables such as ritual vessels, and were brought out only for services. Even then, the Bibles were sometimes chained to pillars so no one would run off with them.

By the 1500s, when the printing press entered the scene and generated more books for less money, lower-income people started buying books. They could not usually afford the elegant cover artwork, so the covers became simpler, lighter and more practical – making Bibles less a showpiece and more a source of guidance and inspiration.

Ornate cover of a Gospel book, *Brevarium Magdeburgense*, the pouch book of Princess Margarete von Anhalt (who died in 1530).

The Bible Comes to Britain

A Bible for battle

An Irish copy of the Psalms, from the 500s, is one of the oldest surviving Bible manuscripts from the British Isles. The book was called the *Cathach*, or 'Battle Book', because the clan of O'Donnell is said to have carried it into battle three times to spur them to victory.

❦

'I saw the God of hosts violently stretched out. Darkness with its clouds had covered the Lord's corpse.'

EXTRACT FROM 'THE DREAM OF THE ROOD', AN ANGLO-SAXON POEM IN WHICH THE ROOD, OR CROSS, TELLS OF CHRIST'S DEATH

Illumination of Mark the evangelist from the *Lindisfarne Gospels*, which were copied and illuminated by Bishop Eadfrith of Lindisfarne around the start of the eighth century.

A medieval legend says Christianity arrived in the British Isles when Joseph of Arimathea – the man who buried Jesus – came on a mission to convert the people. The legend adds that Joseph brought the holy grail, the communion cup Jesus used at the last supper. Unfortunately, there is no evidence to support any of this.

A more likely account is the one reported by the eighth-century British monk and historian, the Venerable Bede, whose *History of the English Church and People* is known for its detail and accuracy. Bede said Christianity arrived in AD 156, about a century after the Romans invaded. Lucius, one of the British kings, wrote to the bishop of Rome, 'asking to be made a Christian by his direction'. The king apparently wanted his conversion to be directed by the highest official in the Church (bishops of Rome later came to be known as popes). By the 300s, church scholar and Bible translator Jerome was able to report that 'Britain in common with Rome, Gaul [or France], Africa, Persia, the East and India adores one Christ.'

Pope Gregory (540–604), who sent a missionary team of 40 monks to Britain. Ivory panel.

WHEN CHRISTIANITY LEFT

Sadly, just as Christianity had arrived with the Romans, it also left with them – at least to a great extent. Rome recalled its armies to fight a doomed war to protect the empire against invaders. Roman soldiers had occupied the south-eastern area of the British island (now England and Wales), protecting Britons from raiders in the north and west, in what is now Ireland and Scotland. But Rome's sudden withdrawal left Britain defenceless. For protection, the Britons in 449 appealed to three Germanic, or northern European, tribes famed for their fighting ability: Jutes along with Angles and Saxons (Anglo-Saxons). True to their reputation, these fierce warriors drove off the attackers. But then they turned on the Britons. Bede said the former saviours 'established a stranglehold over nearly all the doomed island', imposing their culture, language and Norse religion on the Latin-speaking, Christ-loving Britons.

About 150 years later, Pope Gregory decided to send missionaries there. Legend says that

---

Two ancient Gospels of Britain

Two of the most famous Bible texts from ancient times are from the British Isles. They are the *Book of Kells* and the *Lindisfarne Gospels*.

The *Book of Kells* is a lavishly illustrated, colourful collection of the four Gospels, and is thought to be the work of four men. Possibly created by Irish or Scottish monks during the 700s, it contains some of the most beautiful calligraphy from the Middle Ages. On just about every page with text there are detailed illustrations, often elaborate initial letters and pictures of animals and people. The pictures reflect the style of art in medieval Ireland, Scotland and northern England. Unfortunately, the attention the monks gave to the artwork did not extend to the Latin text, which is full of mistakes.

The *Lindisfarne Gospels* is another beautifully illustrated copy of the four Gospels, written in Latin in about 700 to commemorate a former bishop of Lindisfarne, a tiny island off the north-eastern coast of England.

There are 259 pages in this book, each of which is made of vellum, the finest grade of animal skins.

A note added to the book about 250 years later says the volume was copied and illustrated by Eadfrith, who was bishop of Lindisfarne, serving from 698 until he died in 721. But the copying of text as well as the painting of many detailed illustrations – which drew heavily on Irish, Viking and Anglo-Saxon motifs – may have been the work of a team of English monks, perhaps under the supervision of Eadfrith at the Lindisfarne monastery. The Latin text was translated into Anglo-Saxon in the 900s, with the new text – presented in a literal, word-for-word translation – inserted above each of the original lines. This became the first known translation of the Gospels into any form of English.

when Gregory once saw some blonde, light-skinned boys at a slave auction and asked who they were, he was told they were Angles. 'Not Angles,' he replied, 'but angels.' Gregory sent to Britain a team of about 40 monks with a supply of books, probably including at least one copy of the Bible in Latin.

Bede reports the monks 'began to imitate the way of life of the apostles', preaching, praying and living simple lives. Their mission was a huge success, perhaps aided by the fact that the wife of Jute ruler Ethelbert, king of Kent, was already a Christian who employed a bishop as her personal religious guide. The monks eventually converted the king, followed by thousands more Jutes, Angles and Saxons. To continue their ministry, the monks were given a home in Canterbury, and their leader – Augustine – became the first archbishop of Canterbury.

BIBLE BEGINNINGS IN BRITAIN

How and when the Bible first made its appearance in the British Isles remains a mystery. Christian monks had been ministering in Ireland and parts of Scotland uninterrupted by the Anglo-Saxons, who were unable to conquer them. These monks probably had copies of sacred Christian literature early in the British Christian movement.

In 597, Pope Gregory launched his Britain missionary endeavour. Within 75 years part of the Latin Bible was being translated into Anglo-Saxon, an ancient English dialect known as Old English. This began in the 600s, with a song. According to Bede, an illiterate cowherd named Caedmon had a vision to sing of 'the beginning of created things'. The result was a hymn that praised God for creation. Monks, impressed by the song, taught Caedmon stories from the Bible, which he crafted into Anglo-Saxon lyrics and set to music.

About this time, Anglo-Saxon notes and translations began appearing above the main text in Latin Bibles. This helped priests in Britain because as the Latin language of the defunct Roman empire waned, fewer priests in the islands understood it.

Although it was not until the 1300s that the entire Bible was translated into English, there were many earlier translations of parts of the Bible into ancient English dialects. King Alfred the Great, in the 800s, is said to have translated parts of Exodus, Psalms and Acts into Anglo-Saxon – incorporating parts of biblical law into his kingdom law. About a century later, an English monk named Aelfric created a shortened translation of the first seven books of the Old Testament. A short time later, an unknown scholar also translated the Gospels.

By the time the Normans invaded in 1066, temporarily imposing the French language on the people of the British Isles, Bible scholars had made considerable progress in translating the Bible into their own language.

England was Angle-land

In the early fifth century, tribes from northern Europe – most notably the Angles and Saxons, or Anglo-Saxons – invaded the island the Romans had called Britannia (Latin for 'Britain') and settled there. These invaders so dominated part of the island that this area became known as Angle-land, or England.

This ornamental page begins Luke's Gospel in the *Lindisfarne Gospels*.

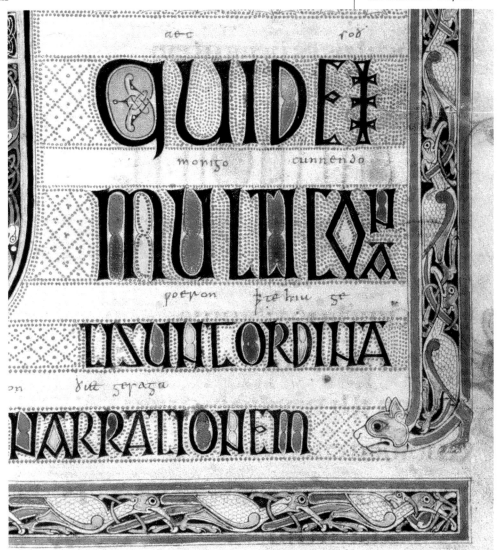

Irish Monks Make Their Mark

From the fifth to the eighth century Europe was overrun by barbarian Germanic tribes, who destroyed many manuscripts and succeeded in almost completely wiping out European civilization as it had been known up until then. The Irish, however, were untouched and Irish monks continued to copy biblical texts and other theological and secular works.

THE CHRISTIANIZING OF IRELAND

When the barbarian invasions of western Europe

Columba and his heritage

A man of fierce determination, the Irish monk Columba always accomplished what he set out to do – and often more. He was born in Ireland in 521 of a princely family, and might have had a chance of becoming a king. Instead, he became a monk. But he had a great love of books, and this got him into trouble. When he heard that his former teacher, Finian, had Ireland's first copy of Jerome's Latin translation of Psalms, Columba 'borrowed' it without permission and copied it.

began, Ireland was still a rural land of farmers and warriors with no knowledge of how to read or write, although they had a brilliant oral tradition of literature. But then, in about 401, a young Briton named Patrick was captured and brought to Ireland as a slave. Six years later Patrick escaped and went to Gaul, which was already under assault by barbarians. He studied at a monastery there – especially scripture – and returned to Ireland as a missionary. Over the next 29 years he succeeded in converting most

on to the pain of this humiliation. Soon after, when one of his men was killed by command of the king, Columba gathered an army and went to war with the king. He won, killing 3,001 of the king's men, but losing only one of his own – and recovering the Psalter.

Because monks were forbidden to take up arms, Columba was excommunicated for a time, then given a heavy penance. He must leave Ireland and save as many souls as were killed in his war with the king. Fired with determination to complete his penance, Columba set out with 12 other men in 564 (about a century after Patrick's death) and sailed to the island of Iona, off the coast of the land now known as Scotland. There he built a monastery, which quickly became famous as a centre of learning. It was on Iona that the *Book of Kells* was created. Columba also worked at converting the local Scots and Picts. His converts flocked to Iona, and when the monastery reached capacity (150 monks), Columba sent some of the monks out to establish another monastery, and then another. In this way, by the time of his death in 597, Columba had established 60 monasteries across the face of Scotland – minstering to far more than the 3,001 souls he had set out to save.

The opening of St Adomnan's *Life of St Columba*, showing a list of bishops. Adomnan (627–704) was the abbot of Iona.

Angry, Finian took Columba to court and demanded the original as well as the copy. The judge granted Finian's request, saying, 'To every cow its calf; to every book its copy.'

Being an aristocrat to the bone, Columba held

of Ireland and in building many churches and monasteries. In the years after his death, more monasteries were built, and they became centres of learning. It was in those monasteries that the Irish learned to read.

In the century after Patrick, a particularly enterprising Irish monk, Columba, travelled to Scotland, where he established numerous monasteries and converted the local people. Following his example, other monks went into northern England, where they converted the Angles and built monasteries. The monasteries established by the Irish not only became havens for local people but also for many foreign monks, who were fleeing the barbarians in Europe. These European monks, well-versed in the ways of the Roman Church, helped raise the level of education for the Irish and their neighbours, while absorbing much of Ireland's own culture themselves.

CREATING A NEW STYLE

Throughout the sixth and seventh centuries, the monks of Ireland, Scotland and northern England worked hard at copying manuscripts in their many monasteries. Meanwhile such work came to a standstill in Europe, where few manuscripts were copied until the time of the emperor Charlemagne in the eighth century. But the Anglo-Irish scribes were not satisfied with simply imitating their European brothers. They boldly initiated changes in both writing style and illumination. The style of their manuscripts came to be known as 'insular' (meaning relating to an island) because they originated in the British Isles.

In the seventh century, the Anglo-Irish monks developed their own form of script, called insular majuscule, which can be seen in the *Book of Kells*. The most important aspect of this script remains with us today – separating the words in the text. Until that time all the words were jammed together, making it difficult to read. Before this script was developed, the monks had to read the texts they were copying aloud to understand them, and so they generally murmured to themselves as they worked. After the innovation of separating the words, however, reading aloud was unnecessary and the monks were required to work in total silence.

The illuminations in insular manuscripts are characterized by decorative embellishment rather than narrative illustration. A page of pure ornamentation called a carpet page precedes the text, and large initials, together with their frames and sometimes the parchment ground, are filled with intricate, densely packed decoration. The ornamentation is composed of spiral patterns, interlacing knotwork and intertwined animals. These motifs are based on Anglo-Saxon and Celtic

Part of an ornamental page from the third volume of the Irish *Book of Durrow* from the seventh century.

metalwork, which in turn was copied from stone engravings found in tombs in the Boyne Valley that date to the third millennium BC – about the time of Stonehenge.

The first masterpiece of insular illumination, the seventh-century Irish *Book of Durrow*, contains miniatures as well as carpet pages. Portraits of the four evangelists based on early Christian models but translated into the stylized insular idiom are also found in the *Lindisfarne Gospels*. A culmination was reached in the profusely decorated eighth-century *Book of Kells*, which has narrative illustrations in addition to portraits.

In time, the Anglo-Irish monks began to travel beyond the British Isles, and wherever they went, they brought their books. Consequently, the art of copying and illuminating manuscripts was revived in Europe, where Irish motifs were often copied, so that the insular style became incorporated into the older style of European manuscripts. Ironically, though, by the time European culture was re-established under Charlemagne, Ireland was being raided by Vikings, and the Irish had to hurry to hide some of their precious manuscripts, including the *Book of Kells* and the *Lindisfarne Gospels*.

Beehive huts

Early Irish monasteries were not big sprawling buildings like the ones in Europe. Rather, they were composed of a group of small beehive-shaped huts, or cells – one for each monk. There was also a chapel, a refectory (communal dining room) and a kitchen. Larger monasteries included other buildings needed for farming work, and perhaps a scriptorium and library. But monks were also known to copy manuscripts in their cells, or even outdoors.

Bibles for Europe

By the time the church scholar Jerome had got around to translating the Bible into Latin, the official language of the Romans, the Roman empire was on its last legs. Jerome finished his work in about AD 405. At that moment in history, Latin was the perfect language for the Bible in Europe. Latin was the language of choice for literature, and was widely understood, especially by people in cities.

Five years later, Rome was sacked by tribal warriors, and the empire was dead by the end of the century. Yet Latin lingered for several centuries, just as Greek had done earlier. Although fewer and fewer people spoke Latin, it remained the preferred language of the Church and the Bible. Unfortunately, this meant that in time, people were listening to Bible readings in church services without understanding a word.

Alba: the Jewish-Christian Bible

When a wave of anti-Jewish sentiment swept through Spain in the early 1400s, one church official came up with an idea for promoting understanding between Christians and Jews. Don Luis de Guzmán asked Rabbi Moses Arragel to translate the Hebrew Old Testament into Castilian Spanish, the common language of the day. Earlier Spanish translations, from the 1100s, were hard to understand, so there was a genuine need for a new translation. But there was also a need to ease the religious tensions, and Guzman thought this project might do that if the rabbi included commentary to help Christians understand the Jewish perspective on the life of faith.

The rabbi declined, saying he was afraid the Jewish view of the Old Testament was different enough from the Christian view that the clash might spark even more tension. Guzman eventually convinced the rabbi to comply, and assigned two monks to work with him. The result of this collaboration was a masterpiece, illustrated with 334 pictures and filled with commentary drawing on the wisdom of ancient Jewish rabbis.

Unfortunately, this Bible did not accomplish Guzman's goal. Completed in 1430, it was apparently scrutinized by church scholars for several years, probably until 1433, and then was passed along for examination by church scholars elsewhere, leading to public debate. In 1492, the Jews of Spain were forced to convert to Christianity or leave. Rabbi Arragel does not appear on the list of those who converted. The Alba Bible disappeared until it resurfaced in 1622 in the Spanish palace library of the Grand Duke of Alba. In 1922, the Duke of Alba commissioned 500 copies of the Alba Bible and presented them to the king in recognition of Jewish contributions to Spain.

In this scene from the Alba Bible, the translator Rabbi Moses Arragel presents the Bible to Don Luis de Guzmán, who commissioned it.

Eventually, even the less-educated priests did not understand the words they were reading from the Bible, or reciting in liturgies.

To communicate God's message in this new era, the nations needed to produce Bibles in their native languages. Beginning in the 600s, Europeans began to see at least parts of the Bible, especially the Gospels and Psalms, in their own languages. Translating the entire Bible was a monumental task, and there are no known copies of it in any European language before the 1200s.

At first, translators took tiny steps. They would copy the Latin Bible, and then add above each line notes that scholars call glosses. These could be explanatory notes, but were often word-for-word, literal translations of the Latin text. These glosses did not provide smoothly flowing prose. For example, the Latin phrase, 'Damnant quod non intelligent' is usually translated, 'They condemn what they do not understand.' A word-for-word translation would be, 'Condemn what not understand.'

BIBLES IN GERMAN AND FRENCH

In the late 900s and early 1000s, a German monk and teacher named Notker Labeo, who was equally proficient in Latin and German, began translating some Latin writings for his students. Among his many translations were the book of Psalms, which survives, and the book of Job, which Labeo said took him five years to complete, but which has been lost. In each of these, Labeo wrote a section of Latin scripture, followed by his German translation along with some of his comments about the passage.

Bibles were time-consuming and expensive to copy, so most people did not own one. Instead, people relied on hearing excerpts read or recited to them in church. Some religious groups (forerunners of the Reformation) said this was not enough – that church leaders were reading only passages that supported their views. Beginning in the 1100s, groups such as the Beghards and Beguines in Germany and neighbouring countries, along with the Waldensians in France, started urging Christians to read the Bible for themselves.

Bible translations were suddenly in great demand. Surprisingly, many church leaders were not happy about this. They feared heresies would show up in the translations, or that the people would not know how to interpret what they read accurately. The concern was serious enough that in 1199, Pope Innocent III ordered an investigation into the translating of Bibles. He concluded, 'The desire to understand holy scripture and the attempt to encourage others to live in accordance with its teachings... is indeed praiseworthy.' But 30 years later, a council of

This 13th-century Italian fresco depicts Pope Innocent III (1161–1216), who declared it acceptable to translate the Bible into the languages of the common people instead of into Latin, a dying language. Many church leaders disagreed, fearing that heresies might show up in the new translations, or that people would misinterpret what they read.

bishops in France ordered that members of the clergy were the only people who could own a Bible – no matter which language it was written in. Immediately after that council meeting, King Louis IX (St Louis) of France showed how he felt about the matter: he ordered the translation of a French Bible. Scholars collected various translations and completed a French version. Still, most church leaders did not agree with the king. Bible translations remained a controversial issue for centuries.

BIBLES FOR SPANIARDS AND ITALIANS

The Spanish church, famed for its intolerant and repressive Spanish Inquisition in the 1400s and 1500s, kept a close eye on any religious activity that could be viewed as heretical – including the translation of the Bible, which could give translators unprecedented freedom to express their interpretations of scripture.

Even so, Jews began translating their Hebrew Bible into Spanish as early as the 1100s. And 100 years later, Christians were translating the New Testament – not from the original Greek, but from Jerome's Latin translation, the Vulgate.

Italians did not have Bibles in their own language until the mid-1200s. That may seem odd, since Rome was an international hub of Christian scholarship. But the Italians may not have needed the Bible much earlier because early Italian dialects were similar to Latin, once the native language of this nation. Even the poor understood the Latin Bible readings and the liturgy. As Italians gradually began speaking Tuscan and Venetian, scholars provided Bible translations in those dialects.

By the end of the Middle Ages – a millennium stretching from about the AD 400s to the 1400s – the entire Bible had been translated into many of the major European languages.

Medieval Worship

'Let the Gospel be read, as the seal of all the scriptures; and let the people listen to it standing upon their feet, because it is the glad tidings of the salvation of all humankind.'

CANONS OF ADDAI,
THIRD CENTURY

Official Church prayers

The official prayers and rites of the Church make up what is known as the liturgy, or 'work of the people', to distinguish them from private prayers. The liturgy includes the eucharistic service, prayers and rites used in the administration of the other sacraments, and the Office of the Hours.

Manuscript illumination depicting the nativity from the Book of Hours of Charles V.

In the early days of the Church, when Christianity was often outlawed, there was less communication between communities and almost no uniformity in worship services. Although the basics of reading from scripture and celebrating the eucharist were common, the prayers and reading selections varied greatly. After Constantine gave official sanction to Christianity in 313, Christian worship moved into the open, taking place in large spaces, such as converted pagan temples, and more uniformity in worship was sought.

CYCLE OF SEASONS

Part of the reform in worship centred on a cycle of seasons that focused on major events in the life of Jesus. The first of these seasons, Easter, went back to the early Church. The first Christians observed the crucifixion and the resurrection on the same day, but before long, they began remembering the crucifixion separately, on the Friday before Easter. About the same time, a celebration of the last supper developed,

including a re-enactment of Jesus washing his apostles' feet.

By the fourth century, when Christians no longer feared persecution, pilgrims visited the Holy Land to re-enact the events leading up to the resurrection. The fourth-century pilgrim Egeria described a celebration of Holy Week (the week ending with Easter) in Jerusalem. Eventually, Holy Week became part of the Christian calendar. It begins with Palm Sunday, celebrating Jesus' triumphal entry into Jerusalem, moves on to Maundy Thursday, marking the last supper, and Good Friday, remembering the crucifixion. It ends with the celebration of Jesus' resurrection on Easter. The Easter season itself was eventually expanded to last 50 days, ending on Pentecost, which celebrates the descent of the Holy Spirit upon Jesus' disciples.

Because Easter is such a great feast, a period of fasting and preparation was always observed. In early times, it ranged in length from a few days to a few weeks, then in the fourth century it was extended to 40 days (excluding Sundays) –

Books for worship

Complete Bibles were too expensive and unwieldy to be used in churches for celebrating the eucharist. Consequently the Bible was broken into separate volumes, including the all-important book of the Gospels, Psalters (for reading or chanting psalms during the eucharist service or the Office of the Hours), and selections from other books of the Bible that were used in worship services. Later, all the biblical selections used in worship were combined into lectionaries. Prayers used in offering the eucharist and in administering other sacraments were bound together into sacramentaries, and material meant to be sung was put into antiphonaries. In the 10th century, the materials formerly found in lectionaries, sacramentaries and antiphonaries were combined into books known as missals.

Because the role of the lay person in worship was so diminished during the Middle Ages, educated lay people looked for ways to worship privately. In the 13th century, when the production of books moved to private professional scribes and artists, books for private devotion appeared, and quickly became popular among people of means. The most common of

these were Books of the Hours, which were commissioned by wealthy patrons, especially women. These books, which were as simple or elaborate as the person commissioning them could afford, varied in content, but generally contained certain elements. They opened with a calendar of the church year and quotations from the Gospels and featured the Hours of the Virgin, a series of psalms and other texts devoted to Mary, the mother of Jesus. Some of these volumes also included prayers for the dead.

While the wealthy had beautifully illuminated prayer books to read from, the poor had to rely on memorized prayers and devotions and their own thoughts and words. One popular devotion was the rosary, a series of 150 Hail Marys (the standard prayer to Jesus' mother), one for each of the 150 psalms. These prayers were divided into groups, or decades, of 10 Hail Marys, and each decade was introduced by the Lord's Prayer. During each decade the person praying was supposed to meditate on one of the 15 'mysteries' or events in the life of Jesus and his mother, Mary.

remembering Jesus' own 40-day fast in the desert. In the fourth century, the 40 days were used to prepare adults for baptism at Easter (although this practice waned in later centuries when infant baptism became the norm). Readings during this period, called Lent, focused on prayer and fasting and preparation for baptism.

There is no record of any celebrations of Christmas in the early Church, but Christmas festivities probably began in the third century. By 336, Christians in Rome were celebrating Christmas on 25 December (replacing a pagan feast of the birthday of the sun god), and the practice spread through the Christian world. Readings for worship services during the Christmas season focused on the birth and infancy of Jesus.

The observance of Advent may have begun during the fourth century in Spain, where it was used as a period of preparation for adults who were to be baptized during the Christmas season, just as Lent was used to prepare for Easter baptisms. Later the observance of Advent (which included four Sundays) spread throughout the Western Church and was kept as a period of fasting and prayer. Readings at worship services focused on the coming of Jesus both as a child in Bethlehem and at the end of time.

The periods between these seasons are known as 'ordinary time', because they do not include the extraordinary seasons discussed above. Readings for these times, were chosen with an eye to including as much of the New Testament in the year's cycle as possible.

ORDER OF WORSHIP

Each day's eucharistic celebration began with some preparatory prayers and a procession of the clergy to the altar. Then a lector, often a deacon, read two biblical excerpts to the people. The first reading was from the Old Testament or from one of the New Testament books other than the Gospels, and the second was a passage from one of the Gospels. The first reading was chosen to show that Jesus' coming was foretold by the prophets, or to underline a theme found in the Gospel reading for the day. After the Gospel reading the priest gave a sermon, telling the people how they should apply what they had heard to their everyday lives. The eucharistic celebration followed the sermon, and then the priest blessed the people and sent them home.

In the Middle Ages, the average person could not read, and was exposed to the Bible only in church. Even this exposure lessened in time. Although the people in the congregation had played a large part in worship in earlier times, they were put more and more into the background as the Middle Ages progressed. In time, the emphasis on the reading of the word lessened as the priest wore exotic vestments and performed ritualistic movements (carried over from earlier cultures) and muttered most of the prayers of the service to himself with his back turned to the congregation. To make matters worse, the entire service – and often the sermon as well – was in Latin, no longer the language of the common people. This situation continued until the time of the Reformation, when both Protestants and Catholics reformed their worship services, once again bringing the entire congregation and clergy together in praising God.

This 14th-century French book illumination shows a congregation at worship. Taken from *History of the King of England, Richard II.*

English book illumination from 1435 showing monks at a service.

The Bible in Plays

Early Christian leaders condemned the theatre, and for good reason. Roman plays were often lewd, crude and laced with profanity. People who craved entertaining stories that glorified murder, adultery and other kinds of immorality could get their fill at the Roman theatre.

Christians stayed away, and for centuries kept theatre out of the Church. But by the AD 900s, theatre gradually began making its way into the Church – with astonishing results that energized congregations.

The first Bible play

The empty tomb of Jesus is the scene for the first-known Bible play. Monks in Winchester, England, preserved the short play – complete with stage directions – in about AD 965. Performed on Easter mornings, the play was called *Quem Quaeritis*, Latin for the first words of the play: 'Whom do you seek?' Here is a translation of it, with the dialogue in bold type and the stage directions slightly condensed:

When the third lesson is being recited, four of the monks will get ready. Let one, wearing a long white robe, go discreetly to the place representing the tomb and sit quietly, holding a palm branch. When the third response to the recitation is being sung, let the other three enter, dressed in colourful capes worn over white robes and carrying censers filled with burning incense. They should approach the tomb with hesitation, as though searching. All of this is to imitate the angel seated on the tomb and the women coming with spices to anoint Jesus' body.

When the seated one sees the three approaching, let him begin to sing in a sweet and moderate voice: **Whom do you seek in the tomb, O followers of Christ?**

Let the three answer with one voice: **Jesus of Nazareth, who was crucified, O dweller of heaven.**

Angel to the others: **He is not here. He has risen as he had foretold. Go, tell others that he has risen from the dead.**

At this command the three should turn to the choir and sing: **Alleluia. The Lord has risen.**

The angel calls the three: **Come and see the place.**

The angel stands and lifts the veil that had wrapped the body of Jesus, to show he is not there. Seeing this, the three lay down their censers in the tomb, take hold of the linen and lift it before the prior [one of the leading monks], to show that the Lord has risen and is no longer wrapped in it.

The three sing: **The Lord has risen from the tomb.**

Then the three lay the linen on the altar. The prior rejoices with the three by starting the hymn, 'We Praise You O God'. When this is sung, all the church bells ring in unison.

ADDING DRAMA TO CHURCH

The Church needed something to awaken the sedate congregations. Many worshippers were sedate because they did not understand Latin, yet the Church followed tradition by conducting rituals such as Mass in Latin. What priests did to enliven the Mass – a ritual of communion (also called the eucharist or the Lord's supper) intended to help Christians remember the price Jesus paid for humanity's salvation – seemed to provide the seed for theatre. When the priest raised high the bread and cup of wine, representing the broken body and spilled blood of Jesus, many were deeply moved. They may not have understood the words the priest spoke, but they understood that Jesus suffered for them.

In time, music added to the drama of the rituals, with choirs and instruments enhancing the worship experience. As early as the 400s, some churches took yet another step towards plays: They included living scenes to illustrate Bible stories, such as the birth or the death of Jesus. People dressed in costume stood quietly – as in live nativity scenes today – while the choir sang or the priest conducted worship.

These scenes developed into short plays. The earliest known play is about the resurrection, and was preserved by Benedictine monks in England for use on Easter morning in the late 900s. A translation of the play appears in the boxed text. More than 400 versions of it survive.

The play was in Latin, meaning worshippers still did not understand the dialogue. But they knew the story it told, and were able to follow along in the same way people today follow an opera sung in a foreign language. The worshippers responded so enthusiastically that plays emerged for other important days in the church calendar, such as Christmas and Pentecost (the day the Holy Spirit filled the disciples). Plays about the life of Jesus and other characters in the Bible were also presented, although again in Latin. Still, the plays were so popular that they spread throughout much of Europe. Clergy acted all the roles, and the plays were usually conducted in the church. In time, the church could not hold all the people who wanted to see the plays. So the presentations moved outside, on to church grounds.

PLAYS ON WHEELS

By the 1300s, the Church developed an ingenious idea for using plays to teach

Passion plays

Modern-day passion plays, which tell the story of Jesus' suffering, death and resurrection, are a remnant of the Bible plays popular in medieval times.

---

townspeople about the Bible – in their own language. The Church would set aside one day a year to stage a succession of plays performed on high floats that could be wheeled from one location in the city to another. Often, there would be 25 to 50 plays covering Bible stories such as creation, Cain killing Abel, Daniel in the lions' den, the birth of Jesus and Judgment Day. There was one play per float, with the top level of each wagon serving as a stage and the lower level draped in curtains as a dressing room.

Spectators would park themselves at one of the stopping points for the floats, such as the town square, and watch one play after another, presented in the order the stories appear in the Bible. The plays were carefully synchronized to keep the parade of plays flowing. This was especially important in York, England, where up to 57 plays were presented in a single day, each at a dozen locations. The plays were often held in the summer, when days are longest. But torches and lanterns allowed some plays to continue into the night.

The sheer volume of plays meant that the Church needed to reach beyond the clergy for actors. And the cost of the plays led to trade guilds sponsoring plays associated with their trade. In York, shipbuilders staged the play about Noah and the ark. Special effects could sometimes get out of control, with the flood scene soaking spectators who did not know they were in the splash zone, fire igniting the set, or the actor portraying Christ actually getting hurt.

CROWDS FLOCK TO TOWN

The plays were often conducted on the feast of Corpus Christi (Latin for the 'body of Christ'), which usually fell in June. People came from all around – neighbouring villages and countryside, as well as distant cities and countries. The mood was festive during what became one of the busiest – and most profitable – days of the year. One city record said the plays were 'to the greater glory of God, and to the profit and increase of the city'.

By the late 1500s, the plays seem to have run their course. Many of them became more entertaining than educational. They added story-lines not from the Bible, such as portraying the devil with a tail that is pulled to make fun of him – while the crowd roared with laughter. Also, plays began to focus more on the Virgin Mary and the saints, something Protestant reformers criticized as 'idolatrous'. As a result, church plays grew more rare. Secular plays picked up the slack, however, producing perhaps the greatest playwright of all time – William Shakespeare – who began writing his plays at that very moment in history.

'I think I heard of that man you speak of [Jesus] once in a play at Kendall, called Corpus-Christi's play, where there was a man on a tree and blood ran down.'

AN ELDERLY ENGLISHMAN, 1644

The Bible Goes to College

The Church led the way in education during the Middle Ages, and established the first universities – teaching students to use the Bible to understand the world.

Before the 1100s, about the only way a person in western Europe could get a formal education was to attend classes in monasteries and church schools, which were taught by monks and priests. But during that pivotal century, there emerged a revival in faith and learning, partly because the era of invasions by the Vikings and others had given way to a time of peace, trade and prosperity. The intellectually curious now had the time and means to study, and the Church accommodated them by expanding its educational system.

Children under the age of 13 – almost exclusively boys – could attend what became known as grammar schools. There, they studied grammar, maths and other basic subjects. For those who wanted to continue their studies – typically boys aged 13 to 16 – there was advanced learning in what became known as universities, which sprang up in major cities. Among the earliest universities were those of Paris, along with Oxford, England and Bologna, Italy. Since the setting was in a church or monastery, it is not surprising that theology was considered one of the most important university subjects studied. Students also took classes in logic, public speaking and other subjects. In time, students could also pursue doctoral studies in law, medicine and theology – with theology presented as the 'Queen of the Sciences'.

RELIGION AND SCIENCE

It might seem odd to classify theology as a science, but it made perfect sense to the clergy teaching the classes. Medieval Christian scholars sought knowledge, whether it came from the natural world or was divinely revealed in the Bible. As far as they were concerned, there was no division between the sacred and the secular. God was Lord of all. An educated person in that day was generally trained to think in Christian terms and to see the world through Christian eyes.

Out of this kind of thinking emerged a movement called Scholasticism. Students were encouraged to seek knowledge and truth, but they were also encouraged to search beyond the Bible and Christian faith. Faith and scripture were important, but not the only sources. As an added resource, they were to use their God-given powers of reason.

Perhaps the greatest challenge the Scholastics faced was in how to handle the rediscovery of some major works of Aristotle, a Greek philosopher famed for his insights into logic but whose teachings sometimes clashed with the Bible. Generally, the Christian scholars used what seemed reasonable to them, and dropped any of Aristotle's teachings that conflicted with the Bible.

'I believe in order to understand.'
ANSELM, SCHOLAR AND CHURCH LEADER (c. 1033–1109)

The School of St Thomas Aquinas by the workshop of Fra Angelico. St Thomas Aquinas (1225–74) was an Italian philosopher and theologian sometimes called the Prince of Scholastics. He taught his students at the University of Paris that reason and faith were not enemies, but allies that could lead them to truth.

Dividing the Bible into chapters and verses

Bibles today are divided into chapters and verses. But that is not how they were written. The divisions came much later, mainly to help scholars find the passages they were looking for.

Chapter divisions came in about the early 1200s, when a university of Paris lecturer named Stephen Langton introduced them into the Latin Bible. Langton, later appointed Archbishop of Canterbury and one of the authors of the Magna Carta, had certainly developed a great Bible reference tool. Over the next two centuries, others began using his system in new copies of the Bible – in Latin as well as other languages.

Within a few decades, the chapters were divided – but by letters instead of verse numbers. Probably the same scholar who developed the first-known Bible concordance, Cardinal Hugo of St Cher in France, subdivided most chapters into seven parts labelled from the letters A through G. Short chapters, such as some in Psalms, did not need all seven letters.

Numbered verses began in about 1440, when a rabbi named Isaac Nathan added them to the Jewish Bible so he could produce an accompanying Hebrew concordance. The New Testament verse divisions we have today were introduced by a Christian scholar named Robert Stephanus (or Robert Estiennes, his French name), who in 1551 published a Greek and Latin edition of the New Testament. Four years later, Stephanus published the first whole Bible with chapter and verse divisions.

For example, Aristotle said the universe had no beginning or end, but the Bible says God created it from nothing and would one day destroy it to make a new heaven and earth. Thomas Aquinas, educated in Paris during the 1200s, responded by arguing that reason alone has its limits, and that it was faith that led him to accept the Bible. Faith and reason, Aquinas said, supplemented each other – the two were not opposites.

Still, Aristotle had a great influence on the Scholastics. The Greek philosopher's writings about logic provided some of the basic methods of Scholastic investigation. Perhaps the most important was a classroom exercise called dialectics, in which the students used dialogue as a way to separate truth from error. As an example, the teacher might raise a theological question from sources such as the Bible, a commentary or a papal order. The debate that followed was an attempt to find an answer based on reason. Aristotle gave Scholastics the philosophical tools to merge the sacred and the secular, while at the same time opening the door to a new world of questions.

SCHOLARS AT WORK

With this open attitude towards learning, scholars began digging deeper for answers to their questions. Working just with Latin translations of the Bible was now considered inadequate. The best scholars wanted to read the Bible in the original languages of Hebrew and Greek. By the 1300s, all the major universities had departments that featured classes in both languages.

University scholars also began turning out a wide range of books to shed light on the Bible – commentaries on selected Bible books, atlases and background on plants and animals in Bible lands. In 1230, one scholar developed the first-known concordance for the Latin Bible. A concordance is an alphabetical list of words in the Bible, and where they can be found. This was especially helpful for scholars who were studying certain Bible topics, such as 'judgment', and who wanted to read every Bible passage where the word appeared.

One of the most important works was Aquinas's *Summa Theologica* ('Summary of Theology', 1267–73), a three-part treatise about God, the moral life of humanity and Christ. In this monumental endeavour, the Italian theologian provided a rational base for the mysteries in the Bible, showing that faith and reason are complementary ways of understanding the world. His insights are models that guide many Christian scholars even today. Yet the third part of his work was left unfinished. After a mystical experience Aquinas said, 'All I have written is as straw beside the things that have been revealed to me.' And he wrote no more.

'Dumb Ox'
Because Thomas Aquinas was heavy set and quiet, his fellow students at the University of Paris called him 'Dumb Ox'. But one of his teachers predicted, 'this ox will one day fill the world with his bellowing'.

Francis, a Living Gospel

A Franciscan nativity

In the town of Greccio, in 1223, and again in 1224, Francis set up a crib at midnight Mass, depicting the birth of Jesus as described in the Gospels of Matthew and Luke. In this way, he hoped to demonstrate the love God had for us all by becoming a helpless infant. The tradition of a Christmas nativity scene caught on, and is continued to this day.

The Church was not at its best at the close of the 12th century. It was, in fact, in total moral disrepair. Priests sworn to celibacy were living openly with women, others were vying for powerful positions in the Church and paying for them, and bishops were living in splendid palaces surrounded by wealth. None of the gospel values was in evidence. A few individuals called for reform, but were quickly silenced. But then, one simple man – Francis of Assisi – managed to repair the Church solely by the power of his example.

REBELLIOUS YOUNG MAN

Francis Bernardone was born in Assisi, Umbria (in central Italy), in 1182. His father, Pietro, was a wealthy cloth merchant who hoped Francis would take over the business. Once the boy was old enough Pietro took him on his annual trips to Champagne and Provence in France to acquire merchandise for sale in Assisi. In Provence, Francis fell in love with the songs of the troubadours, telling of knights in shining armour and the ladies they loved. Francis proved to be a poor businessman because he was filled with dreams of becoming a knight himself and because he became the centre of a group of young men who devoted themselves to parties – financed by Francis.

Perfect joy

Francis believed in laughter and song and was always joyful, even at the time of his death. But his idea of joy extended beyond that of most people. For Francis perfect joy was to be like Jesus. When discussing this with Brother Leo one night on the road, Francis indicated that even if all his friars were perfect, that would not be perfect joy. However, Francis said, if he and Leo arrived home on this cold, windy, snowy night and the porter refused them entrance, calling them frauds and robbers of the poor box, and they accepted this without complaint, that would be perfect joy. If they were forced to stay outside all night racked with hunger, yet did not complain, that would be perfect joy. If they persisted and knocked again and the porter insulted and slapped them and told them to go the hospital, and they remained cheerful and humble, that would be perfect joy. And if they were even further abused, but accepted all by thinking of the sufferings of Christ, that would be perfect joy. For Francis, such rejection by his own friars was similar to Jesus' rejection by his disciples on the night before he died. To be rejected as Jesus was rejected was to be more like Jesus, and so was perfect joy.

In 1202, Francis went to war in the neighbouring town of Perugia, but was captured and spent a year in prison. When released he was severely ill, but once he recovered he returned to his life of parties and frivolities. Then, in 1204, he had a chance to fight in the pope's army at Apulio. Francis outfitted himself with a suit of armour so elaborate that it brought smiles to the faces of his fellow, more weathered, soldiers. But on his first night away from Assisi, Francis had a strange dream in which he was told to serve the master rather than the servant. Confused, he returned to Assisi, where he led a more austere life.

The following year, while praying in the chapel of San Damiano, a voice spoke to him from the crucifix, saying, 'Repair my house.' At first Francis took the message literally, bought materials, and began to repair the chapel. But because he had sold some of his father's cloth to finance the repairs, Pietro grew angry. Eventually, unable to appease him, Francis stripped himself naked in the public square, disowned his earthly father in favour of his heavenly Father, and went on to live a life of dire poverty. For Francis the beloved lady in the troubadour's songs, which he still loved, became Lady Poverty.

A SECOND CHRIST

Jesus, as represented in the Gospels, was everything to Francis, and Francis did all he could to emulate him. Francis was especially inspired by what Jesus told the rich young man: 'If you wish to be perfect, go, sell your possessions, and give the money to the poor… then come, follow me' (Matthew 19:21). Francis refused to keep any personal possessions, went around barefoot, wearing only a simple coarse habit, and begged for scraps of food on the streets. At first, he was scoffed at by the people, but later he gained their respect as he exhibited great holiness in all he did.

Soon, Francis attracted followers. When there were 12 of them, Francis dubbed them Friars Minor and wrote them a Rule based on the Gospels. He then travelled to Rome and ask for Pope Innocent III's approval. Reluctant at first, Innocent was soon completely captivated by Francis and finally approved the Rule.

Francis's popularity spread like wildfire, and hundreds – eventually thousands – of men joined his order. In 1209, Francis founded a Second Order for women with Clare, a young woman of Assisi, and that order prospered, and became known as the Poor Clares. Finally, about 1221 Francis wrote a Rule for a Third Order of lay men and women who were unable to leave their families and live a communal life. This Order became extremely popular and even counted kings and queens among its members. Because Third Order members refused to go to war, they helped erode the power base of medieval lords, leading to the downfall of the feudal system.

Always keeping the Gospels as his focus, Francis travelled far, joyfully preaching love of Jesus and love of one another. He even travelled to Egypt during the Fifth Crusade in an attempt to convert the sultan, who gently sent him away unharmed. Francis so closely imitated Jesus, as seen in the Gospels, that he was known as 'the other Christ', and his teachings and example could not be ignored even by corrupt clergymen, who were forced to mend their ways, establishing reform in the Church. Francis desired to feel everything that Jesus had suffered, and one day in 1224, while at prayer, the wounds of the crucified Jesus (stigmata) appeared on his body. He joyfully endured the pain of these wounds until his death.

Francis had a great love of nature and of everything created by God. He is famous for preaching to the birds and is known to have pacified wild animals. One day, it is said, he moved a worm from the centre of a road to keep it from being squashed underfoot. In the last years of his life, Francis wrote a song of praise to all God's creatures, and urged his friars to sing it when they went out preaching. This 'Canticle of Brother Sun' sees and praises all elements of nature as Francis's brothers and sisters. Shortly before his death, Francis added a verse welcoming 'Sister Death':

All praise be yours, my Lord, through Sister Death,
 From whose embrace no mortal can escape.
Woe to those who die in mortal sin!
 Happy those she finds doing your will!
 The second death can do no harm to them.
Praise and bless my Lord, and give him thanks,
 And serve him with great humility.

Francis died on 3 October 1226, surrounded by his followers.

'When God gave me some friars, there was no one to tell me what I should do; but the Most High himself made it clear to me that I must live the life of the gospel.'

FRANCIS OF ASSISI,
THE TESTAMENT

Pope Innocent III Approves Franciscan Rule by Giotto di Bondone (c. 1267–1337).

End-Time Fever

Right: This illustration of a seven-headed dragon is from *Book of Figures* by Joachim of Fiore, a 12th-century Italian monk who predicted that the end was near. Joachim claimed that the seven-headed dragon of Revelation 12 represented seven leaders. He believed that the sixth head stood for the Muslim warrior Saladin, who controlled Jerusalem, and that the Antichrist would be the seventh head.

A nun's end-time picture book

In the mid-1100s, a German nun named Hildegard of Bingen wrote a beautifully illustrated book of end-time visions she said she had received at the age of 42. Titled *Scivias*, meaning 'know [the way of the Lord]', the book covered sacred history from creation to the end times. One of its most famous images shows the birth of the Antichrist – portrayed as a monstrous head – from the Church. In the same picture, this beastly head was then placed between the legs of a kingly figure who floated above the ground – representing the belief that the Antichrist would try to prove his deity by ascending into heaven.

In medieval times, the end of the world was near. That is what a growing number of monks and priests said, beginning on the eve of the first millennium and continuing for several centuries afterwards. This led to an escalating sense of worry among the masses, widespread persecution of Jews (who some Christians thought would become soldiers of the Antichrist), fervour for the Crusades aimed at recapturing the Holy Land, and war between the rich and the poor in an effort to set up a godly kingdom on earth.

To support their claims, clergy used a surprising mix of evidence. Some used astrology, arguing that the Bible says in the last days there will be signs in the heavens (Acts 2:19). Others pointed to the catastrophes on earth that are predicted in scripture: wars, earthquakes and epidemics, such as the Black Death, a plague that began in the 1300s and is estimated to have killed about a third of western Europeans.

Many of the clergy reversed the Church's long-time tradition of interpreting the Bible's apocalyptic books – such as Revelation and Daniel – symbolically instead of literally. In the 400s, Augustine had managed to turn the Church away from its preoccupation with a literal apocalypse by convincing leaders that the prophecies were a figurative way of portraying the spiritual struggle we all face between good and evil. But an increasing number of church leaders in the Middle Ages disagreed.

A MONK WITH A VISION

The one person who, perhaps more than any other, drove up the apocalyptic fever was an Italian monk named Joachim of Fiore (c. 1132–1202). After wrestling for many months trying to understand the book of Revelation, he said he woke up one Easter morning with spiritual insight. He said world history fell into three overlapping eras, one for each member of the Trinity, with each era spanning 42 generations. The Old Testament was the time of the Father. The New Testament was the time of the Son – a time when much of God's hidden wisdom was revealed. Yet to come was the utopian era of the Holy Spirit, which Joachim said would begin sometime between 1200 and 1260, and end with the coming of the Antichrist.

Joachim said the seven-headed dragon of Revelation 12 represented seven leaders. He added

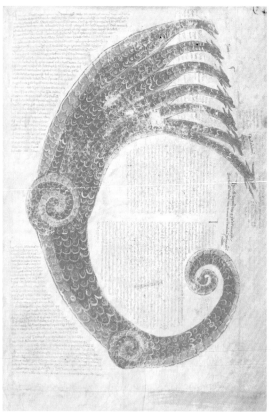

that Saladin – who had captured Jerusalem from the crusaders in 1187 – was the sixth head and that the Antichrist would be the seventh. Although Joachim lived on a lonely mountaintop monastery, he became the apocalyptic advisor to popes in the last two decades of his life. And Richard the Lionheart, on his way to try to capture Jerusalem from Saladin, stopped to ask Joachim for any word about what might happen. One account says Joachim predicted victory, but some scholars say Joachim was probably vague enough to allow for the failure that resulted. Richard fought Saladin to a stalemate before making a truce that left Jerusalem in Muslim control.

JEWS PORTRAYED AS ANTICHRISTS

Jews were often portrayed as a people opposed to Christ – antichrists in the broader sense. This made them logical allies of the coming Antichrist and natural enemies of apocalyptic-minded Christians. As a result, Jews were often persecuted and even driven out of various countries, including Spain and Germany.

Jews were systematically persecuted in Frankfurt in 1241, the year the Mongols invaded eastern Europe. The invasion apparently caused

Antichrist AD 1000

On the brink of the first Christian millennium, in about AD 950, Queen Gerbera of France asked a French monk named Adso to give her details about the Antichrist. Here are excerpts from his letter of response, which summarized many popular beliefs:

The Antichrist will be born from the Jewish people...

At the very beginning of his conception the devil will enter his mother's womb... just as the Holy Spirit came into the mother of our Lord Jesus Christ...

The Antichrist will have magicians, enchanters, diviners and wizards who at the devil's bidding will raise him and instruct him in every evil, heresy and wicked art...

He will come to Jerusalem and with various tortures will slay all the Christians he cannot convert... He will attack the places where the Lord Christ walked...

To those who believe in him he will give great wealth. Those he is not able to corrupt with gifts, he will overcome with terror. Those he cannot overcome with terror, he will seduce with signs and miracles. Those he cannot seduce with miracles, he will cruelly torture and miserably put to death...

He will circumcise himself and say to the Jews, 'I am the Christ promised to you...' At that time all the Jews will flock to him, in the belief that they are receiving God, but rather they will receive the devil...

That Antichrist will be killed on the Mount of Olives in his tent and upon his throne...

After Antichrist has been killed the Judgment Day will not come immediately... the Lord will grant former believers 40 days to do penance because they were led astray by the Antichrist.

Detail from *The End of Mankind* by Luca Signorelli (c. 1441–1523). Fresco from Capella Nuova, Orvieto Cathedral, Italy.

Christians to fear that Gog and Magog – apocalyptic destroyers described in Revelation – were upon them. During the Black Death, Jews were accused of poisoning the water, and were killed in large numbers.

The violence was not limited to Christians against Jews and Muslims. Sometimes Christians fought Christians, for example during peasant revolts against the rich in England in 1381 and in Germany about 150 years later. One leader of the German revolt was a minister named Thomas Münzer (or Muentzer). He convinced many peasants that the rich were the evil ones whose destruction is foretold in Revelation, and that it is possible to create a godly society – heaven on earth.

In a showdown that became the Battle of Frankenhausen on 15 May 1525, about 8,000 ill-equipped peasants gathered on a hillside outside of town and took their stand against the coalition army of several German princes. Before the battle, Münzer delivered a passionate speech, assuring his people that Christ would intervene and the people would catch the bullets and cannonballs in their sleeves. One report said the princes tried to negotiate their way out of the battle. But a rainbow appeared in the sky, rousing the peasants. Münzer's flag carried a rainbow, which was the sign of promise that God gave Noah. The knights charged, slaughtering 5,000 peasants. Münzer was found hiding under a bed and was later beheaded.

Battle near Liegnitz, 1241, at which Mongols defeated Polish-German knights, causing many Christians to fear that the apocalyptic destroyers of Revelation – Gog and Magog – had come. Engraving by Matthäus Merian (1630).

Thomas Münzer (1490–1525), a minister who led peasants in a disastrous revolt. Coloured engraving from 1608 by Christopher van Sichem.

'Now is the time of harvest. God has appointed me for this task. I've sharpened my sickle.'

THOMAS MÜNZER

Terror at midnight

At midnight on 31 December 999 – the turn of the first Christian millennium – a crowd of pilgrims in St Peter's Basilica in Rome trembled in terror as Pope Silvester II presided over what many feared would be their final Mass before the world ended.

A King's Bible

Facing page: a gold-covered page from the *Bible moralisée*, which was completed between 1226 and 1240. Uniquely for its time, each of the four Bible passages here has a commentary beneath it that links it with contemporary medieval life. Each Bible passage and each commentary is accompanied by an illustration to its right or left.

It was not only a gift fit for a king, it was designed for a king. The sumptuous *Bible moralisée*, or moralized Bible, was a lavish book of biblical passages and commentary with 5,000 illuminations. Every page contained gold. The original book, which was later copied for other royal patrons, was probably produced sometime between 1226 and 1240 and presented to Louis IX, the young king of France. Louis was a devout Catholic, who would have welcomed this gift. In fact, he was so spiritual that he was declared a saint after his death. In life, he was a member of the Third Order of St Francis and in death became a patron saint of the order. The book was intended to teach, and Louis would have been an apt pupil.

LAYOUT OF THE BOOK

Each of the gold-coated pages of a *Bible moralisée* follows the same pattern. It features four passages from the Bible (or the Apocrypha),

A humbler picture book

Kings were not the only Christians with picture-book Bibles. A much simpler book that used Bible illustrations to teach Christian morals was *The Mirror of Human Salvation* (or, in the original Latin, *Speculum humanae salvationis*). It was probably created by Ludolph of Saxony in the early 14th century. Each of the book's more than 40 chapters illustrates a single New Testament scene and is accompanied by three scenes that predict or lead up to the New Testament event shown. Unlike other illustrated Bible books, which counterpose New Testament scenes with Old Testament scenes, or (in the case of the *Bible moralisée*) with contemporary scenes), *The Mirror of Human Salvation* also uses scenes from history and legend – both Christian and pagan. An example of such extrabiblical events is the death of Codrus, the last king of Athens, who, reacting to an oracle, deliberately brought about his own death in order to save his people from defeat by the Dorians – anticipating Jesus' dying on a cross for the sins of all. The overall point of *The Mirror of Human Salvation* is that all history manifests God's plan for humanity.

including the text and a brief commentary. Both biblical text and commentary are graced with illustrations that are set off in circular frameworks, or roundels. All this material is arranged in two columns. The first biblical passage appears in the upper left-hand corner of the page with its accompanying illustration to its right. The commentary on the passage and its illustration appear just below. A second passage with commentary and illustrations fill in the bottom of the first column. The right-hand column contains two more biblical passages with their commentary and illustrations in the same order as the first column.

NATURE OF THE COMMENTARIES

The nature of the commentaries and their illustrations is what makes the *Bible moralisée* unique for its time. Generally, in medieval commentaries, Old Testament passages are tied into New Testament texts, showing how the New Testament fulfils the Old. Often prophecies are shown to predict Jesus' coming or an event in his life. At other times characters or stories are seen as earlier versions, or 'types', of Jesus or his words or actions – for example, Abraham's readiness to sacrifice his son Isaac is seen as a 'type' of God the Father's willingness to let Jesus die for our sins.

The commentaries in the *Bible moralisée*, on the other hand, ignore any New Testament parallels and interpret the Bible for contemporary times. Instead of focusing solely on biblical times, they point out how the Bible foreshadows their surrounding (medieval) social situations and so give pertinent moral instructions to the reader. They accomplish this through the use of allegory. Old Testament characters or situations are used to show how medieval men and women fulfil or neglect their Christian duties.

Blockbooks Printed from Wood

'Very deft his hand, from long practice, as he cuts so conscientiously what he seems to see.'

W.J. LINTON, HISTORIAN, DESCRIBING BLOCKBOOK WOOD ENGRAVER HANS LUTZELBURGER

Before books were printed from movable type, they were printed from immovable type carved into page-size blocks of hard, fine-grained wood. Words and pictures were both delicately carved into the wood that was used as templates to produce bound volumes called blockbooks.

The process often started with an artist, who drew the pictures and hand-lettered the text. This artwork was then given to a woodcutter charged with the job of carving the words and pictures into flat blocks. Each page in the book had to be carved on a separate block.

Next, the block was painted with ink and covered with a sheet of paper. When the raised, ink-covered lines on the wood carving came into contact with the paper, the design on the wood transferred to the paper. To make sure the entire page was evenly transferred, the printer would rub the top of the sheet with a rounded burnisher, which often looked a bit like a spoon. Another option was to use a printing press that squeezed the wood and paper together.

The printer could not flip the page and put another image on the back without damaging the front. So printers sometimes glued two pages together so there was no blank side, or they bound the books with the blank pages exposed side-by-side – so the reader would see two printed pages followed by two blank pages. The pictures resembled simple black and white sketches, but were often hand-painted later to make the books more attractive.

THE MONEY MOTIVATOR

Blockbooks became popular because they were cheaper than hand-copied manuscripts. Though it took a long time to produce enough wood carvings to fill a book, each woodcut carefully handled could be printed tens of thousands of times. Volume sales made the work profitable.

The printer also had the flexibility to store the woodcuts and bring them back out when a customer wanted one or more copies. And with paper in short supply, it was great to have the flexibility to print only enough to fill an order. This was an advantage that the woodcuts had over the movable metal letters in Johann Gutenberg's printing press. After finishing the job with metal letters, the printer needed to take the print forms apart to reuse the metal

The making of paper

The Chinese invented paper. Legend says that a eunuch in the court of the emperor developed the process in AD 105, using bark from mulberry trees. The earliest surviving paper was made from rags in about AD 150.

Paper-making was a secret the Chinese guarded for about 500 years, which assured them a monopoly. To make the paper, they gathered material made of fibres that could be broken down in water: bark, straw, leaves and rags. These were put in a vat and hammered to break down the fibres. Then they were soaked in water until the fibres became suspended in the solution. Paper-makers then dipped a page-sized mould into the vat. The mould had a tightly woven mesh bottom, so the water could drain out, but the fibres would stay behind – forming a thin sheet. Next, this sheet was put in a press to squeeze out more water, and then it was hung out to dry.

Arabs discovered the secret from Chinese prisoners of war, and passed on the knowledge as they expanded their empire. Europe's first paper-making mill was set up in Spain in about 1150. From there, paper making spread throughout the rest of Europe. At first, Europeans resisted the idea because it came from the Moors, people of the Muslim faith. Also, most of the paper was often of poor quality. But by the time of the blockbooks and Gutenberg's printing press, paper-makers had perfected their art. Pages in many books from that century remain crisp and white.

Woodblock printing, in which text and pictures are carved into blocks of wood that are covered with ink, then pressed against paper.

letters for other jobs. So it was uneconomical to print just a few copies at a time.

In spite of its advantages, the blockbook technology was soon replaced by books printed with movable type. Both book publishing methods developed about the same time, in the 1400s, although woodcuts were used earlier to make playing cards, patterns for fabrics and eventually books. The blockbook process was centred mainly in Germany and the neighbouring Netherlands, with the heyday of production running from about 1550 until 1575.

A BIBLE FOR THE ILLITERATE

Perhaps the most famous Bible produced by the blockbook method was the *Biblia pauperum* (Bible for the Poor). Technically, it was not a Bible since it contained only very limited excerpts from the Bible. Nor did it target the poor – most of whom could not read. Instead, this book was more like a tool to help clergy minister to the poor by providing a wealth of Bible scenes in pictures.

People today who open one of the more than 120 surviving copies or fragments of this book are often surprised by the format. The pictures and text do not follow the order of the Bible. Instead, the book is arranged by themes, to reinforce an ancient Bible interpretation method called typology. Ministers taught that many Old Testament stories were 'types' or a foreshadowing of Jesus.

So in the centre of one page, there is a picture of the archangel Gabriel telling Mary she will give birth to Jesus. Beside that picture are two distantly parallel stories from the Old Testament. One is the snake tempting Eve. The other is Gideon dressed in armour and praying to God. Each is a one-to-one discussion that produced notable consequences. On that same page are four short quotes from the Old Testament: Isaiah 7:14 (the prediction that a virgin will give birth to a son named Immanuel); Psalm 71:6 (praise to God for giving us life); Ezekiel 44:2 (a prophecy about God returning to the temple); and Jeremiah 31:22 (a prophecy about God making a new creation on earth).

On the next page is a picture of the nativity, alongside scenes of two dramatic Old Testament miracles: Moses at the burning bush and the almond staff of Aaron blooming. Accompanying these are four more short excerpts from the Prophets. Typically, there are between 30 and 40 illustrated pages in this book, varying from one edition to another.

It is impossible to know when this book was created. The paper used in a Dutch copy dates to sometime between 1460 and 1470. But that was only when the paper was produced. The woodcut may have been created many years earlier.

Pictures play a prominent role in the Bible for the Poor, as seen on this page from an edition published in the 1400s, in what is now Germany. This book is not really a Bible as we know it. Instead, each page is a collection of related stories, often intended to show how Old Testament stories foreshadowed the life and ministry of Jesus. On this page, Queen Jezebel plots to kill the prophet Elijah (left), and King Nebuchadnezzar demands the death of Daniel (right). In the centre is a picture of Jesus before Pilate, who ordered the crucifixion.

4

THE BOOK OF THE REFORMATION

IHESVITÆ.

Countering resistance from the Church, a number of nations translated the Bible into the language of their people. During the Reformation – the 16th-century religious revolution that split the Church into Catholic and Protestant – reform-minded Protestants tried to make the Bible available to all Christians. Protestants argued that the Bible, not the Church, was God's voice on earth.

The timing was perfect because the reform movement got a big boost from the German invention of a printing press. Earlier reform movements had gone nowhere because there was no way to get the message out quickly to a wide audience. The printing press changed that.

This reform movement generated many great Bible translations, most notably Luther's influential German-language Bible and England's King James Version. Even the Catholics gave in and translated the Bible into English. American Indians got their own Bibles, too.

Luther, with his supporters, confronts Pope Leo X, together with monks and papal theologians. Woodcut from 1568.

Wycliffe and His Bible

Page from the first English Bible, the translation of which was instigated by John Wycliffe in the late 1300s.

J ohn Wycliffe, the Oxford scholar behind the first English Bible, instigated so much trouble in the Church that, 43 years after he died, church leaders ordered his bones to be dug up, burned to ashes and thrown in a river.

This unlikely end sprang from an unlikely start. Wycliffe was born in about 1330 on a sheep farm, deep in the hinterlands of England, some 125 kilometres (200 miles) north of London. Had he stayed there, content with the education he probably received from his parish priest, the world might never have heard of him. But aged about 16, he left home to continue his studies at Oxford University. There he later joined the teaching staff and earned his reputation as the most brilliant theologian in England's first and highly prestigious university.

CRITICIZING THE CHURCH

As Wycliffe studied the Bible, he came to believe that many leaders in the Church were not practising what the Bible preached. So he spoke his mind, especially during the last decade of his life. With his lectures, sermons and writings, Wycliffe launched a vigorous campaign against the Church, paving the way for the Reformation a century later.

When the Catholic Church demanded financial support from England, a nation struggling to raise money to resist a possible French attack, Wycliffe advised Parliament not to comply. He argued the Church was already too wealthy, and said Christ called his disciples to poverty, not wealth. In fact, the clergy was estimated to have a third of the nation's wealth.

Wycliffe even criticized the pope. When Urban and Clement were each claiming to be the pope and were excommunicating each other, Urban called for war. Wycliffe replied, 'How dare he make the token of Christ on the cross (which is the token of peace, mercy and charity) a banner to lead us to slay Christian men, for the love of two false priests.' The pope, Wycliffe said, was not the voice of God on earth – the Bible was. The pope, he added, may not even be among those chosen for heaven. Wycliffe also rejected the doctrine of transubstantiation, which says that during Mass the bread and wine become the actual body and blood of Jesus. This teaching, Wycliffe said, was not in the Bible.

THE FIRST ENGLISH BIBLE

Driven by his lack of confidence in the authority of the Church, as well as his respect for scripture, Wycliffe started pushing for an English translation of the Bible – one to replace the Latin version that only the well-educated clergy could read. 'The laity ought to understand the faith,' Wycliffe said, 'and, as doctrines of our faith are in the scriptures, believers should have the scriptures in a language they fully understand.'

Wycliffe may not have translated much or any of the Bible that bears his name. But at the very least he was the motivational force behind the project. Working from the Latin Vulgate, Wycliffe's followers produced two English

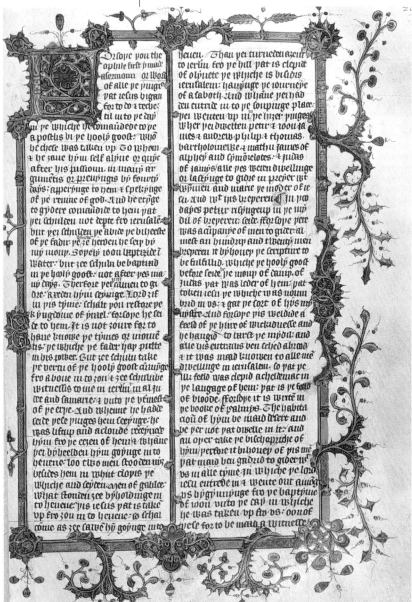

Readings from Wycliffe's Bible

England had three main dialects in Wycliffe's day. Wycliffe and his followers chose to translate the Latin Bible into the Midland English dialect that was popular in the region around London. His Bible helped unite the English language. Here are excerpts from two familiar passages in Wycliffe's Bible, compared with the same passages in the King James Version, translated more than two centuries later:

Forsothe God so louede the world, that he gaf his oon bigetun sone, that ech man that bileueth in to him perische not, but haue euerlastynge lyf.

For God so loved the world, that he gave his only begotten Son, that whosoever believeth in him should not perish, but have everlasting life.
JOHN 3:16

If I speke with tungis of men and aungels, sothli I haue not charite, I am maad as bras sownnynge, or a symbal tynkynge.

Though I speak with the tongues of men and of angels, and have not charity, I am become as sounding brass, or a tinkling cymbal.
1 CORINTHIANS 13:1

IOANNES WICLEFVS ANGLVS.
*Quanta fuit rabies odijque potentia ves tri,
Pontifices olim, carnificesque truces!
Ossa in humata diu vobis inuisa virorum
Sanctorum, requie non potuere frui!* *Cum priuillegio.*

Religious reformer John Wycliffe (c. 1380–84), who taught philosophy at Oxford University and became the driving force behind the first English Bible.

translations. The first was a small pocket edition completed in about 1382. One surviving copy says an associate of Wycliffe, Nicholas of Hereford, translated the Old Testament. The New Testament translator is not named, but has traditionally been assumed to be Wycliffe. Many scholars, however, doubt Wycliffe had a direct hand in the work because the finished product was more stilted than the Bible quotations Wycliffe used in his sermons. The translation was hard to read because it was a literal translation of the Latin. A revised and more reader-friendly version came out about a decade later – after Wycliffe's death – translated by his friend and secretary, John Purvey.

Wycliffe commissioned a group of his followers – later given the derogatory name of Lollards ('mutterers') – to become travelling ministers who read the Bible and presented its teachings to people throughout the land.

Church leaders bitterly opposed the English Bible. Henry Knighton, a Catholic writer of the time, summed up the Church's position:

Christ gave his gospel to the clergy and the learned doctors of the Church so that they might give it to the laity... Wycliffe, by thus translating the Bible, made it the property of the masses and common to all and more open to the laity, and even to women who were able to read... And so the pearl of the gospel is thrown before swine... The jewel of the clergy has been turned into the sport of the laity.

One pope issued five bulls (official letters) ordering Wycliffe's arrest. Two popes summoned him to Rome, and the Catholic Church in England tried him three times. But his friends protected him and he was never in his lifetime convicted as a heretic.

The Church regretted this, and in 1428, at the pope's command, ordered his body to be unearthed. British historian Thomas Fuller, writing some 200 years later, describes what happened next:

They burnt his bones to ashes and cast them into the Swift, a neighbouring brook running hard by. Thus the brook hath conveyed his ashes into Avon; Avon into Severn; Severn into the narrow seas; and they into the main ocean. And thus the ashes of Wycliffe are the emblem of his doctrine which now is dispersed the world over.

The dignified look

Wycliffe was summoned to London in 1377 to answer charges of heresy. A writer of the day described the scholar's physical appearance this way:

... a tall thin figure, covered with a long light gown of black colour, with a belt about his body; the head, adorned with a full, flowing beard, exhibiting features keen and sharply cut; the eye clear and penetrating; the lips firmly closed in token of resolution – the whole man wearing an aspect of lofty earnestness and replete with dignity and character.

Bible Heretics

'The Pope is not the true and manifest successor of Peter... if he be avaricious, then he is the vicar of Judas Iscariot.'

JAN HUS, CZECH REFORMER
(c. 1372–1415)

This 19th-century engraving depicts Peter Waldo, the founder of the Waldensians.

John Wycliffe was not the first to defy the Church and criticize the pope for his wealth and misuse of authority, nor would he be the last. The movement back to leading a life of poverty started before Wycliffe's time, even before the birth of Francis of Assisi.

ARNOLD OF BRESCIA AND WALDO

In the 1130s, Arnold, the abbot of the monastery in Brescia, Lombardy (in northern Italy), reacted strongly against the vice of greed that was so common among the clergy. He considered this vice a result of the Church's attempt to rule the world, and called for the Church to reform. He urged church leaders to give all their wealth to the state and return to gospel values. They should live in poverty and share their few possessions as the apostles did in the early days of the Church, as described in the Acts of the Apostles. This call to lead the life of the apostles, or *vita apostolica*, was the first of many to come in the centuries that followed. Arnold himself, however, was not content to beg for change peacefully. He defiantly gave his full support to the Roman senate in its rejection of the temporal power of the popes. He was eventually hanged and burned and his ashes were thrown into the River Tiber.

The next major figure to call for a return to the *vita apostolica* was Peter Waldo (or Valdes), a rich merchant from Lyons, France. In 1170, or shortly thereafter, Waldo was converted when he heard a street performer tell the story of St Alexis, a fifth-century Roman patrician who had given all his wealth to the poor and lived the life of a beggar, hoping to gain true happiness in the next life.

When Waldo spoke to a priest about the impact the story of St Alexis had made on him, the priest quoted the gospel passage in which Jesus tells the rich young man: 'If you wish to be perfect, go, sell your possessions, and give the money to the poor, and you will have treasure in heaven; then come, follow me' (Matthew 19:21). In response, Waldo promptly transferred his wealth to his wife and put his daughter in a convent. Unable to read Latin, he had parts of the Bible translated into French for him and memorized long passages from it. He then set out

The Humiliati

Another group of Christians who wished to live like the apostles was the Humiliati. Living in voluntary poverty, these men and women banded together to live lives of prayer and manual labour. Like Arnold before them, the Humiliati came mainly from Lombardy in northern Italy. In their communities, they lived simply and devoted themselves to caring for the sick and poor. But they also felt the obligation to preach, and this brought them into conflict with church authorities, who insisted that only clergymen should preach. Because they persisted in their preaching, the Humiliati were condemned for their disobedience to the church hierarchy at the Council of Verona in 1184.

The Humiliati, however, were less defiant than Arnold and Waldo had been, and in 1201 Pope Innocent III, the pope who was soon to approve the Franciscan Rule, had the group investigated. Innocent wholly approved the Humiliati's way of life and accepted them back into the Church. He even gave them permission to preach, provided they avoided theological matters and simply urged their hearers to lead good Christian lives. Unlike the Waldensians the Humiliati bent to the authority of the Church and were allowed to survive.

Francis of Assisi was to be successful, where others had failed, because he never defied the Church, but rather always sought its sanction for his three Orders. He transformed the Church solely by his example, while others had flown in the face of the Church, provoking anger and rejection. The Humiliati had taken a middle ground, and they survived until the 16th century. By that time, however, the group had succumbed to the very faults it had earlier fled from. It became very rich. In 1571, when the venerable churchman Charles Borromeo attempted to reform the group, they attacked him, and the Humiliati were permanently suppressed.

on a life of begging, performing works of charity, and preaching that all Christians should imitate Christ by living in poverty.

Waldo soon attracted followers, who came to be known as the Poor in Spirit. Following the example of Jesus in the Gospels, he sent his followers out two by two to teach the scriptures. In 1179, when the archbishop of Lyons ordered Waldo to stop his preaching, he refused. Two years later he went to Rome to appeal to Pope Alexander III. The pope approved of the Waldensian lifestyle but not the translation of the Bible and the preaching of laymen. Consequently, he craftily gave the Waldensians permission to preach, but only if they were invited to do so by the local bishop. Since this was not likely to happen, the Waldensians were still not permitted to preach.

Waldo refused to submit to the ban and continued to send his followers out to preach. The Waldensians were excommunicated, and in 1184, the Council of Verona condemned them as 'pertinacious and schismatic'. But even this official condemnation failed to stop them. Waldo died sometime between 1205 and 1218, but after his death his followers continued in their work, often advocating views that were considered heretical by the Church. During the Reformation the Waldensians formed their own Church, which still survives to this day.

JAN HUS

Jan Hus was a peasant from Bohemia who left his family to study and became a priest and a leading scholar. He was noted for his preaching in the Czech language at Bethlehem Chapel in Prague. While in Prague he discovered the writings of John Wycliffe and found himself in full agreement with the reformer. From then on he incorporated Wycliffe's ideas into his sermons, holding that scripture should be the supreme authority for Christians and not the church hierarchy. He also, with Wycliffe, attacked the right of the Church to own property rather than living according to gospel values.

At first Hus was supported by the archbishop of Prague, but later his violent sermons against the immorality of the clergy provoked hostility. In 1407, they were denounced in Rome and the archbishop of Prague was ordered to forbid Hus to preach. But Hus had the protection of the emperor, who made him rector of the university in Prague, which was heavily pro-Wycliffe. In 1410, Pope Alexander V ordered the destruction of all of Wycliffe's books, and tried to keep Hus from preaching. In 1414, Hus travelled to the Council of Constance, with a safe-conduct from the emperor. At the Council the following year, he was thrown into prison, despite his safe-conduct, and put on trial. He was convicted of heresy and burned at the stake. His martyrdom made him a great hero in Bohemia, and his followers – the Hussites – fought other religious factions in Bohemia for years to follow. For a time, they even joined with the Waldensians in their wars.

Jan Hus is burned at the stake, from the *Chronicle of Ulrich of Reichental*.

The Christian Renaissance

To raise money to support his lavish tastes, Pope Julius II (1443–1513) sold church jobs and forgiveness for sins. Such impropriety drove many in the Church to call for reform. This portrait of Julius is by Raphael (1483–1520).

A scholar's wish

In the preface of his Greek New Testament, Erasmus said he undertook the project so everyone might one day read the Bible: 'Would that these were translated into each and every language... Would that the farmer might sing snatches of scripture at his plough, that the weaver might hum phrases of scripture to the tune of his shuttle.'

To shoot a clergyman's blood pressure heaven-high in the 1400s and 1500s, a person often needed only to mention the word 'humanism', the name of a literary and cultural movement that emerged from the enlightened age called the Renaissance. Tradition-minded church leaders felt threatened by Christian humanists – and understandably so, since humanists insisted on using human wisdom and learning to re-evaluate and reform Christianity.

Although universities started as church schools that emphasized religion and philosophy, classes began to emerge on less spiritual topics: classical literature, history and ancient languages. Christian humanist scholars wanted to take the insight they discovered in their studies of the classics and use it to correct distortions preached and practised by many in the Church.

GOOD CHURCH GONE BAD

Scholars decided it was time to start calling for reform in the Church. Even common citizens, more and more, were seeing the Church as their enemy – a hostile institution committed to its own wealth and prestige at all costs. One of the low points came when the Church elected as its pope Roderigo Borgia, a priest who had fathered 10 illegitimate children. Taking the name Alexander VI, he cultivated a reputation for opulence, corruption and murder. Some say he probably died of a poison he intended for one of his cardinals.

His successor, Julius II, had dreams better suited to Julius Caesar. This pope dressed his troops in silver armour and set out to secure his kingdom on earth. Like his predecessors, Julius explored creative ways to get money to fund his wars and massive building projects. He created new administrative jobs, which he sold to the highest bidder. He also sold indulgences, which promised to shorten or eliminate a person's time in purgatory (a temporary place of punishment, according to Roman Catholic teaching, where the souls of godly people are purified for heaven) – sending the buyer or the buyer's loved one more quickly to heaven.

Scholars studying the original languages of scripture saw no justification for such practices. In fact, they began arguing that centuries of misunderstanding about the Bible had led to the distorted teachings, useless rituals and scandalous

Erasmus, the illegitimate son of a priest

The first person to compile and publish the New Testament in its original language was Desiderius Erasmus, the illegitimate son of a Dutch priest and a physician's daughter. Erasmus grew to become a reluctant cleric who, after the death of his parents, was forced into a monastery.

Erasmus said the guardian who put him there believed that catching boys for the monastic life was 'offering to God an acceptable sacrifice'. Even so, Erasmus stayed long enough to be ordained a priest by about the age of 26. But he grew to hate monastery life, rigid rules and closed-minded theologians. He wanted to travel. And he wanted academic elbow room. But he also wanted to remain in his Augustinian Order.

A French bishop offered him a way out, taking him on as his Latin secretary, and then helping fund his theological studies in Paris. From there Erasmus began a career of writing and travelling that took him to most countries of Europe. Although he often complained of poor health, he seemed driven by a desire to seek out the best theological minds of the day, and study with them. It was this that drew him to England six times, in spite of what he described as their bad beer, barbarism and inhospitable weather. There, scholars inspired him to learn the Greek language in which the New Testament was written. The result was his most memorable work – the Greek New Testament.

Erasmus wrote many books and essays criticizing the Church and that encouraged Martin Luther and other reformers to do the same. Erasmus initially supported Luther, but backed away when he saw the Church begin to split. Of the bickering and intolerance on both sides, Erasmus wrote to Luther, 'Had I not seen it, nay, felt it myself, I should never have believed anyone who said theologians could become so insane.'

some obvious errors – that when he printed the book again in 1527, he replaced his Latin version with the corrected Vulgate.

Some of his corrections to the Latin Bible raised dramatic questions about church rituals. In Mark 1:15, the official Latin Bible quotes Jesus as saying, 'Do penance, and believe the gospel.' But Erasmus quoted Jesus as saying, 'Repent [be sorry] and believe the gospel.' If Erasmus was right, Christians did not need to go to confession and do acts of penance to make amends to God for their sins.

Protectors of church tradition were not impressed. Nor were they comforted by the humanist reasoning that a more accurate version of the Bible would produce better Christians.

Although Erasmus never wanted a theological revolution – and later resisted the radical changes Martin Luther demanded – the Dutchman had set the stage. To quote a popular saying in church circles during the 1500s: 'Erasmus laid the egg and Luther hatched it.'

Left: Desiderius Erasmus (c. 1466–1536).

A page from Erasmus's New Testament in Latin and Greek, published in 1516.

behaviour. To correct the errors, they turned for guidance to the original sources of early Christian faith – ancient Hebrew and Greek manuscripts of scripture instead of the Church's traditional Latin translation.

REVISING THE BIBLE

The first Christian humanist on record to correct mistakes in the revered Latin Vulgate translation was Lorenzo Valla, a scholar from Italy, where the humanist movement began. In 1455, he wrote *Annotations on the New Testament*, a work that angered theological conservatives but which inspired the scholar who became the 'Prince of Humanism' – a Dutchman named Desiderius Erasmus.

Erasmus was about 40 years old when he came across Valla's work, in 1504. The book impressed him so much that he reprinted it the next year and began writing a barrage of his own works – stories, essays and satires – mostly aimed at correcting abuses within the Church. He wanted reform, not revolution. Yet he was not beyond belittling the pope to get it. In one satire, he told of Pope Julius II being locked out of heaven by Peter, the first pope.

Erasmus's most influential work was his first Greek edition of the New Testament, published in 1516. He created it by drawing from newly discovered Greek manuscripts, and then he added to his book a corrected version of the Latin Vulgate translation. Many fellow scholars were delighted. Two years later he published a second edition, replacing the Latin Vulgate with his own Latin translation. But he drew so much criticism for his translation – partly because of

The Bible Goes to Press

Church pension

The archbishop of Mainz gave Gutenberg a pension, starting in January 1465, three years before the printer died. This was probably in recognition of his contribution to the Church, through printing the Bible and religious documents. The pension provided him with grain, wine and clothing, and exempted him from some taxes.

❦

Reconstruction of the first printing press, which was invented by Johannes Gutenberg between 1397 and 1400. In the foreground are early editions of a book from that era, along with printing blocks. Hanging in the background are pages, showing how Gutenberg dried pages that were wet with ink.

A German metalworker not content with the family business probably takes as much responsibility as Martin Luther for the religious revolution that split the Church into Catholic and Protestant. His name was Johann Gutenberg, and he was a pioneer in printing with movable type.

Only a century before Luther, John Wycliffe and Jan Hus had stirred up sparks of reform. But the fire did not spread. Luther's reform message, however, quickly swallowed up Germany, engulfed other nations of Europe, and kept growing. The critical difference between Luther and earlier would-be reformers is that Luther had access to Gutenberg's newly invented printing technology. Luther could cheaply publish his message in books and pamphlets, and then distribute it to hundreds of thousands of people. More importantly, he could publish the Bible in his people's own language so they could see for themselves that many church leaders were distorting the Bible's message.

SECRET EXPERIMENTS

Little is known about how Gutenberg came up with his printing idea and honed the technology into an art. That is because, like many emerging inventions, it was a guarded secret. Gutenberg grew up in Mainz, Germany, near the western border with France. He earned what was probably a comfortable living at the family trade as a goldsmith, working with precious metals making coins, jewellery and other objects. But around the early 1430s, when he was about 40 years old, he left Germany after a bitter clash between trade guilds and leading citizens in Mainz. He moved

The printer's art

Gutenberg made his type by hand-cutting individual letters onto the tip of hard metal rods. In branding-iron fashion, he then pressed each letter into soft metal, such as copper – perhaps aided by the tap of a hammer. He then filled the punched out area with a strong, molten alloy, such as iron and tin. When the alloy hardened and was removed, it formed the mirror view of a letter and was stored in an organizer box.

To build a page, printers pulled letters from the box, arranged them in a metal frame, and locked the frame so it held the letters tightly together. It might seem that the type would have been hard to proofread, because all the letters looked inverted, like a mirror image, but printers quickly developed a knack for reading it.

Thick ink was dabbed on the letters by using ink balls: handheld leather pads stuffed with wool or horsehair and covered with a removable sheepskin. Using a rocking motion, the printer dabbed the ink onto the metal type.

With the text plate ready, the printer clamped a damp sheet of paper into a holder above it. Damp sheets received the ink more evenly than dry ones. A huge vertical screw, much like smaller screws that push car jacks up today, drove the press. The printer would push a bar attached to the screw. This lowered a plate of metal, pressing the inked type and paper together. If text was to appear on both sides of the paper, this had to be done right away before the damp sheet dried. Two pressmen working together could print about 250 sheets an hour.

The sheets for books were hung to dry, folded and assembled into the order they would be bound. The binding was usually done elsewhere.

about 65 kilometres (100 miles) southwest, to the French city of Strasbourg, near the German border.

It was there, many historians say, that he got involved in expensive and secret experiments with printing. There is no written record of what went on, except for hints from a lawsuit against Gutenberg. Witnesses testified that a carpenter had loaned him money for the building of a screw-driven wooden press, and a goldsmith had provided printing materials for 'new art'. The suit was brought by heirs of a Gutenberg partner who had died; they wanted to be in on the deal. Although they lost the suit, Gutenberg's secret about a new invention was out.

Historians speculate that with the help of a Paris-educated scribe, Peter Schöffer, Gutenberg designed and cut the metal letters he would later use to produce printed works that looked like handwritten manuscripts. Here, too, is where Gutenberg probably refined the entire printing process, including the development of paste-thick ink (perhaps oil-based, made from soot and varnish) that would adhere to the metal letters.

THE PRINTING STARTS

Gutenberg and his associate returned to Mainz in the late 1440s and set up shop. His earliest printing jobs included a poem about Judgment Day, calendars for 1448, and – quite ironically – indulgences for the Church.

By 1450, Gutenberg needed financial backing, perhaps to help him buy the supplies he needed to print what became known as the Gutenberg Bible, using the revised Latin Vulgate translation, the best version available at the time. He turned to a wealthy banker, Johann Fust, who over the next several years loaned him 1,600 guilders – enough money to pay the salary of a skilled artisan for about 10 years. In 1454, Gutenberg showed samples of his forthcoming printed Bible at a German trade fair, and announced that all 180 copies he planned to print had buyers. This created great excitement. But in late 1455, as the Bible project was wrapping up, the banker and the printer had a mysterious falling out. Fust wanted his money back with interest – to the tune of about 2,020 guilders. The case went to court and Gutenberg was forced to give the banker his equipment – as well as the Bible. Fust and Gutenberg's assistant, Peter Schöffer, finished printing the Bible. Schöffer later married Fust's daughter.

Forty-eight copies of the Bible still exist. It is a two-volume book, with 1,282 pages. Each page has two columns and, usually, 42 lines (which is why many historians call it the '42-Line Bible'). Eleven surviving Bibles were printed on vellum – the finest parchment made of animal skins – and

the remaining 37 on paper. Gutenberg went to great lengths to make the text look handwritten. Instead of developing one style of letter, he created many to imitate the variety seen in the work of scribes (he had eight versions of the lower case letter 'a'). In all, he designed a total of 270 letters, plus 125 symbols and abbreviations.

Although Gutenberg never signed his work, many believed he opened another shop and printed a 36-line Bible in 1458. The art of printing spread rapidly, and by the century's end – on the eve of Luther's clash with the Church – there were printing shops in nearly every major European city.

A page from the Gutenberg Bible, with hand-painted initials and decorations, showing Psalms 1 to 4. The name is misleading, as Johann Gutenberg did not finish the project himself. In the midst of the job, his partner, a banker, took him to court. The judge ordered Gutenberg to give everything to the banker, to settle a debt. It was the banker and Gutenberg's assistant who actually finished printing the Bible.

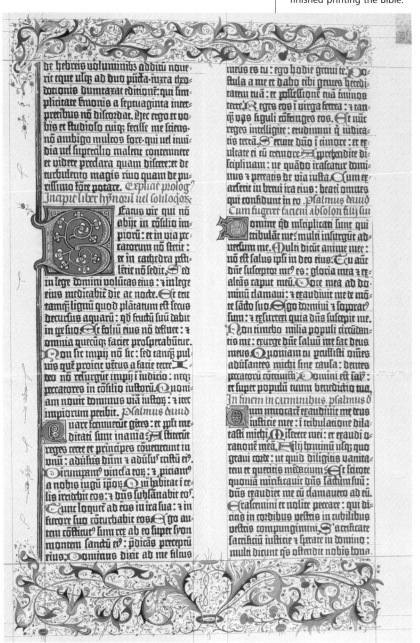

Beyond Gutenberg

Throughout history, few inventions have caught on as quickly as the printing press. In earlier times, books had to be copied and decorated laboriously by hand and only one book could be done at a time. The introduction of blockbooks allowed publishers to print multiple copies of a book, but the work of carefully carving texts and illustrations into blocks of wood was tedious, time-consuming and likely to produce errors that were almost impossible to correct without starting all over again. And when all was said and done, the prints in blockbooks were generally rough and unattractive. But Gutenberg's press used movable type that could be used over and over whether reprinting the same pages or creating entirely new ones. It was a publisher's dream come true.

EARLY PRINTED BIBLES

Beginning in the late 1450s prospective printers descended on the shop formerly owned by Gutenberg in Augsberg, Germany to learn how

The Psalter produced in 1457 by Gutenberg's former associates, Johann Fust and Peter Schöffer, was the first book to be printed in three colours.

to build and use a printing press. Once trained these new printers set up their own shops throughout the country, and shops soon appeared in Italy. Venice was a particularly busy printing centre, and in the 1470s its books dominated the market. Eventually printing spread throughout Europe, and by the end of the century there were printing shops in some 250 cities and towns across Europe.

Along with other books, Bibles were printed in large numbers. By 1500, more than 90 editions of the Latin Vulgate Bible had appeared. Two translations from the Vulgate were printed in Venice in 1471 alone, one by Vindelinus de Spira and the other by Nicolé Malermi. The Malermi translation was edited 10 times before 1500 and frequently afterwards. But even though Latin Bibles predominated a number of Bibles in local languages also appeared. The first Bible to be printed after Gutenberg's was produced in Strasbourg in 1466 and was in German. Its last edition appeared in 1773. The first printed Czech translation of the Bible, made from the Vulgate, was published in 1475.

The first printed biblical book to appear in Hebrew was a book of Psalms, published in Bologna, Italy, in 1477. The first complete Hebrew Bible to be printed was published by Joshua Solomon in 1488, and is known for its delicate Hebrew lettering and intricate geometric designs.

DECORATING PRINTED BOOKS

The earliest printed books were generally not illustrated or decorated, although the printer usually left space for such art work to be added after printing. Artists often added coloured letters and designs to a text after printing, as in the Latin Bible published by Bernhard Richel of Basel, Switzerland, in 1472. Even more noteworthy, de Spira's 1771 Italian translation of the Vulgate contained lavish initial letters, paintings, and designs that were added by the anonymous artist known as the Master of the Putti.

Even in the early years of printing, however, some multicolour work was done on the press. For example, in 1457, Johann Fust, who had taken over Gutenberg's press in payment of a debt, joined with Peter Schöffer, who had helped Fust complete the printing of the Gutenberg Bible, to produce an elaborate book of Psalms. In this Psalter, certain accented letters were printed in red, and some background designs, possibly etched into soft metal like copper, were printed in blue. In order to produce the three separate colours (black, red and blue), the printers had to put the pages through the press three times. After printing the black text, they had to clean the black ink from the plates, add red ink to the letters requiring it, and print the pages again. They then had to repeat the process for the blue backgrounds. It was a time-consuming job.

The first Bible with printed illustrations was published by Gunther Zainer of Augsberg, Germany, in about 1475. It contained woodcuts of initial letters and illustrations, but it was not printed in colour. The colour had to be added by hand after purchase. Then in 1478, German printer Heinrich Quentel produced the Cologne Bible, which was lavishly illustrated with woodcuts, but used colour sparingly. Once a woodcut had been prepared for printing it could be used an indefinite number of times with little loss in detail, accuracy, form or vigour. Woodcuts were to be used extensively in printed books in the centuries to come.

By 1500, the printing and illustrating of books were of such high quality that printing came to dominate publishing. The art of copying and illuminating manuscripts by hand, which had flourished in the Middle Ages, gradually died off. It was the end of one era and the beginning of another.

Craft of the bookseller

Trade in books goes back to ancient Egypt, when scribes copied down the words of orators and poets and sold the copied texts to anyone who could afford them. Later, in Rome, when it became popular to have a library, booksellers set up shops in various parts of the city. On the doors or sideposts of these shops, they posted lists of the books available.

With the spread of Christianity biblical and other sacred books were in demand, and travelling booksellers were common. In the 12th century, meeting the demand of the universities, booksellers, who generally worked on commission, appeared in Paris and Bologna, probably operating from outdoor stalls. They gradually spread to other university towns. By the 14th century, when the task of copying and illuminating manuscripts moved from the monasteries to lay professionals, the number of booksellers increased along with the literacy of the new affluent middle class. In 1300, Paris alone boasted of 30 booksellers. In the 15th century, many of these booksellers had formed guilds and often positioned their stalls against the walls of the city's cathedral. In addition to books, they sold copies of popular prayers.

The modern system of bookselling arose just after the introduction of printing. The earliest printers sold their own books – Gutenberg had customers for every copy of his proposed Bible after printing and showing only a few sample pages of his work. Soon, however, printers employed agents to sell their work. For example, it is said that Anton Koberger, who introduced printing to Nuremberg, Germany, in 1470, had agents to sell his books 'in every city in Christendom' in addition to his own 16 shops. From that time on, bookshops were a common sight throughout Europe.

This detail from an Italian illumination shows a 14th-century bookshop.

Luther and His Bible

A portrait of Martin Luther (1483–1546) by Lucas Cranach the Elder.

'If God had wanted me to die thinking I was a clever fellow, he would not have got me into the business of translating the Bible.'

MARTIN LUTHER, PROTESTANT REFORMER (1483–1546)

German Bible scholar Martin Luther, a one-time monk, is most famous for starting a Church-wide reform movement – the Reformation – that ended up splitting the Church in two: Catholic and Protestant. But he also translated the Bible into German, which helped unify the nation and its dialect-diverse language. Astonishingly, he took only 11 weeks to finish the first draft of his German New Testament – part of a Bible translation so plain-spoken that revised copies of it are still popular among Germans today.

Luther was born of stern peasants who beat him with a ferocity that today would be called abusive. His father was a copper miner who later managed to buy several mines and smelters, providing a comfortable living for his family. Luther's father apparently recognized his son's extraordinary gift of intelligence. For instead of pulling him into the family business after elementary school, the young Luther was sent on to secondary school and then to a university where he received a bachelor's degree followed by a master's degree. From there, Luther began to study law – as his father wished. With a law degree, Luther would have been able to provide handsomely for his parents and extended family.

'I WILL BECOME A MONK!'

About a month into law school, Luther took a leave of absence from school to go home – perhaps to consult with his parents about his future. On the trip back to school, caught in a dangerous thunderstorm, Luther cried out to the patron saint of miners: 'Help me, St Anne! I will become a monk!' Several weeks later, he entered a monastery – a decision that changed the history of Christianity.

As required by the strict Augustinian Order he joined, he gave up all his possessions, including his cherished lute, which he could play quite well. He prayed, fasted and deprived himself using common ascetic practices among the monks – beating himself and going without sleep and without a blanket on cold nights. Yet he never felt good enough to please God.

'My conscience would never give me assurance,' he wrote. 'I was always doubting and said, "You did not perform that correctly. You were not contrite enough. You left that out of your confession."'

His mentor, Johann von Staupitz, who was a fellow monk as well as dean of the theological faculty at the University of Wittenberg, tried to assure Luther of God's love and mercy. But it did not work. So Staupitz, apparently hoping Luther would discover the truth for himself in scripture, ordered him to become a Bible professor at Wittenberg. Luther objected, 'It will be the death of me.' 'Quite all right,' Staupitz replied. 'God has plenty of work for clever men like you to do in heaven.'

During his studies for lectures and sermons, Luther became captivated by the Bible's teaching that Christians are saved not by obeying church rules, confessing sins to a priest, doing penance, or performing acts of kindness – they are saved simply by trusting God. One verse summed it up for him: 'The one who is righteous will live by faith' (Romans 1:17). His studies convinced him that he did not need to earn God's salvation. He simply needed to accept it as a gift.

HEAVEN FOR SALE

Luther's new insight could not have come at a worse time for the Church. Excesses of Pope

Excerpts from the Ninety-Five Theses

When Martin Luther nailed his Ninety-Five Theses to the church door in Wittenberg, he was protesting against several practices of the Roman Catholic Church, mainly the selling of indulgences. Here is a sampling of the theses, which Luther hoped would spark debate and reform:

1. When our Lord and Master Jesus Christ said, 'Repent,' he willed the entire life of believers to be one of repentance.

2. This word [repent] cannot be understood as referring to the sacrament of penance, that is, confession and satisfaction, as administered by the clergy...

27. They preach only human doctrines who say that as soon as the money clinks into the money chest, the soul flies out of purgatory...

32. Those who believe that they can be certain of their salvation because they have indulgence letters will be eternally damned, together with their teachers...

36. Any truly repentant Christian has a right to full remission of penalty and guilt, even without indulgence letters...

45. Christians are to be taught that he who sees a needy man and passes him by, yet gives his money for indulgences, does not buy the pope's indulgences but God's wrath...

51. Christians are to be taught that the pope would do better to sell St Peter's Church [which was being built by money raised from selling indulgences] and give it to the poor who are being pressured into buying indulgences.

Leo X, like those of popes in the recent past, had spawned a financial crisis. To raise money, the pope created more than 2,000 church jobs that he sold, and he approved the sale of indulgences – spiritual fast-pass tickets into heaven, shortening or eliminating time spent in purgatory doing penance for sin. The argument supporting the sale of indulgences was that the Church had a vast spiritual treasury built up by the good works of Jesus, the apostles and the saints. The pope could draw on these resources to release people from penance in the after-life realm of purgatory, and send them on their way to heaven.

In Germany, about half the money raised went to the pope. And with the pope's permission, the other half went to a German prince – so the prince could pay off the massive debt he had incurred when he had bought several of the pope's church jobs, including that of archbishop of Mainz.

The travelling salesman who hawked the indulgences in Germany was a hard-sell monk named Johann Tetzel. 'Listen to the voice of your dear dead relatives and friends,' Tetzel told the crowds that gathered around him, 'beseeching you and saying, "Pity us, pity us. We are in dire torment from which you can redeem us for a pittance."' He often ended his pitch with a jingle: 'As soon as the coin in the coffer rings, the soul from purgatory springs.'

In response, Luther wrote his famous Ninety-Five Theses – statements against the sale of indulgences, against abuses within the Church, and against teachings that salvation requires confession to a priest as well as penance. He nailed these to the door of All Saints' Church in Wittenberg on 31 October 1517, hoping to spark a debate that would ignite a cleansing blaze of reform. Instead, he was shown the door of the Catholic Church – he was excommunicated.

Three and a half years after posting the Ninety-Five Theses, Luther thought he was finally going to get the debate he requested. The Holy Roman Emperor Charles V, who had resisted the pope's request to burn Luther as a heretic, called a meeting that is known, unappetizingly, as the Diet of Worms (meeting in Worms, Germany). Luther quickly discovered that the meeting was not a debate at all, but a trial. Given the offer to recant his teachings, he replied, 'Unless I can be instructed and convinced with the evidence from the holy scripture or with open, clear and distinct grounds of reasoning... then I cannot recant.'

The emperor ruled: 'A single friar who goes counter to all Christianity for a thousand years must be wrong. I have decided to mobilize everything against Luther – my kingdoms and dominions, my friends, my body, my blood, and my soul.' As agreed before the trial, Luther was promised safe passage home. But the prince of his

A portrait of Pope Leo X (1475–1521) by Raphael. As a fundraising strategy, Leo approved the sale of indulgences – spiritual tickets to heaven that were believed to shorten or eliminate a person's time in purgatory.

'We are now sweating over a German translation of the Prophets. O God, what a hard and difficult task it is to force these writers, quite against their wills, to speak German. They have no desire to give up their native Hebrew in order to imitate our barbaric German. It is as though one were to force a nightingale to imitate a cuckoo.'

MARTIN LUTHER

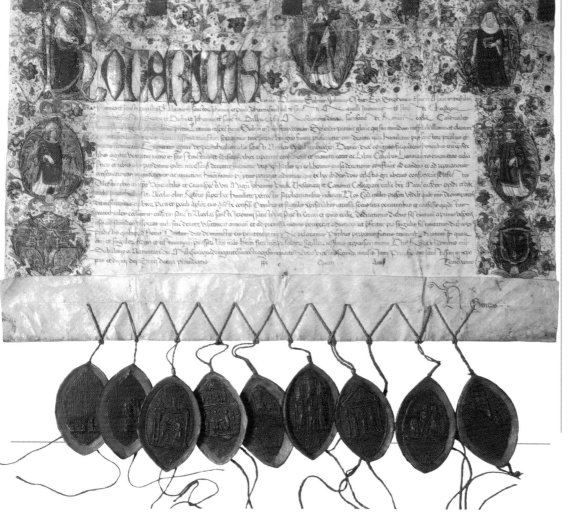

Letter of indulgence from 1484. Such letters were sometimes sent to individual churches, and they granted partial indulgences to all who visited the church on a certain feast day, and full indulgences to those who visited it regularly and performed certain prayers or rituals there. Hanging from the bottom are papal seals.

region did not trust the promise. Since Luther was a convicted outlaw, anyone could kill him and expect nothing but gratitude from powerful people. So the prince kidnapped Luther on the trip home, put him in protective custody in a castle, and gave him a new identity – Knight George.

A NEW BIBLE IN 11 WEEKS

During the 10 months Luther spent in the castle, he wrote. Among his writings was one book destined to transform his teachings into a movement. Working from a Greek edition of the New Testament the Dutch scholar Erasmus had created about five years earlier, Luther translated the New Testament into German – completing the first draft in a mere 11 weeks.

Perhaps one reason the translation moved so quickly was that Luther refused to make a literal translation that rigidly followed the Greek word patterns. Instead, he wanted scripture to read the way Germans talk. 'To translate properly', Luther explained later, while working on the

Old Testament, 'is to render the spirit of a foreign language into our own idiom. I try to speak as men do in the marketplace. In rendering Moses, I make him so German that no one would suspect he was a Jew.'

Luther submitted his translation for review by a committee of gifted scholars he dubbed the Sanhedrin, after the Jewish high council in Bible times. His New Testament – *Das Neue Testament Deutzsch* – was published in September 1522 and priced at about a week's salary for a typical worker. A printer's masterpiece, with beautiful type and woodcut illustrations, it sold an estimated 5,000 copies in the first two months, and more than 100,000 in Luther's lifetime.

The Old Testament came next, but it took 12 years because Luther worked from a variety of Hebrew texts, and he was not as familiar with Hebrew as he was with Greek. In addition, he also took pains to understand topics that were unfamiliar to him. When writing about sacrificial

The analytical John Calvin

The theological father of Southern Baptists, Presbyterians and several other Protestant Churches in the Reformed tradition, John Calvin was a French theologian whom Martin Luther admired, though never met.

The two had much in common, with Calvin considered the second most important reformer, after Luther. Both were encouraged by their fathers to study law. Both were brilliant thinkers. And both severed ties with the Roman Catholic Church – Calvin in 1534, a couple of years after having a spiritual awakening he seldom spoke about.

Calvin had one of the most analytical minds in the Church, which he put to use developing the first carefully reasoned, systematic, Bible-based theology for Protestants. Calvin became best known for his doctrine of predestination – the teaching that God decides who will and will not be saved, and that there is nothing humans can do about it.

Luther defends his beliefs before Holy Roman Emperor Charles V at a hearing convened in Worms, Germany (17–19 April 1521). Charles condemned Luther as a heretic, although he granted him safe passage home. *Luther at the Diet of Worms* by Anton von Wrener (1843–1915).

rituals, he had the town butcher cut up a sheep so he could study its organs.

Luther wrote many books, articles, scholarly essays and even hymns – the most famous of which is 'A Mighty Fortress is Our God'. But he said his greatest contribution to the world was his translation of the Bible: 'I'd like all my books to be destroyed so that only the sacred writings in the Bible would be diligently read.'

Perhaps the reason he felt this way is because it was the Bible – not the Church – that helped him find peace with God. Contained within this book, Luther believed, is God's truth available to everyone. 'A simple layman armed with scripture,' Luther said, 'is to be believed above a pope or a cardinal without it.'

Martin Luther's New Testament in German contains beautiful illustrations. This is the first page of the letter to the Romans, with a woodcut by Hans Schautelein.

Reformation timetable

1512: Martin Luther earns doctorate in theology.

1515: Luther lectures on Romans, teaching salvation through faith.

1517: A German monk starts selling indulgences – spiritual tickets to heaven. In protest, Luther posts his Ninety-Five Theses.

1519: In a public debate, Luther says the Bible has more authority than church leaders.

1520: Pope excommunicates Luther.

1521: Holy Roman Emperor condemns Luther as a heretic.

1522: Luther publishes German New Testament.

1527: First Protestant university started (Marburg, Germany).

1529: Name 'Protestant' first used.

1534: Luther publishes entire German Bible.

Polyglot Bibles

The insights of scripture

Scripture is filled with 'insights which cannot become known from any other sources than from the very fountain of the original language' (Complutensian Polyglot Bible Prologue).

Cardinal Francisco Ximénez de Cisneros (1436–1517), Archbishop of Toledo, Primas of Spain and Grand Inquisitor. Relief by Felipe Bigarny (d. 1543).

The Church was generally against having Bibles translated into the languages of the people, as it was feared that lay men and women would seriously misinterpret what they read and fall into heresy. Church leaders were, however, concerned with ascertaining the most accurate form of the biblical texts, and even though they had declared the Latin Vulgate of Jerome to be their official Bible, they allowed revisions and corrections to be made in the translation over the centuries.

The new universities promoted even more interest in securing an accurate text, and from the 13th century, scholars began examining the Bible in its original languages – Hebrew and Greek. Beginning in the 16th century, books were printed that contained the biblical texts in the original language together with ancient translations. They were called polyglot Bibles. They earned this name because 'poly' means many and 'glot' means language.

ORIGINS OF POLYGLOT BIBLES

The idea of publishing a polyglot Bible originated with Cardinal Francisco Ximénez de Cisneros, archbishop of Toledo in Spain. He may have derived the idea from the sixfold Bible (Hexapla) of the third-century Christian scholar, Origen. Although Origen had copied out ancient biblical texts into six columns (one column for each version), he included only Hebrew and Greek versions. Cardinal Ximénez added Latin and Aramaic.

The work on the first polyglot Bible was done by a team of scholars between 1514 and 1517 (the year Luther nailed his Ninety-Five Theses to the church door in Wittenberg). The scholars worked together at the university Ximénez had founded in Alcalá de Henares, Spain. The Latin name for the city of Alcalá, Complutum, gave its name to the work – it is known as the Complutensian Polyglot.

In the completed polyglot, the Old Testament is printed in three columns, containing texts of the standard Hebrew (Masoretic) version, the Greek Septuagint (the earliest Greek translation of the Old Testament) and the Latin Vulgate. For the first five books of the Bible (the Pentateuch) Aramaic targums (paraphrases), printed in Hebrew characters, are included at the bottom of each page along with Latin translations of the targums. The New Testament texts are printed in two columns, one for the original Greek and the

The man behind the first polyglot Bible

Francisco Ximénez de Cisneros rose from humble beginnings to become one of the leading churchmen of the 16th century and a powerful statesman. It was under his direction that the first polyglot Bible came into being. Ximénez was born in Castile (Spain) in 1436, the son of a poor tax collector. He studied at the University of Salamanca and was ordained a priest. After a number of years in Rome, he returned to Spain, where he eventually served as vicar general of the diocese of Siguenza under Cardinal Pedro de Mendoza.

In 1484, he unexpectedly left this work to become a Franciscan at a friary in Toledo. His life of strict austerity there began to attract crowds, and he moved to a secluded friary, where he lived quietly. But his life of seclusion was short-lived. He was appointed confessor of Queen Isabella of Spain in 1492 (the same year in which Isabella sponsored Christopher Columbus's voyages of discovery). Ximénez's advice was soon sought on matters of state as well as on spiritual issues. In 1494, he was made head of the Franciscans of Castile and in 1495 he was named archbishop of Toledo, the leading church office in Spain. As archbishop, Ximénez sought to reform Christian life in general and succeeded in reforming the Franciscan and other religious orders. He also led a campaign to convert the Moors.

After Queen Isabella's death in 1504, King Ferdinand left Castile, and for a while Ximénez was the virtual ruler of Castile. He later served as regent for the young Charles V. Ximénez was made cardinal in 1507 and in 1508 he used his private income to found the University of Alcalá de Hernares, to which he brought leading scholars from Paris, Bologna and Salamanca. He then financed, sponsored and oversaw the publication of the Complutensian Polyglot Bible. He died in 1517. Although accused of being a harsh taskmaster, Ximénez was an outstanding promoter of learning and one of the great political geniuses of the golden age of Spain.

other for the Latin Vulgate. The Bible was published in six volumes. The final volume contained a brief Hebrew grammar and Hebrew and Aramaic vocabulary lists.

LATER VERSIONS

In the second half of the 16th century, the enterprising French printer Christopher Plantin succeeded in acquiring the patronage of King Philip II of Spain, who awarded him a monopoly on the printing of liturgical books distributed in Spain's dominions. Plantin set up a shop in Antwerp in western Flanders (now part of Belgium), which was then occupied by Spanish forces. Inspired by the Complutensian Polyglot Bible, Plantin persuaded Philip to finance a new, more elaborate version (although Philip's slowness in paying almost bankrupted Plantin). To prepare the texts for the new Bible, King Philip appointed Benito Arias Montano, a Spanish theologian and specialist in Eastern languages who had studied in Alcalá. Montano followed Ximénez in his work, but he added a version of the New Testament in Syriac (an Aramaic dialect used as the liturgical language in some Eastern churches) – along with a Latin translation of the Syriac.

The Antwerp Polyglot, as Plantin's Bible is known, was published in eight volumes between 1569 and 1572. Plantin's beautiful design and printing were highly regarded. Montano, on the other hand, was accused of tampering with the biblical texts, but he was soon cleared of these charges.

Between 1629 and 1645, a 10-volume polyglot Bible was published in Paris. It is inferior in design and printing to Plantin's version, but it included Arabic versions of the Bible as well as the first complete printed version of the Samaritan Pentateuch. The Samaritans were Israelites who had intermarried with Assyrians after the Assyrians conquered the northern kingdom of Israel in the eighth century BC, and who kept their own version of scripture. The Samaritan version of the first five books of the Bible (the only books the Samaritans accept) had come to be known in Europe only a few years before work on the Paris polyglot Bible was started. It differs slightly from the standard Masoretic text of those books, and so was important to the study of the development of the Bible.

The last great polyglot Bible was published in London between 1654 and 1657 in six volumes. It was also the first to be published by Protestants. It was prepared under the direction of the English scholar Brian Walton. The London Polyglot Bible contained texts in nine languages: Hebrew, Aramaic, Samaritan, Greek, Latin, Ethiopic, Syriac, Arabic and Persian. It is generally considered to be the finest of all the polyglot Bibles.

A new polyglot Bible

In 1514, the same year in which work began on the Complutensian Polyglot Bible, an Italian Dominican scholar, Agostino Giustiniani, began work on his own polyglot Bible. He lived to complete only the book of Psalms, which appeared in 1516, including Hebrew, Greek, Arabic and Aramaic texts.

Christopher Plantin's printing works, shown here, are preserved in a museum in Antwerp, Belgium.

Tyndale – Fugitive Translator

Sampling 1526 English

Here is how Tyndale translated Romans 12:1 in the first edition of his New Testament. The original spelling is retained, in phrasing that is a taste of English translations to come:

I beseeche you therefore brethren by the mercifulness of God, that ye make youre bodyes a quicke sacrifise, holy and acceptable unto God which is youre resonable servynge off God.

Found guilty of heresy in 1536, William Tyndall is tied to a stake, strangled with a rope, and then burned. Woodcut from 1563, published in *Acts and Monuments* by John Foxe.

For a priest who wanted little more than a quiet place to translate the Bible, William Tyndale had uncommon adventure in his life. He was hunted throughout Europe by secret agents, and raided while printing his underground English New Testament. He was eventually kidnapped by a spy and executed in his early forties as a heretic – all because he translated the Bible into English.

His Catholic superiors did not approve of the project. They associated it with the growing Protestant movement, which taught that the Bible, not the Church, was God's voice on earth.

FROM PRIEST TO FUGITIVE

Although educated at Oxford and Cambridge, then ordained a priest, Tyndale wanted nothing more than to translate the Bible from its original languages of Hebrew and Greek into English. A gifted linguist, he seemed perfect for the job. He had mastered at least seven languages, including the ancient biblical languages.

In 1523, at about the age of 30, he went to London and asked permission of Bishop Cuthbert Tunstall to start working on the translation. This was a shrewd move because the bishop was a scholar and a friend of Erasmus, the Dutch theologian who published the first Greek edition of the New Testament and who wrote in the preface that he wished the Bible would be translated into every language. Tunstall, however, rejected Tyndale's request – apparently fearing that a Bible the common people could understand would encourage the reform movement started by Martin Luther, who had been excommunicated just two years earlier. This rejection led Tyndale to conclude 'not only that there was no room in my

lord of London's palace to translate the New Testament, but also that there was no place to do it in all of England'.

With the financial backing of a wealthy cloth merchant, Tyndale set sail from England the next year to find a safe place to work. He never saw England again. He moved to Hamburg, Germany, and by August 1525, he had finished translating Erasmus's Greek New Testament into English. Tyndale found a printer in Cologne, but the print job was interrupted when opponents of the Protestant movement raided the print shop. Tyndale, however, heard of their plans, salvaged the pages printed so far, and escaped. A printer in the more reform-minded city of Worms finished the job, and the 6,000 copies were smuggled into England, in barrels of flour and bolts of cloth.

BURNING THE BIBLE – AND THE TRANSLATOR

Bishop Tunstall was horrified when he found out about the Bibles. He ordered all copies in his

The Martyrdome and burning of Master *Wilham Tindall* in *Flanders*, by *Filford* Castle.

Answering his critics

For readers of his English New Testament who were wondering if it was right to ignore the Church's order banning the book, William Tyndale offered the following assurances:

They tell you that scripture ought not to be in the mother tongue, but that is only because they… desire to lead you blindfold and in captivity.

They say that scripture needs a pure and quiet mind, and that laymen are too cumbered with worldly business to understand it. This weapon strikes themselves: For who is so tangled with worldly matters as the prelates [religious leaders]?

They say that laymen would interpret it each after his own way. Why then do the curates [parish priests] not teach the people the right way?

They say we need doctors to interpret scripture because it is so hard… There are errors even in Origen and Augustine… if the curates will not teach the gospel, the layman must have the scripture, and read it for himself, taking God for his teacher.

diocese burned. Then he secretly arranged to buy out Tyndale's remaining inventory. 'The books are erroneous and naughty,' he told a merchant he believed had connections, 'and I intend surely to destroy them all.' The merchant did have connections – he was a friend of the translator. Tyndale agreed to sell the Bibles and use the money to pay for improved editions, which he published in 1534 and 1535.

By that time, Tyndale was well underway with a translation of the Old Testament. He finished the first five books of the Bible as well as Jonah and all the books from Joshua to 2 Chronicles. But he never lived to see them printed.

Tyndale moved around to evade English and church agents sent to arrest him. While living in Antwerp, Tyndale was set up by an English agent who claimed to favour the emerging Protestant beliefs. The agent convinced Tyndale to take a walk through town, then as they entered a narrow alley signalled two waiting soldiers, who seized Tyndale and whisked him off to the state prison near Brussels, which was 16 kilometres (25 miles) away.

Sometime during Tyndale's year and a half in prison, he wrote a letter that sounds remarkably like one of Paul's messages to Timothy – a letter that hints he was still working on his Old Testament translation. It was written in Latin and sent to some unnamed person in authority:

I beg your lordship... request the commissary to have the kindness to send me, from the goods of mine which he has, a warmer cap; for I suffer greatly from cold in the head... a warmer coat also, for this which I have is very thin; a piece of cloth too to patch my leggings... But most of all I beg... to have the Hebrew Bible, Hebrew grammar and Hebrew dictionary, that I may pass the time in that study.

Tyndale was tried not simply for publishing an English New Testament, but because of his Luther-like beliefs. Introductions and marginal notes in his Bible revealed his theology. He taught salvation through faith, not the Church; he denied purgatory existed; and he argued that the Virgin Mary and the saints do not intercede for us, and we should not pray to them.

In August 1536, Tyndale was found guilty of heresy. Two months later, he was chained to a stake where an executioner publicly strangled him with a rope, then burned his body. His final words were, 'Lord, open the King of England's eyes,' and even as he spoke, the mood was changing in England. King Henry VIII, who had been unable to secure the pope's approval to divorce Katharine of Aragón, his 'Spanish cow', was backing away from the Catholic Church.

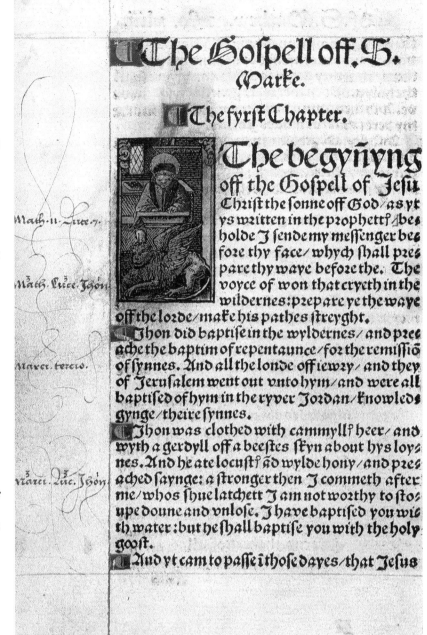

Within a year of Tyndale's death, Bibles that drew heavily on his work circulated in England – with the king's approval. Within two years all parishes were encouraged to have a copy for their people. And within five years the churches faced fines if they did not comply.

The opening of the Gospel of Mark from William Tyndale's English Bible.

'If God spares my life for a few years, I'll see to it that a boy pushing the plough knows more of the Bible than you do.'

WILLIAM TYNDALE, SPEAKING TO CLERGY (c. 1494–1536)

More Reformation-Era Bibles

When Martin Luther published his German translation of the Bible, he created a tidal wave of new publications. Although scripture continued to be published in its original languages, Bibles in the languages of the people began to surface throughout Europe.

BIBLE TRANSLATIONS FROM FAR AND WIDE

In view of the success of Luther's Bible and of the Church's failure to suppress it, Catholics brought out their own German translations. Ironically, these were mainly adaptations of Luther's work. The first, by Hieronymus Emser, simply brought Luther's translation more in line with the Latin Vulgate. The second, a revision of Emser's work by Johann Dietenberger, used Luther's Old Testament, a translation by Anabaptists (a radical Protestant group) and a Bible that had been published in Zürich in 1529. Dietenberger's version became the standard German Catholic Bible.

Spurred by the Reformation, a number of Bibles also appeared in Dutch. The most notable was published by Jacob van Liesveldt in 1526. This translation became so popular that in 1548, the Catholics published their own Dutch Bible.

Meanwhile, in Denmark, a mere two years after the publication of Luther's New Testament, a Danish version was made at the request of exiled King Christian I. In 1550, a complete Bible was published on command of King Christian II. It was revised in 1589 and again in 1633.

After achieving independence from Denmark in the early 16th century Sweden published its own New Testament, based on Luther, the Vulgate and the Greek New Testament of the Dutch humanist scholar Desiderius Erasmus. The first official complete Bible followed in 1541. Iceland published a New Testament, based on the Vulgate and Luther, in 1540, and a complete Bible in 1584.

In Poland, a New Testament translation was made from the original Greek by the Lutheran scholar Jan Seklucjan in 1553. A complete Bible made at Brest from the original languages followed in 1563. A revision of the Brest Bible was made for the Unitarians, and yet another revision, the Danzig Bible of 1632, became the official Bible of all the Evangelical Churches in Poland.

A Serbo-Croatian New Testament appeared in 1562–63. Because the Serbo and Croatian literary languages are identical, only a single translation was needed, but since they use different alphabets, they had to be published separately in Glagolithic and Cyrillic. Responding to the spread of Lutheranism, a complete Bible in Slovene was published in 1584 for the Slovene-speaking provinces of Austria. A New Testament was translated into Hungarian from the Greek in 1541, but the occupation of the Turks and opposition of the Catholics resulted in a halt to printing Bibles in Hungarian. The first complete Hungarian Bible was not issued until 1590, when it became the Bible of the Protestant Church in Hungary.

In Spain, the Inquisition forbade the publication of the Bible in the language of the people, so no Spanish Bibles were published until the 18th century. Portugal fared little better, publishing only a New Testament in 1681. The first complete Portuguese Bible did not appear until 1748–53. The first Protestant Bible in Italian was made by the Greek and Hebrew scholar Giovanni Diodati. It was published in Geneva in 1607, revised in 1641, and frequently reprinted.

Although basically a Catholic country, France issued a number of French Bibles that were influenced by the Reformation. The New Testament, which was probably the work of the reformer Jacques LeFèvre d'Étaples, was published in Paris in 1523. A French Old Testament appeared in Antwerp in 1528 and the two Testaments were published together as the Antwerp Bible in 1530. In 1535, a true Protestant version was prepared by Pierre Robert, known as Olivétan. It was frequently revised, notably by the reformer John Calvin in 1546 and by the French printer-scholar Robert Estienne in 1553. In response, Catholics published a new version, known as the Louvain Bible, in 1550.

MAKING THE BIBLE USER-FRIENDLY

In the early days of printing, it was often difficult to read a Bible comfortably over a period of time because of the monotony of the unbroken blocks of text of heavy black letter type. Generally, the entire Bible was printed with little or no space between chapters or even books. Gradually a number of improvements were made.

Chapters had been indicated from the beginning of printing, but often this was done merely by using enlarged initial capital letters, either plain or decorated. Sometimes a discrete chapter number was placed at the end of the

PROMPTE · · ET SINCERE ·

IOHANNES · CALVINVS · ANNO · ÆTATIS · 53 · · B ·

Fourteenth-century portrait of the Protestant reformer John Calvin (1509–64).

first line of the chapter or right above it. Verses were not separated or numbered, although some early Bibles printed capital letters in the margins every 15 lines or so, but these appeared in different places, depending on the sizes of the pages and type.

In the early 16th century, page headings identifying the book of the Bible printed below were introduced. Clear divisions between the Old and New Testaments were also added. Later, divisions were made between books of the Bible and then between chapters. Eventually, the heavy black lettering used in most early printed Bibles was replaced with a lighter, more readable type, known as roman. Although it had been used in some earlier Latin and Italian Bibles, roman became the standard typeface after 1516, when Erasmus used it in his New Testament. Erasmus also introduced the use of page numbers.

Perhaps the most important innovation was made by the French printer Robert Estienne in a French-language Bible he printed in Geneva in 1553 – separating and numbering the verses of each chapter. In 1528, the Italian Dominican Santi Pagnini, one of the most important Catholic biblical scholars of his time, had numbered the verses in his Latin Bible, but Pagnini's numbering system never caught on. The system developed by Estienne did, and was a tremendous help to preachers and scholars who could refer to passages in the Bible by chapter and verse, making it easy for others to find the passage. Estienne's verse numbers are still in use today.

The most user-friendly of all the early Bibles was the French Genevan Bible of 1559. In this edition, each book begins with an introduction running across the page, which is otherwise divided into two columns. Each chapter is prefaced with a summary of the chapter's contents. Many notes fill the margins, either concerning the text itself or the theology behind it. Printed at the front of the Bible are Robert Estienne's summary of Christian doctrine and Calvin's article 'That Christ is the End of the Law', which had first appeared as an introduction to the New Testament in Olivétan's French Bible of 1535. The French Genevan Bible also included folding maps, diagrams and an index. This remarkable edition was the one that came closest to our modern study Bible.

Robert Estienne, printer

One of the most innovative Bible printers of his time, Robert Estienne (Staphanus in Latin) was born to his craft. His father, Henri Estienne had founded a family print shop at Paris in 1502 and Robert, who was born the following year, learned the printing craft directly from his father. Robert took over the business in 1526, and published complete Latin Bibles, based on the Vulgate, in 1528, 1532 and 1540. During that same period, Estienne published a Latin dictionary that quickly became a standard work.

In 1539, King Francis I made Estienne his printer for all books in Latin and Hebrew, and later for Greek works as well. Estienne prepared the first printed editions of many of the Greek and Latin classics, including a notable edition of the works of the Roman poet Virgil. He also printed the works of early Christian writers and more Bibles, but the annotations in his Bibles created a stir because of their Protestant overtones.

Under attack by Catholic scholars at the Sorbonne (the University of Paris), Estienne moved to Geneva, where he became a Calvinist. There, in 1551, he published a New Testament that introduced the system of dividing the biblical chapters into numbered verses that is still in use today. Estienne later published reformer John Calvin's monumental *Institutes of the Christian Religion*. He died in 1559.

Lay Catholic Bible-reading

Even though Protestants, from the beginning, have been encouraged to put the Bible at the centre of their lives, lay Catholics were discouraged from reading the Bible on their own well into the 20th century. Today, however, all Catholics are encouraged to read and study the Bible, and classes in scripture and its interpretation are widely available.

A Catholic Response

Portrait of Pope Paul III (1468–1549) by Titian.

Seven sacraments

The Catholic Church accepts seven sacraments, holding that they are necessary for salvation even though 'not all the sacraments are necessary for each person'. These are: baptism, confirmation, the eucharist, penance (confession to a priest for forgiveness of sins), extreme unction (the anointing of the sick), order (ordination of deacons, priests and bishops) and matrimony.

Faced with the spread of Protestantism, the Catholic Church was forced to look into itself, acknowledge its faults and initiate needed reforms. Many Catholics called for a general church council to deal with these issues, but when Emperor Charles V asked Pope Clement VII to call one, he refused. The pope was afraid that such a council might contend for control of the Church and issue decrees that would reduce the pope's power – and income. Entertaining the same fears, Clement's successor, Paul III attempted to make reforms on his own, but then, bending under pressure from Charles V, he finally consented to call a council. After a few false starts the council opened at Trent, in northern Italy, in December 1545. It continued – with two long interruptions – until December 1563.

RESPONSES TO PROTESTANTISM

During its 25 sessions the Council of Trent reaffirmed many of its old beliefs and practices and condemned Protestant doctrines that opposed the Catholic views. First, however, the council reaffirmed that the basis of faith was to be found in the Nicene Creed (which had been formulated at the councils of Nicea and Constantinople in the fourth century). But then the council went on to reject Martin Luther's doctrine of justification by faith, insisting that good works increased grace and were also necessary for salvation.

Much time was spent on the sacraments. The council reaffirmed that Christ had instituted seven sacraments, opposing the view of the Protestants, who claimed that only baptism and the eucharist had any basis in scripture. In addition, the presence of Jesus in the eucharist was said to be real and not symbolic, despite claims by some Protestants to the contrary. Near the end of the council, decrees were promulgated justifying the existence of Purgatory, invocation of the saints in prayer and veneration of relics and images. Although Luther had been violently opposed to indulgences, the council declared them valid. However, moderation was urged and the taking of fees for granting indulgences was forbidden.

TRENT'S PRONOUNCEMENTS ON SCRIPTURE

Decrees on scripture came in the fourth session, held in 1546. Countering Luther's doctrine that the source of Christian truth was to be found in

Protestants and the Apocrypha

At the time of the Reformation, opinions were divided about whether to include the Apocrypha in the Old Testament canon. At the Council of Trent the Catholic Church declared them part of the biblical canon. Protestants differed.

In his great German translation of the Bible, Martin Luther grouped the Apocrypha together and positioned them between the Old and New Testaments. Although he did not define the limits of the Old Testament canon, Luther thus indicated that the Apocrypha are separate and distinct from the scriptures.

Other early reformers agreed. In the Zürich Bible of 1529 and the English Geneva Bible of 1560, the Protestant editors separated the Apocrypha from the rest of the Bible and gave them special headings. Although they did not totally reject these works – which had enjoyed wide use in the Church through the centuries – they did not treat them as equal to the other books.

In the years that followed, attempts were made to have the Apocrypha removed from Protestant Bibles, but these efforts failed. They were, however, grouped separately by the Gallican Confession of 1559, the Anglican Confession of 1563 and the Second Helvitic Confession of 1566. The Puritan Confession was less tolerant, holding that the Apocrypha were of purely secular character.

Reformation Bibles – including the first edition of the King James Version – placed them apart from the accepted books in a kind of appendix. The 1629 edition of the King James Version left them out completely, but otherwise the practice of printing them separately continued. Then, in 1825, the Edinburgh Committee of the British and Foreign Bible Society convinced the Society's leaders that the Apocrypha should no longer be included in Bibles taken by missionaries to the 'heathens'. Over the next 100 years the Apocrypha were generally left out of Protestant Bibles, but many of today's Bibles, including the New Revised Standard Version used in this book, print them separately.

scripture alone, the council upheld the validity of tradition as well:

Following then the example of the orthodox fathers, it [the Catholic Church] receives and venerates with the same sense of loyalty and reverence all the books of the Old and New Testaments… together with all the traditions concerning faith and practice as coming from the mouth of Christ or inspired by the Holy Spirit and preserved in continuous succession in the Catholic Church.

The traditions in question cover a wide variety of topics believed to have been passed down from the apostles, including the Church's teaching on the sacraments and the primacy of the pope.

The same decree enumerates the books of the Bible accepted by the Catholic Church. They include the books Protestants regard as the Apocrypha – books that appear in the Septuagint (the ancient Greek translation of the Hebrew scriptures) but not in the standard Hebrew Bible (the Masoretic text). In the fourth century, Jerome in his Vulgate had been the first to label these books Apocrypha, noting that they should not be considered part of the Old Testament canon. However, over the centuries Jerome's reservations had been forgotten and these books had come into general use within the Church. Trent then declared them canonical and they remain so today for Catholics.

In another decree, the council named the Vulgate the authoritative text of the Bible. Because it had been 'preserved by the Church for so many centuries', it was to be used in all 'public readings, disputations, sermons and expositions'. The same decree also declared the Catholic Church to be the only legitimate interpreter of scripture 'to restrain irresponsible minds' from distorting the meaning of God's word. In naming the Vulgate the official Bible of the Church, however, the council acknowledged that it contained imperfections by demanding that it be printed 'in the most correct version

possible'. After the council ended, scholars began work on a revised Vulgate, which was finally published under Pope Clement VIII in 1592. This Clementine Vulgate has remained the official Latin version of the Bible ever since.

Fresco of the Council of Trent in the Vatican, Rome (1512).

Cathedral colleges

Among other things, the Council of Trent decreed that each bishop sponsor a special college in his cathedral to train young men for the priesthood. Until then, candidates for the priesthood had been responsible for their own education. The new colleges were called seminaries, and their use continues to this day.

Bibles from Exile

The 16th century was a period of religious upheaval in England. In 1534, King Henry VIII broke away from the Catholic Church when the pope refused to acknowledge his divorce from Katharine of Aragón and his remarriage to Anne Boleyn. For the remainder of his reign Henry adopted a form of high Protestantism that emphasized worship rituals. When he died in 1547, he was succeeded by his son Edward VI, who was still a boy. During his six-year reign, Edward made a number of reforms, remaining within the Protestant tradition, but he was succeeded in 1553 by his half-sister Mary I, who reinstated Catholicism as the state religion. When Mary died in 1558, she was succeeded by Elizabeth I, who had been declared illegitimate by the Catholic Church, which had never accepted Henry's marriage to her mother, Anne Boleyn. Elizabeth, predictably, reinstated Protestantism as the state religion.

THE GENEVA BIBLE FOR PROTESTANTS

Queen Mary so fiercely attacked the Protestants of England that she came to be known as Bloody Mary. For their own safety, many Protestant scholars fled the country and settled in Geneva, Switzerland, where they gathered together under John Knox, the Scottish reformer, who was pastor of an English church there. Queen Mary had forbidden the publication of English Bibles in her realm and so the Protestant exiles decided to prepare their own.

The work of translating was left mainly to William Wittingham, who had been a Fellow at Oxford. His English version of the New Testament was published in Geneva in 1557. When Mary died and the Protestant Elizabeth I came to the throne, many of the English exiles returned home, but Wittingham remained in Geneva to complete his work. The Old Testament was published there in 1560.

The Geneva Bible was not published in England until 1576, but copies were freely imported from Geneva and the book became enormously successful. Its popularity ultimately overshadowed that of the Great Bible (see box on page 177), which had been placed in every church in England by royal decree. The Geneva Bible was compact and relatively inexpensive and it contained features that made it easier to read – including clear type, verse numbers, vivid illustrations, maps, notes and prefaces. It was also the best English translation to date.

The Geneva Bible remained popular even after the publication of the King James Version. It was the Bible of the great writers of the 17th century – including Shakespeare, Bunyan and Milton – and it was taken by the Puritans to the English colonies in America.

THE DOUAI-RHEIMS BIBLE FOR CATHOLICS

Just as Protestant scholars fled from England during the reign of Mary, Catholic scholars fled from the staunchly Protestant Elizabeth's reach. They settled first in Douai (then a part of

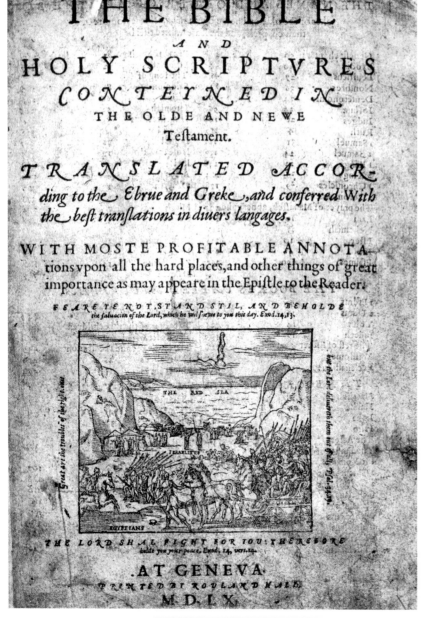

Title page of the Geneva Bible of 1560, the Bible of Shakespeare and Milton, and long the favourite of Puritans.

Flanders, but later ceded to France). There they established an English college under the direction of William Allen, an Oxford scholar and later a cardinal.

In 1578, Allen was granted approval to prepare an English translation of the Bible in order to counter 'the corruptions whereby the heretics have so lamentably deluded almost the whole of our countrymen'. Gregory Martin, another Oxford scholar, did the translating, while Allen and another colleague, Richard Bristow, checked and revised Martin's work.

In 1582, the New Testament was published in Rheims, France, were the college had moved temporarily. However, the Old Testament – perhaps because of financial difficulties – did not come out until 1609, when it was published in Douai.

In a preface, the translators insist that they followed only the Latin Vulgate version approved by the Church, although it is obvious that they also made use of the Greek and Hebrew texts and even the 'heretical' translations they condemned, especially the Geneva Bible. They also tell us that they made their translation as literal as possible. 'Moreover we presume not in hard places to mollify the speeches or phrases, but religiously keep them word for word and point for point for fear of missing, or restraining the sense of the Holy Ghost to our fantasy.'

For the most part, the translation is an excellent one, but faithfulness to the text resulted in a number of strange expressions. Some of these became part of the English language, including 'advent', 'character', 'evangelize' and 'victim'. Others remained indecipherable, such as 'potestates', 'longanimity' and 'correption'. And Matthew's version of the Lord's Prayer reads in part, 'give us this day our supersubstantial bread'. In time, some of these expressions were replaced, but not 'supersubstantial bread'.

The Douai-Rheims Bible was to remain the official English translation for Catholics until well into the 20th century, and it was both attacked and defended staunchly. Protestants claimed that the translators had deliberately 'darkened' the language to keep it from being understood. In 1587, Mary Stuart, the Catholic Queen of the Scots, on the night she was put to death for allegedly plotting against Elizabeth I, swore her innocence on a Douai-Rhaims Bible. When the Protestant Earl of Kent scolded that she had sworn 'a valueless oath on a false book', she responded: 'Does your lordship think that my oath would be any better if I swore on a translation in which I do not believe?'

Other English Bibles

In addition to the Bibles translated from exile, a number of other English Bibles appeared during the reigns of Henry VIII and Elizabeth I. The first was translated by Miles Coverdale, who had worked with William Tyndale on his Old Testament translations. Not knowing enough Hebrew or Greek to translate from the original languages, Coverdale relied on the Latin Vulgate and on translations by Luther, Tyndale and others. The influence of Coverdale's Bible, which appeared in 1535, was limited. Matthew's Bible, which was printed in 1537, was more successful. It was edited by John Rogers, a friend of Tyndale's, although he published the Bible under the name Thomas Matthew. Rogers did not translate the Bible anew, but used Tyndale's New Testament and as much of the Old Testament as Tyndale had completed. For the rest, he used Coverdale's translation. Henry VIII's chancellor, Thomas Cromwell, convinced the king to approve this Bible. Then, in 1538, Henry called upon clergymen to produce a large-sized Bible that could be placed in churches for the people to read. Matthew's Bible was rejected for this purpose because many of its notes reflected a radical Protestantism that was not acceptable. Consequently, Cromwell assigned Coverdale to revise Matthew's Bible and financed the project himself. The result, in 1539, was the Great Bible, named for its size – over 25 centimetres (14 inches) tall.

Later, under Elizabeth I copies of the new Geneva Bible appeared in England and were enormously successful. But because of the Puritan bent of its notes, conservative churchmen sought to prepare a more acceptable translation, based mainly on the Great Bible. The work was farmed out to 16 scholars, mainly bishops. The resulting Bishops' Bible, published in 1568, proved to be far inferior to the Geneva version. Some translations were excellent, but others were not. For example, instead of 'Cast thy bread upon the waters', the Bishops Bible reads, 'Lay thy bread upon wet faces.' The Bishop's Bible soon gave way in popularity to the Geneva Bible.

Mary I, queen of England from 1553 to 1558, promoted Catholicism and persecuted Protestants. Portrait by Master John (1544).

Elizabeth I, queen of England from 1558 to 1603, promoted Protestantism and persecuted Catholics. Portrait after Nicholas Hilliard (c. 1575/80).

King James Version

'The noblest monument of English prose.'

JOHN LIVINGSTON LOWES, A HARVARD ENGLISH PROFESSOR, DESCRIBING THE KING JAMES VERSION OF THE BIBLE

King James I of England (1566–1625) arranged for the best scholars in the country to create a new English Bible translation. Portrait by Paul van Somer.

When James VI of Scotland became James I of England in 1603, he was greeted with a petition signed by 1,000 Puritans.

They were not happy with the Church of England, or with either of the two popular English Bible translations. The Church, they argued, needed to be purified of leftover Catholic influences, such as the offices of bishop, clerical robes and the heavy emphasis on rituals. As for the popular Bibles of the day – the Geneva Bible (1560) and the Bishops' Bible (1568) – Puritans said they were not accurate.

James liked the Church of England as it was. He liked its bishop-led hierarchy, its rituals and especially its description of the king as 'Defender of the Faith', since James believed it was God's will that he rule. But James agreed with the Puritans on one point: he wanted a new Bible translation. The Puritans did not like the Bishops' Bible, which was the preferred version for reading in church; it was not Protestant enough. James, on the other hand, hated the Geneva Bible, which was the most popular among the people and was probably the version that William Shakespeare drew from for his plays. Its running commentary was too Protestant. Besides, it did not show enough respect for kings. For example, a note in the margin beside Exodus 1 said Hebrew midwives in the time of baby Moses were right to disobey the Egyptian king's order to kill newborn boys. And a note beside 2 Chronicles 15 criticized King Asa for not executing his idol-worshipping mother.

KING JAMES CALLS A MEETING

In January 1604, during his first year on the throne, James called a meeting to evaluate the state of the Church in England. Gathering at the king's command in Hampton Court Palace were Church of England bishops, ministers and professors along with four Puritan church leaders. The purpose, as James explained it, was 'for the hearing, and for the determining, things pretended [claimed] to be amiss in the Church'.

The conference was almost a total failure for the Puritans. They did not get the Protestant-friendly reforms they wanted for the Church of England. In fact, King James said they had better learn to accept the Church as it was or he would 'harry [force] them out of the land'. One thing the Puritans did get, however, was the king's approval for a new Bible translation.

King James said he would like an accurate translation to replace the other English versions – to become the only version read in church. He wanted the work done by England's best Bible scholars and linguists. And he did not want any commentary added to the margins.

Work began that year. The king wrote to Richard Bancroft, bishop of London, reporting that he had chosen 54 men for the project, though only 47 are known to have taken part. These men, representing both the Church of England (Anglicans) and the Puritans, were divided into six translation teams working at three cities in southern England. Two teams worked at Oxford, two at Cambridge, and two at Westminster, in what is now London. At Oxford, a team of seven men translated Isaiah to Malachi, while a team of eight translated the Gospels, Acts and Revelation. At Cambridge, eight worked on 1 Chronicles through Ecclesiastes, while seven others translated the Apocrypha. At Westminster, 10 were assigned Genesis to 2 Kings and seven worked on Romans to Jude. After each group finished its translation, their work was reviewed by a committee of 12 scholars, made up of two men from each of the translation teams.

A set of 15 general rules guided the translators. Among the most important were these:

❧ The new version was to follow the Bishops' Bible as much as possible. Scholars were to make only the changes necessary for accuracy.

❧ Translators were free to draw from many other versions in an attempt to find the best way of expressing the message contained in the original Bible languages.

❧ There would be no marginal notes except those needed to clarify Hebrew and Greek words or to point out related Bible passages. This was to allow the Bible to speak for itself, and to keep translators from inserting their own interpretations.

❧ Translators were to retain traditional church office terms instead of substituting terms that many Protestants preferred. For example, the translators were to use 'priest' instead of 'elder' and 'church' instead of 'congregation'.

A NEW BIBLE IN 1611

It took about three years for each of the translation teams to finish their initial drafts, sometimes working individually and sometimes in conference. Another three years were spent in review and revision. The translators were meticulous, and made no apologies for being more concerned about the quality of their work than the speed.

'We did not disdain to revise that which we had done,' they later explained, 'and to bring back to the anvil that which we had hammered: but having and using as great helps as were needful, and fearing no reproach for slowness.'

this version took its name. The translation also came to be known as the Authorized Version, although there is no surviving evidence that the king formally gave it his stamp of approval, declaring it the official Bible of England. He did, however, permit it to be published.

CRITICS AND SUPPORTERS

Not everyone immediately warmed to the King James Version. In fact, the popular Geneva Bible

This painting from 1605 shows King James I in the House of Lords. The previous year, the king had commissioned a definitive English Bible, which became known as the King James Version of the Bible.

The result of their tedious work was a black-letter edition measuring 41 centimetres (16 inches) by 27 centimetres (10.5 inches), published in London in 1611.

'We never thought from the beginning', the translators wrote in the preface, 'that we should need to make a new translation.' Because they drew so heavily on previous versions, they said they were simply making 'out of many good ones, one principal good one'.

The scholars dedicated their work to the man who ordered the project: 'the most high and mighty prince, James, by the grace of God, King of Great Britain, France and Ireland, Defender of the Faith'. It was after the king that

– which King James so desperately wanted his new version to displace – lived on in continuing reprints for more than 30 years. Many Puritans preferred the staunchly Protestant Geneva Bible, and in 1643, printed excerpts of it in the Soldier's Pocket Bible issued to the army of Puritan leader Oliver Cromwell. And it was the Geneva Bible – not the King James Version – that many Puritans carried with them to the New World of America.

One scholar of the day was especially vicious in his criticism of the King James Version – Hugh Broughton, a renowned professor who had argued for a new translation and who must have been upset that the king did not appoint him to help in the project. 'Tell His Majesty,' Broughton wrote in a letter to the palace, 'I had rather be rent in pieces with wild horses, than any such translation by my consent should be urged upon poor churches… The new edition crosseth me. I require it to be burnt.'

Despite its detractors, by the end of the 1600s the King James Version had become the Bible for English-speaking people. As Roman Catholic priest Alexander Geddes put it in 1792, 'if accuracy, fidelity, and the strictest attention to the letter of the text, be supposed to constitute

Common phrases from the Bible

Many words and phrases we use today are from the King James Version of the Bible. Here is a sample:

Man does not live by bread alone (Deuteronomy 8:3).

Skin of my teeth (Job 19:20).

You cannot take it with you (Ecclesiastes 5:15).

A leopard cannot change its spots (Jeremiah 13:23).

A good Samaritan (Luke 10:29–37).

Blind leading the blind (Matthew 15:14).

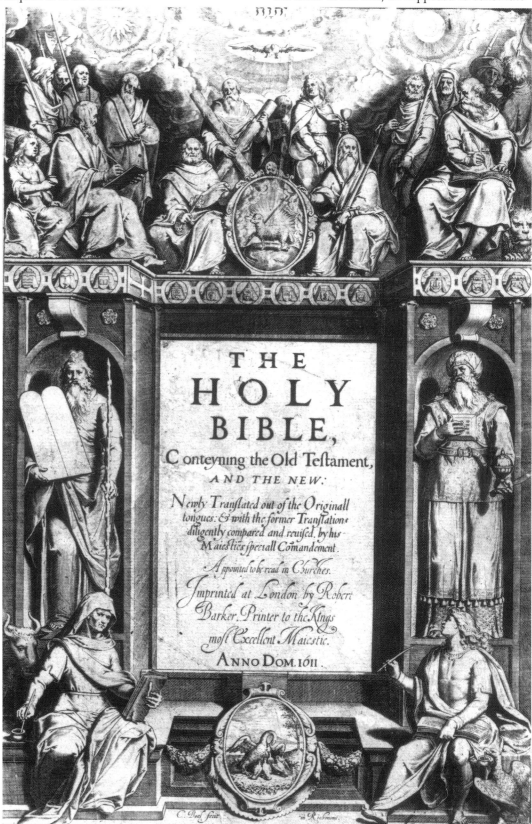

Lavishly illustrated title page of the King James Version (1611). The inscription says this translation was made at the king's command, using the original languages of the Bible as well as other translations. This new translation is 'Appointed to be read in Churches'.

the qualities of an excellent version, this of all versions, must, in general, be accounted the most excellent'.

The King James Version was revised in later editions, to correct mistakes. These corrected versions often became the new standard. In 1629, the first King James Version printed in Cambridge dropped the Apocrypha – a practice that caught on because it reduced the cost of the Bible by eliminating the section considered least reliable.

Throughout the years, the King James Version's elegant language and rhythmic prose made it a delight to read and to hear read. It also made the verses easier to memorize. And without editorial comments in the margin, this Bible allowed a variety of interpretations, drawing a broad following from Protestant to Catholic.

It was more than 250 years before a serious attempt was made to displace the aging version with an updated translation – the English Revised Version (1881–85). From this revision sprang an American variation called the American Standard Version (1901), followed by the Revised Standard Version (1952) and the New Revised Standard Version (1989).

Revisions like these were necessary because language continually changes. In time, the King James Version became hard to understand – much like the works of William Shakespeare, of the same vintage. The average reader today probably would not realize that 'I prevented the dawning of the morning' (Psalm 119:147, King James Version) means 'I got up before dawn'. Still, the King James Version has had an incredible effect on the English language. Many of our most common sayings come directly from this version of the Bible: 'forbidden fruit' (Genesis 2:17), 'at wits' end' (Psalm 107:27), 'going a second mile' (Matthew 5:41).

In time, some scholars say, the King James Version will eventually become a historic piece, like the Geneva and Bishops' Bibles – too archaic for most people to understand. Others warn that there have been many attempts to bury the King James Version, but announcements of its death have been premature. Some four centuries after it was created, new copies are still being printed and sold.

The King James Version had its detractors. Many Puritans preferred the strongly Protestant Geneva Bible, and they took this with them to the New World of America rather than the King James Version. *The Landing of the Pilgrim Fathers, 1620* by George Henry Boughton (1833–1905).

The changing English Bible

The King James Version, many scholars say, was not so much a new translation as a revision of earlier English Bibles. To illustrate this, here is a comparison of how several English versions translated the first two verses of Psalm 23:

The Lord gouerneth me, and no thing schal faile to me;
in the place of pasture there he hath set me.
He nurshide me on the watir of refreischyng.
WYCLIFFE BIBLE, 1388 EDITION

The Lord is my shepherd, I shal not want.
He maketh me to rest in grene pasture
& leadeth me by the stil waters.
GENEVA BIBLE, 1560

God is my sheephearde, therfore I can lacke nothing;
he wyll cause me to repose my selfe in pasture full of grass,
and he wyll leade me vnto calme waters.
BISHOPS' BIBLE, 1568

The Lord is my shepheard, I shall not want.
He maketh me to lie downe in greene pastures:
he leadeth me beside the still waters.
KING JAMES VERSION, 1611

Reflections in Poetry

In about 1210, German poet Wolfram von Eschenbach wrote the epic poem *Parsifal*, his own version of Chrétien de Troyes's *Perceval*. Centuries later, Eschenbach's epic was turned into an opera by Richard Wagner. The hero is depicted here by Franz Stassman.

Almost from the beginning, the Bible inspired works of poetry outside the realm of religion. In the early Middle Ages, most of these poems were in Latin. But by the seventh century, works in the language of the people began to appear. Since most Christians were unable to read Latin (the language in which most Bibles were printed), this poetry helped spread the message of God's word. Later poets used the Bible to delineate characters, by referring to their use or misuse of scripture, or by criticizing various points of view.

MEDIEVAL POETRY

Almost as soon as literature began to be written in the language of England (Old English, or

Anglo-Saxon), poems inspired by the Bible appeared. The earliest was probably a hymn exalting the creation by Caedmon, an illiterate herdsman of the second half of the seventh century. The masterpiece of this period was 'The Dream of the Rood', in which the poet dreams that the rood (the cross of Christ) speaks to him, telling what it was like to bear the Son of God, Jesus Christ, who is portrayed as a typical Anglo-Saxon hero.

Poems were also inspired by objects that appear in the Bible. In about 1175, the French poet Chrétien de Troyes wrote 'Perceval', a long narrative poem about the knights of the Round Table under King Arthur and their search for the

holy grail. The grail was the cup from which Jesus drank at the last supper, and which was apparently used to catch blood from his pierced side at the crucifixion. At the end of the poem Perceval is rewarded with sight of the grail because his heart is pure.

Comic poems also used the Bible, as seen in *The Canterbury Tales*, written by the English poet Geoffrey Chaucer in the late 14th century. In one lively episode, the wife of Bath banters on about the Samaritan woman at the well in chapter 4 of John's Gospel. To justify her own many marriages, she points out that the woman at the well had five husbands, but then professes not to know what Jesus meant when he said that the Samaritan woman's current husband was not her husband.

RENAISSANCE POETRY

The first masterpiece of the Renaissance was the Italian poet Dante Alighieri's *Divine Comedy*, which was completed by 1321. In this great three-volume epic, the poet is given a tour of hell, purgatory and heaven. The work is filled with allusions to the Bible, and characters from the Bible appear in all three books. For example, in the *Inferno*, Dante shows Judas locked in the jaws of Satan at the frozen bottom of hell. Among the persons in the *Purgatorio* is Michal who heaped scorn on her husband, King David, for dancing in front of the ark of the covenant. And the *Paradiso* is full of the good people of the Bible, including Adam and Eve and even Rahab, the prostitute of Jericho who hid the invading Israelites from her own people.

The 16th-century English poet Sir Edmund Spenser, in his Sonnet 68, uses the Bible for seduction. Spending 12 lines on the greatness of Christ's love for us in dying on the cross, the sonnet ends with a couplet in which the poet invites his beloved to make love, as the Lord has taught that love is good.

The plays of William Shakespeare are filled with the language of the Bible, and Shakespeare used the Bible for his own purposes. For example, in *The Merchant of Venice*, the Jewish villain, Shylock, refers to the patriarch Jacob's cheating his father-in-law Laban (Genesis 30:25–33). He also refuses to dine with Christians because they eat pork (which is forbidden to Jews), reminding them that Jesus drove the devil into a herd of pigs (Matthew 8:32). Shakespeare's use of biblical language is clearly seen in *Antony and Cleopatra*, which is filled with references to the book of Revelation. For example, Cleopatra is described as the great harlot of Revelation 17 and Antony himself describes his passion for Cleopatra as a 'new heaven' (Revelation 21:1).

By the time Shakespeare ended his career, two great playwrights on the Continent were beginning theirs. The French playwright Racine wrote *Esther* in 1689, based on the biblical book of the same name; and in 1691, he wrote *Athalie*, the story found in 2 Kings 11:1–16 of Athaliah, who murdered 42 princes of the house of David to gain the throne. *Athalie* is widely considered the most perfect example of French classical tragedy. Towards the end of his career, the Spanish playwright Pedro Calderón de la Barca, wrote a number of plays focusing on the vanity and emptiness of life, reflecting the book of Ecclesiastes.

In the drama *Samson Agonistes*, the English Puritan poet John Milton, who became blind at the age of 43, focuses on the captured, blinded Samson of the book of Judges, and uses Samson's blindness to meditate on his own. In *Paradise Lost*, Milton tells the story of the Fall, as recounted in Genesis, but he elaborates on the story, adding – among other things – the story of the fall of the angel Lucifer and his cohorts. Lucifer's story, however, is not told in the Bible, although it may be alluded to in Revelation 12:7–9 and Luke 10:18. Milton turned the tale from Genesis into a towering epic modelled on the epics of Homer and Virgil. It is one of the greatest masterpieces of English literature.

Caiaphas in hell

In *Inferno*, the first part of his *Divine Comedy*, Dante is led on a tour of hell by the Roman poet Virgil. Among the biblical characters whom Dante sees suffering there is Caiaphas, the high priest. Caiaphas had advised the Sanhedrin, the Jewish court, to put Jesus to death to avoid the wrath of the Romans, saying: 'it is better for you to have one man die for the people than to have the whole nation destroyed' (John 11:50). When Dante first spots Caiaphas in hell, he is addressing two 'Jovial Brothers', but stops his remarks to them in mid-sentence:

'O brothers, your evil...' I began,
but then I stopped: I saw a figure
crucified by means of three stakes
along the ground; on seeing me
he moans into his beard, writhing.
Brother Catalan was watching this
and says, 'You're wondering at him:
he it was advised the Pharisees
"one man should die for the people".
He's laid naked across the way
as you can see, and has to bear
the weight of everyone who passes.
His father-in-law suffers likewise
in this pit, and all that council
the Jews owe their misfortunes to.'
I could see Virgil was stupefied
by this, a soul spread on a cross
in the dirt, exiled for eternity.
CANTO XXIII

This scene from Canto VIII of *Inferno*, part one of Dante's *Divine Comedy*, shows the wrathful in the Styx. Sienese illumination, c. 1438/44.

Bibles in the New World

The mission shown here was built by Christian missionaries near the Copper Canyon in Mexico in 1680. From there the missionaries worked to spread the gospel message to local Indians.

When the first European explorers sailed to the New World of North and South America, they brought Christianity – and Christian missionaries – with them. Later, when Europeans began to settle in the New World, they brought their Bibles with them. Some even developed Bibles for their neighbours, the Indians.

MISSIONARIES TO THE NEW WORLD

After Christopher Columbus sailed out, under the sponsorship of the pious Queen Isabella of Spain, and discovered a new world in 1492, he sought to Christianize the people he found there, whom he called Indians. Consequently, on his second voyage, in 1493, Columbus brought along a Benedictine monk and five priests to evangelize the Indians. Most of the European explorers who followed Columbus to various parts of the New World followed suit.

Beginning in 1524, after the Aztecs of Mexico had been forcibly converted by Hernán Cortez, a

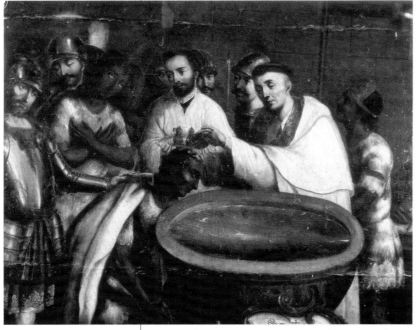

Dominican missionaries sailed to the New World from Spain to bring the gospel to the Indians. In this painting, the friars baptize some Indian converts.

group of Franciscan missionaries, known as the Twelve Apostles, established almost 400 missions in Mexico and eventually built thousands of churches there. In 1539, they had a printing press set up – it was probably the first in the New World – and produced catechisms and other texts. Because the Catholic Church discouraged Bibles for the people, the Catholic missionaries did not print any Bibles.

Spain's Francisco Pizarro overthrew the Incas

of Peru between 1531 and 1535, and was helped, unwittingly, by a Dominican missionary, Vicente de Valverde. When De Valverde approached the Inca emperor Atahualpa, and asked him to submit to Pizarro, the emperor asked for evidence of his authority. The missionary responded by handing him a copy of the Bible. Unaware of its significance, Atahualpa threw the book to the ground, scandalizing the Spanish troops, who proceeded to massacre the thousands of Indians in attendance. Other missionaries soon moved in to convert the Incas, and a Dominican missionary established the first university in the Americas at Lima.

Starting in 1549, Portuguese Jesuits worked at converting the Indians of Brazil, where they established missions in hostile interior regions. Spanish Jesuits established their first missions in Paraguay in 1568, setting up disciplined Christian villages there for the Indians. Although they did not provide Bibles, the missionaries passed on biblical material by word of mouth, as in the earliest times.

The Dutch settled in Guiana in 1580, followed by the French and English. The Dutch also settled in the West Indies and in New Netherlands (now New York State), where they established the Dutch Reformed Church. They worked with the Indians in New Netherlands until the English took over the missions early in the 18th century.

French and Spanish explorers brought Dominican, Franciscan and Jesuit missionaries to various other parts of North America as well, and missions were established in Florida, Texas and the southwest, and along the Mississippi River. In 1615, missionaries from the French Order of Récollets sailed to the new province of Quebec, Canada, and tried to Christianize the Indians, but the missionaries remained aloof and ineffectual. In 1625, French Jesuits moved into Quebec and adopted some of the ways of the Indians in their efforts to reach them and teach them gospel values through preaching and example. They succeeded in part, but many of the Indians held on to their old beliefs. When a plague broke out and the Jesuits baptized the dying but not the living, the Indians blamed the Jesuits for causing the plague, and a number of Jesuits were tortured and killed by Indians.

BIBLES IN THE ENGLISH COLONIES

The English Puritans who settled in Massachusetts in the early 17th century brought their Bibles with

John Eliot, apostle to the Indians

The first man to publish a Bible in the New World was John Eliot. He was born in Widford, Hertfordshire, in England, in 1604 and was educated at Cambridge University. In 1631, he sailed to Boston, and the following year he became pastor of a church in nearby Roxbury. Supported by his congregation and some fellow ministers, Eliot began preaching to the local Indians. In 1650, he convinced some Indians to move into a new 'praying town', where they built and lived in European-style houses and followed a biblical code of laws. Eliot supplied the Indians with food and clothing, while they tended gardens, raised cattle, and studied English, crafts and the Bible. When they were ready, they were baptized as Christians.

Meanwhile, back in England, Eliot was so admired for his work that a new organization was formed to help finance his efforts. This Company for Propagating the Gospel in New England and Parts Adjacent in North America was the first of many missionary societies. In 1654, Eliot published a catechism in the language of the Indians under his care. He followed this in 1658 with a translation of the entire Bible. By 1674, Eliot had established 14 'praying towns' which housed some 4,000 Indian converts. The following year, however, war broke out between the

colonists and the Indians, and because Eliot's Indians refused to fight, they were persecuted by both sides, and were nearly wiped out. Eliot later tried to revive the towns and even prepared a new edition of his Bible in 1685, but without his former success. He died in 1690.

John Eliot preaching to Algonquin Indians.

'O that I could address the Indians in their own language! My ardent soul longs to be sounding salvation in the ears of these red men.'

JASON LEE, MISSIONARY TO OREGON

them. Most of the earliest settlers preferred the popular Geneva Bible, but by 1700, they were all using the King James Version, which had become the official English Protestant Bible. Unfortunately, however, the King James Version was copyrighted and could only be printed by the King's Printer or at the Universities of Oxford or Cambridge. This prevented the Puritans from printing their own copies of scripture, and they had to import them.

When Harvard College was established in 1636, a printing press was set up in Harvard Yard. Because it seemed fitting that the first book to be printed in the colony should be scriptural, a decision was made to publish a new version of the Psalms. Three Puritan scholars – Richard Mather, John Eliot and Thomas Weld – made a fresh translation of the Psalms from the Hebrew original. Although they realized their translation lacked elegance, they insisted that it was faithful to the original. And so *The Whole Booke of Psalmes Faithfully Translated into English Metre*, which came to be known as *The Bay Psalm Book*, was printed at Harvard in 1640.

The first full Bible to be printed in North America was in an Indian dialect. It was prepared by the missionary John Eliot in the Massachusetts

Bay Indians' own language, Massachuset – a dialect of the Algonquin Indians. Because Massachuset had never been written, Eliot had to begin by devising an appropriate writing system.

In making his translation, Eliot did not try to be literal, but rather did all he could to make the biblical text understandable to the Indians. For example, he transformed the parable of the 10 virgins (Matthew 25:1–12) into the parable of 10 chaste men because the Indians considered chastity to be a virtue required of men, but not of women. The New Testament appeared in 1661, and the entire Bible in 1663.

In the years that followed, scripture was translated into various other Indian dialects throughout North America, but no Bibles were published in the colonies in European languages until 1743. Then, Christopher Sauer, a German Baptist immigrant, published an edition of Martin Luther's translation of the Bible in Germantown, on the outskirts of Philadelphia. When the American Revolution broke out, American printers considered their ties with England broken and began printing the King James Version. In the new nation of the United States, Bibles in various translations were freely published.

5

THE BIBLE IN THE MODERN WORLD

Over the past 200 years or so, missionaries with the help of Bible translators and Bible distribution societies have intensified the work of spreading scripture throughout the world – a mission still underway. Scholars continue to develop new tools and techniques to study the Bible and determine what the original writers intended to communicate. Countless new translations of the Bible are published, in an effort to better capture the meaning of scripture and express it in today's languages. As the message of the Bible spreads, so does its influence on such far-reaching institutions as law, literature and theatre.

Still from Cecil B. DeMille's 1927 film epic *King of Kings*, in which Jesus (played by H.B. Warner) addresses Peter at the last supper.

Enlightenment Dims the Bible

'Have courage to use your own reason.'

IMMANUEL KANT

Portrait of Voltaire (1694–1778), the French writer who was at the forefront of the Enlightenment.

A German biblical epic

Reacting against the negative treatment given to the Bible by many thinkers of his day, the German poet Friedrich Gottlieb Klopstock tried to create a German biblical epic in the style of Milton's English masterpiece. Drawing material from the New Testament and Milton's *Paradise Lost*, Klopstock's *Der Messias* (*The Messiah*) depicts the passion, death, resurrection and enthronement of Jesus Christ. It was published in 1773 and, in revised form, in 1800. Sadly, where Milton triumphed, Klopstock met with only moderate success.

❧

In the 18th century, during the period known as the Enlightenment, human reason was elevated above everything else and was even seen to limit God himself. In the 17th century, philosophers and scientists, such as Galileo Galilei and Sir Isaac Newton, had demonstrated that the universe was governed by natural laws. Philosophers of the 18th century concluded that they could come to understand the workings of nature by close observation and the application of reason.

They included the Scottish philosopher David Hume, the German philosopher Immanuel Kant and the French writers Jean-Jacques Rousseau, Voltaire and Denis Diderot. Diderot went so far as to compile a vast encyclopedia covering all fields of knowledge. A number of Enlightenment thinkers concluded that, since the universe is governed by strict laws, even God himself must abide by those laws, resulting in a limit to his powers. Some claimed that, since creating the universe, God has avoided all contact with humans, and so revelation, as presented in the Bible, is a fiction. In his satirical novel *Candide* (1759), Voltaire considers all biblical theology bankrupt.

QUESTIONING THE BIBLE

For those who did not reject the Bible altogether, the rule of reason seriously influenced its interpretation. A number of elements were questioned.

First, the miracles described in the Bible were said to represent a break in the order God had established at the creation. Attempts were made to explain them away as literary devices – for example, when Joshua asked that the sun stand still (Joshua 10:12–13), he was merely expressing in poetic terms his hope of conquering his enemy before dark, and that is what happened; the sun did not literally stand still. Other miracles were seen as exaggerations of natural phenomena. And so, the manna found by Moses and the Israelites in the wilderness (Exodus 16:4) was not really bread from heaven but a sugary substance excreted by insects that burrow into the bark of a desert shrub.

Prophecies that accurately predicted the future or prefigured the coming of Jesus were also questioned. In an ordered world, this could not happen, Enlightenment thinkers claimed. In response, one believer, Thomas Sherlock, held that prophecy had two meanings – the one intended by the prophet himself and another, imposed by God, that would be understood only after it was fulfilled. For example when Isaiah prophesies that a 'young woman' (which can also be read in Greek as 'virgin') will bear a son who will be called Immanuel (Isaiah 7:14), he is referring to a young woman of his day, perhaps the king's wife; but in New Testament times, God's deeper meaning emerges: the woman is seen as the Virgin Mary and the child as Jesus.

Studies in geology indicated that the earth was far older than indicated by the Bible and that living creatures had appeared on earth over a vast period of time; they were not created in a single day, as described in Genesis. (Irish archbishop James Usher had calculated that the creation occurred in the year 4004 BC, but observable evidence showed that the earth is far older.) In response, it was suggested that the Genesis account was a myth and not in the least historical. This elicited a huge cry of protest from traditional Christians, for even though many in the 18th century had turned away from their faith, many others clung to it with great fervour.

DEVOTIONAL APPROACHES TO THE BIBLE

Reaction against the rationalist treatment of the Bible led to a spread of Pietism in Germany. This movement had been introduced in 1677 by Lutheran minister Phillip Jacob Spener with the publication of a set of six proposals for restoring true religion. Spener called for an increase in the 'practice of piety', emphasizing an intensified study of scripture to enhance personal devotion. The influence of Pietism soon spread across Europe and into America.

Strongly influenced by Spener, the German Lutheran scholar Johannes Albrecht Bengel published penetrating commentaries on the New Testament, which were greatly admired by John Wesley, the founder of the Methodist movement. In England, between 1708 and 1712, the Presbyterian minister Matthew Henry published biblical commentaries that were personally meaningful. In his commentaries, Henry sought to provide the general reader with biblical ideas and images that gave meaning to his or her individual life. Henry's approach was adopted by John Wesley in his *Notes on the New Testament*, published in 1754 and 1765.

Bach, Handel and the Bible

Inspired by the soul-searching Pietism of Johannes Albert Bengal, the German Lutheran composer Johann Sebastian Bach created vast numbers of compositions based on the Bible. The bulk of them consists of hundreds of cantatas that were composed for performance at church services. These sacred cantatas consist of citations, paraphrases or allusions to the Bible passages being read in church that day, including emotionally wrought arias, which give a personal perspective on the biblical passage, and choruses. Bach also composed two long pieces, *The Passion According to Matthew* and *The Passion According to John*. In these compositions, a narrator declaims the full text of the Gospel in recitative, a kind of speech song, with others singing the words of Jesus and other figures. As in the cantatas, arias and choruses comment on the text. Once again these are highly emotional, as Bach believed that music should appeal to the emotions of the laity. The emotion felt by the composer should be relived by the performer, and so communicated to the listener.

The German-born English composer George Frideric Handel also wrote a large number of biblically based pieces. His masterpiece is *Messiah*, which meditates on the life of Christ, from predictions of his coming to his resurrection. It resembles an extended cantata in form, but all the text (even for the arias) is taken from the Bible, especially from Isaiah, Psalms, the Gospels and the letters of Paul. *Messiah* includes many impassioned arias and memorable choruses, including the ever-popular 'Hallelujah Chorus'. In addition to *Messiah*, Handel composed oratorios on other biblical figures, but most of these are in a more dramatic form than *Messiah*, resembling plays set to music. They include: *Samson*, *Joshua*, *Esther*, *Israel in Egypt* and *Saul*.

To bring these ideas to the people, small study groups appeared throughout the Western world. Earlier, Spener had established devotional circles for prayer and Bible reading, which met in his home. At Oxford, in 1729, John Wesley organized what came to be called the Holy Club. Its members sought a deepening of their personal faith and relied heavily on readings from the Bible. The Holy Club developed into a number of overlapping groups throughout England and America. Seeking to escape the scholarly approach to the Bible, which fostered rationalist ideas, many groups of traditionalists met for private study without the interference of trained theologians.

Other popular movements can also be seen as reactions to Enlightenment views on religion and scripture. In the American colonies, between

1720 and 1740, a religious movement known as the Great Awakening spread across the land. The preacher George Whitefield travelled throughout the colonies and preached to crowds who were so large they had to meet in open fields. Whitefield brought out the emotions of his audiences, stressing the 'terrors of the law' to sinners and 'new birth' in Jesus Christ. At the same time, Jonathan Edwards, a Congregationalist preacher, attempted to help those who heard him at revival meetings to separate the true works of the Spirit of God from the false. Revival preachers were soundly criticized by church leaders for stimulating emotional excesses and dangerous religious delusions.

The wide diversity of views on religion and the Bible led to a broader toleration. In the 19th century, a new wave of popular interest in the Bible emerged, and the older Puritan approach to the Bible gave way to a new Evangelicalism, which favoured a strongly conservative approach to biblical interpretation. Also, 19th-century scholars found new ways to study the Bible in response to the questions raised by Enlightenment thinkers. The pessimism of Enlightenment views on the Bible was thus diminished.

John Wesley (1703–91), the founder of Methodism, preaching while standing on his father's tomb. Wesley's Holy Club focused on Bible reading as a way to deepen personal faith.

Jonathan Edwards (1703–58) was a prominent American clergyman and theologian. During the Great Awakening, Edwards emerged as the champion of evangelical religion and preached the need for a 'new birth'. He also worked as a missionary to the Indians at Stockbridge, Massachusetts, and served as the president of Princeton College.

Nineteenth-Century Bibles

A physician's translation

Most Bible translators were either biblical scholars or missionaries who were specially trained for the purpose. A notable exception was B.J. Bettelheim, a Hungarian Christian of Jewish birth. While working as a physician in the Ryukyu Islands – a Japanese Island chain that includes Okinawa – Bettelheim translated the New Testament into the local Japanese dialect. He later revised the translation, with the help of native speakers of Japanese, to put it into standard Japanese.

Before Braille

In 1836, the New York Asylum for the Blind issued a New Testament with raised letters. This appeared almost 20 years before the development of the Braille system.

Charles Taze Russell (1852–1916), founder of the Jehovah's Witnesses.

The 19th century was characterized by a renewed interest in the Bible. Old translations were revised, new translations were made, and other Bibles appeared to appeal to particular denominations or to the average Christian.

BIBLES IN EUROPE

By the start of the 19th century, scripture had been translated into 48 European languages, including all the major languages of the continent, except Russian. Consequently, most of the activity in translating in the years that followed was devoted to revising earlier translations. In some cases, however, fresh translations were made. Often this seemed necessary because the language of the old versions became outdated, but people who cherished these versions did not want to see them changed, preferring to have new versions that could be used along with the older ones. In addition, improved versions of the Bible in its original languages called for new versions to incorporate the latest scholarly findings.

First-time translations into European tongues started with a full Bible in Gaelic, a language spoken by some people in Scotland, and similar to the native Irish tongue, also called Gaelic. The Scottish Bible was published in 1801.

The first Bibles in Russian were also published in the 19th century. Until then, Russian Bibles were editions of the ancient translation made by Cyril and Methodius in the ninth century. This Old Slavonic translation had been retained for church use long after Slavonic ceased to be the language of the people, much as Latin was retained for use in the Catholic Church. Then, in 1815, Paul's letter to the Romans was published in a bilingual edition – Old Slavonic and Russian. The New Testament was published in 1821 and the Old Testament in 1867. The first complete one-volume Bible in Russian appeared in 1877, although it is known as the version of 1876.

Meanwhile, Unitarians set about 'correcting' the Bible. The Unitarians, who reject the doctrine of the Trinity and the divinity of Jesus, had their origins in the Reformation. They were first established as an organized community during the 16th and 17th centuries in Poland, Hungary and England, and soon spread to other parts of the world. In the 19th century, Unitarians turned to making their own translations of the Bible in order to restore the spirit of the original biblical texts, while at the same time purging the Bible of what they considered to be error. They considered all biblical passages that supported the concept of the Trinity – and other doctrines they disapproved of – as 'spurious', claiming that they were added to scripture at later times by copyists.

In 1808, the English Unitarian Thomas Belsham published an 'improved version' of the Bible. Then Abner Kneeland prepared an American version of the New Testament, basing

Jehovah's Witnesses

The worldwide movement now known as Jehovah's Witnesses was formed in the 1880s by the American laypreacher Charles Taze Russell as the Watch Tower Bible and Tract Society. Russell claimed that Jesus Christ, a perfect man, had returned invisibly to earth in 1878 to prepare for the kingdom of God, which would be inaugurated after the battle of Armageddon in 1914. Russell urged all people to study the Bible, and to warn as many people as possible of the impending end of time, so that they might survive a first judgment, Jesus' 1,000-year reign on earth, and a second judgment, when only 144,000 people from all of human history would be taken into heaven. Russell drew these observations from his own interpretation of the book of Revelation. After 1914, when Armageddon didn't materialize as

Russell had predicted it would, the prophecies were reinterpreted. Russell died in 1916 and his successor, J.F. Rutherford, soon turned the movement into a 'theocratic' one, dedicated to the truth and demanding the full commitment of its members. Later in the 20th century, Jehovah's Witnesses focused on missionary outreach, and worked hard, often going from door to door of people's homes, to distribute copies of their biblically based magazines, *The Watchtower* and *Awake*. The movement has its own translations of the Bible, which reinforce its emphasis on preparing for the end time. There are currently about four million Jehovah's Witnesses in more than 200 countries.

it on Belsham's Bible, but adding more 'corrections'. Kneeland published his New Testament in Greek and English in 1823, in the hopes of 'correcting some of the monstrous errors that now exist in the Christian Church'. A large number of other Unitarian translations appeared throughout the 19th century.

BIBLES IN NORTH AMERICA

Because the population of Latin America was overwhelmingly Catholic, little Bible translation took place, because it was discouraged by the Church. During the 19th century, however, Protestant missionaries and others translated portions of the Bible into 12 Indian dialects. A complete New Testament was translated into Sranan, a dialect used by black Creoles in the coastal area of Dutch Guyana (now called Surinam).

In the newly founded nation of the United States, the King James Bible remained the Bible of choice for most Christians. In fact, it was so revered that American Christians rejected a new edition of the King James Version, which corrected errors that had crept into the translation over the years. Nevertheless, various new Bible translations appeared, including one by Charles Thomson, secretary of the Second Continental Congress (1775–81). After losing political favour, Thomson retired to work out his bitterness in translating the Bible. In his version, published in 1808, he attempted to capture the 'spirit and manner' of the original texts, while making it clear to the readers of his day.

Moving in another direction, Joseph Smith, a young man from Elmyra, New York, said he had a vision of the Angel Moroni, who showed him a long-lost book that told about Jesus' visit to North America just after his resurrection, to advise a group of Israelites who had fled there to escape the Babylonians in 586 BC. In 1830, Smith published the text. The Book of Mormon still serves as scripture for Smith's Church of Jesus Christ of Latter-Day Saints (the Mormons).

While work was progressing on new versions of scripture, and additions to it, the Bible was being rearranged and repackaged in various ways. First of all, in 1803, US President Thomas Jefferson created his own version of the Gospels. He cut out passages that presented Jesus' 'true message' and arranged them in four columns, one each for English, Greek, Latin and French texts.

Throughout the century (and beyond), Family Bibles were highly prized in America, as elsewhere. Each family kept a large Bible with blank pages on which they entered family statistics, such as births, baptisms, marriages and deaths. Sometimes personal thoughts were recorded and one young woman even sewed pieces of her wedding gown into the Family Bible. In the evenings, families often gathered together and read from the Bible.

During the Civil War, portions of the Bible were carried by soldiers in their breast pockets, and stories began to circulate about lives being saved when bullets aimed at the heart were stopped by a Bible. These tales were so widespread that humorist Mark Twain quipped that a bullet had saved him from a near-fatal Bible. While walking down the street one day, he elaborated, a Bible fell from an upstairs window and struck him, but was deflected by a 'lucky bullet' he always carried in his breast pocket.

Towards the end of the century, Elizabeth Cady Stanton and other women's rights activists studied the Bible from women's point of view, hoping to prevent men from using the word of God to discriminate against women. Their Woman's Bible consists of excerpts from the Bible, together with feminist commentaries. In discussing the two stories of the creation, they declare that the version in Genesis 1, which shows that the man and woman were created together and seem equal, to be 'more worthy of an intelligent woman's acceptance' than Genesis 2, which holds that man was created first, and then woman was created from one of his ribs.

While serving as President of the United States, Thomas Jefferson (1743–1826) put together his own unique version of the Gospels. Portrait by Rembrandt Peale.

Joseph Smith has a vision of the Angel Moroni delivering a long-lost book to him. Smith's vision led him to found the Mormons.

Elizabeth Cady Stanton (1815–1902), an American women's suffrage leader, helped produce a Woman's Bible.

The Bible Heads Far East

Bibles for Asia

By 1800, part or all of the Bible had been translated into 13 Asian languages. Within 30 years, the total had risen to 43. In 1837, Prussian scholar Karl Gutzlaff translated John's Gospel into Japanese – the oldest surviving Japanese translation.
❦

Spanish priest Francis Xavier takes the gospel to fishermen of India and then to Japan. Scene from *The Life of St Francis Xavier*.

Christianity reached the Orient long before the Bible existed. Legend says the apostle Thomas took the good news to India in the first century. When Catholic missionaries arrived there some 1,500 years later, they found a small but strong community of Christians who traced their faith to Thomas.

In the AD 400s, China received a group of Christians condemned as heretics. Called Nestorians, after deposed Archbishop Nestorius whose teachings fuelled the movement, these Christians refuted the traditional doctrine that Jesus was one person with two natures – divine and human. Instead, they said Jesus was two people, divine in heaven and human on earth. That meant Mary was not 'the Mother of God', as many Christians of the day called her. The cast-off Nestorians fled east. Centuries later, explorer Marco Polo made note of their churches scattered from Baghdad to Beijing.

EARLY MISSIONARY EXPEDITIONS

In 1493, Pope Alexander VI drew an imaginary line on a map, dividing the world in two. The boundary was the Azores, a group of islands about 1,300 kilometres (800 miles) off the coast of Portugal, in the Atlantic Ocean. Spain could claim land to the west. Portugal could claim land to the east. As explorers set off in search of trade and treasures, missionaries eventually joined them, hoping to expand the treasures of heaven by converting people to Christianity.

Francis Xavier, a Spanish priest who ministered in Portugal as part of the newly created Society of Jesus (Jesuits), boarded a ship in the Portuguese capital of Lisbon in April 1541. He made the long and dangerous journey around Africa to Portugal's new colony on the western coast of India. Working among the lower castes, especially fishermen and pearl divers, he converted thousands and became known as the Apostle of the Indies. After three years he travelled further east, arriving in Japan in 1549. There, he studied the language, translated a catechism into Japanese and made many converts. But without a Bible, the people of India and Japan did not fully understand Christianity. When Xavier died of illness in 1552, their faith languished. In 1597, Japanese fears that the missionaries were the first wave of a European invasion led authorities to expel the missionaries. Within 30 years, there was almost no trace of the faith.

Xavier had wanted to go to China, which was closed to foreigners. He even persuaded Portuguese authorities to send an embassy to the Chinese emperor, and include him among the group. But he died on a small island off China's coast. Another Jesuit, an Italian named Matteo Ricci, entered China about 30 years later. In this nation of people deeply suspicious of foreigners, Ricci came up with a mission strategy that is used today: he dressed like the people of his host nation and tried to fit in with their culture. He wore the robes of a Confucian scholar, and showcased in his home impressive European objects, such as gold-covered books, paintings and clocks. He also immersed himself in Chinese culture, and found common ground between Christianity and Chinese beliefs, which

he used to present his faith. All this earned him the respect of China's elite, who influenced the peasants and generated thousands of converts.

Ricci learned several Chinese dialects, conducted Mass in Chinese and translated the ten commandments and a catechism. But success in China was also short-lived. When the pope ruled in 1704 that Mass had to be conducted in Latin, the Chinese emperor was deeply offended; he expelled the missionaries and outlawed Christianity.

PROTESTANTS BRING THE BIBLE

By the late 1700s, European explorers had mapped outlines of most continents, started colonies in far-distant locations throughout the world, and spread exciting stories of their adventures and the people they met. Protestants saw an opportunity to fulfil Jesus' commission to take the good news 'to the ends of the earth'. Dozens of missionary societies were born. Support became especially strong in Britain, France, Germany and Belgium.

One of the most famous missionaries was a poor English shoemaker named William Carey, stirred to missions after reading *The Last Voyage of Captain Cook*, a sailor's journals from the South Seas. Carey became a cobbler's apprentice at the age of 14, but his gift was learning languages. His employer soon saw this and said, 'I do not intend you should spoil any more of my leather, but you may proceed as fast as you can with your Latin, Greek and Hebrew.' With his salary continued, Carey did as he was told, adding French and Dutch.

In 1793, the newly formed Baptist Missionary Society agreed to send Carey to India. Within eight years of his arrival, Carey had completed

the first New Testament translation into an Indian language – Bengali. In the years that followed, he translated the entire Bible into six Indian dialects – Bengali, Oriya, Marathi, Hindi, Assamese and Sanskrit – and parts of the Bible into 29 other languages.

Many Indian-language experts agree that Carey's translations were wooden and at times impossible to understand. His work had to be immediately and significantly revised, but it opened the door to giving the Indians the Bible in their own language.

Hudson Taylor in China

The Scottish missionary Robert Morrison translated the Bible into Chinese in 1823. Thirty years later, English missionary Hudson Taylor, dressed in Chinese clothes and with a bag of Chinese Bibles and tracts slung over his shoulder, visited tiny villages along the banks of the Huangpu River, which runs from the seaport of Shanghai towards China's interior.

After seven years of ministry, he returned to England to recover from a disease. But he still worked frantically, translating the Bible into Chinese dialects and recruiting missionaries. There were 90 Protestant missionaries in China, and Taylor wanted to add 22 new ones – two for each of China's 11 inland provinces. In 1865, he set up the China Inland Mission (now known as Overseas Missionary Fellowship International). He added 16 missionaries within a year, and in 1887 there were 102 new missionaries.

The deadly Boxer Rebellion broke out in 1900, in which the Chinese reacted against abusive trading and treaties imposed on them by foreign nations, killing foreigners and 30,000 Chinese Christians. The China Inland Mission lost 58 missionaries and 21 of their children, which devastated the elderly Taylor. The uprising was quelled, with China forced to pay reparations, but Chinese resentment continued to build for another 50 years, until the communists expelled all 'foreign devils'. Christians responded by smuggling Bibles into the country. Today, the Chinese are more open to Christianity and even publish the Bible in Chinese.

Left: This engraving shows Italian priest Matteo Ricci (1552–1610) (left), founder of the Catholic missions in China. Ricci decided that since the Chinese were so suspicious of foreigners, he would dress like them and conduct Mass in the Chinese dialects.

*'Expect great things!
Attempt great things!'*
WILLIAM CAREY (1761–1834),
MISSIONARY TO INDIA

William Carey (1761–1834), English missionary to India, with his native language instructor. Carey translated the Bible into six Indian dialects. The manuscript he is holding in this portrait is the Sanskrit version of Acts 2:11: 'We hear them declaring the wonders of God in our own languages.'

Hudson Taylor (centre), with colleagues, in a photo from 1905.

Bibles in the South Pacific

As the first moon landing captivated the world's imagination in 1969, the discoveries of the British captain James Cook did the same for his countrymen some 200 years earlier. Colourful tales of his voyage in 1768 to the other side of the world – far-distant destinations such as Tahiti, New Zealand and Australia – enticed explorers and traders, as well as British leaders who understood the value of trade. (For a time, tax on imported Chinese tea generated up to 10 per cent of the British government's revenue.)

Christians saw something entirely different: an opportunity to give instead of get – to present the good news about Jesus to people who had

Captain James Cook landing in New Zealand at Queen Charlotte's Sound in 1778–79.

English circumnavigator Captain James Cook (1728–79), whose expeditions to the South Pacific inspired Christian leaders in Britain and the United States to send missionaries. Portrait by Nathaniel Dance.

never heard it. But this raised a troubling question: where was the missionary mechanism to deliver the gospel? Jesus told his followers to be his witnesses 'to the ends of the earth' (Acts 1:8). That is how Christianity spread in the first place. But now, as the Europeans discovered those distant ends of the earth, there were no Christians ready to go.

THE MISSION STARTS

Later expeditions, including one by the infamous Captain William Bligh and mutineers on the *Bounty*, came back with stories of South Sea islanders who were cannibals, sexually promiscuous and thoroughly heathen. British preacher Thomas Haweis responded in 1795 by organizing the London Missionary Society. Some 200 Christians showed up for the first public meeting, paid the guinea membership fee, and elected a London-based board of 12 members to meet monthly. Their objective: to spread the gospel to the South Pacific. Their primary target:

Tahiti. This was partly because its culture was among the best-documented by Cook and others. Also, sailors on the *Bounty* had already compiled a partial dictionary of Tahitian words.

Missionary fervour erupted in an outpouring of cash donations – 3,500 pounds sterling in the first four weeks alone. Within a few months, the Missionary Society bought a ship, the *Duff*, for 4,800 pounds. A team of missionaries set sail on 10 August 1796 for the seven-month, 27,000-kilometre (17,000-mile) voyage around Africa's Cape Horn and east towards Australia. There were 30 men, along with their six wives and three children. Only four were ordained ministers; the rest were chosen for their practical skills as much

Welcomed in Samoa and Hawaii

The Christian message was well received in both Samoa and Hawaii, and there were wholesale conversions, partly because some key Bible stories were similar to stories in Samoan and Hawaiian religions.

Samoans said that their god, Nafanua, predicted the coming of a newer, better and stronger religion, and it was clear to them that European Christians had greater wealth and firepower, which implied they had a greater god. John Williams and Charles Barff became the first two missionaries in Samoa, converting many. Samoa and the nearby islands became known as 'the Bible belt of the Pacific'.

The American Board of Commissioners of Foreign Missions sent a group of missionaries to Hawaii in 1820. Queen Kaahumanu converted after she became seriously ill, and a missionary wife nursed her back to health. Hawaiian chiefs and their subjects followed. Within about 10 years, more than 50,000 Hawaiians were enrolled in missionary schools, where they learned to read, and studied the Bible. As in other South Sea Islands, the missionaries had developed a written language into which to translate the Bible, and within 20 years of arriving in Hawaii, they had completed the first edition of the Hawaiian Bible. The Bible's story of creation sounded much like a Hawaiian legend: the gods 'formed man out of the red earth and breathed into his nose, and he became a living being'.

as for their religious convictions. The team included six carpenters, two bricklayers, two tailors, two shoemakers, a gardener, a surgeon, a harness maker and a printer.

Defending the lack of formally educated ministers, Haweis said, 'A plain man with good natural understanding, well read in the Bible, full of faith and of the Holy Ghost, though he comes from the forge or the shop, would, I own, in my view, as a missionary to the heathen, be infinitely preferable to all the learning of the schools.'

Assigned to Tahiti were 17 missionaries, including all the ones who were married. The remaining missionaries were assigned to neighbouring islands of the Marquesas and Tonga, where some were murdered and the rest abandoned the ministry within three years. Tahiti was the only mission station where the work survived – though only seven missionaries remained; the others disappeared or left.

The *Bounty*'s Tahitian dictionary proved a disappointment, so bricklayer Henry Nott began creating a written language for the Tahitians based on phonetics. With this, and the help of King Pomare II, who said, 'I want to learn the talking marks,' the missionaries started translating the Bible. Since one of the missionaries was a printer who had brought his press, the Bible was printed in sections, as it was translated.

OUTBACK AND EAST

English minister Samuel Marsden was chaplain to the Australian settlement of British convicts when he decided to take the gospel to New Zealand, 1,930 kilometres (1,200 miles) east. The trouble was that Marsden could not find a captain willing to take him. The ferocious Maoris who lived in New Zealand had a reputation for killing and eating visitors. Just five years earlier, in 1809, they had overrun, killed and eaten the 67 crewmembers sailing on the *Boydó* – one of many such incidents.

With money he raised, Marsden bought a ship, the *Active*. On 19 November 1814 he set sail with a crew of Christians and Aborigines and a cargo of animals. On 19 December there to greet him was a New Zealander he had once taken into his home and nursed back to health. But even this friend warned Marsden not to land. 'It is high time', Marsden replied, 'to make known the glad tidings in these dark regions of sin and spiritual bondage.' On Christmas Day, Marsden preached New Zealand's first Christian sermon, using his friend as a translator. Marsden's text was from the first Christmas message: 'Fear not: for, behold, I bring you good tidings of great joy which shall be to all people.' After settling three missionaries on the islands, Marsden returned home, but he often took his ship back to New Zealand, with supplies and more missionaries. He made seven trips in total.

Translating the Bible into Maori began with missionaries creating a written language out of the spoken words. A Maori dictionary was published in 1820, followed seven years later by Bible passages from the Gospels, Genesis and Exodus. It took another 40 years before an entire one-volume edition of the Bible was published.

In 1907, the Governor of New Zealand unveiled a cross in Marsden's honour, located on the spot where the missionary delivered his Christmas message.

Samuel Marsden lands in the Bay of Islands (North Island) and is met by native Maoris in New Zealand. Engraving from c. 1880.

'We prepared to go ashore to publish for the first time in New Zealand the glad tidings of the gospel.'
SAMUEL MARSDEN (1764–1838), MISSIONARY TO AUSTRALIA AND NEW ZEALAND

Bibles Come to Africa

Right: This crucifix, made from bronze and wood, originates from Central Africa, and dates from the 18th to 19th centuries.

Robert Moffat (1795–1883), a missionary in Africa who translated the Bible into Tswana, a South African dialect.

North Africa played a vital role in the history of the early Church. Egypt and Ethiopia were Christianized in the earliest days of the new Church, and Christianity later spread west along the Mediterranean coast to cover all of the parts of Africa under the rule of Rome. Throughout the second and third centuries AD, Alexandria, in Egypt, was one of the three leading centres of Christianity, along with Antioch and Rome, and in the fourth century, North Africa nurtured the great theologian Augustine of Hippo.

The African Church's accomplishments and vigour were severely undermined by attacks from the barbarian Vandals, in 429, but after a period of about 100 years, it once again prospered for a time. Then, in the later seventh century, the rise of a new religion, Islam, led to an Arab takeover of much of northern Africa. Most of the people eventually became Muslims, and the few surviving Christians, mainly in Egypt and Ethiopia, barely survived in the centuries to come.

EUROPEAN MISSIONARIES TO AFRICA

By the 15th century, the entire continent of Africa was basically non-Christian. This enticed large numbers of missionaries to try to convert the people to Christianity. The first group of missionaries followed Portuguese explorers. In the kingdom of Kongo (now in Angola and Zaïre), Portuguese missionaries converted the king to Christianity. Later the king's son became a bishop. Other missionaries evangelized the people of the Niger river delta and set up missions along the Zambezi River, which flows from what is now Zambia to Mozambique.

By the middle of the 18th century, British, Danish and Dutch traders had set up numerous forts along the gold coast, and Protestant missionaries were sent there by the Society for the Propagation of the Gospel and other groups to bring the word of God to the people. Missionary activity increased at the end of the 18th century and evangelical missionaries came to Africa under the sponsorship of Britain's Baptist Missionary Society and similar groups. They converted thousands of local Africans.

In 1868, a new order of French Catholic missionaries was founded. Members of this Society of Missionaries of Africa, commonly known as the White Fathers, not only preached the gospel, but followed gospel principles in their work. While living in often primitive conditions, they devoted themselves to teaching, trained the people in trades and agricultural skills, and cared for the needy. Beginning their work in Algeria and Tunisia, the White Fathers soon spread south. They continue to work in Africa today.

During the same period, Protestant missionaries travelled deep into the interior of the continent to reach the people. In these remote areas, they often had a problem in communicating. Generally, they used converts, whom they taught to read European languages, to impart the words of scripture to their fellow Africans. But even this proved problematic, as the African cultures were so vastly different from European culture. For example, for these Africans the word 'spirit' referred to the spirits of the dead, and so it was difficult to transmit to them the idea of the Holy Spirit.

BIBLES IN AFRICAN LANGUAGES

As missionary activity intensified in Africa during the 19th century, the need for Bibles in the languages of the peoples became increasingly more pressing. In response, translators went to work early in the century and the numbers of translations accelerated steadily over the years. The first scripture to be translated into a modern African language was the Gospel according to Matthew, which was published in Bullom, the language of southern Sierra Leone, in 1816. A complete New Testament was translated into Amharic, the official language of modern Ethiopia, in 1829. The first complete

Ancient Coptic and Ethiopic Bibles

Christianity came to North Africa in its earliest days. This was particularly true of Egypt, which had a large Jewish population, and Ethiopia: the Ethiopian eunuch baptized by the apostle Philip (Acts 8:25–39) is said to have established the Ethiopian Church. In the early years, the Christians of Africa used Greek Bibles, but before long translations into the languages of Egypt and Ethiopia were made.

Until the early Christian era, Egyptians had used a simplified form of hieroglyphs for writing. But as the language took in a lot of Greek words and came to be known as Coptic, a new alphabet, based on Greek, was developed for use in the five dialects of Coptic. A translation of the Old Testament into the Sahidic dialect of Upper Egypt was made in about the year AD 200. A translation into Boharic, the dialect of the Delta region of Lower Egypt, was made at a later time, and Boharic eventually became the dialect of the Coptic Church.

In Ethiopia, the Old Testament was probably translated into the local language, Old Ethiopic, in the fourth century. It may have been made by African Jews who were descended from Israelites who migrated to Ethiopia around the time of

Solomon. The Old Testament canon of the Ethiopic Church is the largest of all. In addition to all the books found in the Catholic Bible, it includes the books of Enoch, Jubilees and

3 Baruch. The earliest New Testament in Ethiopic appeared sometime between the fourth and seventh centuries. Then, with the coming of the Muslims, no more Bible translations were made for many centuries.

Pages from an Ethiopic Bible in the Ge'ez script.

Bible in an African language (Malagasy) appeared in Madagascar (now the Malagasy Republic) in 1835.

Several missionaries devoted themselves to translating scripture into the languages of Africa. In 1857, Robert Moffat, the father-in-law of the well-known Scottish explorer and medical missionary David Livingstone, translated the Bible into Tswana, a dialect of South Africa. In the 1870s, Jonathan Ludwig Krapf, a German missionary, translated scripture into Galla, another dialect of Ethiopia. And the Anglican bishop of Natal, John William Colenso, published a harmony of the four Gospels in Zulu in 1857. Late in the century, a complete Zulu Bible appeared.

Not all the translators were missionaries, however. Some were African. One important African Christian and translator, Samuel A. Crowther, was born in Nigeria. When he was about 13, he was captured and put aboard a ship for exportation and sale as a slave. Fortunately, the ship was stopped by the British at Sierra Leone

and Crowther was freed. He was then converted and educated by the Christian Missionary Society. After studying theology in London, he was ordained and returned to Africa, where he worked diligently as a clergyman. In 1864, he was named bishop, and so became the first African bishop in the Anglican Church. During the 1860s and 1870s, Crowther worked hard at translating scripture, and he rendered most of the New Testament into Yoruba, his native language.

By the end of the 19th century, there were complete Bibles in 14 different African languages. Translation in the next century proceeded even more quickly. By the end of the 20th century, there were complete Bibles in more than 100 African languages, complete Testaments (Old or New) in about 100 more, and smaller portions of scripture in more than 225 languages. In all, by the end of the 20th century, at least some portions of scripture appeared in more than 500 African dialects.

Former slave Samuel Crowther (1809–92) ultimately became an Anglican bishop and a Bible translator.

The Bible and Slavery

'When some Midianite traders passed by, they drew Joseph up, lifting him out of the pit, and sold him to the Ishmaelites for twenty pieces of silver.'

GENESIS 37:28

'We were at times remarkably buoyant, singing hymns and making joyous exclamations, almost as triumphant in their tone as if we had already reached a land of freedom and safety.'

FREDERICK DOUGLASS, ESCAPED SLAVE AND ABOLITIONIST

This engraving depicts an African slave praying. American slave traders used certain Bible passages to justify slavery.

When the apostle Paul wrote to Philemon, he hinted that Philemon might wish to free his slave Onesimus, but he did not insist on it. In fact, in two other letters Paul advised slaves to obey their earthly masters (Ephesians 6:5 and Colossians 3:22–25). In the centuries that followed, Christians used Paul's failure to demand the release of Onesimus and his advice to slaves to obey as justification for slavery – although they often ignored Paul's order that masters treat their slaves 'justly and fairly' (Colossians 4:1).

Citing the Old Testament, which condones the buying and selling of non-Israelite slaves (Leviticus 25:44–46), some Christians even considered it permissible to grow wealthy in the slave trade. Early explorers of the Americas made slaves of the people they found there, despite the objections of the Catholic Church. Then, after Europeans first ventured into the 'dark continent' of Africa for profit, commerce in African slaves began to thrive and continued to do so for centuries.

TRADE IN AFRICAN SLAVES

In the 18th century, a number of missionaries to Africa strongly opposed slavery, and some of them ministered to slaves who had been freed and returned home to Africa. Many of these missionaries encouraged free trade in Africa, hoping that it would replace the slave trade. But still the traffic in slaves continued.

Throughout the 19th century, slave trade was an enormous business in Africa and countless African men and women were shipped abroad and sold into bondage. Many of the slaves were brought to the United States, especially to the agricultural southern states, where manpower was needed to work in the fields. Missionaries continued to denounce the lucrative slave trade, as did the Catholic Church. At the Congress of Vienna in 1815, Pope Pius VII demanded the suppression of the slave trade and in 1839 Pope Gregory XVI condemned slavery once again. But these protests had no effect – the slave trade continued to flourish.

SLAVERY IN AMERICA

When they came under attack, American slave traders defended themselves by referring to the Bible. Not only did they cite Paul's writings and the laws of Leviticus, but they pointed out that the patriarchs themselves had held slaves – Abraham even had a child with his wife's slave, Hagar. And what is more, the jealous sons of the patriarch Jacob even sold their own brother Joseph into slavery for a mere 20 pieces of silver. The slave traders' chief argument, however, was that Jesus never preached against slavery.

The advocates of anti-slavery were horrified by the slave traders' abuses of scripture, finding them at total odds with the main message of the Bible – universal brotherhood and love of neighbour. They pointed out that the New Testament shows that we are all the children of the same Father in heaven, and that even though Jesus said nothing about slavery, he always championed the poor and oppressed. And Paul, they claimed, did not condone slavery, but tried to instil in both masters and slaves the Christian spirit of love for one another.

A BIBLE OF HOPE FOR SLAVES

In contrast to the slaveholders, the slaves themselves took something entirely different from scripture: consolation and hope. Most slaves were not Christians when they arrived on American shores, but many of them soon

Release through music

The blacks who were sold into slavery in America were musical people, and when they became Christians it was only natural that they expressed their religious feelings in music. During their night-time Bible meetings, slaves often danced and sang songs now known as spirituals. The whole group generally participated, joining in repetitive choruses and supplying sung responses to the lead singer. Some of the songs were mournful, but others were joyful and full of hope. Often the spirituals reflected a silent acceptance of the life of a slave by meditating on Jesus' passion, as in:

They crucified my Lord an' he
*   never said a mumblin' word;*
they crucified my Lord an' he
*   never said a mumblin' word;*
not a word, not a word, not a word.

In other spirituals, the slaves yearned for freedom. Some of the lyrics, such as those of 'The Gospel Train', even allude to the Underground Railroad, an organization that helped slaves escape by train or chariot, providing 'stations' along the way where they could find food and shelter. The popular spiritual 'Swing Low, Sweet Chariot' even mentions one of the 'stations' by name. Other spirituals reflect the slaves' longing for freedom either from slavery or from life on earth. One of the most popular of these was 'Go Down Moses', which evoked the freeing of the Israelites from slavery in Egypt. The original lyrics of this spiritual are as follows:

Go down Moses,
*   way down in Egypt land.*
Tell ole Pharaoh
*   to let my people go.*
When Israel was in Egypt land.
*   Let my people go.*
Oppressed so hard they could not stand.
*   Let my people go.*
'Thus spoke the Lord,' bold Moses said.
'If not, I'll smite your first born dead.
*   Let my people go.'*

converted. Some slaveholders were reluctant to have Christianity taught to their slaves because they did not consider them human and they were afraid that Christianity would make them less submissive. Other slaveholders offered limited religious instruction, and slaves were required to attend their master's church, where they heard carefully selected Bible texts and sermons that would not disturb the status quo.

On their own, however, many of the slaves developed a hunger for scripture. Because they were not taught to read and write, they passed along stories from the Bible by word of mouth and some slaves even memorized passages from the Bible. Often at night slaves grouped together and held their own worship services, freely exchanging information about the Bible passages they knew, singing spirituals and dancing.

The suffering of Jesus evoked the compassion of the slaves, who saw in Jesus' suffering a reflection of their own. They also clung to stories of hardship and slavery, such as the story of Joseph, who was sold into slavery by his brothers. The biblical book the slaves discussed most, however, was probably Exodus. The African slaves in America fully identified with the Israelite slaves in Egypt, who were forced to work beyond their capacity. They loved hearing how Moses faced Pharaoh and demanded that he let the Israelites go to the wilderness to worship, and how Moses eventually led his people to total freedom, crossing through the miraculously parted waters of the Red Sea. These stories, including the recurring demand of the Lord through Moses that Pharaoh 'let my people go' (Exodus, chapters 7–12) buoyed the spirits of the American slaves and made them look for their own hero, who, like Moses, might liberate them from slavery.

At the outbreak of the American Civil War in 1861 the slave population of the United States totalled some four million. At the end of the war, in 1865, all slaves were freed. However, racism prevailed into the 20th century, and civil rights leaders, such as Martin Luther King, Jr, looked to the Bible for messages of relief, as the slaves before him had done. Adopting the slogan and song 'We shall overcome', significant advances were made in the fight to make all Americans equal.

The Underground Railroad

In the true spirit of the Bible, numerous abolitionist groups sought to end slavery in America and often helped slaves escape. One such group, the Underground Railroad, was organized by Quakers and Mennonites to help runaway slaves move from one point to another. The Underground Railroad's most renowned worker, Harriet Tubman, was originally a slave herself. After first walking to freedom herself, she returned to slave territory 19 times, leading more than 300 individuals out of slavery.

Doomsday Specialists

Breeding a holy cow

Some Christians believe that before Christ can return the Jews must rebuild their temple. With the encouragement of some Orthodox Jews in Israel, Mississippi cattle rancher and Pentecostal preacher Clyde Lott has been trying to breed a perfect red heifer, which Jewish ritual says must be sacrificed to purify the grounds of the temple mount in Jerusalem before the temple can be rebuilt. On the temple mount now is the Dome of the Rock, a 1300-year-old mosque-like shrine – one of the most revered in Islam.

A rapture missed

Author and end-time specialist Hal Lindsey boldly predicted in 1970 that the rapture of Christians into heaven would occur by 1988 – within a 40-year generation of Israel's emergence as a nation in 1948. Lindsey based this on Jesus' teaching that the 'end of the age' would come before 'this generation' was over (Matthew 24:34). Lindsey said the generation Jesus meant was the one after the rebirth of modern Israel. Others say Jesus was talking about his own time, perhaps referring to the fall of Jerusalem in AD 70 – about 40 years after his ministry.

I *have eaten almost nothing since yesterday noon. It is the last day of the year 1842, which according to Mr Miller could be the last year of the world.*

So reads an entry from the diary of Julia Smith, one of thousands once captivated by the end-time teachings of a New England farmer-turned-lecturer named William Miller.

By linking cryptic numbers in the apocalyptic books of Daniel and Revelation, Miller concluded that the 2,300 'days' mentioned in Daniel 8:14 should be considered 'years', and that they mark a cosmic countdown that started in 457 BC, which he said was when Persia's king gave the Jews permission to rebuild Jerusalem. Subtracting 457 from 2,300, Miller calculated that the world would end in about 1843. When it did not, he said he had not allowed for the year zero between 1 BC and AD 1, so he bumped back the date to 1844. After this prediction failed, most of his followers abandoned what had become the 'Adventist' movement (from a word meaning 'to come'). Miller died five years later, but some of his lingering followers went on to claim that his predictions were about an event in heaven, not on earth, and they founded the Seventh-Day Adventist Church.

Miller was just one of the first in a long line of modern-era Christians who specialized in searching the Bible for clues about when the world will end.

LOOKING FOR DOOMSDAY

The Bible repeatedly says human history will one day end. Jesus said the date of the apocalypse is something 'no one knows... only the Father' (Matthew 24:36). Yet, convinced the time is short, many Christians search for clues. They sift mainly through perplexing passages in Revelation, Daniel and Ezekiel – passages that many scholars say were once read as poetry symbolizing the ongoing war between good and evil, or perhaps as coded messages to comfort God's people in past times of crisis. All three books were probably written when Israel was occupied and when it would have been dangerous to speak out against the invaders.

Even Jesus' disciples wanted to know when the end was coming. Although Jesus said he did not know, he said there would be signs: false messiahs would come, there would be wars and rumours of wars, along with famines and earthquakes. These would signal the beginning of the end.

Apocalyptic signs

1945: Atomic bomb falls on Hiroshima. Suddenly, prophecies of a scorched earth no longer seem far-fetched: 'The day of the Lord will come like a thief... the elements will be dissolved with fire' (2 Peter 3:10).

1948: After nearly a 2,000-year absence, Israel re-emerges as an independent nation, seeming to fulfil the prophecy that the nation of Israel will 'be born in one day' (Isaiah 66:8) and develop into a world power.

1962: Telstar 1, the first television satellite, is launched. People soon realize how it will be possible for everyone to see the second coming: 'Look! He is coming with the clouds; every eye will see him' (Revelation 1:7).

1970: *The Late Great Planet Earth*, a best-selling book by Hal Lindsey, shows how current events seem to fulfil ancient prophecy.

1978: The Reverend Jim Jones orders his people to commit mass suicide at Jonestown, Guyana – an apocalyptic jungle community he built to escape 'a corrupt world'.

1992: Thousands of South Koreans gather for what they are told will be their rapture into heaven by midnight, 28 October.

1993: A stand-off in Waco, Texas, between federal agents and the Branch Davidians, an end-time cult led by David Koresh, results in the death of some 80 cult members. Koresh taught that the US government was the evil Babylon described in Revelation.

1997: Thirty-nine members of the Heaven's Gate cult commit suicide in a California mansion. They believed a spaceship was travelling behind the Hale-Bopp comet, and that they could leave their physical bodies and ascend to an extraterrestrial 'Kingdom of Heaven'.

1999: The world awaits Y2K disaster at the turn of the millennium. When the time comes, nothing happens.

One scholar claimed the end could come at any moment. A few years after Miller's failure, a brilliant British theologian named John Nelson Darby emerged with a new end-time message, which involved no date setting but kept Christians on the alert. Called Dispensationalism, this teaching said human history could be divided into several eras or dispensations – such as the era of law (Moses to Jesus) and the era of grace (from the Holy Spirit's arrival until the rapture).

His scenario, drawn from a literal reading of Bible prophecy, was dramatic. The first scene is the rapture, when Christians are suddenly taken to heaven. For those left behind, seven horrific years of tribulation follow, led in Jerusalem by the Antichrist whose followers wear 666 on their forehead. Next, a massive northern army invades the Middle East, starting the battle of Armageddon. Jesus returns in the second coming, destroys the Antichrist and his armies, restores the Jerusalem temple, and rules for a millennium. Afterward comes Judgment Day, followed by eternity in heaven or hell.

SEEING PROPHECY IN THE NEWS

In 1970, a campus preacher named Hal Lindsey popularized Darby's theology in a book that became the decade's non-fiction bestseller, *The Late Great Planet Earth*. What Lindsey did that so captivated readers was to link current events to ancient prophecy, declaring that what the Bible writers spoke about is happening in modern times. The Bible predicted fervent heat would decimate the planet (2 Peter 3:10), and nuclear bombs can now accomplish that. The Bible said the entire world would see the dead bodies of two end-time martyrs (Revelation 11:7–9), and satellites can now broadcast those images worldwide. The Bible said Israel would be restored, and after a nearly 2,000-year absence Israel re-emerged in 1948 as a sovereign nation.

Others soon saw the tremendous market for prophecy themes, which have become a big business. Apocalyptic images were suddenly everywhere – in sermons, bookstores, television and theatres.

AWAITING THE RAPTURE IN SOUTH KOREA

South Korean author and Protestant minister Jang Rim Lee started a wave of end-time hysteria in 1987, when he published *Getting Close to the End*. In this book, Lee reported what he said were interviews with South Korean children and adults who had had visions of a 1992 rapture – with Jesus coming in the sky to take the godly home. Lee set the date of Jesus' return as 28 October.

This spawned a worldwide movement known as *Hyoo-go* (rapture) or *Jon Mal Ron* (end-time

theory). Estimates of the movement's size ranged from about 20,000 to 100,000. But millions followed the events in news reports.

As the day approached, some believers quit their jobs, burned their furniture and other possessions in huge bonfires, and donned white robes. In Seoul alone, more than 5,000 left their jobs to gather in churches for the rapture. Some women reportedly had abortions because they feared they might be too heavy to be carried up to heaven. South Korean students and others scattered around the globe returned home to be lifted up with family and friends.

On 28 October, thousands of believers gathered in Seoul. Police officers were on hand to deal with any violence or attempted suicide after the prediction proved wrong. When midnight passed, the believers wept and the ministers sent them home.

Lee was later sentenced to two years in prison for fraud. South Korean police said he had over four million dollars that had been donated by his followers, and that he had invested some of it in bonds that matured in May 1993.

Many believers abandoned the movement, but some *Hyoo-go* churches live on, claiming that Jesus delayed his return to test believers, and warning that the end is near.

British theologian John Nelson Darby (1800–82) taught that this dispensation, or era, in human history is the last one, and the end could come at any instant.

Hitler and the apocalypse

According to William Shakespeare, even 'the devil can cite scripture for his purpose' (*The Merchant of Venice*, act 1, scene 3). Certainly evil individuals have done so. Most notably, Adolf Hitler used apocalyptic language to feed his political propaganda to German citizens. Hitler made several allusions to apocalyptic books of the Bible.

His '1,000-year Reich' refers to a 1,000-year empire that parallels the millennium, the 1,000-year reign of Christ, when, according to Revelation 20, the world would be at peace.

Some European Christians thought of the Holy Roman Empire of Charlemagne as the first Reich (empire), and the German empire set up by the Kaisers as the second. They longed for a third age, which they believed would unfold as the era of harmony described by the Bible at the end of time, when God would create a new heaven and a new earth. Hitler called this the 'third Reich'.

'The Jew would devour the peoples of the earth.' With this statement, Hitler paraphrased Daniel 7:23, which says the Beast [not the Jew] 'shall devour the whole earth'. Ironically, many people came to think of Hitler as the Beast.

In this 1930s poster, Adolf Hitler and his followers carry the swastika, the emblem of the German Nazi party. Hitler used the Bible's apocalyptic language to fuel Nazi propaganda. *Long Live Germany* by K. Stauber.

Bible Societies Worldwide

During the 19th and the early 20th centuries, it was not unusual to find travelling salesmen trekking from one place to another to sell Bibles to the local people at very low prices. In the early days, they travelled by foot, and later on bicycles. In the end, they also travelled in special vans. These Bible sellers were known as *colporteurs*, from the French name for hawkers who carried their goods on their backs.

Colporteurs were dedicated men and women. They were not out for profit, but sought only to fulfil the mission of their national Bible societies to distribute Bibles to everyone within their reach. The Bible societies they worked for – organizations devoted to distributing Bibles to people everywhere – are found in countries throughout the world.

EMERGENCE OF BIBLE SOCIETIES

Bible societies first appeared in the early years of the 19th century, but earlier organizations had prepared the way for them. Spurred by the Evangelical movement that spread throughout Europe and America in the 18th century, and which emphasized the importance of the Bible in reaching and teaching, a number of organizations for distributing Bibles was formed.

In the 1920s, colporteur Samuel Benson walked through New York state, from Niagara in the north to New York City in the south, to sell his Bibles.

People buying scriptures from a van belonging to the Bible Society of Côte d'Ivoire (Ivory Coast), after a special lunchtime prayer service.

The Canstein Bible Institute of Halle, Germany, formed in 1710, was the first organization devoted to producing inexpensive Bibles. A number of British societies also evolved, including the specialized Naval and Military Bible Society, founded in 1780 to distribute Bibles to seamen and military personnel. In 1805, the French began to distribute French Bibles throughout their country, although the French Bible Society was not formed until 1946.

The most influential of all these societies, and the one that was to provide a pattern for organizations worldwide, was the British and Foreign Bible Society. It was founded on 7 March 1804, when a group of nearly 300 British Protestant laymen met in a London tavern to discuss the place of Bible distribution in their work. Despite doctrinal and episcopal differences, these Christians formed a society whose sole purpose was to print copies of scripture 'without note or comment', and to distribute them without financial gain throughout the world.

In the next 10 years, hundreds of auxiliary societies were formed throughout Britain. At the same time, Bible societies sprang up in all parts of Europe, including Germany, Switzerland, Scandinavia, the Netherlands, Russia and France. They also appeared in Canada, and in numerous areas of the United States. In 1816, most of the local US Bible societies banded together to form the American Bible Society.

The British and American Bible societies used colporteurs from the beginning to distribute Bibles. By the 1880s, colporteurs were also hawking Bibles throughout Latin America. In the following decade, France began to use them and soon they were being sent out in all parts of Europe and beyond. By 1900, nearly 2,000 colporteurs were at work for various Bible societies in nearly all the countries of the world.

REACHING TO THE ENDS OF THE EARTH

From its inception, the British and Foreign Bible Society was committed to distributing scripture to the far parts of the earth, and they sponsored

many new translations, including an early Chinese edition. Most other Bible societies limited themselves to working within their own nations. Exceptions were the Netherlands Bible Society, the National Bible Society of Scotland and the American Bible Society. These three Bible societies also went beyond their own borders to translate and distribute Bibles in the nations evangelized by the missionaries of their national Churches.

The Bible societies have established a reputation for careful scholarship in preparing the Bibles they distribute. Through the years they have translated scripture – either complete Bibles or parts of Bibles – into an incredible number of languages, often taking many years to produce a single version. They have also maintained an open attitude, accepting all Christians, regardless of denomination, to work with them and use their Bibles. They manage this by holding to their original policy of publishing scripture 'without note or comment', thus avoiding conflicts over interpretation among the numerous denominations.

As the British, Dutch and American Bible societies spread out throughout the world, some overlap occurred in the areas they were serving. As a result, during the 20th century they made attempts to work together to increase their efficiency. At first, only the British, American and Dutch societies worked to coordinate their efforts. Then, in 1939, at a conference in Amsterdam, the Netherlands, a proposal was made to create a kind of world council of Bible societies. Unfortunately, the outbreak of the Second World War delayed implementation of the plan, but after the war, in 1946, 14 European, British and American societies joined to form the United Bible Societies. This loose federation serves as a valuable centre for

A colporteur offers pages from the Bible to a young Cantonese in China, c. 1900.

coordinating and planning the work of Bible translation and distribution in all parts of the globe.

At the start of 2001, the United Bible Societies incorporated 137 national societies. Together, these societies, which work in more than 200 countries and territories, distribute more than 500 million Bibles – or parts of Bibles – each year.

Gideon Bibles

The shortage of hotel rooms led to the formation of one of the most important organizations for distributing Bibles, Gideons International. One night in 1898, when John H. Nicholson, a businessman, tried to check into a hotel in Boscobel, Wisconsin, he was told he would have to share the room with another man. When his roommate, the salesman Sam Hill, asked if it were all right to leave on the light for a while so he could read from his Bible before going to sleep, Nicholson asked him to read it aloud.

The two men became firm friends and a year later they formed an association of businessmen and professionals, naming it after the Old Testament hero, Gideon. The sole purpose of the association was to 'put the word of God into the hands of the unconverted'. In the years that followed, the Gideons placed copies of the Bible in hotel and hospital rooms, schools and prisons around the world. They also sponsored new translations in order to provide Bibles in all the languages they needed.

In their first 100 years of existence, the Gideons distributed more than 770 million copies of the scriptures in 172 countries. Today, when you check into a hotel room you are almost sure to find a copy of a Gideon Bible in the bedside table for your use.

Wycliffe Translators

'Translation is profoundly related to the original conception of the gospel: God, who has no linguistic favourites, has determined that we should all have the good news in our native tongue.'

LAMIN SANNEH,
GAMBIAN HISTORIAN

Bible Translation Day

In 1966, the US Senate passed a resolution requesting President Lyndon B. Johnson to proclaim 30 September as Bible Translation Day. The day was proclaimed in an elaborate ceremony that year and repeated the following year. The Wycliffe Translators have continued to carry on the tradition of an annual Bible Translation Day ever since.

Dr Kenneth Lee Pike (1912–2000) was one of the first Wycliffe translators to go into the field. Pike (left) is shown here during one of his signature 'monolingual' demonstrations on how to learn new languages in 1981.

One day in the early 1930s, while William Cameron Townsend was working hard at a mission in Guatemala to bring Christ to the Cakchiquel Indians, a local asked him a simple question: 'If your God is so great, why doesn't he speak my language?' The question moved Townsend profoundly.

GETTING STARTED

After thinking long and hard about the implications of the question he had been asked by the Cakquichel man, Townsend became convinced that every man, woman and child should be able to read God's word in his or her own language, and he resolved to do something about it. In 1934, he established a linguistics school for training future Bible translators. Inspired by the work of the pre-Reformation hero, John Wycliffe, who was the first to translate the Bible into English, Townsend named the school Camp Wycliffe.

Once students completed their training, Townsend sent them into the field to develop writing systems for languages that lacked them and to translate scripture into those languages. His sole aim was to supply Bibles to peoples who had none in their own language. Camp Wycliffe grew rapidly, and in 1942 Townsend split it into two interdependent organizations – the Summer Institute of Linguistics (SIL) and the Wycliffe Bible Translators.

One of the first of the Wycliffe translators to go into the field was Kenneth Lee Pike. In 1935, Pike travelled to Mexico, where he committed himself to learning Mixtec, an Indian dialect, with the help of an old Mixtec man. Pike's efforts to learn Mixtec were almost foiled from the beginning. When he asked to be taught the numbers in Mixtec, Pike was dismayed to discover that the words for 'one' and 'nine'

The Summer Institute of Linguistics

The Wycliffe Bible Translators' sister organization, the Summer Institute of Linguistics (SIL), is dedicated to working with people who speak the world's lesser known languages. The SIL was incorporated separately from its sister group in 1942 so it could present itself as a secular linguistics institute, thus enabling its workers to enter countries that prohibit missionary activity.

Because the SIL concentrates on small communities who have no written language, the people they work with are generally among the poorest and least educated in the world. In addition to developing writing systems and translating the Bible, SIL personnel help train the people in the skills they need for survival – such as farming and health care. They often cooperate with governments and with local, regional and national agencies in developing education programmes in the languages of the people.

In addition to the Bible, SIL personnel translate materials on health care, agriculture, spiritual growth, nutrition, sanitation and other topics requested by the local communities. The SIL also maintains a web page, www.ethnologue.com, which disseminates information about all the currently known languages of the world and offers help to scholars in the fields of anthropology and language-related studies.

SIL workers come from more than 40 countries and have diverse backgrounds, but they are united in the belief that every person is created in the image of God and has value and dignity. They are rigorously trained in linguistics and the other skills they will need in their work by a professional staff with a broad range of field experience and a commitment to high academic standards. Courses are offered in many parts of the world, including the United States, Canada, Australia, New Zealand, France, Germany, the United Kingdom and Kenya. In the first 60 years of its existence, SIL carried out linguistic investigations in 1,320 languages spoken by 350 million people in more than 50 countries. And its work is just beginning.

sounded exactly alike to his ears. They differed only in pitch, and Pike was unable to master the tone problem either in Mixtec or any other language. Finally, he received help from a former linguistics professor, Edward Sapir, who explained his own system for analysing the tones of Navajo. Using Sapir's technique, Pike returned to work on learning Mixtec. Finally, some 10 years after he had started, he was able to crack the Mixtec system. With the help of Donald Stark of Wycliffe, Pike translated the New Testament into Mixtec. It was published in 1951, the first of hundreds of Wycliffe translations. Pike went on to become one of Wycliffe's foremost teachers and writers, sharing his experience and skills with hundreds of future translators.

WORK PROCEDURES TODAY

Wycliffe Translators International works hard to identify cultures that have no written language, to develop writing systems for them, and to translate the Bible into those languages. Sometimes requests for help come directly from the people themselves. For example, in about 1970 a group of Kuna Indians from Panama asked for help in translating the Bible. In response, Keith and Wilma Forster were sent to a Kuna village in 1972, where they developed writing systems for two Kuna dialects. With help from a Kuna pastor, Lino Smith, they translated the New Testament into two dialects, publishing the first in 1993 and the second in 1996. The team is now at work on a Kuna Old Testament.

More often, however, needy people are identified through Wycliffe surveys. Young Christian men and women trained by Wycliffe drive and hike through remote areas of the world for days or weeks at a time, combating foul weather, leeches and insects. On their travels they interview dozens of people to determine which groups truly need scripture in their own language. The neediest groups are later visited by translators who develop writing systems and publish scripture in the language of the people.

Translating scripture for unknown cultures is not easy. To begin with, translators must organize a way of dealing with the specific sounds of a language. In addition to the tonal problems that gave Pike trouble in the beginning of his work with Mixtec, symbols need to be found for sounds not used in European languages. These include a sound made in West Africa by flapping the lip rather than the tip of the tongue, the clicking sounds used in other African languages, and a sound made with the tongue sticking out and down towards the chin, as used in Pirahá, a Brazilian dialect. Today, computers are often used to chart and organize sounds and find symbols to represent them.

The actual work of translating presents other problems. It is often not possible to find an appropriate word in a remote dialect for one used in Hebrew or Greek. For example, Isaiah's statement that our sins 'shall be like snow' would be meaningless to people in jungle cultures who had never seen snow – even if they had a word for it. On the other hand, some languages contain many words with various shadings of meaning for a single Hebrew or Greek word. The Eskimos, for example, have many different words for snow, describing different grades of the frozen white precipitation. Care must be taken to choose the right word to fit the biblical context. In addition, some languages lack words that seem essential to

us. Languages in Papua New Guinea have no words for 'before' or 'after'. Translators must carefully structure their sentences to suggest the proper sequence without being able to state it directly. Consequently, instead of saying 'Peter went to the village after having supper at home', a speaker would have to say, 'Coming home and eating supper, Peter went to the village.'

Today, the Wycliffe Bible Translators, together with the Summer Institute of Linguistics, have translated at least parts of scripture into 500 languages, and translations into more than 1,000 other languages are in progress. However, they claim, more than 3,000 other languages are still waiting for translations of the Bible. Through a campaign called Vision 2025, Wycliffe translators hope that by the year 2025 they will have translation projects started – although not necessarily completed – in every language that needs one.

'Now you have God's word in your own language. The word of God is like rain that brings forth growth. God brings new life. Put God first, and everything will work better.'

BISHOP SENEMONA OF ZAÏRE, 1996

A Wycliffe Bible translator working with the Karabaro people of Burkina Faso in the early 1990s. They received their full New Testament in 1994.

Digging Up the Past

'Maybe we should stop digging and digest the stuff we have.'

PHILIP KING, BOSTON COLLEGE ARCHAEOLOGIST

Archaeologist Sir Flinders Petrie (1853–1942) arranges some of the pottery he found in Southern Palestine.

Excavating a burial site south of Gaza, in the region where Philistines once lived. This coffin, designed to resemble a human, is the kind commonly used among Philistines. It dates from about the 1300s to the 1200s BC, roughly when the Israelites and Philistines are both thought to have started settling in what is now Israel and the Palestinian Territories.

Treasure hunters are about the closest thing we had to archaeologists 200 years ago. These adventurers looted ancient tombs and dug up city ruins, taking gems, gold and anything else that looked as if it could be sold to museums or private collectors. Left behind in the damage and disarray of a frenzied hunt were bones, fragments of pottery and mysterious symbols etched onto stone and scrolls – clues to the past that modern archaeologists value more than gold.

FROM TREASURE HUNTING TO SCIENCE

Over the past two centuries, archaeology has gradually evolved into a science. In the process, it has generated a wealth of information about Bible times. It has filled in gaps of unrecorded history, restored meaning to long-lost words in the Bible, confirmed Bible history, and on occasion clashed with Bible accounts – stirring up questions no one had thought to ask.

Unlike the pyramids of Egypt and the Parthenon temple ruins in Athens, most remains from past ages in Bible lands are buried. Cities and villages were destroyed or abandoned, their ruins covered by wind-swept soil. In many cases, however, a new generation levelled the rubble and rebuilt. This could happen many times, producing what has become a common feature on the Middle East landscape – large mounds that look like gently rolling hills but that actually cover layer upon layer of past civilizations. Archaeologists call these mounds tells, the Arabic word for 'small hill' or 'mound'.

The first serious attempt to move beyond treasure hunting came in 1838, when two American scholars – Edward Robinson and Eli

Smith – travelled throughout the Bible lands recording the names of towns and villages. They made a second trip in 1852. Armed with these names, and the proposition that ancient names cling tenaciously to places even though the people and languages change, the scholars proposed the location of many Bible sites. For example, in the name of the Arab village of Jib, they heard a shortened version of Gibeon, where the Bible says the sun stood still during one of Joshua's battles.

The first scientific excavation of a Holy Land site took place in 1890. British scholar W.M. Flinders Petrie, began digging on a mound known as Tell el-Hesi, about 45 kilometres (30 miles) southwest of Jerusalem. Here, at what many scholars believe was once the Canaanite village of Eglon defeated by Joshua, Petrie convinced the academic world that tells were not natural hills but were layers of past villages built one on top of the other.

Petrie also started developing a pottery chronology – a list of the kinds of pottery made at different times in history. Pottery on top layers is usually newest, and pottery at the bottom of the mound is oldest. Classifying pottery has become one of the most accurate ways for archaeologists to date a site. The reason – just as cars from various decades look different, pottery from different centuries look different. And fortunately, fire-baked pottery lasts nearly as long as rocks – unlike wood, cloth and parchment, which decay with time. The pottery is usually found in pieces, but those pieces can often be reassembled well enough to tell what era they are from.

Bible scholars started leading archaeological expeditions to what they thought might be key sites in Bible lands. Often, their goal was to locate sites mentioned in scripture and to find other evidence supporting the Bible. This has changed in recent decades. Starting with preconceived notions – such as the hope that the mound was once a certain Bible site – has occasionally led archaeologists to jump to wrong conclusions. So today, most archaeologists aim for objectivity. They try not to bring their own questions and theories to the site as much as they allow the site to speak for itself.

To help interpret all this information, archaeology draws on many specialists: geologists, linguists, climatologists, anthropologists, zoologists, engineers, computer programmers, statisticians and biblical scholars. The list goes on. There are

even specialists who devote their life to studying a particular culture's social life, or government, warfare, architecture, furniture, fabric – you name it. New technology helps, too: ground-penetrating radar, satellite photography and computer reconstruction of everything from sprawling capital cities to tiny figurines.

KEY DISCOVERIES

In the last few decades, archaeologists have unearthed weapons of war and treaties of peace. They have gently brushed the dust off 4,000-year-old paintings and statues that put faces and fashions to the ancient people. From Iran to Egypt, archaeologists have not only uncovered ancient books and entire libraries, they have deciphered them – Egyptian, Sumerian, Akkadian (used by Assyrians and Babylonians), Hittite and Persian, to name just a few.

The Rosetta Stone was discovered in 1798. It has the same words written in Greek and two forms of Egyptian, including hieroglyphics. This allowed scholars to later decipher the hieroglyphics.

The Nineveh library, which was uncovered in the mid-1800s, included 25,000 clay tablets from the palace of the Assyrian king Ashurbanipal, along with tablets from Sennacherib. Both rulers are mentioned in the Bible.

In the late 1920s, some 20,000 clay tablets written in the wedge-shaped letters of cuneiform were discovered in northern Iraq. Referred to as the Nuzi tablets, they reveal much about life in Abraham's homeland of the Persian Gulf during his lifetime and beyond.

The Dead Sea Scrolls formed a library of ancient Jewish scrolls that included copies of the Old Testament 1,000 years older than those used to translate the King James Version of the Bible. First discovered in 1947, the scrolls were uncovered in dozens of caves about 24 kilometres (15 miles) east of Jerusalem, near the Dead Sea. These scrolls represent part of the library of a Jewish sect overrun by the Romans in about AD 68. (For more about this remarkable discovery, turn to page 218.)

Today, most archaeologists are not looking for spectacular discoveries. Instead, they are carefully sifting through the slightest of clues to what life was like in Bible times. They scrutinize bones, seeds, even pollen. 'What is interesting to me is certainly not interesting or spectacular to the average person,' said Jodi Magness of Tufts University. 'I get excited over little pieces of Byzantine pottery if they come from the right context.'

Confirming the Bible

Archaeology has confirmed the Bible on many points once disputed by scholars. For example, the Bible refers to people called Hittites, although the name never appeared outside the Bible. Scripture also said Belshazzar was king of Babylon in Daniel's day, although the records of history said the king was Belshazzar's father, Nabonidus. Some critics even questioned the existence of King David, suggesting he was nothing more than a heroic legend – like King Arthur.

Remnants of the Hittite civilization started turning up around 1900. An inscription showed that Belshazzar and Nabonidus ruled jointly for a time. And in 1993, a fragment of a stone from King David's day was uncovered in Israel; the inscription included the phrases, 'The House of David' and 'King of Israel'.

Here are some other notable discoveries:

❧ In 1990, Israeli park employees found an ornately decorated burial box in a previously unknown cave in Jerusalem. Etched into the limestone box from the first century was the name of Caiaphas, the high priest who tried Jesus. This box was found with 11 others, one of which held a coin dating to 10 years after the crucifixion. Many archaeologists say this cave was probably the family tomb of Caiaphas.

❧ A fishing boat from the days of Jesus was found buried in the mud beneath the Sea of Galilee. The boat could have held about 15 men, more than enough to accommodate Jesus and his 12 disciples who sailed on the lake one stormy night.

❧ Other Bible characters whose names have been found on objects dating from their eras include Pontius Pilate, the apostle Paul and Baruch, who was Jeremiah's assistant.

The Rosetta Stone helped archaeologists decipher Egyptian hieroglyphics. The stone inscription from 196 BC bears a message written in three languages: Egyptian hieroglyphic (top), Egyptian demotic (middle) and Greek (bottom).

Biblical Criticism Emerges

Biblical criticism
The term biblical criticism is not meant in any negative way. The aim of such studies is not to criticize and find fault with the Bible, but to examine the texts of the Bible to ascertain exactly what the human authors of scripture were trying to express. Although the findings of biblical criticism have sometimes contradicted long-held assumptions about the Bible, they have generally verified the major theological doctrines drawn from scripture by theologians throughout the ages.

Differences in the number of animals Noah took aboard the ark led scholars to believe Genesis had more than one author. *Noah's Ark* (1846) by Edward Hicks.

The field of study known as biblical criticism started with the Enlightenment and blossomed in the 19th and 20th centuries. The severe religious scepticism of Enlightenment thinkers, who tended to condemn the Bible – or large parts of it – as an affront to reason, created a strong reaction from traditional Christians. Many Christians reacted to these views by returning to a more personal interpretation of scripture, spurning any idea of looking at the Bible critically. To them the Bible was the word of God that spoke to them in their hearts and it should be accepted at face value. Nothing less was acceptable. At the same time, some scholars were adopting a middle ground, hoping to understand better what the writers of the biblical books were trying to say.

TWO GOALS OF BIBLICAL CRITICISM

Biblical criticism has two basic aims. First, it works to establish biblical texts that are error free and as close to the original texts as it is possible to get. Because none of the original texts of scripture survived antiquity, scholars must prepare new editions of the Bible by sorting through hundreds of old hand-copied versions, trying to find the most correct ones through rigorous detective work. This type of biblical scholarship, known as textual criticism, goes back to at least the early third century, when Origen assembled his Hexapla, a sixfold version of the Old Testament in which he placed the Hebrew and various Greek translations of the Bible in parallel columns to arrive at the best text (see pages 90–91).

The other major aim of biblical criticism is to examine the established texts for linguistic and literary style to ascertain the intentions of the original authors. Most biblical critics see the Bible as the word of God, but realize that God's word is expressed in human language (mainly Hebrew and Greek). Although inspired by the Holy Spirit, human writers wrote the texts using the tools available to them at the time. Consequently, they expressed themselves in the conventions of the literature of their time. By studying the literary conventions of biblical times and by trying to identify the Bible's human authors and their sources, modern readers can better grasp what the biblical authors were trying to communicate to the people of their time.

Such historical approaches to Bible studies are generally referred to as exegesis, from the Greek word for 'draw out', or 'explain'. Using exegetical findings as a basis for reading the Bible as it was originally intended, other scholars, teachers and preachers can relate the texts to their own time to make the Bible meaningful to today's believers. This branch of biblical criticism is known as hermeneutics, from the Greek word for 'interpret'. It endeavours to present the ancient texts in a way that is faithful to its historical settings, but that does not imprison us in them. Thus it allows today's believers to apply the messages of scripture to their own lives and nourish the faith they share with others.

IDENTIFYING AUTHORS AND SOURCES

Although biblical criticism developed during the era of the Enlightenment, and used the new tools for historical investigation that were honed during that period, it was not an entirely new concept. Questions had arisen from early times about seeming contradictions in the Bible. Did Noah take two of each ritually clean (kosher) animal aboard the ark (Genesis 7:8–9) or seven (Genesis 7:2–3)? In about AD 400, Jerome, who was translating the Bible into Latin, questioned the tradition that Moses had written the Pentateuch, the first five books of the Bible, holding that those books did not receive their final form until centuries after the time of Moses.

The Tübingen School

Nineteenth-century scholars at a number of European universities were active in applying the historical methods of criticism to the New Testament, but writers from the University of Tübingen, Germany, were probably the most influential. Two Tübingen scholars in particular influenced the biblical scholarship that followed. They were David Friedrich Strauss and Ferdinand Christian Baur.

In 1835, Strauss published his *Life of Jesus*, radically interpreting the Gospel accounts. Unlike previous biographies of Jesus, which had either followed tradition in accepting God's intervention into human history or used rationalist arguments to explain away any supernatural events, Strauss suggested a mythical interpretation. He held that the Gospels contained historical truths that the Church had embellished and transformed. It was impossible to construct a true life of Jesus, he wrote, because the Gospels offer only disconnected fragmentary views, imposing their own order on the material. In response, other writers went to extremes, either discounting the historic basis for the Gospels and offering a totally fictitious Jesus, or considering the supernatural elements in the Gospels unreal and offering a purely human Jesus.

In 1853, Baur, the founder of the Tübingen School, held that most of the books of the New Testament were not written until the second half of the second century. Adopting the philosophy of Georg Wilhelm Friedrich Hegel, Baur viewed the early history of Christianity as a dialectical development in which there was tension, struggle and then reconciliation. The tension rose out of Paul's view that Jesus freed us from the Jewish law against the insistence of Peter and others on a narrow adherence to the Jewish law. Baur held that out of this thesis-antithesis the Catholic Church emerged and the New Testament was written, smoothing away the differences by placing Peter and Paul on equal footing, as reflected in the Acts of the Apostles. Later scholars showed that the New Testament was completed early in the second century, making Baur's views untenable. But even though few of his views are accepted today, the questions Baur posed were of enduring significance and his scientific methods of scholarship were widely adopted.

During the Reformation, when the Bible was held up as the sole authority for Christian thought, Martin Luther applied his doctrine of justification by faith alone to cast doubts on the authenticity of the letters of James, Jude, Hebrews and the book of Revelation – denying they were apostolic in origin.

Jerome was not the last to doubt that Moses had written the Pentateuch. In later centuries, other scholars found the idea implausible because the last of the five books describes the death of Moses, its supposed author, and because the Pentateuch contains different versions of the same stories and references to events that occurred long after the time of Moses. Consequently, scholars analysed the texts of the Pentateuch, and gradually began to see that the Pentateuch was made up of four distinct narratives that were not fully united until at least the time of the Babylonian captivity. In 1878, the German theologian Julius Wellhausen, brought together all the related theories about the Pentateuch and added his own, formulating the so-called Documentary Hypothesis, which is still widely accepted today. (For a fuller discussion of this hypothesis and its development, see 'Sources of the Pentateuch', pages 28–29, and 'Shaping the Pentateuch', pages 30–31.)

Authorship and sources of the New Testament books were also questioned in the early years of biblical criticism. At first, scholars began to believe that not all the letters attributed to Paul were actually written by him. Some of them may have been written by disciples who borrowed Paul's name to give more authority to their writing (a common practice in Bible times). Soon there were almost as many ideas about which letters were authentically Pauline as there were scholars speculating on the subject. Scholars also began to wonder who really wrote the Gospels and when, pointing out that the names of the evangelists – Matthew, Mark, Luke and John – were not applied to the Gospels until the second century and may not be accurate. Consequently they closely examined the Gospels for internal evidence of authorship and the sources on which the authors based their work. Work in this area was to bear much fruit in the 20th century, when scholars uncovered a great deal about how the Gospels had been written.

'Seeing that, in sacred scripture, God speaks through men in human fashion, it follows that the interpreter… should carefully search out the meaning which the sacred writers really had in mind.'
SECOND VATICAN COUNCIL

Bringing together current theories about the authorship of the Pentateuch, Julius Wellhausen (1844–1918) developed the widely accepted Documentary Hypothesis, which holds that the Pentateuch is made up of four separate narratives.

Some scholars maintain that Paul did not write the letters to Timothy found in the New Testament, although Timothy is pictured with the letter-writing Paul in this 14th-century manuscript illumination from the French *Bible historiale* by Guiart Desmoulins.

Critics Get Back to Basics

Hermann Gunkel (1862–1932) led the field in investigating the historical circumstances in which small units of the biblical texts may have been written.

By the end of the 19th century, biblical critics had thoroughly explored and analysed the sources of most of the biblical books, but work remained to be done. A new form of historic criticism, known as form criticism, soon emerged, with the purpose of studying the various literary forms found in the Bible. By going back to the basics of literary style used in biblical times, these scholars hoped to understand better what the biblical authors meant to convey.

FORM CRITICISM AND THE OLD TESTAMENT

The German theologian Hermann Gunkel approved of the earlier work done in studying biblical sources, but he considered it limited in scope. Until then, scholars had dealt with the Bible in terms of material that had been handed down in written form but, Gunkel held, much of the biblical material originated in the oral tradition, being passed along by word of mouth for long periods of time – centuries for parts of the Old Testament, and decades for the Gospels. In his groundbreaking commentary on Genesis, published in 1901, Gunkel held that to understand the Old Testament writers, it was necessary to investigate thoroughly the history behind the biblical texts that have come down to us.

Gunkel realized that it is impossible to trace down the actual authors and dates of composition for most of the Old Testament books, but in order to ascertain the original meanings he thought it necessary to separate units of early tradition from material that had been added in later times. To accomplish this separation, Gunkel set about determining the literary form in which a particular thought had been expressed. After closely examining stylistic elements in the writing, he broke the text down into types of forms, such as songs, prophecies, miracle stories and folk tales.

In the days when biblical stories were being handed on by word of mouth, these forms were developed to tell certain types of stories. They served partly to aid the teller's memory and partly to trigger recognition in the listener. A story of a certain type, therefore, always followed a particular pattern – sometimes with variations. (See the accompanying boxed feature 'Annunciations of births'.)

In order to determine the literary form of a biblical passage, it is necessary to delve into what Gunkel called the *Sitz im Leben* (life-setting) that gave rise to it. By *Sitz im Leben*, Gunkel meant all the circumstances surrounding the person telling the story and his audience – or of the writer and his first readers, in later stages of the story's development. What type of person was passing on the story, and to whom was he transmitting it? What was going on around them at the time? Was it a time of war or peace, famine or prosperity, upheaval or stability? What types of literary forms were prevalent in that time? Such circumstances, Gunkel believed, would be strong influences on how a storyteller shaped his material and give clues as to what literary forms might be in use – such as history or moral story.

Annunciations of births

One of the basic forms found in the Bible is that used to announce the birth of a special child. These annunciation stories follow a simple pattern, with variations, which helped the storytellers and preachers remember them, and helped others to recognize that an exceptional birth was imminent. Old Testament annunciation stories relate the coming births of Ishmael (Genesis 16:7–13), Isaac (Genesis 17:15–21, and another version in Genesis 18:1–15) and Samson (Judges 13:2–23). In the New Testament, annunciations precede the births of John the Baptist (Luke 1:5–20) and Jesus (Luke 1:26–37 and Matthew 1:20–21).

The elements of an annunciation story are generally as follows:

* an angel of the Lord (or sometimes the Lord himself) appears to the prospective mother or father

* the future parent is afraid or falls prostrate

* the angel calls the parent by name and says not to be afraid

* the angel announces the upcoming birth

* the angel gives the name of the child, explains the meaning of the name, and predicts what the child will later accomplish

* the future parent objects that the birth is impossible, or asks for a sign that what the angel said is true

* the angel gives a sign to reassure the parent.

After isolating the forms and placing them within a *Sitz im Leben*, Gunkel then proceeded to trace the progress of the stories from their oral origins to their development into larger cycles or groups of stories and ultimately into the form in which they appear in the Bible today. To help him in this long and tedious process, Gunkel relied on recent archaeological findings that reflected life in Bible times and on the literature of nearby civilizations. He especially examined the literature of the Babylonians, which often contained parallels to forms found in the Bible, although without the emphasis on Yahweh (the Hebrew name for God) as the only God and saviour.

In his last years, Gunkel made important studies of the psalms, focusing on the literary characteristics and historical development of the psalm genre. He began his evaluation by classifying the individual psalms into standard types, including psalms of praise, thanksgiving, national lament and individual lament (there are 40 of these).

After classifying all the psalms, Gunkel then analysed each type, breaking it into its individual parts. For example, he found that the individual lament contained a number of common elements – a summons in the name of Yahweh and a call for help, the complaint itself, a petition, a statement of confidence in God and a promise to praise God. In comparing the types of biblical psalms to Egyptian and Babylonian poetry, Gunkel found striking resemblances and realized that the psalm was not a distinctive type of Hebrew poetry, as formerly believed, but one that was common in that era. He also saw that some of the psalms were quite ancient, pre-dating the time of David, and that they had gone through various stages of change to fit the needs of the times. Other psalms were written centuries later, at the time of the Babylonian exile.

FORM CRITICISM AND THE NEW TESTAMENT

In 1919, the German scholar Martin Dibelius published *From Tradition to Gospel*, applying form criticism to the Gospels – and creating the term 'form criticism' in the process. Two years later Rudolf Bultmann published his highly influential *History of the Synoptic Tradition* in which he classified all the stories of Jesus in the first three Gospels according to their types and common patterns. His broad categories were: sayings of Jesus, miracle stories and other stories about Jesus, including the infancy, passion and Easter narratives. Bultmann then divided each of these categories into subtypes and sometimes further divided the subtypes, creating a kind of collection of Chinese boxes.

Studies of the psalms show that they were written over a long time span, and therefore not all of them could have been written by the musical King David, who is shown here in an illustration from a 12th-century Psalter.

Bultmann and others held that these types were often influenced by the needs of the early Church, including teaching, preaching and worship. They held that the units were developed in three stages, reflecting:

❧ The *Sitz im Leben*, or situation in the life, of Jesus (under what circumstances did Jesus act or speak).

❧ The situation in the life of the early Church (often how the apostles and others shaped the events they had witnessed to suit what was happening in the Church at that time).

❧ The situation in the life of the evangelist, who selected and shaped the material to suit his first readers.

The job of the form critic is to pare away the influences of the second and third stages of transmission to arrive at a more exact representation of the words and deeds of Jesus. Along the way, the form critic can also study the early Church, discovering the needs and events that made the evangelists shape the Gospels as they did.

Writers and Revisers at Work

Jesus of Babylonia

Scholars sometimes let bias get in the way of good judgment. In 1902, Friedrich Delitzsch, a German specialist in Babylonian culture, claimed that the Babylonian religion was older than Judaism and superior to it. Among other things, he contended, the Babylonians initiated the celebration of the sabbath and first used the name Yahweh for God. He later rejected the Old Testament as scripture and declared that Jesus was not a Jew but a Babylonian. His theories were debunked, but not before they fuelled the anti-Semitism of the Nazis.

The practice of form criticism of the Bible concentrated only on small parts of a biblical book and how these units were reworked at later times. Scholars give the name 'redactor' both to the writers who originally put two or more traditions together and to editors who later revised such accounts. Ultimately a new form of scholarship – which came to be called redaction criticism – evolved in biblical studies. Its purpose is to discover the intentions of the various biblical redactors and to identify the theological emphases those redactors may have contributed to the traditions they worked with. Redaction criticism came to the fore in the 1950s, when three German scholars used it in studying the Gospels of Matthew, Mark and Luke.

REDACTION CRITICISM IN THE NEW TESTAMENT

Gunther Bornkamm was the first scholar to examine the work of a Gospel redactor. In 1948, he published an article showing how the author of Matthew's Gospel took the account of Jesus quieting the storm from Mark's Gospel and gave it a new theological meaning. In Mark, Bornkamm holds, the calming of the storm serves mainly to show that Jesus has power over nature. Matthew uses the miracle to show Jesus as the 'Messiah of deed' after having shown him as the 'Messiah of the word' in the Sermon on the Mount, which almost immediately precedes the storm passage. Furthermore, since the account follows two sayings on discipleship (Matthew 8:19–22), Matthew turns Jesus' rebuke to the disciples into a comment on discipleship – so adding a new dimension to the passage.

Bornkamm continued his studies, and in 1954 he presented a book on the entire Gospel of Matthew. Applying redaction criticism to Jesus' discourses, he brought out Matthew's ideas on the Church and its relationship to the imminent second coming of Jesus.

In 1953, Hans Conzelmann published *The Theology of St Luke* in which he goes through the entire Lukan Gospel, trying to separate out Luke's own editorial material from that of his sources. Conzelmann then examines the Lukan material for theological motivation. By putting all the pieces together, he arrives at a revolutionary view of Lukan theology.

Redaction criticism was first used in a study of the story of Jesus calming the storm, shown here in a 1695 painting by Ludolf Backhuysen (1631–1708): *Christ in the Storm on the Sea of Galilee.*

In the past, Luke had generally been seen as a historian, in the modern sense of a chronicler of events. Through his redactional studies, however, Conzelmann demonstrates that Luke was much more a theologian than a historian. Even time and geography have theological purposes in Luke, and may not reflect the actual locations or times that particular events occurred. In fact, Conzelmann demonstrates that Luke divides time into three major periods: the period of Israel (including the ministry of John the Baptist); the period of Jesus' ministry (including his post-resurrection appearances); and the period of the Church from Jesus' ascension until his second coming. Conzelmann goes on to show how Luke used this time frame and other tools to explain the delay in the second coming, which at Luke's time was seen as past due.

In *Mark the Evangelist* (1956 and 1959), Willi Marxsen, the first to use the term redaction criticism, investigates Mark's contributions to the Gospel traditions. He studies the life situation (*Sitz im Leben*) of the evangelist to establish the evangelist's purpose and point of view in writing his Gospel. He focuses mainly on Mark's treatment of John the Baptist, Mark's geographical references, the concept of Gospel and the material on the end times (chapter 13).

REDACTION CRITICISM IN THE OLD TESTAMENT

Scholars also used redaction criticism in studies of the Old Testament. In *Reading the Old Testament*, published in 1984, John Barton gives the example of how a redactor tied together the early chapters of Genesis and the Abraham story. The redactor's use of genealogies – once thought to be only a device for tying together distinctly different sources – actually serves an important theological function in the case of the Table of Nations in Genesis 10. In the ancient Near East, the creation was regarded as occurring in a timeless realm unconnected with the time frame used to relate human history. In response to this belief, the redactor of Genesis used simple genealogies to tie together accounts of the creation to the history of the Israelites. As a result, the text makes clear that 'one and the same God is responsible both for creating the world and for directing its subsequent history – which in many religions is not the case'. It also shows that God 'has a purpose which is already implicit from the moment the world is formed, a purpose which works itself out over an immensely long period of time but which is never frustrated'. That purpose, of course, is to establish Abraham's descendants in Palestine.

Other scholars studied the redactors of the prophets, concluding that the prophetic books went through various revisions before arriving at

Types of biblical criticism

So many forms of biblical criticism have been employed in recent times that the terms can become confusing. Following is a list of the chief forms of biblical interpretation in use today, together with the focus of each:

❧ Historical criticism looks back to the origins of the biblical texts in an attempt to understand how the sacred authors proceeded and what they meant to convey. This school includes many of the following types of biblical scholarship.

❧ Textual criticism sorts through the various ancient versions of the Bible to establish the most accurate text.

❧ Source criticism seeks to trace any oral or written sources used by the biblical authors.

❧ Literary criticism examines the Bible for literary aspects of the Bible, examining types of writing and literary style.

❧ Form criticism examines the literary forms and small units that make up the Bible.

❧ Redaction criticism looks at the work of the original authors and editors of the Bible to better understand their viewpoints.

❧ Canonical criticism studies biblical books in their context as part of the entire Bible.

❧ Semiotics or structuralism seeks meanings that arise from the relationships between words, patterns and ideas.

❧ Interpretation history studies biblical interpretations through the centuries to help us better understand the Bible today.

❧ Liberation theology sees the Bible as a mandate to engage in the struggle to liberate the oppressed.

❧ Feminist interpretation examines how women are represented or misrepresented in the books of the Bible.

❧ Fundamentalist interpretation focuses on the verbal inerrancy of scripture.

the text we have today. Most important, perhaps, Martin Noth developed a widely accepted theory that the books Joshua to 2 Kings formed a single work, with Deuteronomy as its prologue, retelling the history of the Israelites to show that they had lost their land and been taken captive because they had not been faithful to God's covenant. Later scholars built on this theory. (For a discussion of their findings, see 'History with a Viewpoint', pages 36–37.) On the whole, redaction criticism has helped us understand the theology of the biblical writers and has filled in our knowledge of the theological history of Judaism and early Christianity in a way that was formerly impossible.

Biblical Scholarship Today

Jewish scholarship

A number of the more astute biblical scholars from the past made good use of Jewish biblical learning to acquire a better understanding of scripture. Among these scholars were Origen in the third century and Jerome, who translated the Bible into Latin in the fourth century. Today many biblical scholars follow their example, and often Jewish and Christian scholars work together.

Earlier in the 20th century biblical scholars used the techniques of historical criticism to focus on how the biblical books were written and revised until they attained the form in which they now appear. In the second half of the century, a number of different types of biblical criticism arose, ranging from the simple to the highly complex.

CONCENTRATING ON THE FINAL FORM OF SCRIPTURE

In 1970, Brevard S. Childs expressed his dissatisfaction with the results of historical criticism in *Biblical Theology in Crisis*. To supplement historical criticism he proposed a biblical theology that would be based firmly on the canonical, or final, form of the text – that is accepted as authoritative for belief and life in the community of faith. In his 1974 commentary *The Book of Exodus*, he applied his new method, beginning with a textual and historical-critical study of the text, continuing with a history of its interpretation, and ending with a theological reflection on the official canonical form of the text. In 1985, Childs further applied his methods in *The New Testament as Canon*.

Childs was criticized by some for giving too much attention to the relationship of one biblical book to the other books of the Bible, while totally ignoring what the book meant to the original author and his first readers – long before it was considered part of the Bible. In contrast, James A. Sanders wrote a series of works that investigated the process by which books became canonical. As part of this process, he holds, certain traditions and values became authoritative and so were preserved by the community of faith, which found its identity and direction for its lifestyle in them. Sanders' critics have asked whether it is legitimate to use the interpretation process that led to the formation of the canon as the guiding principle for interpreting scripture today.

A far more complex form of biblical criticism, semiotic analysis – formerly known as structuralism – concentrates on an analysis of the biblical text as it comes before the reader in its final state. It originated in the work of the Swiss linguist Ferdinand de Saussure, who developed a theory that all language is a system of relationships that obey fixed laws. Semiotics (from the Greek for 'observing symbols') seeks to uncover the meanings that emerge from the relationships between words, patterns and ideas. It was used especially in studies of the passion narratives – notably by the French-Canadian scholar O. Genest in *The Christ of the Passion* (1978) and the American scholar L. Marin in *The Semiotics of the Passion Narrative* (1980).

Other scholars have looked at the history of how the canonical texts have been interpreted over the centuries. Such investigations seek to assess the development of interpretation as influenced by the concerns readers have brought to the text over the course of time. For example, a history of the reading of the Song of Solomon would show how the book was regarded by the Fathers of the Church, by monks of the Middle Ages (especially Bernard of Clairvaux), and by mystics, such as John of the Cross. The approach helps uncover all the dimensions of meaning in the text. However, it might also uncover false and harmful interpretations from the past, such as interpretations of the Bible that promoted anti-Semitism or slavery. Consequently, discretion must be employed in evaluating findings.

Archbishop Oscar Romero of San Salvador put liberation theology into practice by preaching against the oppression of his people by the totalitarian government. He was assassinated in 1980 while celebrating Mass.

BIBLICAL INTERPRETATION AND SOCIAL CONCERNS

Sometimes scholars bring their own social concerns into the fore in interpreting the Bible. Inspired by biblical passages that show deep concern for the oppressed, a new school of thought, known as liberation theology, surfaced in 1968. It gained impetus with the publication in 1971 of *A Theology of Liberation* by the Peruvian theologian Gustavo Gutierrez. In reading the Bible, liberation theologians draw from the situation of the people around them. They hold that God is present in the history of his people, bringing them salvation. Because he is the God of the poor he cannot tolerate oppression or injustice. As a result, biblical interpretation cannot be neutral but must take sides on behalf of the poor, in imitation of God, and engage in the struggle to liberate the oppressed. Reacting to liberation theology, missionaries and local clerics in Latin American and elsewhere engaged in political activities against regimes who oppressed the poor. Many of them were put to death.

Branching off from liberation theology, a new school of feminism gathered strength in the 1970s. Feminist interpretation of the Bible usually

Quest for the historical Jesus

Since the era of the Enlightenment in the 18th century, scholars have been trying to discover the 'historical' Jesus (Jesus as he was in real life) in the belief that the Jesus described in the Gospels is coloured by the theological views of the early Church. In 1853, David Friedrich Strauss held that it was impossible to construct a true life (historically accurate biography) of Jesus, but countless theologians, including Strauss himself, proceeded to try. Lives, or biographies, of Jesus have gone through a number of stages, the last of which began in the late 20th century and is still going strong.

Using the techniques of historical criticism, writers have presented a dizzying number of portrayals of the historical Jesus. These include pictures of Jesus as a cynic; a wandering preacher who shocked people into fresh thought about themselves; a teacher who envisioned a reborn community whose sins would be forgiven under a renewed covenant; a reformer who refused to work within normal categories and insisted that the urgency of the moment should override some provisions of Jewish law; a non-political figure; a political figure who opposed Israel's nationalist cause because he believed it would end in social and military disaster; and a Jewish man who overcame the stigma of an illegitimate birth to become a rabbi and a mystic.

Meanwhile, the Jesus Seminar, a group of prominent American scholars have been meeting to discuss the historicity of Jesus' sayings. Using a set of guidelines, to help them, these scholars discuss, debate and vote on the authenticity of Jesus' sayings according to a scale of probability. In the end, all the diversity of opinions about the historical Jesus go further in reflecting the personalities of these scholars than they show what Jesus was really like.

criticizes the biblical writers for being male-centred and covering up the true status of women in biblical times. Feminists use the tools of historical criticism in their work, but add to it a general principle of suspicion. Because history was written mainly by the victors, feminists hold, scholars can establish the full truth only by distrusting the texts as they stand and looking for signs that may reveal something quite different about women in the Bible.

In her 1978 book *God and the Rhetoric of Sexuality*, Phyllis Trible examined such texts as the book of Ruth to find expressions of affirmation and liberation for women. Ruth and Naomi, she holds, are only two of the many 'valiant women' in the Bible. However, Trible goes on, such a story of joy and celebration must be balanced with the sombre accounts of victimized women, such as the slave Hagar (mistreated by her owner, Sarah) and Jepthah's daughter (who was sacrificed by her father). J. Cheryl Exum later showed that in Exodus 1:8 – 2:10, women act as the saviour of the saviour Moses, and Carol M. Meyers attempted to give a more balanced view of women's status in the biblical texts, which are overwhelmingly patriarchal. Similarly, New Testament studies have sought to rediscover the status and role of women disciples in the life of Jesus and in the churches established by Paul. In those early days, feminists claim, a certain equality prevailed that was later concealed in the New Testament, as men more and more asserted their authority.

Naomi entreats her daughters-in-law Ruth and Orpah to remain in their homelands, as shown in this illustration from 1795 by William Blake, but Ruth follows Naomi to Israel. Feminists saw Ruth and Naomi as valiant women.

Human sciences

In the late 20th century, the human sciences were increasingly put to use in interpreting the Bible. Sociology was used to uncover social conditions in biblical times, showing how a loose confederation of 12 tribes might have become a solid nation and a people bound together by a common religion. Anthropology shed light on the ideas of kinship in the Old Testament, among other things. Psychology and psychoanalysis investigated the meanings of symbols.

The Bible as Literature

'We shall come much closer to the range of intended meanings – theological, psychological, moral or whatever – of the biblical tale by understanding precisely how it is told.'

ROBERT ALTER, *THE ART OF BIBLICAL NARRATIVE*

This wood engraving illustrates the Song of Solomon 2:3–6. Literary critics are interested in the literal and symbolic imagery of the poetry in the Song of Solomon. *The Repose of the Beloved Woman Under the Protection of Her Lover* by Johann Wolfgang von Goethe (1749–1832) from *The Bible in Pictures.*

Books of the Bible have been admired as literary masterpieces from early times, and poets and storytellers have used them as models for their own writing – especially since the time of the Renaissance. During the 20th century, however, critics began to examine the biblical books strictly for their literary merit, putting aside any theological considerations. In the 1960s, high schools and colleges began to teach courses in the Bible as literature, and these were very popular for a time. Subsequently, biblical scholars began to use the tools of literary analysis for interpreting the Bible.

GENERAL PRINCIPLES OF LITERARY CRITICISM

Scholars who study the Bible as literature reject any form of historical criticism. They examine only the biblical text itself. Once a text has been written, they hold, it has a life of its own and may take on new meanings. Therefore, the message the original writer meant to convey is unimportant, they claim. A biblical text should not be seen as a window that reveals something outside it, such as history or doctrine, literary critics contend. Rather, it should be seen as a mirror that has its meaning locked in, for the only legitimate meaning is the meaning contained within the text itself.

In studying a biblical text, literary critics examine it closely in terms of its own literary structure. They are concerned with the world of the text and perceive reality in the terms that the text perceives it. For example, literary scholars generally read the Song of Solomon in terms of a love poem or a series of such poems, as the book closely resembles many ancient Near Eastern love songs.

In studying the Song of Solomon, literary scholars reject past readings that have seen it as a celebration of God's love for Israel or Christ's love for his Church. In fact, they tend to discard any theological interpretations, as the Song of Solomon is one of the only two books of the Bible that do not mention God (the other is Esther).

They also reject the search for cultic origins, such as comparing the text with ancient fertility rites or with ceremonies to ward off death – although both have been proposed by historical critics.

Instead, literary critics focus on the poetry of the Song of Solomon, noting how its rich imagery functions on both a literal and a symbolic level. For example, they see the garden as a place of nurture – whether for plants or in a sexual capacity – and the pasture as a place for feeding the shepherd's flock and for nourishing human intimacy. They also study the use of repetition and the various patterns found in the text.

TECHNIQUES OF LITERARY CRITICISM

When analysing a biblical book, literary scholars use the tools of secular literary criticism. That is, they pinpoint the genre of the work and study the literary style, including the use of imagery, sentence structure and vocabulary. Genres found in the Bible are narrative, poetry (including the psalms), proverbs, visionary writing (including prophecies), gospel, parable, satire, apocalypse, pastoral, oratory, elegy, letter writing and many more.

In 1981, Robert Alter, an American professor of Hebrew and comparative literature, published *The Art of Biblical Narrative*, an influential book on Old Testament narrative. New Testament critics have treated the Gospels as narratives, pointing out that they contain stories with plots, characters and outcomes. They hold that the Gospels are not histories or biographies of Jesus, and offer no means for discovering the historical Jesus.

Literary critics tend to see narrative as a fundamental part of the human experience, because people live in a reality that is story-like. Such a view gives meaning to the smaller stories in which we all participate. This approach can even be seen in Paul's letters, which assume a narrative substructure based on the sacred story of God's saving action, which culminates in Jesus' death on the cross to save sinners. Not only does Paul continually refer to this basic story of salvation, literary critics have pointed out, but he tells his own story as well. By relating his personal story to the basic story, he gives a personal meaning to his letters.

The unity of a biblical book or of the entire Bible is also worth examining. There are many themes that hold the texts together. The most inclusive is the story of how God interacts with humans and brings about their salvation. On a smaller, but still major scale, Luke carefully structured his Gospel and the Acts of the Apostles. Luke begins his Gospel in Jerusalem, the centre of Judaism, and gradually moves out into the lands of the Gentiles, ending Acts in Rome, the centre of Gentile power. Along the way, Luke draws parallels between events described in the two volumes. For example, many of the events in Paul's trial reflect those in Jesus' trial. Smaller literary structures are found throughout the Bible.

Language is also used to bind books together. Often a particular word or phrase serves as a recurrent theme. The formula 'God's mighty hand and outstretched arm' (or a variation on it) is frequently referred to in the Old Testament to describe how God saved the Israelites from their enemies. The word 'light' is frequently used for God, and John's Gospel often refers to Jesus as 'the Word'. Relational descriptions also sometimes make their own points. Michal is described either as Saul's daughter or David's wife depending on her fortunes in the story at the time. Amnon is repeatedly referred to as Tamar's brother in the story in which Amnon rapes Tamar (2 Samuel 13:7–14).

Literary studies of the Bible often bring out meanings that traditional historic or theological approaches do not. Anyone wishing to read the Bible from a theological perspective can still learn much from literary studies, but may want to combine the findings with those uncovered in more traditional methods of analysis.

Repeating a point

Literary critics have noted that the use of repetition in the Gospels often furthers the point being made by the evangelist. For example, in repeating the story of Jesus miraculously feeding a crowd, Mark adds a new dimension to the story by making minor changes. In the first version, Jesus feeds 5,000 in a Jewish region, but in the second he feeds 4,000 in a Gentile region, showing that Jesus was concerned with both Jews and Gentiles alike.

Characteristics of Hebrew poetry

Nearly a third of the Old Testament is in poetic form, including all of Psalms, Proverbs, Ecclesiastes, Lamentations and the Song of Solomon. In addition, poems – especially in the form of songs – are scattered throughout the narrative books, and much of the Prophets and all but the beginning and end of the book of Job are poetry.

Hebrew poetry differs somewhat from modern poetry. It does not make use of rhyme, but it seems to have a definite rhythmic form – although scholars cannot agree on how it works. Lines in Hebrew poetry are composed of two, or sometimes three, short units. Often these short units are broken in two with a pause in the middle. Two short units make up a line and two lines constitute a verse.

The two lines of a verse in Hebrew poetry are generally parallel in sense. The second line may repeat the first with one or more minor variations, or it may give the opposite view – such as stating good people do one thing but bad people do the contrary. In some cases, the second line extends the meaning of the first, as in Proverbs 20:1:

Wine is a mocker, strong drink a brawler,
and whoever is led astray by it is not wise.

In addition, Hebrew verse, like other poetry, plays on words and uses vivid images to heighten its effect. Proverbs 10:26 reads:

Like vinegar to the teeth, and smoke to the eyes,
so are the lazy to their employers.

The Dead Sea Scrolls

'Not only are the scrolls the oldest known copy of the Old Testament, but they belonged to the Essenes, a mysterious ascetic Jewish sect that existed about 2,000 years ago and is believed to have had a great influence on the early Christians.'

MAGEN BROSHI, FORMER CURATOR OF THE SHRINE OF THE BOOK, JERUSALEM

The interior of cave number four, in which 15,000 scroll fragments have been found.

The Temple Scroll, which outlines plans for a new, ideal Jewish temple, is one of only about a dozen Dead Sea Scrolls to survive mainly intact. Most of the approximately 800 scrolls lie in scraps that are still being pieced together.

Not since young David dropped Goliath with a slingshot has the stone of a shepherd boy so captivated the world.

In the winter of 1946–47, a young shepherd was tending his flock along the shores of the Dead Sea, about 24 kilometres (15 miles) east of Jerusalem. As the story goes, he saw a cave in the cliffs above, threw in a rock, and heard the crash of shattering pottery. When he investigated, he found three scrolls that had been protected inside clay pots. One of the scrolls was a complete copy of Isaiah, written about 150 years before Jesus –1,000 years older than any previously discovered copy.

Until that day, the oldest known copy of Isaiah and the rest of the Jewish Bible was from about AD 900: the Masoretic Hebrew text, which was the standard text used in most modern Bible translations including the King James Version.

Archaeologists and local herders began scouring caves in the vicinity of the shepherd's discovery. What they found over the next decade was a hidden library of sacred Jewish writings, dating from about 250 BC to AD 68 – when Roman soldiers overran the desert community that owned the library. Every book in the Old Testament except Esther was represented, though often only in the tiny fragments of scrolls shredded by time, animals or people.

MONSTROUS JIGSAW PUZZLE

Scattered among 11 caves in the cliffs and ravines near the Dead Sea were remnants of some 800 manuscripts, about 200 of which were copies of Old Testament books. Only about a dozen manuscripts were intact. All the rest lay in crumbled scraps – about 25,000 of them – many no bigger than a fingernail. Scholars are still trying to piece them together.

There are three distinct kinds of writing in the

Dead Sea library: biblical books, commentaries on biblical books and general religious writings such as prayer books, rules to live by and collections of visions. One scroll, known as the Copper Scroll because the text is etched into copper sheets, identifies 64 sites of buried treasure, such as gold, silver, perfume and scrolls. Location descriptions seem vague and coded, and may have been intended as reminders only for community leaders familiar with the sites.

To Bible scholars, such treasures are of relatively little interest. They are more curious about the biblical books in this ancient library – such as the collection's most famous document: the complete Isaiah Scroll. What the scholars have discovered is that the surviving biblical books and fragments are remarkably similar to the traditional Masoretic text produced a millennium later. This suggests that Jewish scriptures were becoming standardized by the first century and that scribes preserved the sacred words with remarkable care.

There are, however, some differences – most notably in Psalms, Israel's hymnbook. One scroll that contains the last third of the book of Psalms puts the songs in an unusual order. It also includes three previously unknown songs, as well as seven other songs later eliminated from the Jewish Bible but preserved in the Apocrypha, the Greek collection of sacred Jewish writings. Some scholars speculate that this scroll was a collection of David's songs, while other scholars suggest it was a compilation used in worship rituals.

Commentaries on biblical books such as Isaiah, Habakkuk and Hosea show that the Dead Sea community had its own distinct method of interpreting the Bible. Just as Christianity highlighted references to Jesus in the Jewish Bible, the Dead Sea community called special attention to messages and implications about the end times, when God would conquer sin and set up a righteous kingdom. These people believed the end was near and that they were the 'Sons of Light' who would soon ride with God's army to defeat the 'Sons of Darkness', who were the Romans and all other sinful people.

Other writings in the library reveal even more about the people behind the scrolls. Rule books such as the Rule of the Community show they had high standards of ritual purity, taking ritual baths every day so they would remain pure enough to fight in God's army whenever that day came. The War Scroll seems to contain their battle plan.

The Dead Sea Scrolls have not only helped us see the care that Jewish scribes took to preserve their sacred writings. The scrolls have also provided a window into the life and practices of a group of Jews who lived at the time and near the place where Christianity was born. They were waiting for God. But they did not recognize him when he came.

Since 1965, portions of the Dead Sea Scrolls have been on display in Jerusalem at the Israel Museum, in a pavilion called the Shrine of the Book.

One scroll, known as the Copper Scroll, was inscribed onto a copper sheet. Here, in 1955, a scholar begins the delicate process of unrolling the scroll so it can be read. The scroll contains sketchy directions to buried treasure.

'Texts that you have never seen, have never held, have never been able to see and read, and now you have them telling you about the beliefs of people who are our forefathers from 2,000 years ago. This is really a miracle. This is a tremendous opportunity.'

LAWRENCE SCHIFFMAN, PROFESSOR OF JEWISH STUDIES, NEW YORK UNIVERSITY

Who owned the library?

Most Bible experts say the Dead Sea Scrolls were copied and preserved by a group of monk-like Jews called Essenes ('pious ones'). These Jews – almost exclusively men – lived in a desert community called Qumran. The settlement was a tiny, walled village on a rugged and desolate ridge near the banks of the Dead Sea, a body of water so salty that fish cannot survive in it.

The Essenes apparently severed all ties with other Jews in about 152 BC, when a Jewish leader in Israel's successful war of independence from Syria declared himself the new high priest. Like the Pharisees and the Sadducees, the Essenes represented a distinct branch of the Jewish faith, much like Baptists, Anglicans and Catholics represent different forms of Christianity.

When they withdrew from Jewish society, the Essenes took with them sacred Jewish writings, which they preserved by making copies of them. Leaders in the group added new works, such as predictions about the approaching end times. Ironically, what came was the end of their community. Roman solders crushing a nationwide Jewish rebellion decimated the settlement in AD 68. The Essenes had a good vantage point on the high ridge and could probably see the army advancing from miles away. It was perhaps in those frantic moments that the settlement leaders ordered the scrolls hidden in the nearby caves. Most scrolls – more than 500 – were stashed in Cave 4, just across a steep ravine from the settlement.

Burnt walls and Roman arrowheads found at the ruins of Qumran confirm the settlement's violent end.

In Search of a Reliable Text

'The task of text criticism is to scrutinize all variant readings throughout the history of the text, and to separate the true variants from the pseudo-variants. True variants are those that survive the tests of textual analysis... Pseudo-variants arise from early attempts to update the text and make it understandable to a specific community, or from unintentional errors in copying.'

JAMES A. SANDERS,
TEXTUAL CRITIC

Resorting to conjecture

When comparing ancient versions fails to clear up a verse that makes no sense in the original language, scholars have to resort to conjecture. The original Hebrew version of Amos 6:12 translates as 'Does one plough in the mornings?' This makes no valid point, but by changing the Hebrew word *babbeqarim* to *bebaqar* the verse can be translated as 'Does one plough the sea with oxen?' Today scholars often adopt this conjecture, which was first made in 1772.

❧

Biblical scholars were exhilarated by the discovery of the Dead Sea Scrolls, especially the ones with biblical texts. These manuscripts were far older than any other surviving copies of the Old Testament books, and spurred scholars on to studying the basic biblical texts with renewed vigour. For the most part, these early texts agreed with the later ones, but some had minor variants, while others were radically different. Consequently, questions arose about which versions were the most authentic.

OLD TESTAMENT VARIATIONS AND ADDITIONS

Sometime after AD 70, when the Romans invaded Jerusalem and destroyed the temple, the Jews established the canon of their scriptures and accepted the texts they had at that time as standard, allowing no further changes to be made to them. These texts were carefully reproduced by Jewish scribes over the years and eventually came to be known as the Masoretic texts, after the scribes who copied them.

Before AD 70, however, the Hebrew scriptures were often altered and even expanded. The Septuagint, the Greek translation of the Old Testament that was started in the third century BC, contains books that do not appear in the Jewish canon and versions of the canonical books that differ radically from the Masoretic texts. The Dead Sea Scrolls also contain earlier versions of the Hebrew scriptures, some of which may have been used by the Septuagint translators.

Variations are even found in the Pentateuch, the first five books of the Bible, which are considered the most sacred of the Hebrew scriptures because they constitute the law. For example, in all Bibles the ten commandments are listed twice, first in Exodus and then in Deuteronomy. In Exodus 20:11, the reason given to remember the sabbath day is that God created the universe in six days and rested on the seventh day, blessing and consecrating that day. In Deuteronomy 5:15, the reason for observing the sabbath day is that the Lord commanded it when he delivered the Israelites from slavery in Egypt. In a version of Deuteronomy found among the Dead Sea Scrolls, both reasons are given for observing the sabbath, adding text from Exodus to Deuteronomy.

Textual critics examine such variants to determine whether or not they are legitimate. They generally discount the above variation as a scribe's attempt to smooth out and harmonize the texts by combining the two justifications for the sabbath into one, long commandment. But this variant serves to show that before AD 70, Jews must have considered the general message of the scriptures to be more important than the precise words. The words could be manipulated, updated and even added to without detracting from the authority of the writing.

In another Dead Sea Scroll, seven entirely new lines are added to Miriam's song (Exodus 15:21), which celebrates God's victory in leading the

The standard biblical texts

Before making a new translation of the Bible from the original languages, translators must determine which version of the ancient texts to use. Although they will probably consult other versions and even other translations, they must settle on a single basic text. Despite some contrary views, most scholars are generally in agreement over the best versions of the Hebrew and Greek scriptures.

The standard version of the Old Testament is the Biblia Hebraica Stuttgartensis, published in Stuttgart, Germany, in 1966–77, the fourth edition of a version edited by Rudolf Kittel in 1902. The biblical text is that of the *Leningrad Codex*, which dates to 1010, making it the oldest complete Hebrew Bible in existence, but it also incorporates notes on variant readings, including some from the Dead Sea Scrolls. A new edition, with even more variants, is being prepared and will be published in about 2005.

The standard New Testament text is the fourth edition of the Greek New Testament, published in 1993. This version was prepared by an international panel of scholars under the auspices of the United Bible Societies. It includes a basic text plus evaluations of readings that differ from it in various early manuscripts, citations from the Church Fathers and ancient translations into Syriac, Coptic, Latin, Armenian, Georgian and Old Church Slavonic.

Israelites to freedom through the parted waters of the Red Sea. In deciding on the authenticity of these added lines, textual critics have noted they were not retained by later scribes and not quoted or referred to elsewhere in Jewish writings. Consequently, some critics have dismissed them as scribal additions and not authentic. The extra lines were probably a scribe's way of extending and emphasizing for a new generation of readers the theological message that God was Israel's liberator at the Red Sea, not Moses.

Other variations help clarify single words or phrases in the Masoretic texts that seem out of place or even incorrect. The Masoretic text often questions such texts in the margins, but keeps the traditional reading, letting the reader decide if it is authoritative. Today's scholars try to establish a firm basis for interpreting or translating problematic passages by consulting other ancient copies of the scriptures, such as the Dead Sea Scrolls, and by looking at early translations of these passages. They then choose whether to use the standard, problematic text or substitute a variant.

DEALING WITH VARIATIONS

Unfortunately there is no equivalent of the Masoretic text for the New Testament. In fact, there are more than 5,300 New Testament manuscripts and it is estimated that they contain more variants among them than there are words in the entire New Testament – although some say that 95 per cent of these variants are unlikely to change the true meaning of the text. Scholars have had to sift through these manuscripts, identify the ones most likely to be accurate, and compare these versions to arrive at what are hopefully the original readings.

Over the years textual critics have developed general guidelines to help them establish the accuracy of passages in both Old and New Testament texts, although these guidelines do not always lead to the best readings. Discretion must be used in applying them. One of the tenets of these guidelines is that the shorter the reading the more likely it is to be the original. Scribes often added material in order to make a passage more comprehensible to their readers,

but they seldom deleted anything, for they considered the scriptures to be the sacred word of God. Another tenet is that the more difficult the reading is to understand the more likely it is to be the original, as scribes often simplified texts to clarify them for their readers but were not likely to muddy the readings.

Textual critics also look for substitutions of words that sound alike or look very much alike in order to root out unintentional scribal errors. In addition, they watch for passages a scribe may have skipped by jumping a line or going from one use of a word to a later use of the same word, thus accidentally eliminating words in between.

Although textual problems in the Old Testament continue to need solutions, the dependability of the Masoretic texts has made the work of scholars easier. The overwhelming number of variant readings in New Testament manuscripts, however, guarantee that textual critics will remain hard at work for a long time to come.

This coloured woodcut by Julius Schnorr von Carolsfield (1794–1874) shows God resting on the sabbath, the seventh day, having created the universe in six days. Exodus 20:11 cites this as a reason to observe the sabbath, but other passages differ. Textual critics study such variations for legitimacy. From *The Bible in Pictures*.

Recent European Translations

*'God is the great linguist –
he speaks your language
and he speaks mine.
It is to enable all peoples
to hear God speak their
own language that we
translate the Bible.'*

MILLER MILLOY OF THE UNITED
BIBLE SOCIETIES

*'A nation that receives
the Bible in its own
language will never
be the same again.'*

MARTIN BUBER

Renowned Jewish
philosopher Martin
Buber (1878–1965), shown
here in the garden of his
Jerusalem home, sought to
give his German translation
of scripture the feel of the
original Hebrew text.

Dutch medieval texts

While most of the
efforts in publishing
European Bibles over
the past half-century
were concentrated on
new translations, in the
1970s, C.C. de Bruin of
the Netherlands edited
the texts of a 14th-
century Dutch version of
the Bible. The project
was part of a larger
collection of major
medieval Dutch biblical
texts. A companion
series of minor texts
included three Gospel
harmonies (1970) and a
life of Christ (1980).

As the world moved into a new millennium, the work of Bible translation was at an all-time high. New translations appeared throughout Europe and many others were in progress. Often they were made by interdenominational committees.

FRENCH TRANSLATIONS

The most important Bible to come out of France in the 20th century was the Jerusalem Bible, which appeared shortly after the end of the Second World War (see the boxed feature

opposite). The Jerusalem Bible is not only noted for the excellence of its translation, but for the high quality of its scholarly notes and other features. The volume contains introductions to individual books of the Bible or groups of books (such as the books of Wisdom or the Prophets). Notes in the margins call attention to other biblical passages that were cited or alluded to in the passage at hand. Explanatory and linguistic notes are found at the foot of the pages. Other features include maps, an index of persons in the Bible and tables giving modern equivalents of biblical money, measurements and months of the year.

In 1956, the year the Jerusalem Bible was completed, the Pléiade translation of the Bible was published by Gallimard Press in Paris. It was prepared by a group of leading biblical scholars. In addition, between 1974 and 1977, a 26-volume Bible appeared. Translated by André Nathan Chouraqui into Hebrew-flavoured French, it was the first French Bible translated by a Jewish scholar to include the New Testament. Finally, in the year 2000, the *Parole de Vie* was published by the French Bible Society, following the basic translation principles recommended by UNESCO. It uses only 3,000 words of vocabulary.

SPANISH AND ITALIAN TRANSLATIONS

The first Bible to be translated into Spanish from the original languages was made under the direction of the Pontifical University of Salamanca in 1944, and it went through numerous editions. A Spanish translation based on a 1961 Italian Bible was published in 1969. In 1971, a Latin-American Bible appeared in Spanish, and in 1992, a Spanish translation based on the English New International Version was brought out.

Italy published the *Bibbia Concordata* in 1968. This interconfessional version was translated by a committee of Catholic, Protestant and Jewish scholars and reviewed by the Dominican Biblical School in Jerusalem. An interfaith Common Language Translation of the New Testament appeared in 1976, which sought to translate the original Greek text into everyday Italian. In the 25 years after its publication, more than 10 million copies of various editions of this translation were distributed, playing a major role in developing dialogue between the various churches in Italy after centuries of tension and confrontation.

GERMAN TRANSLATIONS

A historic German translation of the Old Testament was published in Berlin between 1925 and 1937. This 15-volume edition was translated by the Jewish philosophers Martin Buber and Gotthold Salomon, who attempted to give the translation the feel of the Hebrew original. The New Testament was translated into everyday German in 1967 and revised in 1977. This translation, the *Gute Nachricht für Sie*, was based on the English Good News Bible as reworked by a committee of Catholic and Protestant scholars. A full Bible was completed in 1980, translated by a committee commissioned by Catholic bishops of Germany, Austria, Switzerland, Luxembourg and Lüttich. Protestant scholars were included in the committee for revising the New Testament, which appeared in 1980. A German New Testament published in 1999 differed in that it arranged the books in chronological order.

DUTCH TRANSLATIONS

The first Catholic Bible to be translated into Dutch since the 16th century was published by the Peter Canisius Society between 1929 and 1939. A fresh translation of the New Testament into modern Dutch followed in 1961. Today's

Dutch Bible, an interconfessional common language version, was completed in 1983 and revised in 1996. A new translation of the Bible was being published in individual books at the start of the new millennium.

SLAVIC TRANSLATIONS

At the start of the new millennium, the Bible Society of Russia was working on translations into Russian and six minority languages spoken in Russia. Greek-Russian and Hebrew-Russian interlinear editions were also in progress, as was a critical edition of the Old Slavonic Gospels.

In 2001, a New Testament in Polish was published as part of a projected full Bible. The work is being done by a team of 30 scholars with the cooperation of Catholic, Orthodox and Protestant churches, marking a milestone in Polish ecumenical efforts.

SCANDINAVIAN TRANSLATIONS

In 1931, a royal commission in Denmark produced a new Danish translation of the Old Testament. The New Testament followed in 1948 and the Apocrypha in 1957. In 2000, the Danes published Bibles in Danish, Faroese and Greenlandic, using a matching format with tailpiece and cover designs created by Queen Margrethe II. It was felt that the uniform format showed that Denmark, the Faroe Islands and Greenland form a spiritual community.

In Norway, the Bible was translated into modern Norwegian in 1978, and revised in 1999.

In 1999, Sweden published *Bibel 2000*, a modern Swedish version of the Bible. It was so successful that within weeks of its publication, one in every ten people in Sweden had bought a copy. The popularity of the volume owed a great deal to its award-winning advertising – posters juxtaposed biblical texts with life's great questions to encourage people to think.

TURKISH TRANSLATIONS

Turkey also produced a popular Bible. In 1941, an old Turkish translation had been put into the new Turkish alphabet, which had replaced Arabic characters. However, the translation still contained many Arabic words, so by the 1970s, young Turks were finding it difficult to understand. Consequently, a new translation was started in 1979. The New Testament was published in 1989, and the text was said to flow 'like music'. In 2001, the entire Bible appeared, and it was warmly received, in contrast to 1974, when a Bible advertisement had brought threats of violence to the newspaper that printed it. Five newspapers, two television stations and a radio station ran stories about the new Bible, pointing out that it was the first new translation of the Bible into Turkish in more than 300 years.

All in all, there has been a lot of recent activity in translating the Bible into modern languages throughout Europe. According to the United Bible Societies, complete Bibles had been translated into 62 different European languages by the start of 2002, single Testaments (Old or New) had appeared in 31 additional languages, and smaller portions of the scriptures had been rendered into 110 other European languages.

In 1942, Pope Pius XII (1876–1958) signed a letter calling for more accurate translations of the Bible.

The Jerusalem Bible

Historically, the Catholic Church had been reluctant to approve translations of the Bible into the languages of the people. But this attitude changed in 1942, when Pope Pius XII issued an encyclical (official letter) calling for a more historic approach to biblical studies and for new and more accurate translations of the Bible.

The timing of the encyclical was ideal for Father Thomas Georges Chifflot, a Dominican priest and publisher in Nazi-occupied Paris. Father Chifflot had recently determined that the time had come for a new translation of the Bible, which would comfort, inspire and instruct French Catholics. Encouraged by the pope's encyclical, he wrote to scholars at the Ecole Biblique, a famous biblical studies institute in Jerusalem, asking them to undertake a translation based on the original Hebrew and Greek texts of the Bible and not on the Latin Vulgate that earlier Catholic translators had used. Because the Second World War was still raging, he got no response to his letter until 1945. Then, with the war ended, work on the translation began and progressed rapidly.

Preliminary translations of sections of the Bible were published between 1948 and 1954, and each was thoroughly revised (some more than once). Finally, a one-volume edition of the new translation was published in 1956 as the Jerusalem Bible. A revised version, based on later scholarly findings, was issued in 1973.

Not only was the translation of high calibre, but scholarly notes and introductions and other extra features made the Jerusalem Bible invaluable. It served as a model for future study Bibles. Germany produced a version of the Jerusalem Bible in 1966, Spain followed suit in 1967, and a version in the language of the Cree Indians of Ontario, Canada, followed between 1976–87.

England produced a Jerusalem Bible in 1966 and revised it in 1985 to incorporate the changes made in the revised French version. Although the revised English version – the New Jerusalem Bible – relied more on the original Hebrew and Greek texts for its translations than on the French, it closely adopted the French introductions and notes, as did versions in other languages.

The influence of the Jerusalem Bible spread far beyond Europe. In Africa, a version in Swahili was started in 1967. A Vietnamese New Testament appeared in 1986.

Popular Bibles in English

There are more than just a few English translations of the Bible. There are hundreds. And more are coming.

Each translation has a unique slant or purpose. Many are theologically distinct, intended for evangelical Protestants, Catholics, Eastern Orthodox or Jews. Some target people at a certain level of reading ability: scholars, average readers, children or adults learning English as a new language. Others are written for people in different English-speaking areas of the world, drawing on words unique to that region – such as Great Britain, the United States or Australia.

Most translations have at least one thing in common – they are trying to keep pace with the ever-changing English language. Words popular a generation ago mean nothing today, or have picked up entirely different meanings. And new words constantly emerge. For this reason, some popular translations are periodically updated.

TEN NOTABLE ENGLISH BIBLES

Ten of the most influential, best-known Bibles in the English language are as follows.

King James Version, 1611

This is the most famous and perhaps most artistically written English Bible of all – the top-selling Bible until 1988, when the more popularly written New International Version bumped it to second place. Called the Authorized Version in many countries, the King James Version was commissioned by King James I of England as a revision of earlier English translations that had become hard to understand. Although beloved for its poetic rhythms and majestic style that left an enduring mark on the language, the Shakespearean English is hard for people today to understand. (See pages 178–81.)

Revised Standard Version, 1952 (updated in 1989 as the New Revised Standard Version)

This is a descendant of the King James Version, two translations removed. The English revised the King James Version with the English Revised Version in 1885. But the phrasing was too British for many Americans, so they responded in 1901 with their own update – the American Standard Version. The Revised Standard Version was an update of the American Standard Version. Unfortunately, many Christians considered it too liberal. For one thing, the translation team of Protestants, Catholics and Reform Jews was sponsored by the National Council of Churches, which some Christians, during the communist witch hunts of the 1950s, accused of having communist leanings. Also, many Christians objected to the translation of Isaiah 7:14, a passage generally considered a prophecy about Christ's birth. The reference to the child's mother had been changed from 'virgin' to 'young woman', and many saw this as an attack on the doctrine of the virgin birth. Still, this translation is perhaps the most widely approved English Bible, endorsed by Protestants, Catholics and Eastern Orthodox. The 1989 revision drew from older and more reliable ancient manuscripts. It also substituted gender-inclusive language for the original words intended to refer to both sexes. For example, instead of using 'sons' to describe the people of Israel, the revision uses 'children'.

New American Bible, 1970 (revised 1986)

The official translation of the Roman Catholic Church, this is the first American Catholic Bible translated from the original languages. It outsells another Catholic Bible – the New Jerusalem Bible (originally the Jerusalem Bible, 1966, revised and renamed in 1985). French Catholic scholars in Jerusalem translated the Jerusalem Bible into their language, as the first Catholic Bible from the original languages. It was translated into English and many other languages.

New English Bible, 1970 (revised in 1989 as the Revised English Bible)

The first British Bible to break from the

tradition of the King James Version, this translation drew directly from the original Hebrew and Greek languages. It was translated by a team of British scholars from all the major Christian denominations in the UK.

New American Standard Bible, 1971 (revised 1995)

Because so many Christians thought the Revised Standard Version was too liberal, a foundation in California arranged for a team of 32 scholars to produce another update of the 1901 American Standard Version. The New American Standard Bible retains 'virgin' in Isaiah 7:14. Many readers complain that this Bible translation is too literal and hard to read. Many scholars, however, prefer it because it so accurately reflects the wording of the original languages.

Good News Bible (Today's English Version), 1976

Easy to read, and generally considered quite accurate, this translation uses words that even people unfamiliar with the Bible and church can understand. For this reason, it has been a favourite source for translators wanting to produce Bibles in other languages. Many Bible stories in this translation read as smoothly as a novel. It is published by the American Bible Society.

Tracking Bibles in English
1611: King James Version
1885: English Revised Version
1901: American Standard Version
1952: Revised Standard Version
1958: J.B. Phillips: The New Testament in Modern English
1965: Amplified Bible
1966: Jerusalem Bible
1970: New English Bible
1970: New American Bible
1971: Living Bible
1971: New American Standard Version
1976: Today's English Version (Good News Bible)
1978: New International Version
1982: New King James Version
1989: New Revised Standard Version
1989: Revised English Bible
1993: The Message (New Testament)
1995: Contemporary English Version
1996: New Living Translation

New International Version, 1978 (revised 1984)

This top-selling English translation was prepared by a team of 115 scholars working under the direction of the New York Bible Society (now the International Bible Society). The 'International' of the title demonstrates the translators' intention that their work could be used in any English-speaking country. The translation appears in versions with spellings unique to various countries, such as England and the United States. This Bible is the preferred translation for many evangelical churches. Under development is another revision, called Today's New International Version. Among the changes is the substitution of gender-neutral terms for the original text where the intention was to include both men and women. The New Testament was released in 2002, with the Old Testament scheduled to follow in 2005.

New King James Version, 1982

This does not replace the King James Version, which still outsells it. Instead, the New King James Version attempted to retain the elegant literary style of the King James Version, while eliminating the outdated words, such as 'thee' and 'shalt'. It draws on the same sources used by translators of the original King James Version instead of the older and more reliable manuscripts that have since been discovered.

The Message, 1993

This highly colloquial paraphrase reads more like a novel than a Bible, even omitting verse numbers. The New Testament portion was released in 1993, with the Old Testament following in 2002. This Bible is the work of one man, Eugene H. Peterson, a theology professor retired from Regent College in Vancouver, British Columbia. Although *The Message* is not a word-for-word translation, it seeks to convert the Bible's tone, rhythm, events and ideas into everyday language. So Titus 3:8, 'I desire that you insist on these things,' becomes, 'I want you to put your foot down. Take a firm stand on these matters.'

New Living Translation, 1996

One of the easiest reading translations for adults, this version is described as a thorough revision of the Living Bible, 1971. However, the Living Bible was a paraphrase by one man, Kenneth Taylor, who did not understand the original Bible languages. The New Living Translation is the work of more than 90 scholars from various denominations who translated from the original languages and the oldest reliable manuscripts.

Revising the King James Version

The King James Version did not remain as it was published in 1611. It was revised periodically, to correct obvious mistakes and to keep pace with changes in word spelling. If it had not been updated, the last verse of Psalm 23 would look like this: 'Surely goodnes and mercie shall followe me all the daies of my life: and I will dwell in the house of the Lord for euer.'

Comparing Modern Translations

Translation it is that opens the window, to let in the light; that breaks the shell, that we might eat the kernel.'

KING JAMES VERSION
TRANSLATORS

Long gone are the days when we could walk into a bookstore, ask for a Bible, and walk out with the same translation nearly everyone else had. Many Christians consider this good news, because it means there is a wide variety of Bibles for a wide variety of needs.

For Bible scholars who understand the original Bible languages of Hebrew or Greek, there are Bibles in those original languages. For serious students of the Bible who do not read the original languages but want a good study Bible that follows the original languages as closely as possible, there are such Bibles – including interlinear Bibles, which print the original languages and provide word-for-word translations. For plain-spoken people who want an easy-to-read Bible, there are many from which to choose.

Niche markets abound: Catholics, evangelical Protestants, mainline Protestants, Anglicans, Jehovah's Witnesses, British, Americans, new converts, children, to name a few. People looking for a Bible for themselves or for friends are well-advised to learn about the different Bibles. Only then is it possible to match readers to the Bible best suited to their needs.

COMPARING THE LORD'S PRAYER

Differences between translations can be subtle or extreme. Here are samples of how several versions translate the Lord's Prayer that Jesus taught his disciples (Matthew 6:9–13). The following comparisons begin with the more literal Bible translations, and work towards the most freely phrased versions.

Young's Literal Translation, 1898

Our Father who [art] in the heavens! hallowed be Thy name.
Thy reign come: Thy will come to pass, as in heaven also on the earth.
Our appointed bread give us to-day.
And forgive us our debts, as also we forgive our debtors.
And mayest Thou not lead us to temptation, but deliver us from the evil, because Thine is the reign, and the power, and the glory – to the ages. Amen.

New American Standard Bible, revised 1995

Our Father who is in heaven, Hallowed be Your name.
Your kingdom come. Your will be done, On earth as it is in heaven.

Give us this day our daily bread.
And forgive us our debts, as we also have forgiven our debtors.
And do not lead us into temptation, but deliver us from evil. [For Yours is the kingdom and the power and the glory forever. Amen.]*

*This phrase does not appear in the oldest known manuscripts.

King James Version, 1611

Our Father which art in heaven, Hallowed be thy name.
Thy kingdom come. Thy will be done in earth, as it is in heaven.
Give us this day our daily bread.
And forgive us our debts, as we forgive our debtors.
And lead us not into temptation, but deliver us from evil. For thine is the kingdom, and the power, and the glory, for ever. Amen.

New King James Version, 1982

Our Father in heaven, Hallowed be Your name.
Your kingdom come. Your will be done
On earth as it is in heaven.
Give us this day our daily bread.
And forgive us our debts,
As we forgive our debtors.
And do not lead us into temptation,
But deliver us from the evil one.
For Yours is the kingdom and the power and the glory forever. Amen.

New Revised Standard Version, 1989

Our father in heaven,
hallowed be your name.
Your kingdom come.
Your will be done,
on earth as it is in heaven.
Give us this day our daily bread.
And forgive us our debts,
as we also have forgiven our debtors.
And do not bring us to the time of trial,
but rescue us from the evil one.

New International Version, revised 1984

Our Father in heaven,
hallowed be your name,
your kingdom come,
your will be done
on earth as it is in heaven.
Give us today our daily bread.

Forgive us our debts,
    as we also have forgiven our debtors.
And lead us not into temptation,
    but deliver us from the evil one.

New American Bible, revised 1986

Our Father in heaven, hallowed be your
        name,
Your kingdom come, your will be done,
on earth as in heaven.
Give us today our daily bread;
and forgive us our debts, as we forgive
        our debtors;
and do not subject us to the final test, but
deliver us from the evil one.

New Living Translation, 1996

Our Father in heaven, may your name
        be honoured.
May your kingdom come soon.
May your will be done here on earth,
just as it is in heaven.
Give us our food for today,
and forgive us our sins,
just as we have forgiven those who have
        sinned against us.
And don't let us yield to temptation,
but deliver us from the evil one.

The Message, 1993

Our Father in heaven,
Reveal who you are.
Set the world right;
Do what's best –
    as above, so below.
Keep us alive with three square meals.
Keep us forgiven with you and forgiving
        others.
Keep us safe from ourselves and the Devil.
You're in charge!
You can do anything you want!
You're ablaze in beauty!
    Yes. Yes. Yes.

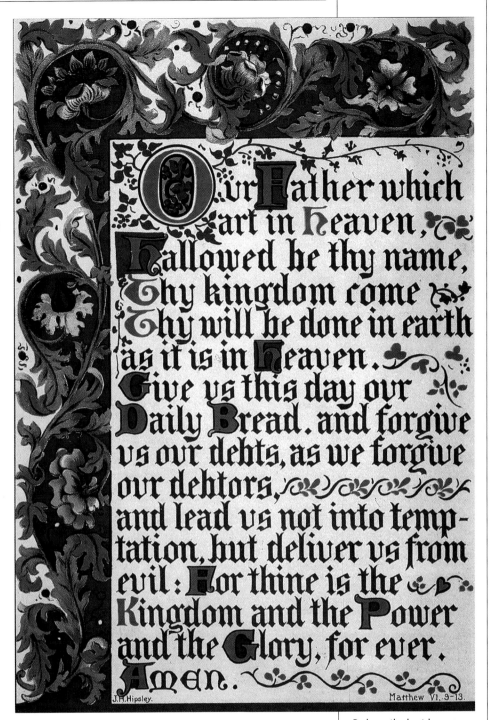

Perhaps the best-known English-language version of the Lord's Prayer is that from Matthew's Gospel in the King James Version. From *The Sunday at Home* by J.H. Hipsley, 1895.

227

Ways to Translate the Bible

THE BIBLE IN THE MODERN WORLD

'It is said that people should not see how either their sausage or their laws are made. Perhaps the same could be said of their Bible translations.'

DANIEL TAYLOR, CONSULTANT FOR NEW LIVING TRANSLATION

Chart of Bible versions showing, from left to right, a progression from the literal towards the paraphrase. The chart also gives an indication of how difficult each one is to read. The easiest (New International Reader's Version) is at the bottom to the most difficult (King James Version) at the top.

Anyone starting work on a new Bible translation has one critical, controversial question to answer: How closely should they follow the ancient text?

If the Hebrew prophecy speaks of a coming sacrificial 'Lamb', is that the term you should use – even if your intended readers are isolated Eskimos who have never seen a lamb? Or should you substitute 'seal pup', as Wycliffe translators once did?

Translators are sharply divided over what should get top priority: preserving the literal words and sentence structure of the ancient language, or presenting the basic ideas in a way that today's reader can understand. The more literal approach is called 'formal equivalence', or 'word-for-word translation'. Examples of this include the King James Version, New King James Version and the New American Standard Bible. The less literal approach is called 'thought-for-thought translation', 'equivalent meaning' or 'dynamic equivalence'. Examples of this include the majority of the best-selling Bibles, including the New International Version, New Revised Standard Version and the New Living Translation.

THE CASE FOR LITERAL TRANSLATIONS

There is one main reason some people prefer word-for-word translations, even though the English phrasing is often awkward and at times impossible to understand – as awkward as it is, this is what the Bible says. For example, Hebrew sayings common in ancient times are kept though they make no sense today. One such saying talks about 'heaping coals of fire' on your enemies. To readers today, this sounds like some kind of torture. But to the Hebrews it meant to make their enemies regret what they did.

Compare these two methods in the translating of Romans 12:20. The first version is from a more literal translation, and the second is from a freer translation:

But if your enemy is hungry, feed him... for in so doing you will heap burning coals upon his head.
New American Standard Bible

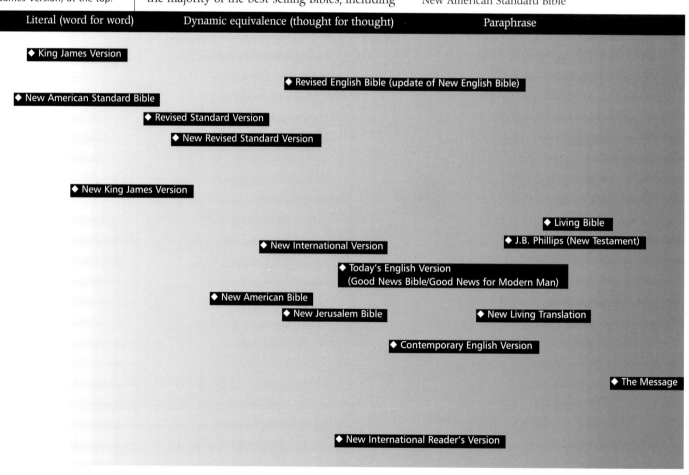

Literal (word for word)	Dynamic equivalence (thought for thought)	Paraphrase

◆ King James Version

◆ Revised English Bible (update of New English Bible)

◆ New American Standard Bible

◆ Revised Standard Version

◆ New Revised Standard Version

◆ New King James Version

◆ Living Bible

◆ J.B. Phillips (New Testament)

◆ New International Version

◆ Today's English Version (Good News Bible/Good News for Modern Man)

◆ New American Bible

◆ New Jerusalem Bible

◆ New Living Translation

◆ Contemporary English Version

◆ The Message

◆ New International Reader's Version

If your enemies are hungry, feed them... and they will be ashamed of what they have done to you.
New Living Translation

Bible students who prefer the more literal versions of scripture acknowledge that these are harder for most people to understand. But the place to clear up the confusion, they insist, is not in the Bible text, but in notes added to the margin of the Bible or in accompanying commentaries and dictionaries. This approach is said to help protect the Bible from translators weaving their own theological preferences into the text. Critics of the Living Bible, for example, say Kenneth Taylor took extraordinary measures to make sure texts conform to his conservative beliefs – to the point of adding comments. For example, the King James Version describes the sinful cities of Sodom and Gomorrah as 'an example, suffering the vengeance of eternal fire' (Jude 7). The Living Bible adds: 'Those cities were destroyed by fire and continue to be a warning to us that there is a hell in which sinners are punished.'

Confessions of a Bible translator

When Bible scholars and writing specialists work together to create a new Bible translation, the frailty of humanity sometimes works its way onto the printed page. Daniel Taylor, a communications specialist for the popular New Living Translation wrote in *Christianity Today* magazine,

A phrasing that would die an unlamented death at nine in the morning will somehow survive if it comes up instead at four in the afternoon after a long and tiring day. God willing, it meets its just reward at the next level of review, but I have spent too much time noting the infelicities in existing translations to have overwhelming confidence in that.

Taylor said his stylizing contribution came after the scholars made their initial translation. In an effort to simplify academic and religious jargon by exchanging them for easily understandable words, he offered suggestions, asked questions, and made pronouncements. Taylor explained:

I ponder nuances of meaning, listen to the sound of words echoing off words, feel for their rhythm as they jostle for position. And after doing all that and seeing I still haven't gotten it right, I find myself hoping a colleague across the country is having better luck with the passage than I am.

THE CASE FOR LESS LITERAL TRANSLATIONS

There are serious problems with trying to translate ancient languages, word for word, into modern languages. For one, there are often no matching words. In addition, it is usually impossible to reproduce the rhythm, puns, word sounds and other literary devices that beef up the message in the original language.

In the mid-1900s, a new translation principle surfaced. Scholars started to argue that the most important job of Bible translators is not to preserve the literary structure of scripture, but to communicate clearly what it means. Instead of trying to translate word for word and sentence for sentence, they translated thought for thought. 'As literal as possible, as free as necessary' were the guiding words for the translators working on the New Revised Standard Version published in 1989.

Some translations are freer than others. In fact, Bible scholars will not even call some of them translations. Instead, they call them paraphrases: *The Message*, *The Living Bible* and *The Cotton Patch Version*. In each of these Bible versions, the individual translator focused less on the science of linguistics (if at all), and more on expressing the main ideas to his target audience. And it is the target audience that often determines how literal or how free a translation to produce. If the intended readers are children, adult newcomers to the Bible or the uneducated, the result may not sound at all like the classic King James Version. Longstanding biblical terms such as 'righteousness' and 'sanctification' may give way to more reader-friendly words such as 'goodness' and 'devotion'. But if the intended audience is scholars or biblically savvy lay people, translators may feel as though they can keep many traditional terms – especially in well-known passages, such as the Lord's Prayer.

Most scholars maintain there is no one right way to translate the Bible, but that most translations available today can be helpful to various groups of readers. For today's translator, the challenge is to find that perfect balance between accuracy and readability. But with continuing discoveries about ancient languages, coupled with our ever-changing modern language, that perfect balance remains an elusive goal.

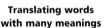

A complaint about scholars

Some Bible translations are harder to read than others, critics say, because scholars doing the translation are too familiar with ancient syntax and dated Christian terms to know that these terms do not communicate. So the scholars keep words they should probably replace – words such as 'cut off' (kill), 'faithfulness' (dependability) and 'unrighteousness' (sin).

Translating words with many meanings

Translators debate how to handle words with various meanings. The Hebrew word *hesed*, for example, can mean devotion, love, kindness, goodness, grace, mercy and loyalty. Some translators say it is best to pick one word and use it throughout the translation. Others say the context of the passage should determine which word to use.

Specialized Bibles Today

New believers who take their first timid steps into a Bible bookshop, looking for a Bible and perhaps another book to help them study it, can be overwhelmed with the thousands of titles that greet them. There are so many Bible-related books to choose from that even bookstore employees have trouble keeping up. Savvy bookstore managers hold classes to teach their staff how to match shoppers to the appropriate books.

Demand for Bibles has grown dramatically in recent years, spawning a steady stream of specialized Bibles and companion products. Study Bibles are a prime example.

STUDY BIBLES

Some study Bibles provide information about ancient times that help us better understand what the writers were saying. For example, the *HarperCollins Study Bible* – which is about 60 per cent Bible text and 40 per cent explanatory notes in the margins – introduces the Pharisees in Matthew 3:7 as 'a Jewish group that rigorously applied the Jewish law to everyday living. They are Jesus' major opponents in Matthew.'

The *Quest Study Bible* uses a question and answer approach. In the margins are answers to more than 6,000 questions a typical person might ask while reading the Bible.

The *Life Application Study Bible*, based on the New Living Translation, is concerned with applying the Bible's message to the reader's life today. Its notes often sound like the insightful advice of a compassionate pastor. In Matthew 6:25, Jesus says not to worry. The notes in the margin of this Bible explain why: worry can damage your health, disrupt your productivity, negatively affect the way you treat others, and reduce your trust in God.

DEVOTIONAL BIBLES

Devotional Bibles are intended to help readers get the most out of their reflective time with the Bible. The *Inspirational Bible*, based on the New Century Version, offers short articles that sum up the passage and add inspiring thoughts and applications. In the margin beside the story of Lazarus, the devotional writer reminds readers who have suffered the death of a loved one that Jesus promised, 'I am the resurrection and the life. He who believes in me will live, even though he dies.'

Some devotional Bibles reorganize scripture to follow a certain reading plan. The *One-Year Bible*

High-art Bibles today

The price tag is about 20,000 pounds, or 30,000 dollars, for the deluxe edition of the two-volume Pennyroyal Caxton Bible, printed by Letterpress and containing 233 black-and-white engravings by illustrator Barry Moser, known for his pensive and startling images. The 1,350-page Arion Bible, 400 copies of which were printed by Letterpress in 2000, sells for about 6,000 pounds, or 9,000 dollars. The typesetting alone took nearly two years. Each book of the Bible begins with a large red initial letter, embellished by abstract patterns created by calligrapher Thomas Ingmire.

Behold, a Virgin Shall Conceive, relief engraving by Barry Moser from the Pennyroyal Caxton Bible, 1999. Steeply priced at roughly 20,000 pounds, or 30,000 dollars, the deluxe edition of this Bible showcases 233 engravings by Barry Moser.

arranges passages into 15-minute readings designed to help people read the entire Bible in a year. Each daily reading draws from Psalms, Proverbs, another Old Testament book and a New Testament book. The *Two-Year Bible* slows the pace.

COMMENTARIES

Bible commentaries are a big step up from study and devotional Bibles, with much more extensive notes. Some fast-paced commentaries cram all the notes into a single volume. Others split into two volumes, one for the Old Testament and another for the New. For the more serious Bible students, there are separate commentaries for each book of the Bible. One complete set could fill several shelves in a home library. Bookstores often sell entire sets at a discount – especially classic works like those of John Calvin (22 volumes) and Matthew Henry (six volumes) for which royalties are no longer paid.

Most Bible students, however, prefer modern commentaries that draw from the latest insights in archaeology, ancient languages and scholarly discussion. These, too, are often sold at a discount when a person buys the entire set. One disadvantage is that a packaged set with many writers may be inconsistent in scholarly accuracy, from one book to another. For this reason, the most serious Bible students look for individual commentaries by scholars well-known for their expertise in a particular area, such as the Gospels or the Prophets.

REFERENCE BOOKS

Supplementing the Bibles and commentaries are many other Bible-background books. Among the most common are: encyclopedias, dictionaries, atlases, parallel Bibles (which have two or more Bible translations printed side-by-side for easy comparison), along with topical Bibles and concordances (both of which help readers do a word or topic study by pointing out every Bible passage in which a particular word or topic appears, such as 'apostle' or 'salvation').

There are also books about Bible plants, animals and people. There are books that focus on mysteries and tough questions in the Bible, such as how the parting of the Red Sea could have happened. And there are books that provide an overview of the Bible. *How to Get into the Bible* by Stephen M. Miller, for example, briefly introduces every book in the Bible, highlighting the big scenes, leading characters and plot.

COMPUTER SOFTWARE

Every kind of product mentioned so far is available on computer software – part of an ever-growing digital library.

Bible videos, tapes and games

One popular method of introducing people to the story of Jesus – especially among mission ministries around the world – is to show a video or film based on the Gospel of Luke. As the actors speak in the original Bible language, the story is read from the Bible in the native language of the people – much like foreign films today that are dubbed or subtitled. Other videos – many with well-known actors – present some of the most fascinating Bible stories. There are also video tours of Bible lands and teaching sessions to help in groups or private study.

For people who do not have the time, energy or ability to read, the Bible is available in a variety of versions on tape or compact disks.

For more exposure to Bible teachings and facts, there are games. Among the many are: crossword puzzles, jigsaw puzzles, card games and table games such as *Bible Trivia* and *Bibleopoly*, modelled after *Monopoly*.

One top-selling software package, *QuickVerse*, has a deluxe edition on four compact disks that contains 18 Bible versions and 108 reference titles. Like other software packages, it includes both modern and classic books: atlases, dictionaries, handbooks, a concordance, several sets of commentaries, a Greek New Testament, biographies of Bible people and the combined works of Josephus, a first-century Jewish historian.

Cost is one of the biggest advantages a digital library has over a printed one. Many software packages offer a collection of Bibles and books for a fraction of the cost it would take to buy in printed form. Another big advantage is the speedy search capability. With a few taps of the keyboard, Bible students can do a topic search in any part of their digital library. Video adds an extra dimension, allowing readers to visit Bible sites.

The continuing growth of Bible products – printed and electronic – suggests that the best-selling book of all time will probably remain one of the best read and most intensely studied.

'We should thank God for the scholarly labour that gives us so rich a range of options for our Bible reading and show our gratitude by soaking ourselves in the version or versions that suit us best.'

J.I. PACKER, THEOLOGY PROFESSOR, REGENT COLLEGE, BRITISH COLUMBIA

The Bible in Literature

Biblical operas

The Bible has inspired opera composers as well as writers. Major operas that dramatize biblical stories include the 1842 *Nabucco* (Italian for 'Nebuchadnezzar') by the Italian master Giuseppe Verdi, *Samson et Dalila* (1877) by French composer Camille Saint-Saëns, and two German operas – *Salome* (1905) by Richard Strauss and *Moses und Aron* (1954) by Arnold Schoenberg. Other operas, such as *Jenufa* (1904) by Czech composer Leos Janacek, have Christlike central figures, but the American singer Jerome Hines composed and starred in *I Am the Way* (1968), an opera about Jesus himself. Rock operas include *Godspell* (1970) by American composer Stephen Swartz and *Jesus Christ Superstar* (1970) by British composer Andrew Lloyd Webber.

Over the past 200 years, as in the more distant past, writers used the Bible as a source of inspiration. Poets, playwrights and novelists adapted biblical stories directly or indirectly, enhanced their style with biblical language, or improvised on biblical themes.

ROMANTIC AND VICTORIAN ERAS

The Romantic poets sometimes used the Bible to bolster their own artistic views. For example, the English poet William Blake mixed pagan mythological language with biblical poetics to create his personal view of a universe of opposites, such as heaven and hell, good and evil, innocence and experience. His most popular poem, 'The Tyger', in *Songs of Experience* (1794), is a meditation on God as creator. In Blake's 'The Everlasting Gospel' (1818), Joseph of Arimathea, the disciple who buried Jesus in his own tomb, freely ruminates on the life of Jesus in rhyming couplets. He ends by comparing the high priest Caiaphas of Jesus' time to the bishops of Blake's own day: 'Both read the Bible day & night, / But thou read'st black where I read white.'

American novelist and poet Herman Melville offers a rich synthesis of biblical narrative in his masterpiece *Moby Dick* (1851), the story of a mad sea captain who wants revenge on the white whale that bit off his leg. The captain is named Ahab, after the king of Israel who opposed the prophet Elijah. The narrator of the entire novel, who is named after the exiled son of Abraham, opens the novel with the words, 'Call me Ishmael'. After hearing a sermon on the story of Jonah (complete with a hymn echoing the words of Jonah in the whale's belly), Ishmael is warned by a madman, named Elijah, not to sail with Captain Ahab. When the expedition ends in disaster, Ishmael is the only one to survive and tell the story. The superscription for the epilogue is from the book of Job: 'And I only am escaped alone to tell thee.'

Russian novelist Fyodor Dostoyevsky portrayed a number of his fictional characters as Christ figures, including Prince Leo Myshkin in *The Idiot* (1868–69) and Alyosha in *The Brothers Karamazov* (1880). In *Les Misérables*, French writer Victor Hugo also created Christ figures in the bishop of Digne and – once converted – the hero Jean Valjean. The French novelist Gustav Flaubert was not so affirming. In 'Herodias', one of his *Three Tales* (1877), he curses all the parties

involved in the beheading of John the Baptist. The writings of the reclusive American poet Emily Dickinson (1830–86) quote from or allude to nearly every book of the Bible. Dickinson's poetic imagery draws heavily from biblical poetry, and a number of her poems centre directly on biblical stories. For example, in Poem 540 Dickinson turns the story of David and Goliath into a reflection of her own inadequacies: 'I aimed my pebble – but Myself / Was all the one that fell – / Was it Goliath – was too large – / Or was myself – too small?'

THE 20TH CENTURY

James Joyce, the Irish expatriate author of the highly influential novel *Ulysses* (1922), evokes the book of Revelation in his last novel, *Finnegans Wake* (1939). Joyce also wrote 'The Joking Jesus', an irreverent satirical poem. In it, Jesus talks jocularly about himself in rhymed couplets, and urges his followers to write down all he did and said, adding, 'And tell Tom, Dick and Harry I rose from the dead.'

The American-born English poet T.S. Eliot, a Nobel prize winner, often turned to the Bible for inspiration. Two of his poems deal directly with events surrounding the birth of Jesus. 'Journey of the Magi' (1927) focuses on the arduous journey the wise men make to visit the newborn Jesus (Matthew 2) and ends with their discomfort in returning to their homes where they are surrounded by 'alien people clutching their gods'. 'A Song of Simeon' (1928) is an expansion of and reflection on the song sung by the ancient prophet Simeon on finally seeing the Messiah with his own eyes (Luke 2:22–32).

The tetrology of novels *Joseph and His Brothers* (1933–43) by the Nobel prize-winning German author Thomas Mann is an elaborate rewriting of Genesis. Mann begins with the patriarch Jacob telling his favourite son, Joseph, stories about his ancestors. There follows the story of Joseph himself, who is sold into slavery by his jealous brothers, taken to Egypt, and eventually serves as an official of the pharaoh, saving the brothers who had harmed him. In Mann's version, the pharaoh Joseph serves is Akhenaton, who defied his times by worshipping only one god – the sun disc Aton. Mann suggests a connection between Akhenaton's religious practices and the emerging monotheism of the Israelites. Mann's additions to the Genesis stories add to the characters' depth and symbolic significance, pointing to both past mythologies and New Testament events. For example, Mann connects Joseph's reappearance after long being thought dead with both Christ's resurrection and the myth of the Egyptian god Osiris, who was resurrected after being murdered by his brother.

The Nobel prize-winning Nigerian author Wole Soyinka (1934–) uses biblical themes, language and archetypes. In his play *The Swamp Dwellers*, he focuses on the parable of the prodigal son but mixes in the larger biblical theme of brothers in conflict. In *Cry the Beloved Country* (1948), on the other hand, South African author Alan Paton fuses the story of the prodigal son with aspects of the story of David and Absalom in a Christian plea for compassion in his country. Another Nobel prize winner, the Australian author Patrick White, often uses biblical symbolism in his novels, and the title character in *Voss* (1957) is gradually revealed as a Christ figure of significant dimensions.

Swedish writer Pär Fabian Lagerkvist focuses on a minor biblical figure. His *Barabbas* imagines what life was like for the criminal who was freed in the place of Jesus. It was published in 1950.

Lagerkvist was awarded the Nobel prize for literature in 1951.

The Greek Passion (1951) by the Greek poet, novelist and philosopher Nikos Kazantzakis brings Christ's passion into the 20th century. The novel focuses on a group of poor Greek villagers living in Anatolia, who are being persecuted by Turkish overlords. Although the villagers are assigned roles in an upcoming passion play, the play is abandoned after a succession of violent events erupt. Instead, the actors play out their assigned roles in real life.

Finally, two American Nobel prize winners wrote novels based on the Bible. John Steinbeck's *East of Eden* (1952) is a reworking of the story of Cain and Abel, set in 20th-century California. William Faulkner's *A Fable* (1954) is an extended parable of Christ's passion set during the First World War.

'Many scriptural poems have been written with so much of scripture in them that what is not scripture appears to be not true.'

SAMUEL TAYLOR COLERIDGE, ENGLISH ROMANTIC POET AND CRITIC

Faust translates the Bible

The German poet Johann Wolfgang von Goethe's two-part masterpiece, *Faust*, tells of a medieval German scholar who despairs in old age and sells his soul to the devil. Goethe drew heavily on the Bible for themes and characters, and the play's 'Prologue in Heaven' is taken from the book of Job, in places almost word for word. At the end of Part 2 (1832), Faust is saved by his wish to do good works and by the enduring love of a good woman, Gretchen, who combines the attributes of Mary, the mother of Jesus, and Mary Magdalene.

In the third scene of Part 1 (1808), a despondent Faust seeks consolation in translating the Bible into German (as Martin Luther was to do). His thoughts follow:

But ah! I feel, though will thereto be stronger,
contentment flows from out my breast no longer.
Why must the stream so soon run dry and fail us,
and burning thirst again assail us?
Therein I've borne so much probation!
And yet, this want may be supplied us;
we call the Supernatural to guide us;
we pine and thirst for Revelation,
which nowhere worthier is, more nobly sent,
than here in our New Testament.
I feel impelled its meaning to determine, –
with honest purpose, once for all,
the hallowed Original
to change to my beloved German.
'Tis written: 'In the Beginning was the Word.'

Here am I balked: who now, can help afford?
The Word? – impossible now to rate it;
and otherwise must I translate it,
if by the Spirit I am truly taught.
Then thus: 'In the Beginning was the Thought.'
This first line let me weigh completely,
lest my impatient pen proceed too fleetly.
Is it the Thought which works, creates, indeed?
'In the Beginning was the Power,' I read.
Yes, as I write, a warning is suggested,
that I the sense may not have fairly tested.
The Spirit aids me: now I see the light!
'In the Beginning was the Act,' I write.

Mephistopheles (the devil) gets God's permission to tempt Faust in the play's 'Prologue in Heaven', shown here in a pen-and-ink drawing by Johann Wolfgang von Goethe (1749–1832), the play's author.

The Bible in Moving Images

The ten commandments are not rules to obey as a personal favour to God. They are the fundamental principles without which mankind cannot live together. They are not laws – they are the LAW.'

CECIL B. DEMILLE, *THE TEN COMMANDMENTS*, 1923

Hollywood – or holy wood of the cross?

It has been pointed out that Hollywood is a natural centre for producing biblical motion pictures. The reason given is that the name 'Hollywood' may be biblical, as it has been seen as a corruption of the term 'holy wood', or the wood of Christ's cross.

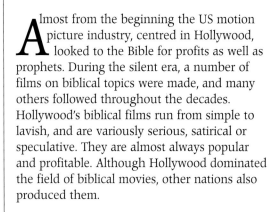

Almost from the beginning the US motion picture industry, centred in Hollywood, looked to the Bible for profits as well as prophets. During the silent era, a number of films on biblical topics were made, and many others followed throughout the decades. Hollywood's biblical films run from simple to lavish, and are variously serious, satirical or speculative. They are almost always popular and profitable. Although Hollywood dominated the field of biblical movies, other nations also produced them.

BIBLE STORIES ON FILM

France was the first to make a biblical motion picture, in 1907. This film, *Moses and the Exodus from Egypt,* ran less than 10 minutes and was followed by a number of similar films in both France and the United States. But it was Hollywood that created the popular genre of biblical epic. The man mainly responsible was Cecil B. DeMille, whose career in movies lasted from 1914 to 1956.

In 1923, DeMille wrote, produced and directed *The Ten Commandments.* The first half of this silent film tells the story of Moses, ending with events surrounding the reception of the ten commandments. The remainder of the film is a morality tale of two 20th-century brothers. One brother respects the ten commandments, while the other tries to break every one of them – with disastrous results. The film's biblical scenes were lavishly produced, and the sets for the Egyptian scenes were based on recent archaeological discoveries, including King Tutankhamun's tomb. DeMille also employed a gigantic cast and made brilliant use of special effects. To stimulate interest he included orgy scenes featuring half naked bodies, which were acceptable at the time only because of their context. All these elements established the pattern for many biblical epics to come.

Encouraged by the success of *The Ten Commandments,* in 1927 DeMille released *The King of Kings,* a sprawling movie on the life of Jesus. Three decades later he returned to the Old Testament for material, producing and directing a spectacular *Samson and Delilah* (1949), which was a huge financial success. He ended his career with a remake of *The Ten Commandments* (1956). In this version, however, DeMille stayed with the story of Moses, but portrayed the Israelites as proto-Americans whom God orders to spread a concept of liberty that closely resembles American political ideals.

A number of other directors took DeMille's lead in producing large-scale biblical films. In *David and Bathsheba* (1951), Henry King offered a romantic version of a low point in the life of the great King David. Richard Thorpe's *The Prodigal Son* (1955) expanded Jesus' simple parable into a sprawling epic, focusing on the corruption of the title character. George Stevens directed a long but vivid version of the Gospels called *The Greatest Story Ever Told* (1965). It had an all-star cast, but some of the big-name actors seemed oddly inappropriate for their roles. Franco Zeffirelli's six-hour *Jesus of Nazareth* (1977), made for television, has authentic settings and verbatim quotes from the Bible.

In 1966, American director John Huston made a heavy-handed film he audaciously called *The Bible,* although it covers only the first 22 chapters of Genesis and ignores the rest of the Good Book. Bruce Beresford directed *King David* (1985), a solid retelling of David's life, beginning with his slaying of the Philistine giant Goliath. It boasts a strong cast, including Hollywood star Richard Gere as David.

The Bible on the home screen

After the 1960s, most of the biblical movies were made for television and continue to be produced in large numbers. In addition to Zefirelli's monumental *Jesus of Nazareth,* they include *Moses* (1996), a two-part mini-series starring Ben Kingsley, as a very human, down-to-earth Moses, and *Greatest Heroes of the Bible,* a series of individual videos. Another series, *The Bible,* includes 'Genesis' (1994) in which an elderly desert nomad tells stories from Genesis, much in the way the stories were probably related before they were written down, and 'Solomon', 'Esther' and 'Jeremiah' (all three released in 2000), which use Hollywood stars for key roles in small-scale dramatized biographies. Yet another series, *The Bible Collection* (1990s), emphasizes the flaws in biblical heroes, who must rely on God.

Greatest Adventure Stories from the Bible is a series of animated Bible stories, including 'Noah's Ark', 'Jonah' and 'The Miracles of Jesus'. There is also a British-Russian series entitled *Testament: The Bible in Animation.*

Other videos help explain the world of the Bible or how the Bible came to be. *Time Travel Through the Bible* (1990) and *Who Was Moses?* (2000) use archaeological finds and history to explore the world of the Bible. *Where Jesus Walked* (1995) traces Jesus' footsteps in today's Holy Land. Reader's Digest's *Jesus and his Times* (1991) shows how people lived at the time of Jesus, and *Who Wrote the Bible?* (1996) is a documentary exploring theories of biblical authorship.

In the wake of Cecil B. DeMille's two versions of the ten commandments, Jeffrey Katzenberg of Dreamworks Studio produced an animated version of the story, *The Prince of Egypt* (2000) in which Moses and the future pharaoh Rameses grow up together but find themselves in opposition over letting the Israelites go.

In reaction to Hollywood's super-spectacular biblical epics, the Italian director Pier Paolo Pasolini created a pared-down, simple rendering of *The Gospel According to St Matthew* (1964), in which he used amateur actors, including his own mother as the Virgin Mary. It is a beautiful, dignified, quiet and sensitive film that goes far in capturing the look and feel of what New Testament Israel must have been like.

A satirical view of the Bible is featured in the *Life of Brian* (1979), directed by Terry Jones, featuring the Monty Python troup of British comics. It tells of Brian, a man who lives a life that runs parallel to that of Jesus. Because he is mistaken for the Messiah, Brian is manipulated, abused and exploited by the religious and political forces of the day. Jesus himself appears only twice, and then in the background. The comedy is not aimed at Jesus or Christianity but at politics and the excesses of some religionists that are still obvious today.

A speculative treatment of the Gospels is given in Martin Scorsese's *The Last Temptation of Christ* (1988), based on a novel by the Greek writer Nikos Kazantzakis. This film created enormous controversy. In its attempt to make Jesus completely human, it portrays him as being tempted to marry Mary Magdalene and abandon his messiahship.

BIBLE-RELATED MOVIES

A number of motion pictures have speculated about what happened to New Testament characters – or even objects – in later years. Henry Koster's *The Robe* (1953), based on a popular novel by Lloyd C. Douglas, imagines that the centurion who wins Jesus' robe while gambling during the crucifixion is haunted by the garment until he finally converts to Christianity. It was the first movie to be filmed in CinemaScope. Mervyn LeRoy's *Quo Vadis* (1951) starts with the apostle Peter's attempt to leave Rome until he is stopped by the voice of God asking 'Quo vadis?' ('Where are you going?'). The bulk of the film, however, depicts Nero's persecution of the Christians. Victor Saville's *The Silver Chalice* (1954), based on a novel by Thomas Costain, tells the story of a silversmith (Paul Newman in his first film role) who is commissioned to make a silver framework for the cup Jesus used at the last supper.

Charlton Heston plays Moses in Cecil B. DeMille's 1957 film *The Ten Commandments*.

One of the most popular stories taken from the margins of the New Testament was *Ben Hur: A Tale of the Christ*, a 1880 novel by Lew Wallace. It tells of an aristocratic Jew who is sent to the galleys as a slave after being falsely accused of trying to murder Palestine's Roman governor. Hur later escapes and competes in a fearsome chariot race with his accuser, a former friend. In the end, Hur meets with Jesus and is converted to Christianity. The story had been popular as a lavish stage play before the time of the movies. It was made into a short film in 1907 and into a high-budget spectacular silent film in 1926. In 1959, William Wyler turned the story into an award-winning extravaganza.

Modern reflections on both Old and New Testament events are also depicted in movies. In the spirit of the second half of DeMille's silent version of *The Ten Commandments*, Polish director Krzystov Kieslowski made *The Decalogue* (1988), a series of 10 one-hour long films first shown on Polish television. Each of the films – one for each of the ten commandments – shows ordinary modern men and women coping with situations that are connected with the commandment being featured, although sometimes loosely. The characters are warmed by the director's sympathetic approach and his eye for poignant detail. In *Jesus of Montreal* (1989), the French-Canadian director Denys Arcand follows a troop of actors as they prepare to present a passion play and become embroiled in controversies that reflect the themes of Christ's passion.

The Bible in vegetables

Veggie Tales, a series of children's videos, offer imaginative retellings of Bible stories, using computer animation. In these videos, all the characters are played by vegetables. For example, 'Dave and the Giant Pickle' retells the story of David and Goliath. When the young David, who is played by Junior Asparagus, is teased because of his small size, he says, 'little guys can do big things, too'. To prove it, Dave battles and defeats Goliath, a giant Philistine pickle who wears boxing gloves.

Using and Abusing the Bible

A woman puts bottles into a bank for recycling. Some Christians say the creation story shows that God has made human beings the caretakers of his world, giving them authority over all other life on the planet.

'Both [Northerners and Southerners] read the same Bible, and pray to the same God; and each invokes his aid against the other.'

ABRAHAM LINCOLN,
1865 SPEECH ABOUT THE
AMERICAN CIVIL WAR

The Bible is a book of authority, widely respected as God's words to humanity. For this reason, when people want evidence to back up their opinion on a controversial matter, they often turn to scripture. They have done so for centuries.

Many have used the Bible fairly, appealing to its teachings as a way to solve injustice, hatred and other problems in the world. Others have abused the Bible – taking it out of context and using it to support causes the Bible does not address, and even to justify evil.

FOR BETTER

People have often used the Bible to protect the poor and the environment.

Helping the poor and oppressed

Advocates for the needy have often appealed to scripture. American civil rights leader Martin Luther King, Jr, in his most famous speech, drew from the prophet Amos's theme of justice for the oppressed: 'I have a dream that one day even the state of Mississippi, a state sweltering with the heat of oppression, will be transformed into an oasis of freedom and justice.'

Peruvian priest Gustavo Guiterrez pointed to Amos and other prophets when he wrote in his book, *A Theology of Liberation*: 'Poverty is not caused by fate; it is caused by the actions of those whom the prophet condemns. As Amos put it, the rich "trample the head of the poor into the dust of the earth". In some places in Latin America, for example, the wealthy own nearly all the land, forcing poor people to work for them in return for the right to live in tiny shacks crowded together. Some churches responded by buying small lots with enough room for little gardens. They built simple cinderblock houses on the lots and gave them to the poor, to help them break out of the cycle of poverty.

Caring for the planet

One of humanity's most persistent questions is, 'Why are we here?' Some believe the answer – at least in part – lies in the creation story. 'Let us make humankind,' God said, 'let them have dominion over the fish of the sea, and over the birds of the air, and over the cattle, and over all the wild animals of the earth, and over every creeping thing that creeps upon the earth'

Abortion and the Bible

The Bible does not directly talk about abortion, which is why people of faith are so sharply divided on the issue. Some see an anti-abortion message in Psalm 139:13, 'You knit me together in my mother's womb.' Others see that as a song of thanks to God for being involved in every detail of our life, not as a song to discourage abortion or to identify conception as the moment God places an eternal soul within us.

If the psalm did oppose abortion, some Christians ask, why in Exodus 21:12, 22 is the punishment for killing a woman death, while the punishment for injuring a pregnant woman so badly that she miscarries is only a fine?

Most Christians would agree that life is a sacred gift of God, and that the Bible calls us to have compassion towards others. But they cannot always agree on how to express that compassion in cases of unwanted pregnancy, especially in situations involving rape, incest and children who get pregnant. The Roman Catholic Church is adamantly opposed to deliberate abortion at any time from the moment of conception. But it will allow a medical procedure to save the life of the mother, even though the procedure may kill the fetus. In this case, the Church considers the procedure both good and bad – good because it saves a life, bad because it takes a life.

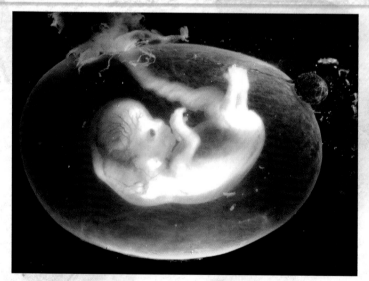

Human embryo at seven to eight weeks old.

(Genesis 1:26). We are caretakers of God's creation.

In recent years, many religious organizations have started saying we need to do a better job. 'We hear God calling our churches to care more intentionally for all of creation,' the United Methodist Church wrote in a resolution for Earth Day 1995, 'living in an economically and ecologically sound way that preserves the future of life on the planet.'

FOR WORSE

Throughout the centuries, many have used the Bible to support their mistreatment of Jews, women and slaves.

Jewish persecution

Many people have turned to the Bible to justify persecuting the Jews: church leaders from popes to pastors, crusaders, politicians, Nazis, neo-Nazis, Ku Klux Klan. They quote passages such as Jesus telling Jewish leaders, 'You are from your father the devil' (John 8:44). And they quote Paul, describing the Jews as evil people 'who killed both the Lord Jesus and the prophets' (1 Thessalonians 2:15). Jesus and Paul, however, were not criticizing the entire Jewish race. They were talking about certain Jewish leaders who opposed God and people doing God's work.

Martin Luther, German father of the Protestant movement, became frustrated at the Jews for not converting to Christianity. And in 1543 he wrote harsh words later used as Nazi propaganda. Luther called the Jews a 'damned, rejected race'. And he called for rulers to shut down the faith by burning the synagogues, taking away the prayer books, outlawing rabbis from teaching, destroying Jewish homes, confiscating their money, revoking their travelling rights, and forcing them into jobs of manual labour. Some Lutheran churches have since repudiated these writings and vow to oppose anti-Semitism.

Oppression of women

The Bible abounds with what seems like bad news for women. In Genesis, God tells Eve that because she ate the forbidden fruit her husband will rule over her. And in several letters, the apostle Paul orders women to submit to the authority of their husbands, to keep silent in church and never to teach in church.

Many Christians take these instructions as timeless, and refuse to let women take leadership roles in the Church. Some vigorously criticize women's rights movements. 'The feminist agenda is not about equal rights,' said televangelist Pat Robertson in 1992, 'It is about

a socialist, anti-family political movement that encourages women to leave their husbands.'

Other Christians say these Bible instructions were not meant for everyone for all time, but were intended for an ancient, male-dominated culture,

and for specific churches with unique problems. In churches where groups of women were causing problems, Paul set up rules to stop them. In other situations, Paul recognized the authority of women church leaders (Romans 16:1–3), some of whom were prophets (Acts 2:17), and one of whom may have carried the New Testament's highest title for a church leader – apostle (Romans 16:7).

Justification of slavery

To justify enslaving black people, many slave owners noted that the New Testament repeatedly orders slaves to obey their masters. And the Old Testament hints that blacks may be cursed – that the mark of Cain may have been black skin, or that Africans are simply living out their fate as descendants of Noah's son Ham, who was cursed by God.

Christians opposed to slavery say the New Testament does not condone slavery. They say church leaders, such as Paul, were simply putting the faith above social change – trying to establish Christianity – and that Paul, in his letter to slave owner Philemon, strongly hinted that Philemon should free the slave, Onesimus, who delivered Paul's letter. As for the mark of Cain, the Bible does not say what it was, other than a mark of mercy to keep people from killing Cain. And the curse of Ham's descendants was directed at his son, Canaan – a prophecy many say was fulfilled when the Jewish people conquered the Canaanites.

During violent protests against racial injustice in 1986, a South African policeman patrols Soweto, a black township in Johannesburg. The white government used this crowded, matchbox-house community of more than half a million blacks as one of many residential centres to segregate blacks from the white minority. This preserved the nation's pro-white policy of Apartheid – Afrikaans for 'separateness'. The Bible, however – as Archbishop Desmond Tutu and other Christian leaders preached – calls for unity, not a racial caste system.

Witches

In 1486, two Dominican priests published what became a guidebook for inquisitors hunting for witches. *The Hammer of the Witches* outsold all other books except the Bible. In this book, the writers explained why women were more likely than men to become witches: 'because being formed from a man's rib, they are only "imperfect animals" and "crooked" whereas man belongs to a privileged sex from whose midst Christ emerged'.

Bible Trivia and Oddities

Entire books have been written about fascinating Bible trivia, oddities and embarrassing misprints. Here is a short collection of just a few choice morsels.

❧ A person reading at a typical pace can read the Bible out loud in about 100 hours or fewer.

❧ 'Bible' is a word that is not in the Bible. It comes from the Greek word *biblos*, after the Phoenician city of Biblos – an important source of papyrus rolls used to make books. In time, the word *biblos* came to mean 'book'. The Bible, then, was simply known as 'the Book'.

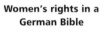

Women's rights in a German Bible

A German Bible from 1580 seems to insert an editorial comment about men. After Eve sinned, God told her that instead of being free to do as she pleased, she would now have to obey her husband: 'Und er soll dein Herr sein', meaning 'And he will be your master'. However, the word 'Herr' was replaced by 'Narr', making the revised phrase read: 'And he will be your fool.' Some historians suspect that the printer's wife made the change.

❧

Adam and Eve by Lucas Cranach the Elder.

❧ Perhaps the most scandalous typographical error ever printed in the Bible was one that appeared in a 1631 edition of the King James Version, published just 20 years after the translation was introduced. That was at a time when people were still trying to get used to this new translation – and many were resisting, preferring the older Geneva Bible. The British printer left out an essential 'not' from the seventh commandment. As a result, the Bible had God declaring that people should commit adultery (Exodus 20:14). This edition became known as the Wicked Bible, or the Adulterer's Bible. When the mistake was discovered, printer Robert Barker was fined the hefty sum of 300 pounds – enough money to buy a 300-acre farm at the time.

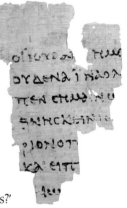

❧ Using the Bible at swearing-in ceremonies – such as before testifying in court or when accepting a political office – comes from the ancient Jewish practice of making a promise and then saying 'remember that God is witness between you and me' (Genesis 31:50). During the Middle Ages, Christians swore by touching a cross, a Bible or a sacred relic believed to have belonged to a godly person.

❧ The oldest surviving Bible text is from a Dead Sea Scroll fragment, found near the shores of the Dead Sea in Israel. Written in about 225 BC, the passage is from one of the Old Testament books of Samuel.

❧ The oldest surviving New Testament text is a piece of the Gospel of John. Written in about AD 125 – perhaps only 30 years after the original – the fragment contains parts of John 18:31–33, including Pilate's question to Jesus: 'Are you the King of the Jews?'

The earliest surviving copy of any New Testament book: part of a copy of John's Gospel written in Greek and dating from about AD 125.

❧ The Bible has been translated and published more than any other book in history.

The most widely translated Bible book is the Gospel of Mark, perhaps because it is the shortest and most action-packed of the four Gospels about Jesus' life and teachings. Mark is available in about 900 languages.

The Bible, in part or whole, has been translated into about 1,500 languages. Translations are needed for about another 3,000 languages, according to Wycliffe Bible Translators.

The word 'God' appears in every book of the Bible except Esther and the Song of Solomon. God's exclusion led many Jewish and Christian leaders to argue that these books did not belong in the Bible. Other leaders saw God in each book. They saw the Song of Solomon as a poetic symbol of God's love for his people. And in Esther, they saw God at work behind the scenes in the remarkable string of 'coincidences' that protected the Jews from a Persian holocaust.

Bible statistics

Although Christians generally spend much more time reading the New Testament than the Old, the Old Testament makes up more than three-quarters of the Bible. The following numbers are based on the King James Version – the most widely distributed Bible translation in history. The numbers of words vary somewhat from one translation to another.

	Old Testament	New Testament	Total
Books	39	27	66
Chapters	929	260	1,189
Verses	23,214	7,959	31,173
Words	592,439	181,253	773,692

The middle chapter in the Bible – Psalm 117 – is remarkably fitting. Also the shortest chapter in the Bible, this two-verse song at the core of the Bible sums up God's message to the world, and the world's appropriate response:

Praise the Lord, all you nations! Extol him, all you peoples! For great is his steadfast love towards us, and the faithfulness of the Lord endures forever. Praise the Lord!

The middle verse in the Bible seems just as fitting, with its spotlight on God's dependability: 'It is better to take refuge in the Lord than to put confidence in mortals' (Psalm 118:8).

The most mentioned human is David, whose name appears 1,118 times.

The oldest man is Methuselah, who was 969 when he died (Genesis 5:27).

The longest name is Mahershalalhashbaz (Isaiah 8:1). It means 'swift to spoil and quick to plunder'. The prophet Isaiah gave this symbolic name to his son to warn the king that if the Jews made a treaty with the Assyrian empire, the Assyrians would invade and take what they wanted.

Angels do not sing in the Bible. Not once. Not even at the birth of Jesus, when the multitude of heavenly hosts praised God '*saying*, "Glory to God in the highest"' (Luke 2:13–14).

Depictions of the angel's annunciation to the shepherds and of Christ's nativity, in an 11th-century manuscript.

Epilogue

Jesus' last words on earth explain why so many people throughout the ages have been willing to die for the sake of the Bible – to translate it, to teach it, and to live by its principles.

'Go into all the world and proclaim the good news to the whole creation,' Jesus told his followers, moments before he ascended into the heavens. 'You will be my witnesses in Jerusalem, in all Judea and Samaria, and to the ends of the earth' (Mark 16:15; Acts 1:8).

The eyewitnesses are gone. They died nearly 2,000 years ago. But their stories live on in the Bible, a book that Christians consider the only reliable testimony of God's good news about salvation.

From Genesis to Revelation – the Bible's first book to its last – scripture follows God as he initiates and works his plan to eradicate sin from his once-perfect creation. God begins by calling a people, the Jews, to obey him and reap the rewards of his protection and blessing. This single nation is to serve as an example that will draw other nations to God, in the way light draws lost people at night. 'All the nations of the earth shall gain blessing for themselves through your offspring,' God promised Abraham (Genesis 26:4). About two millennia later, Jesus is born into a Jewish family. Proclaimed by angels as the Son of God, Jesus announces it is time to take God's message of salvation to everyone.

In a day yet to come, the New Testament promises, God's plan will be accomplished. 'It is done!' God proclaims to John in an end-time vision of a creation where sin is gone:

I am the Alpha and the Omega, the beginning and the end. To the thirsty I will give water as a gift from the spring of the water of life. Those who conquer will inherit these things, and I will be their God and they will be my children... and they will reign for ever and ever.
Revelation 21:6–7; 22:5

There are on this planet an estimated 6,500 languages. The Bible, complete or in part, is available in about 2,300 languages. But the languages already translated are the major ones. Most of the others are regional dialects spoken by relatively few people. About nine out of ten people have at least some part of the Bible in their native language. Even so, many Christians are not satisfied. An estimated 700 scripture translation projects are currently underway.

'To the whole creation,' Jesus said.

Bibliography

Achtemeier, Paul J., *HarperCollins Bible Dictionary*, San Francisco: HarperCollins, 1996.

Achtemeier, Paul J., Green, Joel B., and Thompson, Marianne Meye, *Introducing the New Testament: Its Literature and Theology*, Grand Rapids, Michigan: Wm B. Eerdmans, 2001.

Adler, Joseph, and Alpher, Joseph (eds), *Encyclopedia of Jewish History*, New York: Checkmark, 1986.

Alexander, David, and Alexander, Pat, *New Lion Handbook to the Bible*, Oxford: Lion, 1999.

Anderson, M.W., *The Battle for the Gospel: The Bible and the Reformation, 1444–1589*, Grand Rapids, Michigan: Baker Book House, 1978.

Ayling, S., *John Wesley*, London: Collins, 1979; Nashville, Tennessee: Abingdon, 1980.

Ball, B.W., *Great Expectation: Eschatological Thought in English Protestantism to 1660*, Leiden: Brill, 1975.

Beardslee, W.A., *Literary Criticism of the New Testament*, Minneapolis: Fortress, 1970.

Blenkinsopp, Joseph, *The Pentateuch: An Introduction to the First Five Books of the Bible*, New York: Doubleday, 1992.

Bray, Gerald, *Biblical Interpretation, Past and Present*, Downers Grove, Illinois: Intervarsity Press, 1996.

Bromiley, Geoffrey, *The International Standard Bible Encyclopedia*, Grand Rapids, Michigan: Wm B. Eerdmans, 1959, 1994.

Brown, Colin, *Christianity and Western Thought: A History of Philosophers, Ideas and Movements*, Downers Grove, Illinois: Intervarsity Press, 1990.

Brown, Peter, *Augustine of Hippo: A Biography*, London: Faber and Faber, 2000; Berkeley, Los Angeles: University of California Press, 2000.

Butterworth, C., *The Literary Lineage of the King James Bible 1340–1611*, New York: Octagon, 1971.

Cahill, Thomas, *How the Irish Saved Civilization*, New York: Doubleday, 1995; London: Sceptre, 1996.

Calvin, J., *Calvin's New Testament Commentaries*, tr. T.H.L. Parker, London: T & T Clark, 1993.

Calvin, J., *Calvin's Old Testament Commentaries*, tr. T.H.L. Parker, ed. David W. Torrance and Thomas F. Torrance, London: T & T Clark, 1986.

Calvin, J., *Institutes of the Christian Religion* (1536), ed. J.T. McNeill, tr. F.L. Battles, London: T & T Clark, 1980.

Campenhausen, H. von, *Formation of the Christian Bible*, tr. Baker, J.A., Minneapolis: Fortress, 1972; Mifflintown, Pennsylvania: Sigler, 1997.

Charlesworth, James H., *The Old Testament Pseudepigrapha: Apocalyptic Literature and Testaments*, New York: Doubleday, 1983.

Childs, B.S., *Introduction to the Old Testament as Scripture*, London: SCM, 1979, 1983.

Childs, B.S., *The New Testament as Canon: An Introduction*, Minneapolis: Fortress, 1985; London: SCM, 1994.

Cohn-Sherbok, Lavinia, *Who's Who in Christianity?* London: Routledge, 1998.

Collins, John Joseph, *The Apocalyptic Imagination: An Introduction to Jewish Apocalyptic Literature* (*The Biblical Resource Series*), Grand Rapids, Michigan: Wm B. Eerdmans, 1998.

Collins, Michael, and Price, Matthew, *Story of Christianity: A Celebration of 2,000 Years of Faith*, New York: Dorling Kindersley, 1999.

Congar, Y.M.J., *Tradition and Traditions: An Historical and a Theological Essay*, London: Burns and Oates, 1966.

Couch, Mal (ed.), *Dictionary of Premillennial Theology*, Grand Rapids, Michigan: Kregel, 1996.

Cross, F.L., and Livingstone, E.A. (eds), *The Oxford Dictionary of the Christian Church*, Oxford: Oxford University Press, 1997.

Douglas, J.D., *Who's Who in Christian History?* Wheaton, Illinois: Tyndale House, 1992.

Drane, John, *Introducing the New Testament*, Oxford: Lion, 1999.

Drane, John, *Introducing the Old Testament*, Oxford: Lion, 2000.

Drane, John, *New Lion Bible Encyclopedia*, Oxford: Lion, 1998.

Evans, Craig, and Porter, Stanley, *Dictionary of New Testament Background*, Downers Grove, Illinois: Intervarsity Press, 2000.

Fishbane, M., *Biblical Interpretation in Ancient Israel*, Oxford: Clarendon, 1985.

Freedman, David, *The Anchor Bible Dictionary*, New York: Doubleday, 1992.

Friedman, Richard Elliott, *Who Wrote the Bible?*

Harlow: Prentice Hall, 1988; San Francisco: HarperCollins, 1997.

Frye, N., *The Great Code: The Bible in Literature*, New York: Harcourt, 1983.

Galling, K. Bagoas, and Ezra in *Studien zur Geschichte Israels im persischen Zeitalter*, Tübingen, 1964, pp. 149–84.

Gardner, Joseph L. (ed.), *Complete Guide to the Bible*, New York: Reader's Digest, 1998.

Grant, F.C., *Translating the Bible*, Edinburgh, 1961.

Grant, R.M., and Tracy, D., *A Short History of the Interpretation of the Bible* (second edition), London: SCM, 1984.

Green, Julien, *God's Fool: The Life and Times of Francis of Assisi*, tr. Peter Heinegg, San Francisco: HarperCollins, 1987; London: Hodder and Stoughton Religious, 1986.

Greenspahn, F.E. (ed.), *Scripture in the Jewish and Christian Traditions*, Nashville: Abingdon, 1982.

Grun, Bernard, *The Timetables of History*, New York: Simon and Schuster, 1991.

Gutjahr, Paul C., *An American Bible: A History of the Good Book in the United States, 1777–1880*, Stanford, California: Stanford University Press, 1999.

Hall, Christopher, *Reading Scripture with the Church Fathers*, Downers Grove, Illinois: Intervarsity Press, 1998.

Hamel, Christopher de, *The Book: A History of the Bible*, London: Phaidon, 2001.

Harrop, Clayton, *History of the New Testament in Plain Language*, Waco, Texas: Word, 1984.

Herbert, A.S., *Historical Catalogue of Printed Editions of the English Bible 1521–1961*, London and New York: British and Foreign Bible Society, 1968.

Huber, Robert V. (ed.), *The Bible Through the Ages*, New York: Reader's Digest, 1996.

Hurley, M., '"Sola Scriptura": Wycliff and His Critics', *Traditio* 16:275–352, 1960.

Izbicki, T., 'La Bible et les canonists', in Riche and Lobrichon, 1984, pp. 371–84.

Jedin, H., *A History of the Council of Trent*, tr. E. Graf, Bloomington, Indiana: Indiana University Press, 1997.

Josephus, Flavius, *The Complete Works of Josephus*, tr. William Whiston, Carlisle: STL, 1998; Nashville, Tennessee: Thomas Nelson, 1999.

Keene, Michael, *The Bible* (*Lion Access Guides*), Oxford: Lion, 2002.

Kelber, W.H., *The Oral and the Written Gospel*, Philadelphia: Fortress, 1983.

Kelly, J.N.D., *Jerome, His Life, Writings and Controversies*, London: Duckworth, 1975.

Knowles, Andrew, *The Bible Guide*, Oxford: Lion, 2001.

Kselman, John S., and Whiterup, Ronald D., 'Modern New Testament Criticism' in Raymond E. Brown, Joseph A. Fitzmeyer and Roland E. Murphy (eds), *The New Jerome Biblical Commentary*, Englewood Cliffs, New Jersey: Prentice Hall, 1990.

Kugel, J.L., and Greer, R.A. (eds), *Early Biblical Interpretation*, (Library of Early Christianity, volume 3), Louisville, Kentucky: Westminster John Knox, 1986.

Latourette, Kenneth Scott, *Christianity Through the Ages*, New York: Harper and Row, 1965; Peter Smith, 1965.

Lauterbach, J.Z., *Rabbinic Essays*, New York: Ktav, 1973.

Leclercq, J., *The Love of Learning and the Desire for God: A Study of Monastic Culture*, London: SPCK, 1978.

LeMaire, A., *Les Écoles et la formation de la Bible dans l'ancien Israel* (*Orbis biblicus et orientalis* 39), Freiburg and Göttingen, 1981.

Light, L., 'Versions et revisions du texte bibliques', in Riche and Lobrichon, 1984, pp. 55–93.

Lightfoot, Neil R., *How We Got Our Bible*, Grand Rapids, Michigan: Baker Book House, 1988.

McBrien, Richard P., *The HarperCollins Encyclopedia of Catholicism*, San Francisco: HarperCollins, 1995.

McGinn, Bernard, *Anti-Christ: Two Thousand Years of the Human Fascination with Evil*, San Francisco: HarperCollins, 1994.

McGrath, Alister E., *In the Beginning: The Story of the King James Bible and How it Changed a Nation, a Language and a Culture*, New York: Anchor/Doubleday, 2001; London: Hodder and Stoughton, 2002.

Mack, Burton L., *Who Wrote the New Testament?* San Francisco: HarperCollins, 1995.

McKim, D.K., 'Scripture in Calvin's Theology', *Readings in Calvin's Theology*, Grand Rapids, Michigan: Baker Book House, 1984.

McKnight, E.V., *What is Form Criticism?* Minneapolis: Fortress, 1969.

McNally, R.E., *The Bible in the Early Middle Ages*, Westminister, Maryland: Scholars, 1959.

Marius, Richard, *Martin Luther: The Christian Between God and Death*, Cambridge, Massachusetts, and London: Harvard University Press, 2000.

Martin, Ralph, and Davids, Peter, *Dictionary of the*

Later New Testament and its Developments, Downers Grove, Illinois: Intervarsity Press, 1997.

Mason, Steve, *Josephus and the New Testament*, Peabody, Massachusetts: Hendrickson, 1993.

Maynard, Jill (ed.), *Illustrated Dictionary of Bible Life & Times*, New York: Reader's Digest, 1997.

Metzger, Bruce, and Coogan, Michael, *The Oxford Companion to the Bible*, New York: Oxford University Press, 1993.

Metzger, Bruce Manning, *The Canon of the New Testament: Its Origin, Development, and Significance*, Oxford: Clarendon, 1997.

Miller, Stephen M., *How to Get into the Bible*, Nashville, Tennessee: Thomas Nelson, 1998.

Neusner, Jacob, *The Midrash: An Introduction*, Northvale, New Jersey, and London: Jason Aronson, 1994.

Nida, Eugene A., *Toward a Science of Translating with Special Reference to Principles and Procedures Involved in Bible Translating*, Leiden: Adler's Foreign Books, 1964.

Nida, Eugene A., and Taber, C.R., *The Theory and Practice of Translating*, Leiden: Adler's Foreign Books, 1969.

Norton, David, *A History of the English Bible as Literature*, Cambridge: Cambridge University Press, 2000.

Pagels, Elaine, *The Gnostic Gospels*, London: Penguin, 1990.

Pelikan, Jaroslav, *Luther the Expositor: Introduction to His Exegetical Writing*, St Louis: Concordia, 1959.

Perrin, N., *What is Redaction Criticism?* Minneapolis: Fortress, 1969; London: SPCK, 1970.

Philo, *The Works of Philo, Complete and Unabridged*, tr. C.D. Yonge, Peabody,

Massachusetts: Hendrickson, 1998.

Pontifical Biblical Commission, *The Interpretation of the Bible in the Church*, Rome: Libreria Editrice Vaticana, 1993; New York: Pauline Books and Media, 1993.

Porter, S.E., and Hess, R.H. (eds), *Translating the Bible: Problems and Prospects*, Sheffield: Sheffield Academic Press, 1999.

Pritchard, James B., *Ancient Near Eastern Texts Relating to the Old Testament with Supplement*, Princeton: Princeton University Press, 1969.

Ramsey, Boniface, *Beginning to Read the Fathers*, New York: Paulist, 1994; London: SCM, 1993.

Rogers, J.B., and McKim, D.K., *The Authority and Interpretation of the Bible*, San Francisco: HarperCollins, 1979.

Rogerson, John (ed.), *The Oxford Illustrated History of the Bible*, Oxford: Oxford University Press, 2001.

Reventlow, H. Graf, *The Authority of the Bible and the Rise of the Modern World*, tr. J. Bowden, London: SCM, 1985; Minneapolis: Fortress, 1985.

Schaeder, H.H., *Esra der Schreiber, Beitrage zur historischen Theologie* 5, Tübingen, 1930.

Sharpe, Eric J. (tr.), *Memory and Manuscript: Oral Tradition and Written Transmission in Rabbinic Judaism and Early Christianity*, Grand Rapids: Wm B. Eerdmans, 1998.

Smalley, B., *The Study of the Bible in the Middle Ages*, Oxford: Blackwell, 1983.

Suelzer, Alexa, and Kselman, John S., 'Modern Old Testament Criticism' in Raymond E. Brown, Joseph A. Fitzmeyer and Roland E. Murphy (eds), *The New Jerome Biblical Commentary*, Englewood Cliffs, New Jersey: Prentice Hall, 1990.

Trigg. J.W., *Biblical Interpretation* (*Message of the Fathers of the Church*, vol. 9), Wilmington, Delaware: Michael Glazier, 1988.

Truesdale, Albert, and Lyons, George, *A Dictionary of the Bible and Christian Doctrine in Everyday English*, Kansas City: Beacon Hill, 1986.

Vermes, Geza, *The Complete Dead Sea Scrolls in English*, New York: Penguin, 1998; London: Allen Lane, 1997.

Walsh, K., and Wood, D. (eds), *The Bible in the Medieval World* (*Studies in Church History* Subsidia 4), Oxford: Blackwell, 1985.

Ward, Kaari (ed.), *ABCs of the Bible*, New York: Reader's Digest, 1991.

Wigoder, Geoffrey, *The Encyclopedia of Judaism*, New York: New York University Press, 2002.

Zeolla, Gary F., *Differences Between Bible Versions*, Bloomington, Indiana: 1stBooks Library, 2001.

Index

Picture and Text Acknowledgments

Pictures

Picture research by Zooid Pictures Limited.

AKG London: cover, spine, 2, 6 (left), 6 (right), 8E, 9D (Trinity College, Dublin), 9E, 22 (Erich Lessing), 25 (Erich Lessing [top]), 25 (Erich Lessing [bottom]), 28–29, 30, 34, 37, 42, 45, 48, 49 (Erich Lessing), 52–53 (Gilles Mermet), 59 (S. Domingie – M. Rabatti), 61 (top), 68–69 (Schütze/Rodemann), 73 (top), 74 (Cameraphoto), 84 (Erich Lessing), 85 (Pirozzi), 86, 93 (Erich Lessing), 104–105, 110 (S. Domingie [left]), 111 (Erich Lessing), 118 (British Library [left]), 122 (British Library), 125, 126, 130, 132 (left), 132 (British Library [right]), 133 (British Library), 134 (British Library), 135 (Trinity College, Dublin), 139 (British Library [top]), 139 (British Library [bottom]), 142–43 (S. Domingie – M. Rabatti), 147 (top), 147 (centre), 147 (bottom), 149, 151, 154 (British Library), 160 (Erich Lessing), 161, 162, 165 (top), 166–67, 167, 168 (Erich Lessing/Universidad Complutense, Madrid, Spain), 169 (Erich Lessing), 172, 177 (Erich Lessing [bottom]), 183 (British Library), 184 (bottom), 186–87, 192 (Jean-Louis Nou/Bom-Jesus Church, Old Goa, India), 194 (bottom), 196 (right), 201 (bottom), 209 (top), 216, 221, 233, 235, 237.

American Bible Society Library: 202 (top).

Beinecke Rare Book and Manuscript Library, Yale University: 92.

Bodleian Library, University of Oxford: 78.

Boston University School of Theology Library: 57 (courtesy of Boston University School of Theology Library).

Bridgeman Art Library: 12 (Wallace Collection, London, UK), 62–63 (Bible Society, London, UK), 67 (Private Collection, France), 100 (Este Cathedral, Italy), 163 (Bibliothèque Municipale de Cambrai, France), 165 (Staatsarchiv, Hamburg, Germany [bottom]), 170 (Private Collection), 177 (National Portrait Gallery, London [top]), 179 (St Faith's Church, Gaywood, Norfolk, UK), 181 (Sheffield Galleries and Museums Trust, UK), 212 (Noortman, Maastricht. Netherlands), 215 (Victoria and Albert Museum, London, UK).

British Library: 88, 89 (top), 109, 159 (bottom), 171.

Cambridge University Library: 90, 115.

Corbis UK Ltd: 5 (Bill Ross [left]), 5 (Kim Sayer [right]), 8B (Gianni Dagli Orti), 8C (Bill Ross), 9A (Archivo Iconografico, S.A.), 9B (José F. Poblete), 9C (By kind permission of the Trustees of the National Gallery, London), 9F (David Lees), 9G, 10–11 (Bill Ross), 15 (Archivo Iconografico, S.A.), 16 (Archivo Iconografico, S.A.), 18 (Gianni Dagli Orti), 19 (David Lees), 20 (Wolfgang Kaehler), 21 (Gianni Dagli Orti [left]), 21 (K.M. Westermann [right]), 27 (By kind permission of the Trustees of the National Gallery, London), 33 (Dean Conger), 36 (Adam Woolfitt), 47 (Peter Turnley), 54 (Richard T. Nowitz), 56–57 (Hanan Isachar), 61 (Archivo Iconografico, S.A. [bottom]), 64–65 (Kim Sayer), 66 (Sandro Vannini), 70 (Mimmo Jodice), 73 (Archivo Iconografico, S.A. [bottom]), 77 (Kimbell Art Museum, Fort Worth, Texas), 79 (Archivo Iconografico, S.A.), 80 (Gianni Dagli Orti), 87 (Lowell Georgia), 89 (Dave Bartruff [bottom]), 95 (Archivo Iconografico, S.A.), 96 (Chris Hellier), 98 (Archivo Iconografico, S.A.), 99 (By kind permission of the Trustees of the National Gallery, London), 101 (Archivo Iconografico, S.A.), 103 (Historical Picture Archive [top]), 103 (Archivo Iconografico, S.A. [bottom]), 106–107 (By kind permission of the Trustees of the National Gallery, London) (Dave Bartruff), 108, 110 (Roger Wood [right]), 113 (Archivo Iconografico, S.A.), 114 (Bojan Brecelj), 119 (Archivo Iconografico, S.A.), 120 (Diego Lezama Orezzoli), 121 (José F. Poblete), 123 (Archivo Iconografico, S.A.), 127 (Christie's Images), 128 (Archivo Iconografico, S.A.), 129 (Austrian Archives), 131 (Elio Ciol), 137 (Archivo Iconografico, S.A.), 138 (Archivo Iconografico, S.A.), 145 (Elio Ciol), 150 (Roger Ressmeyer), 157 (Archivo Iconografico, S.A.), 158 (Bettmann), 159 (Archivo Iconografico, S.A. [top]), 164 (David Lees), 174 (Archivo Iconografico, S.A.), 175 (David Lees), 178 (Gianni Dagli Orti), 182 (Archivo Iconografico, S.A.), 184 (Gerald French [top]), 185 (Bettmann), 188 (Archivo Iconografico, S.A.), 190, 191 (Bettmann) (top left), 191 (Bettmann) (top right), 191 (Bettmann [bottom]), 193 (Bettmann [left]), 193 (Bettmann [centre]), 194 (Bettmann [top]), 197 (Diego Lezama Orezzoli [top]), 198 (Bettmann), 200, 203, 206 (Hulton-Deutsch Collection [top]), 208 (Philadelphia Museum of Art), 211 (Bettmann), 214 (Bettmann), 219 (Bettmann), 222 (David Rubinger), 223 (Bettmann), 224 (Nathan Benn [bottom]), 236 (Richard Olivier [left]), 238 (Archivo Iconografico, S.A. [left]), 239 (Sandro Vannini).

Corpus Christi College, Oxford: 146 (Ms255A Fol.7r. By permission of the

President and Fellows of Corpus Christi College, Oxford).

Getty Images: 224 (top), 225.

Hulton Archive: 155, 176, 180, 189 (top), 189 (bottom), 201 (top).

Institut Amatller d'Art Hispanic: 136 (MAS).

John Rylands University Library of Manchester: 51, 238.

Lutherhalle, Wittenberg: 6 (centre), 152–53.

Mary Evans Picture Library: 52, 81, 91, 156, 195, 196 (left), 197 (bottom), 227.

Barry Moser/Pennyroyal Caxton Bible: 230.

Niedersachsische Staats- Und Universitatsbibliothek Göttingen: 209 (bottom), 210.

OMF International: 193 (right).

Rex Features: 238 (centre).

Scala Art Resource: 94 (Pierpont Morgan Library), 118 (right).

Science Photo Library: 236 (Dr G. Moscoso [right]).

United Bible Societies: 202 (Maurice Harvey [bottom]).

Victoria & Albert Museum: 141.

Wycliffe Bible Translators: 204 (Barb Alvarez), 205 (June Hathersmith).

Zev Radovan, Jerusalem: 8A, 8D, 14, 23, 24, 32, 34–35, 38, 39, 40–41, 41, 44, 60–61, 63, 82, 83, 116, 117, 206 (bottom), 207, 218, 218–19.

Text

p. 145: extract from 'Canticle of Brother Sun', from *St Francis of Assisi: Writings and Early Biographies: English Omnibus of the Sources for the Life of St Francis*, edited by Marion A. Habig, fourth revised edition (1991), Franciscan Press, Quincy College, Quincy, Illinois.

p. 183: extract from Canto XXIII of *Inferno* from *Divine Comedy* by Dante Alighieri, translated by Steve Ellis. Published by Vintage, 1995. Translation copyright © 1994 Steve Ellis.

pp. 222–23: With grateful thanks to the American Bible Society for supplying information for this spread, 'Recent European Translations' – in particular to Dr Liana Lupas, curator of the library and archives.

p. 232: extract from Part 1 of *Faust* by Wolfgang von Goethe, translated by Bayard Taylor, 1870. Copyright © 1950 Random House.

Lion Publishing

Commissioning editor:
Morag Reeve

Project editor:
Jenni Dutton

Designer:
Nicholas Rous

Picture researcher:
Laura Derico

Production manager:
Charles Wallis